TEXTS AND THE REPRESSION OF MEDIEVAL HERESY

'Did you see a heretic? When? Where? Who else was there?'. The inquisitor is questioning, and a suspect is replying; a notary is translating from the vernacular into Latin, and writing it down, abbreviating and omitting at will; later there is the reading out of a sentence in public and then, in a few cases, burning. At every stage there is a text: a list of questions, for example, or an inquisitor's how-to-do it manual. The substance and intention of these texts forms the subject of this book. The introduction brings them all together in an historiographical survey of the role of texts in the suppression of heresy, and the volume is crowned by the Quodlibet lecture, in which the doyen of all heresy historians, ALEXANDER PATSCHOVSKY, magisterially surveys the political nature of heresy accusations.

YORK MEDIEVAL PRESS

This is a leaf from the unique manuscript of the inquisitor Bernard Gui's *Book of Sentences*, BL MS Add. 4697, fol. 11v (by permission of the British Library).

It comes from the C–F section of an index devised for the rapid inspection and retrieval of the data in the *Book of Sentences*. Place-names were given in alphabetical order, and listed under each place were its residents, together with their penalties and the numbers of the folios where they could be found. One example, which is discussed in ch. 9, pp. 182–9, can be seen under the fourth place-name shown here: 'Johannes Philiberti presbiter degradandus et post relictus curie seculari – cxxiii°. f. Item degradatus. cxxxvii°' ('John Philiberti, priest, to be degraded and afterwards relinquished to the secular arm – 123rd folio. Item, degraded, 137th.').

York Studies in Medieval Theology IV

TEXTS AND
THE REPRESSION OF
MEDIEVAL HERESY

Edited by

CATERINA BRUSCHI and PETER BILLER

THE UNIVERSITY *of York*

YORK MEDIEVAL PRESS

BT
1319
.T49
2003

First published 2003

A York Medieval Press publication
in association with The Boydell Press
an imprint of Boydell & Brewer Ltd
PO Box 9 Woodbridge Suffolk IP12 3DF UK
and of Boydell & Brewer Inc.
PO Box 41026 Rochester NY 14604–4126 USA
website: www.boydell.co.uk
and with the
Centre for Medieval Studies, University of York

ISBN 1 903153 10 7

ISSN 1366–9656

A catalogue record for this book is available
from the British Library

Library of Congress Cataloging-in-Publication Data
Texts and the repression of Medieval heresy / edited by Caterina Bruschi
and Peter Biller.
    p. cm. – (York studies in medieval theology, ISSN 1366–9656; 4)
Includes bibliographical references and index.
    ISBN 1–903153–10–7 (alk. paper)
1. Heresies, Christian – History – Middle Ages, 600–1500 – Congresses.
2. Heresies, Christian – History – Middle Ages, 600–1500 – Sources –
Congresses. I. Bruschi, Caterina, 1968– II. Biller, Peter. III. Series.
    BT1319 .T49 2003
    273'.6 – dc21   2002010808

This publication is printed on acid-free paper

Typeset by Joshua Associates Ltd, Oxford
Printed in Great Britain by
St Edmundsbury Press Ltd, Bury St Edmunds, Suffolk

CONTENTS

CONTRIBUTORS

John H. Arnold, Lecturer in Medieval History, Birkbeck College, University of London

Peter Biller, Professor of Medieval History, University of York

Jessalynn Bird, Department Associate, Department of History, Northwestern University

Caterina Bruschi, Lecturer in Medieval History, University of Birmingham

James B. Given, Professor of History, University of California at Irvine

Anne Hudson, Professor of Medieval English, Lady Margaret Hall, Oxford

Alexander Patschovsky, Professor of Medieval History, University of Konstanz

Mark Gregory Pegg, Assistant Professor of History, Washington University, St Louis

EDITORS' NOTE

The Centre for Medieval Studies at the University of York and the editors of this volume are grateful to all those who took part in the original conference. The editors are also grateful to the contributors for their patient responses to queries; to each other for support and good humour throughout the editing; and to Pru Harrison and Mark Ormrod for their invaluable help in the final preparation of the text of the volume.

English translation of the Bible is given from the Douay version. We have followed the commonest modern forms of names, except in the case of Occitan names from medieval Languedoc. We have not standardized the forms of Occitan names used by the contributors, but cross-references in the index serve to identify any variously named individuals.

ABBREVIATIONS

ABAW	*Abhandlungen der bayerischen Akademie der Wissenschaften*, Philosophisch-historische Klasse (Munich, 1835–)
AFP	*Archivum Fratrum Praedicatorum* (Rome, 1931–)
AHDLMA	*Archives d'histoire doctrinale et littéraire du moyen âge* (Paris, 1926–)
AHR	*American Historical Review* (New York, 1895–)
Alain, *Contra hereticos*	Alain de Lille, *De fide catholica contra hereticos sui temporis*, PL 210, 306–430
AMN	Analecta Medievalia Namurcensia (Louvain, etc., 1950–)
Arnold, *Inquisition and Power*	J. H. Arnold, *Inquisition and Power: Catharism and the Confessing Subject in Medieval Languedoc* (Philadelphia, 2001)
Audisio, *Dissent*	G. Audisio, *The Waldensian Dissent: Persecution and Survival, c. 1170-c. 1570*, trans. Claire Davison (Cambridge, 1999)
Baldwin, *Peter the Chanter*	J. W. Baldwin, *Masters, Princes and Merchants: The Social Views of Peter the Chanter and his Circle*, 2 vols. (Princeton NJ, 1970)
Berlioz, 'Exemplum'	J. Berlioz, 'Exemplum et histoire. Césaire de Heisterbach (v. 1180-v. 1240) et la croisade albigeoise', *Bibliothèque de l'École des chartes* 147 (1989), 49–86
Bernstein, 'Teaching'	A. E. Bernstein, 'Teaching and Preaching Confession in Thirteenth Century Paris', in *The Devil, Heresy, and Witchcraft in the Middle Ages: Essays in Honor of Jeffrey Burton Russell*, ed. A. Ferreiro (Leiden, Boston and Cologne, 1998), pp. 111–30
Biller, 'Northern Cathars and Higher Learning'	P. Biller, 'Northern Cathars and Higher Learning', in *Essays in Honour of Gordon Leff*, pp. 25–53
Biller, *Waldenses*	P. Biller, *The Waldenses, 1170–1530: Between a Religious Order and a Church*, CS 676 (Aldershot, 2001) [articles identified by Roman numeral]
BISIME	*Bollettino dell'Istituto Storico Italiano per il Medio Evo*, Roma, ISIME (Rome, 1886–)
BL	London, British Library
BnF	Paris, Bibliothèque nationale de France
Borst, *Katharer*	A. Borst, *Die Katharer*, Schriften der MGH 12 (Stuttgart, 1953)

Brenon, *Femmes cathares*	A. Brenon, *Les femmes cathares* (Paris, 1992)
Caesar, *Dialogus*	Caesar of Heisterbach, *Dialogus miraculorum*, ed. J. Strange, 2 vols. (Cologne, Bonn and Brussels, 1851)
CaF	Cahiers de Fanjeaux (Toulouse, 1966–)
CCCM	Corpus Christianorum, Continuatio Medievalis (Turnhout, 1966–)
CCR	*Calendar of the Close Rolls preserved in the Public Record Office 1272–1509*, 61 vols. (London, 1900–63)
Clanchy, *Memory*	M. T. Clanchy, *From Memory to Written Record: England 1066–1307*, 2nd edn (Oxford, 1992)
COD	*Conciliorum oecumenicorum decreta*, ed. G. Alberigo et al., 3rd edn (Bologna, 1973)
Contra amaurianos	Contra amaurianos: *ein anonymer, wahrscheinlich dem Garnerius von Rochefort zugehöriger Traktat gegen die Amalrikaner aus dem Anfang des XIII. Jahrhunderts*, ed. C. Baeumker, Beiträge zur Geschichte der Philosophie des Mittelalters, Texte und Untersuchungen 24, 5/6 (Münster, 1926)
Councils & Synods	*Councils and Synods with other Documents Relating to the English Church II. AD 1205–1313*, ed. F. M. Powicke and C. R. Cheney, 2 vols. (Oxford, 1964)
CPR	*Calendar of the Patent Rolls preserved in the Public Record Office 1216–1509*, 54 vols. (London, 1891–1916)
Crane	T. F. Crane, *The* Exempla *or illustrative stories from the* Sermones vulgares *of Jacques de Vitry* (London, 1890)
CS	Variorum Collected Studies Series (London, Northampton and Aldershot, 1970–)
D	Paris, Bibliothèque nationale de France, MS Collection Doat
DA	*Deutsches Archiv für Erforschung* (formerly *Geschichte) des Mittelalters* (Weimar and Munich, 1937–)
d'Avray, *Preaching*	D. L. d'Avray, *The Preaching of the Friars: Sermons Diffused from Paris before 1300* (Oxford, 1985)
De inquisitione hereticorum	*De inquisitione hereticorum*, ed. W. Preger, 'Der Tractat des David von Augsburg über die Waldesier', *ABAW* 14 (1879), pp. 204–35
Dondaine, 'Manuel'	A. Dondaine, 'Le Manuel de l'Inquisiteur (1230–1330)', *AFP* 17 (1947), 85–194; reprinted in A. Dondaine, *Les hérésies et l'inquisition, XIIe–XIIIe siècles: Documents et études*, ed. Y. Dossat, CS 314 (London, 1990), no. II
Dossat, *Crises*	Y. Dossat, *Les crises de l'inquisition Toulousaine au XIIIe siècle (1233–1273)* (Bordeaux, 1959)

Douais, *Documents*	C. Douais, *Documents pour servir à l'histoire de l'Inquisition dans le Languedoc*, 2 vols. (Paris, 1900)
Douais, *Inquisition*	C. Douais, *L'Inquisition: Ses Origines – Sa Procédure* (Paris, 1906)
Duvernoy, 'Registre de Bernard'	J. Duvernoy, 'Registre de Bernard de Caux. Pamiers, 1246–47', *Bulletin de la société Ariègeoise de Sciences, Lettres et Arts* (1990), 5–108
EFV	*Enchiridion Fontium Valdensium*, ed. G. Gonnet, Collana della Facoltà Valdese di Teologia, Roma, 22 (Turin, 1998), II
EHR	*English Historical Review* (London, 1886–)
Essays in Honour of Gordon Leff	*The Medieval Church: Universities, Heresy and the Religious Life: Essays in Honour of Gordon Leff*, ed. P. Biller and B. Dobson, SCH, Subsidia 11 (Woodbridge, 1999)
Fichtenau	H. Fichtenau, *Heretics and Scholars in the High Middle Ages, 1000–1200*, trans. D. A. Kaiser (Pittsburgh, 1998)
Fournier	*Le registre d'inquisition de Jacques Fournier évêque de Pamiers (1318–1325)*, ed. J. Duvernoy, Bibliothèque Meridionale 3rd s. 41, 3 vols. (Toulouse, 1965)
Frédéricq	*Corpus Documentorum Inquisitionis Neerlandicae*, ed. P. Frédéricq, 5 vols. (Ghent-'S Gravenhage, 1889–1903)
Friedberg	*Corpus iuris canonici*, ed. E. Friedberg, 2 vols. (Leipzig, 1879–81)
Friedlander, *Hammer*	A. Friedlander, *The Hammer of the Inquisitors: Brother Bernard Délicieux and the Struggle against the Inquisition in Fourteenth-Century France*, Cultures, Beliefs and Traditions: Medieval and Early Modern Peoples 9 (Leiden, 2000)
FZ	*Fasciculi Zizaniorum*, ed. W. W. Shirley, RS (London, 1985)
Gerald, *Gemma*	*Gerald of Wales: The Jewel of the Church*, trans. J. J. Hagen (Leiden, 1979)
Given, 'Inquisitor at Work'	J. B. Given, 'A Medieval Inquisitor at Work: Bernard Gui, 3 March 1308 to 19 June 1323', in *Portraits of Medieval and Renaissance Living: Essays in Memory of David Herlihy*, ed. S. K. Cohn Jr and S. A. Epstein (Ann Arbor MI, 1996)
Given, *Inquisition*	J. B. Given, *Inquisition and Medieval Society: Power, Discipline and Resistance in Languedoc* (Ithaca, 1997)
Given, 'Inquisitors'	J. B. Given, 'The Inquisitors of Languedoc and the Medieval Technology of Power', *AHR* 94 (1989), 336–59
Grundmann, *Ausgewählte Aufsätze*	H. Grundmann, *Ausgewählte Aufsätze*, 3 vols., Schriften der MGH 25 (Stuttgart, 1976)
Grundmann, 'Ketzerverhöre'	H. Grundmann, 'Ketzerverhöre des Spätmittelalters als quellenkritisches Problem',

Lambert, *Cathars*	M. D. Lambert, *The Cathars* (Oxford, 1998)
Lambert, *Medieval Heresy*	M. D. Lambert, *Medieval Heresy: Popular Movements from the Gregorian Reform to the Reformation*, 2nd edn (Oxford, 1992)
Lansing, *Power and Purity*	C. Lansing, *Power and Purity: Cathar Heresy in Medieval Italy* (New York and Oxford, 1998)
La parola	*La parola all'accusato*, ed. J.-C. Maire Vigueur and A. Paravicini Bagliani (Palermo, 1991)
Lerner, *Free Spirit*	R. E. Lerner, *The Heresy of the Free Spirit in the Later Middle Ages* (Berkeley and London, 1972)
Maisonneuve, *Études*	H. Maisonneuve, *Études sur les origines de l'inquisition*, 2nd edn, L'Église et l'État au Moyen Âge 7 (Paris, 1960)
Mansi	J. D. Mansi, *Sacrorum conciliorum nova et amplissima collectio*, 31 vols. (Florence, 1759–98)
Merlo, *Eretici e inquisitori*	G. G. Merlo, *Eretici e inquisitori nella società piemontese del Trecento, con l'edizione dei processi tenuti a Giaveno dall'inquisitore Alberto de Castellario (1335) e nelle valli di Lanzo dall'inquisitore Tommaso di Casasco (1373)* (Turin, 1977)
Merlo, *Identità valdesi*	G. G. Merlo, *Valdesi e valdismi medievali II. Identità valdesi nella storia e storiografia: Studi e discussioni* (Turin, 1991)
MGH	Monumenta Germaniae Historica
Molinier, 'Rapport'	C. Molinier, 'Rapport à M. le ministre de l'instruction publique sur une mission executée en Italie', *Archives des Missions scientifiques et littéraires*, 3rd s. 14 (1888), 133–336
Montaillou (1975)	E. Le Roy Ladurie, *Montaillou, village occitan de 1294 à 1324* (Paris, 1975)
Montaillou (1978)	E. Le Roy Ladurie, *Montaillou: Cathars and Catholics in a French Village, 1294–1324*, trans. B. Bray (London, 1978) [= translation of a shortened version of *Montaillou* (1975)]
Moore, *Persecuting Society*	R. I. Moore, *The Formation of a Persecuting Society: Power and Deviance in Western Europe, 950–1250* (Oxford, 1987)
Mundy, *Repression*	J. H. Mundy, *The Repression of Catharism at Toulouse: The Royal Diploma of 1279*, PIMS, Studies and Texts 74 (Toronto, 1985)
MS	*Medieval Studies* (Toronto, 1939–)
Pales-Gobillard, 'Gui Inquisiteur'	A. Pales-Gobilliard, 'Bernard Gui inquisiteur et auteur de la *Practica*', CaF 16 (1981), 253–64
Paolini, *Eresia a Bologna*	L. Paolini, *L'eresia catara alla fine del Duecento* = L. Paolini and R. Orioli, *L'eresia a Bologna fra XIII e XIV secolo*, 2 vols., ISIME, SStor 94–6 (Rome, 1975), I
Parmeggiani	R. Parmeggiani, 'Un secolo di manualistica inquisitoriale (1230–1330): intertestualità e

	circolazione del diritto', forthcoming in *Rivista Internazionale di Diritto Comune* 13 (2002)
Patschovsky, *Inquisition in Böhmen*	A. Patschovsky, *Die Anfänge einer ständigen Inquisition in Böhmen*, Beiträge zur Geschichte und Quellenkunde des Mittelalters 3 (Berlin and New York, 1975)
Patschovsky, *Passauer Anonymus*	A. Patschovsky, *Der Passauer Anonymus: Ein Sammelwerk über Ketzer, Juden, Antichrist aus der Mitte des xiii. Jahrhunderts*, MGH Schriften 22 (Stuttgart, 1968)
Patschovsky, *Quellen zur Böhmischen Inquisition*	*Quellen zur Böhmischen Inquisition im 14. Jahrhundert*, ed. A. Patschovsky, MGH, Quellen zur Geistesgeschichte des Mittelalters 11 (Weimar, 1979)
Patschovsky and Selge	*Quellen zur Geschichte der Waldenser*, ed. A. Patschovsky and K.-V. Selge, Texte zur Kirchen- und Theologiegeschichte 18 (Gütersloh, 1973)
Paul, 'Mentalité'	J. Paul, 'La mentalité de l'inquisiteur chez Bernard Gui', CaF 16 (1981), 279–316
Pegg, *Corruption*	M. G. Pegg, *The Corruption of Angels: The Great Inquisition of 1245–1246* (Princeton, 2001)
PIMS	Pontifical Institute of Medieval Studies
PL	*Patrologia Latina*, ed. J. P. Migne, 217 vols. (Paris, 1857–66)
Pontal, I	*Les statuts synodaux français du XIIIe siècle*, vol. 1: *Les statuts de Paris et le synodal de l'ouest*, ed. and trans. O. Pontal (Paris, 1971)
Pontal, II	*Les statuts synodaux français du XIIIe siècle*, vol. 2: *Les statuts de 1230 à 1260*, ed. and trans. O. Pontal (Paris, 1983)
Puylaurens	Guillaume de Puylaurens, *Chronica Magistri Guillelmi de Podio Laurentii*, ed. and trans. J. Duvernoy, Sources d'Histoire Médiévale (Paris, 1976)
RIS	L. Muratori, *Rerum italicarum scriptores*, new ed. G. Carducci et al. (Città di Castello etc., 1900–)
RS	*Rerum Brittanicarum medii aevi scriptores*, 99 vols. (London, 1858–1911) = Rolls Series
RTAM	*Recherches de Théologie Ancienne et Médiévale* (Louvain, 1929–)
Scharff, *Häretikerverfolgung*	T. Scharff, *Häretikerverfolgung und Schriftlichkeit*, Gesellschaft, Kultur und Schrift, Mediävistische Beiträge 4 (Frankfurt-am-Main, 1996)
SCH	Studies in Church History (London etc., 1964–)
Segl, *Anfänge der Inquisition*	*Die Anfänge der Inquisition im Mittelalter*, ed. P. Segl, Bayreuther Historische Kolloquien 7 (Cologne, Weimar and Vienna, 1993)
Sermones dominicales	Jacques de Vitry, *Sermones in epistolas et evangelia*

	dominicalia totius anni, ed. D. a Ligno (Antwerp, 1575)
SOPMA	T. Kaeppeli and E. Panella, *Scriptores Ordinis Praedicatorum medii aevi*, 4 vols. (Rome, 1970–93)
SStor	ISIME, Studi Storici
Stephen of Bourbon, *Tractatus*	*Tractatus de diversis materiis praedicabilibus*, ed. A. Lecoy de la Marche, *Anecdotes historiques, légendes et apologues tirés du recueil inédit d'Étienne de Bourbon, Dominicain du XIIIe siècle* (Paris, 1877)
Stock, *Implications of Literacy*	B. Stock, *The Implications of Literacy: Written Language and Models of Interpretation in the Eleventh and Twelfth Centuries* (Princeton, 1983)
Tardif, *Processus*	*Processus inquisitionis*, ed. A. Tardif, 'Document pour l'histoire du *processus per inquisitionem* et de l'*inquisitio heretice pravitatis*', *Nouvelle revue historique du droit français et étranger* 7 (1883), 669–78
Texte zur Inquisition	*Texte zur Inquisition*, ed. K.-V. Selge, Texte zur Kirchen- und Theologiegeschichte 4 (Gütersloh, 1967)
Thouzellier, *Catharisme*	C. Thouzellier, *Catharisme et valdéisme en Languedoc à la fin du XIIe et au debut du XIIIe siècle*, 2nd edn (Louvain and Paris, 1969)
Toulouse 609	Toulouse, Bibliothèque de la Ville, MS 609
Vaux-de-Cernay	Peter of Vaux-de-Cernay, *Hystoria albigensis*, ed. P. Guébin and E. Lyon, 3 vols. (Paris, 1926–39)
VMO	*Vita Mariae Oigniacensis*, ed. D. Papebroeck, *AA SS* June V(23) (Paris, 1707), 636–66 (cols. 636–7, 638–9)
Wakefield, *Heresy, Crusade and Inquisition*	W. L. Wakefield, *Heresy, Crusade and Inquisition in Southern France 1100–1250* (London, 1974)
Wakefield and Evans	W. L. Wakefield and A. P. Evans, *Heresies of the High Middle Ages: Selected Sources Translated and Annotated*, Records of Civilization, Sources and Studies 81 (New York and London, 1969)
Waugh and Diehl *Christendom*	*Christendom and its Discontents: Exclusion, Persecution and Rebellion, 1000–1500*, ed. S. L. Waugh and P. D. Diehl (Cambridge, 1996)

Introduction

Texts and the Repression of Heresy: Introduction

Caterina Bruschi and Peter Biller

After its introduction this volume prints the sixth of the Annual Quodlibet Lectures on medieval theology, 'Heresy and Society: On the Political Function of Heresy in the Medieval World', delivered by Alexander Patschovsky on 19 May 2000. It then continues with papers delivered at a conference held by the University of York's Centre for Medieval Studies at King's Manor, York, on 20 May 2000, under the title 'Trials and Treatises: Texts and the Repression of Medieval Heresy', together with two further papers on this theme, written by Caterina Bruschi and Peter Biller.

A word is needed about the origins of this book. Both of us are historians of heresy and inquisition, working in the first instance within the different historiographical traditions of our countries of origin and universities (Italy and Bologna on the one hand, England, Oxford and York on the other), and when beginning to collaborate on Languedocian inquisition records[1] we quickly became convinced that the time was now ripe to gather historians and their ideas on the texts of repression in themselves. Historiography in this field needed to be updated and revised. In this introduction we explain why. We begin by recalling elementary facts: what the texts were. We then identify and address the trend that suggested our book,[2] and describe the contribution it makes. One caveat: we work and write mainly on the high Middle Ages, hence the smaller attention we pay to the very early and late Middle Ages.

Inventory of the Texts

Let us take up position in the high Middle Ages and look around. What are the texts that are already there in the Church's chests of books?[3]

---

[1] See n. 28 below on the results of the collaboration.

[2] See also the introductory historiographical comments in chs. 4, 5 and 8 below.

[3] The following broad-brush summary is based on the standard works in the field: H. Grundmann, 'Oportet et haereses esse. Das Problem der Ketzerei im Spiegel der mittelalterlichen Bibelexegese', *Archiv für Kulturgeschichte* 45 (1963), 129–64, and 'Der Typus des Ketzers in mittelalterliche Anschauung', in *Kultur- und Universal Geschichte. Walter Goetz zu seinem 60. Geburtstag* (Leipzig, 1927), pp. 91–107, reprinted in his *Ausgewählte Aufsätze*, I, 313–27 and 328–63; Borst, *Katharer*, pp. 1–27; Maisonneuve, *Études*; Dondaine, 'Manuel'; Dossat, *Crises*, ch. 1; *Inventer l'hérésie?*,

All around there are the vast numbers of manuscript copies of the standard texts that are present in virtually any library: individual books of *the* text, the Bible, and the inherited texts of the early fathers, in particular Augustine and Isidore of Seville. The Bible established the foundation, that 'there *should* be heresies' and the providential reason for this, 'that those who are approved may be made manifest' (I Corinthians 11. 18–19). It used the principal words, 'heretic' and 'heresy', and 'sect' could also be found in it (I Corinthians 11. 18, Titus 3. 10, and Acts 24. 5 and 14), while at the same time it displayed such alternative and broader terminology as 'false prophets' and 'Antichrists' (e.g. Matthew 7. 15, 24. 11, Mark 13. 22 , and I John 2. 18) and the animal images of 'foxes', 'little foxes' and 'wolves' (Judges 15. 4, Song of Songs 2. 15, and Matthew 7. 15). It established as a mark of false prophets the contrast between their outer sheep-like appearance and inner wolf-like reality (Matthew 7. 15 and II Timothy 3. 5). It specified some heresies – forbidding marriage and the eating of meat (I Timothy 4. 3) – and it described how heretics converted, creeping into houses and leading little women astray (II Timothy 3. 6). At the same time it said what should be done with heretics – variously 'beware' of them, correct them twice and then 'avoid' them, 'take' them, or copy what Solomon did when he caught foxes, namely tie their tails together and apply torches to them (Matthew 7. 15, Titus 3. 10, Song of Songs 2. 15, and Judges 15. 4–5).[4] Augustine's compendious *On Heresies* and his writings against particular heretics and against the Manichees provided a model for the treatise which repressed heresy or heresies, doing this by describing and refuting their doctrines and discrediting them morally. At the same time his writings gave body to a principle established in 'there must be heresies' – their plurality – and they popularised certain labels for heresies, especially *Manichean*. The eighth book of Isidore of Seville's *Etymologies* provided definitions and etymologies of the key-words 'heresy' and 'sect' (VIII.iii.2 and 4), while at the same time providing a long list of heresies (VIII.v.1–70). Here was plurality, once again. Here was a principle, that a heresy took its name from an originating author, such as *Nicolaites*, from an originator called Nicholas; or from a cause, such as the *Angelics*, because they worshipped angels. Here, most of all, was a model for describing and pigeonholing a 'heresy', with its name, a terse account of origin and the crisp formulation of one wrong doctrine or practice.

Each point, of course, had already received very extensive further elaboration and was susceptible to more. For example, the outer sheep was spelled out as moral or doctrinal purity, the inner wolf as inner immorality or doctrinal impurity, disseminated with wolfish cunning.

---

chs. 1 and 4–5; D. Iogna-Prat, *Ordonner et exclure: Cluny et la société chrétienne face à l'hérésie, au judaisme et à l'Islam* (Paris, 1998), chs. 3–4, and Kienzle, *Cistercians*.

[4] While mainly discussing text *and* repression, we do not address the theme of the Bible as a matter of contention between heresy and orthodoxy – its interpretation and the diffusion of its knowledge – and the consequent development of a textual culture, which fuelled textual production in both the Church and heresies.

This inner:outer dichotomy was ordered under the moral category of hypocrisy, while in general 'heresy' – a Latinization of the Greek word for 'choice' – was seen morally as temerity in making one's own choice and preferring one's own opinion, and therefore given its place as a sub-species of one of the seven deadly sins, pride. But the fundamentals are already in place. Set aside the question of the real existence of heresy in itself: there was another reality, the omnipresence of these texts in themselves – and of all the countless other texts into which they flowed. They furnished the minds of Latin readers with the fundamental words, definitions, images and models for them mentally to conceive heresy as a subject, to map it out, and to deal with it.

During the course of the twelfth century, the defining and treating of contemporary persons and movements as heretical added to the corpus of texts in which such language was used. There were the decrees of councils naming and condemning heresies, letters and papal bulls about heresy, and sermons and treatises directed against heretical doctrines. The monastery of Cluny, in particular through its abbot Peter the Venerable, was a producer of texts, while from the 1140s to the early thirteenth century the Cistercians made a great literary contribution to the repression of heresy, mainly through sermons but also via biblical exegesis, didactic stories (*exempla*) and a chronicle of the crusade against the Albigensian heretics. There were Cistercian 'dossiers' of anti-heretical texts, with one Cistercian house, Clairvaux, acting as a repository for the dossier compiled by Bernard. The copying and diffusion of some of these texts was massive, especially conciliar decrees, papal bulls, and Bernard of Clairvaux's *Sermons* on the Song of Songs. The latter's numerous manuscripts disseminated very widely Bernard's highly charged and biblically rhetorical and stereotypical picture of the little foxes who demolish the vine of the Lord.[5] At the same time, there was the rise of schools of higher learning in northern France and Italy and, accompanying this, the production of textbooks and treatises. The presence of heresy in texts expanded, most significantly in the unofficially standard canon-law collection, Gratian's *Decretum*, question 3 of whose Causa 24 brought together and further disseminated heresy's definition and providential explanation and the listing of heresies, following Causa 23's aggregation of the main texts about coercion and repression.[6]

Much of the thirteenth century can be seen simply as the continuation and ever increasing proliferation and expansion of these genres. In canon law, for

---

[5] See n. 15 below.

[6] Since the recent demonstration that the *Decretum* was produced in two stages, a shorter first recension, whose earliest date is 1139, and a longer second recension, certainly before 1158 (A. Winroth, *The Making of Gratian's* Decretum (Cambridge, 2000), pp. 140 and 142), it has become necessary to compare Winroth's list of texts in Causae 23–4 in the first recension (*Making of Gratian's* Decretum, pp. 218–20) with the edition of the second recension of these Causae in Friedberg. The latter's collection of heresy texts is larger.

example, there is the heresy section of the official collection issued by Pope Gregory IX in 1234, the *Five Books of the Decretals*; for some time such collections have been clearer in organisation than Gratian, and the reader always knows how to turn up heresy quickly in book 5 of such texts, always collocated with Jews and followers of Mahomet. Likewise, to take another example, polemical treatises listing and refuting heretical doctrines become more systematic and scholastic, under the influence of the theology of the universities. The most elaborate were now written by members of the new mendicant Orders of Dominicans and Franciscans, they developed most in northern Italy and they reaching their apogee of length and precision in the treatise written against Cathars and Waldensians by the Dominican Moneta of Cremona.

   Set against this background there is one major new development, which accompanied the appearance in the 1230s and then the development of specialised inquisition into heresy. A specialised technical literature comes into existence to help the inquisitor in his job. The manuscripts proliferate, sometimes containing anthologies of useful material – legal consultations, conciliar decrees, and such procedural forms as oaths and sentences – and sometimes containing fully developed inquisitors' manuals. At the same time the inquisitor's job of interrogation and sentencing of heretics produced texts – in particular records of interrogations. Unlike the texts we have so far been inventorising, whose diffusion was vast, the relatively small numbers of still extant manuscripts of most of the technical literature of the inquisitors suggests a much smaller presence. Even smaller was the diffusion of the documentation produced by inquisitors. The textual record might be deposited in a convent belonging to the inquisitor's Order, in Toulouse, for example, in the Dominican convent: often in a unique manuscript and unlikely, except in exceptional cases, to be copied more than once. Plots to steal these records attest, of course, to the very real sense contemporaries had of the awesome power and danger of these pieces of parchment.

Scholarship and the Texts

The history of the post-medieval historical scholarship devoted to medieval heresy and its inquisition is long and varied, and it has been written, most notably in the first chapter of Arno Borst's *Die Katharer*. We are leaving aside the predominant strand in this history, the succession of certain *interpretations* of medieval heresy (such as Protestant continuity and Catholic counter-polemic, the history of Free Thought, the Marxist history of ideological rebels, Occitan separatism, and feminism), and confining ourselves to another strand, the history of what historians did with *texts*. Two points stand out, the longevity of rigorous text-based history, and a twentieth-century change in historians' attitude to texts.

'I have a large volume of hearings, in which 443 Waldensians mentioned by name were examined . . . around 1391': a typical beginning of a sentence written by Matthias Flacius Illyricus, in his *Catalogus Testium Veritatis*, 'Catalogue of Witnesses to Truth'.[7] This was the originating and fundamental text for Protestant history of heresy, demonstrating doctrinal and moral continuity of the true Church, in conformity with prophesy, bridging the dark papal period between the early Church and the Protestant Reformers. To back up and demonstrate his thesis, Flacius had hunted for copies of trials such as the set to which he refers here, and he also edited extracts from inquisitors' treatises in the *Catalogus*. Catholic and Protestant historians of the later sixteenth and seventeenth centuries followed in Flacius's path, seeking out texts and publishing them, trials as well as treatises, even if the latter had pride of place, and their names still haunt the pages of modern scholarship.[8] The achievement was very considerable, and the degree to which the sources at the disposal of, say, Cardinal Bossuet, approach those available today can still surprise the modern historian.

Around 1700 there was a correlative development of method. This area of history supports Anthony Grafton's identification of these years as crucial in the development of the footnote and all that it represents.[9] In Amsterdam in 1692 the Protestant historian and friend of the philosopher John Locke, Philip van Limborch, published his history of the inquisition. At the beginning, just after the preface, he printed a bibliography (not his word) listing his sources, with, in some cases, brief biographical comments on authors. He cited sources in margin-notes, referring to them in a form as short and efficient as the Harvard reference system. The title-page describes his book as *Historia Inquisitionis, cui subiungitur Liber Sententiarum Inquisitionis Tholosanae Ab anno Christi mcccvii ad annum mcccxxiii – History of the Inquisition, to which is appended the Book of Sentences of the Inquisition of Toulouse*: the latter is a collection of sentences delivered principally by the inquisitor Bernard Gui.[10] Limborch edited his manuscript with extraordinary care – it is nigh impossible to find an error of transcription. The text's edition is literally an appendix of evidence Limborch cites and uses. A final flourish of Limborch's scholarly standards is his printing of minor errata and addenda just after the *Historia*'s contents list. Beyond rigour in editing and citing the sources there was also questioning of the veracity of their contents. Protestant historians had been driven to this when confronting accusations of heretics' immoral practices, arguing that these were calumnies and that inquisitors falsified

---

[7] 'Habeo quoque magnum processuum volumen, in quo 443 Valdenses nominatim examinati sunt . . . circa annum Domini 1391'; *Catalogus Testium veritatis* (Strasbourg, 1562), p. 430. On their edition four centuries later by Dietrich Kurze, see below and n. 33.

[8] See for example the index-entries 'Flacius Illyricus' in Patschovsky's *Passauer Anonymus, Inquisition in Böhmen*, and *Quellen zur Böhmischen Inquisition*.

[9] A. Grafton, *The Footnote: a Curious History* (Cambridge MA, 1997), ch. 7.

[10] See ch. 8 below, n. 9.

records.[11] In his *Historia* Limborch carefully described inquisitors using set questions when interrogating suspects, notaries recording questions and answers, and the pressures exerted upon the suspects, including long detention in prison – here he refers to the practice of the inquisition in Toulouse, as shown by Bernard Gui's sentences. His sober and sceptical conclusion was that all this led to people confessing 'everything, even those things that had never occurred to them in their minds'.[12]

Whatever later particular technical developments have occurred in editing texts and source criticism, historical scholarship over the centuries since Limborch has remained unchanged in its principle: that history is reconstruction rigorously based on texts. However, there has been a gradual sea-change in the way the texts themselves have come to be envisaged by historians, largely brought about by the advances of earlier twentieth century technical and positivist scholarship. Consider these examples. First, Herbert Grundmann's descriptions (in 1927 and 1964) of the stereotype of the heretic and New Testament prophesy about heresy which informed the writings of medieval clergymen when writing about heresy, and his analysis of the use of question-lists by inquisitors when interrogating suspects have been fundamental.[13] The result? Study of the stereotype of the heretic, for example, brings in its wake the idea that it was itself part of that past reality, one element in the minds and thoughts of past writers and readers of a particular range of literature. Let us turn to the fundamental studies and editions of inquisition treatises by Antoine Dondaine, Alexander Patschovsky and Lorenzo Paolini.[14] The result? Dondaine's technical study of inquisitors' literature brings in its wake a certain view: inquisitors and their handbooks, professionals making efficient use of highly developed practical guides; the handbooks themselves are now on the historical stage. A modern scholarly edition of Bernard of Clairvaux's *Sermon* on the Song of Songs lists 111 still-extant twelfth or early thirteenth century manuscripts and in many cases their provenance.[15] The result? Where medieval provenance can be shown, principally as we would expect, ownership in Cistercian houses, this brings in its wake the idea that this list provides the (fragmentary) cartography of one past reality, the diffusion of the ideas contained in the treatise.

The texts used to be only 'sources': glasses cleaned and polished and rendered distortion-free by source-criticism, *through* which historians then peered at the past. There has been a seismic shift: the texts and the actions

---

[11] Examples concerning sources bearing on the Waldensians are provided by E. Cameron, *Waldenses: Rejections of Holy Church in Medieval Europe* (Oxford, 2000), pp. 290–2.

[12] P. van Limborch, *Historia Inquisitionis* iv.13 (Amsterdam, 1692), p. 276: 'omnia, etiam quae nunquam ipsis in mentem venerunt'.

[13] The articles cited in n. 3 above and 'Ketzerverhöre'.

[14] See nn. 26–7 below.

[15] Bernard of Clairvaux, *Opera omnia*, ed. J. Leclercq, C. H. Talbot and H. M. Rochais, 8 vols. (Rome, 1957–77), I, xxvi–xxxi.

and mind-sets which produced them have slowly become *themselves* also elements of the past reality which historians need to describe.

Texts Working through Miracle and Diabolic Art

The point that texts themselves were part of the stage, could even sometimes take the leading role, would not have needed insistence in the Middle Ages, as we shall see in two stories, one of miracle and the other of diabolic magic.

In the second half of the twelfth and the early thirteenth century the Church's effort to repress heresy by persuasion often took the form of debates, sometimes very formally organised, with set speakers, exchanges of views, an audience, and judges to decide which side won. At one of the most famous of these, at Montréal in 1207, the debate lasted a fortnight, and the disputing sides exchanged their positions in writings. These writings were 'schedules' containing Cathar or Catholic views, doubtless supported by 'authorities' (biblical quotations) and 'reasons' (logical arguments). By the next decade the actions of this occasion had been changed into a story in which God intervened to demonstrate the true faith. The Catholic and heretical texts were put to ordeal by fire. The fire consumed the heretical text. Although the Catholic text was thrown into the fire three times, it always leapt out unharmed. Essentially, a ritual is performed, in which Church text vanquishes heretical text. During the transformation things have been simplified, the debaters have gone to the side of the stage and the story of the texts has come to occupy its centre, as it continues to do in the later retailing of this performance in the many textual and pictorial representations of St Dominic's life.[16]

As dramatic as this miracle is a slightly later story of diabolic magic, which we quote here more fully from the chronicler Richer de Senones, who wrote it probably around 1264/5.[17]

> There was then at this time a man from Paris who was very learned and brilliant with words, called Robert, of the Preachers' [Dominican] Order, a man of such charm that he was regarded then as second to none. However, according to report he was addicted to worldly ambition and debauchery. He had composed for himself a *cartula* [written text *or* small piece of parchment] with some sort of ⟨magical⟩ art, so that when he placed this *cartula* on top of the head of someone, that person would willy-nilly confess

[16] Vaux-de-Cernai, I, 47–9; *The History of the Albigensian Crusade: Peter of les Vaux-de-Cernay's* Historia Albigensis, trans. W. A. and M. D. Sibly (Woodbridge, 1998), pp. 29–30.
[17] Richer de Senones, *Chronicon* iv. 18, ed. G. Waitz, MGH, Scriptores 25, pp. 307–8. The story was used and translated by C. H. Haskins (*AHR* 7 (1902), 637–8) in an article on Robert an amplified version of which was printed as ch. 10 of his *Studies in Medieval Culture* (Cambridge MA, 1929), where it appears on pp. 225–6. Grundmann used it in 'Ketzerverhöre', pp. 519–21 (364–6 in the article's reprint).

whatever things he [Robert] wanted him to. As it turned out one day when he spotted a shapely woman during his sermon, he lusted after her in his heart and told her to speak to him after the sermon. She came to a certain secret place, where she anticipated wanting to confess to him; he speaks to her, pressing her with menacing and seductive words to do his will. What then? She resists; he insists, threatens: if she won't, he will impose ⟨the charge of⟩ heresy on her and have her burnt by fire. In fact the next day he made her come to him in the presence of all of the women, and, placing his hand upon her he questions in a raised voice, ⟨as follows⟩. 'Are you not of the heretics' sect?' She said, 'Truly I am.' 'Do you wish to return to the Catholic faith?' She replied, however, 'No.' He said, 'Would you rather be burned than deny that sect?' She replied, 'I would.' He said, 'Have you heard how this woman has confessed her foulness?' But they were amazed and said they had never heard such a thing about her; and so she was handed over to custody. This matron had a clerical son, a good-natured youth. Affected by his mother's suffering, he went around neighbours and relatives,[18] consulting them about any possible way to free his mother from the danger of death. Someone who was familiar with this Preacher [Dominican], sympathising a lot, said to him, 'Go tomorrow to the public consistory, because your mother will be examined again. You, in fact, must stand next to her. And when master Robert has placed his hand on your mother and interrogates her again about the faith, you – for you're stronger than him – grab hold of his hand strongly and take the *cartula* you'll have found in it and keep it to yourself. And ⟨then⟩, raise your voice, asking master Robert to question your mother again about the faith.' It happened just like that. And when that cleric had taken the said *cartula* text from that Preacher's hand, that matron, questioned as before, swore in front of everyone that she had never heard those words, nor had she ever been interrogated by Robert, nor had she ever replied to him on any point, nor had she ever heard what was heresy. In fact the son showed that *cartula* to everyone, ⟨demonstrating⟩ that this same Preacher with diabolic skill used to trap whoever he wanted with this *cartula*, and deliver them to death. In fact, hearing this the people tried to kill him, but he was seized by the clergy and put into a stone prison, shut up for ever. And because in order to conceal his wickedness he had used this art, that has been described above, to have father⟨s⟩ and mother⟨s⟩[19] and many others burned as though they were culpable, God decreed the imposition of such a punishment on him in this present life, just in case he might be converted from his wickedness while still alive.[20]

---

[18] Usually meaning relatives by marriage, 'affines' here may mean relatives on his mother's side.

[19] Perhaps meaning the fathers and mothers of girls he had seduced by blackmail or condemned for their resistance.

[20] 'Fuit itaque hiis diebus Parisius vir doctissimus et eloquio clarus Robertus nomine de ordine Predicatorum, qui tantam habuit gratiam, ut nullus ei tunc secundus haberetur. Sed, ut ferebatur, totus glorie mundi et luxurie dedidus erat. Qui quadam arte cartulam sibi composuerat, ut, si quando eandem cartulam capiti alicuius superponeret, quecunque ille volebat, velet nollet, fateretur. Quadam quippe die cum in predicatione sua quandam formosam mulierem conspexisset,

Reluctantly we pass over sexual blackmail[21] and a traditional monk's hostility to the Dominican Order – fascinating topics but not germane to our theme – and we are left with the story of a performance. Robert le Bougre was a zealous and well-known early inquisitor active in northern France. However, there is a contrast to the case of the trial of the books, where we have ordinary accounts of the original episode as well as the miraculous version. We lack an earlier and more sober account of Robert's performance of this particular interrogation, and consequently our investigation is more conjectural, working backwards from the story towards the earlier activity, and then forwards towards this activity's transformation. We do, however, have recent historical investigation of Robert, which has established a sober picture of an inquisitor who did not act alone and who always worked according to rules and procedures.[22] Robert interrogated, and in his

eam animo concupivit, mandans ei, ut post sermonem sibi loqueretur. Que ad quendam locum secretum veniens, ubi sibi velle confiteri expectabat, illam alloquitur, ut voluntatem suam faceret, verbis minacibus et blandis ipsam coartabat. Quid plura? Illa negat; iste instat, minatur: si non faciat, ei heresim opponet et igne comburi faciet. In crastino nempe coram cunctis mulierem illam ad se venire fecit, et manum ei imponens, alta voce interrogat, "Numquid ex secta hereticorum es?" Illa dixit, "Sum vere." "Vis redire ad fidem catholicam?" Illa autem ait, "Non." Ille dixit, "Vis potius comburi quam sectam illam abnegare?" Illa respondit, "Volo." Ille dixit, "Audistis, quomodo ista mulier confessa est turpitudinem suam?" At illi admirantes dixerunt, se de ea numquam tale quid audivisse; et ita tradita est custodie. Habebat illam illa matrona filium clericum, bone indolis adolescentem, qui dolore matris tactum circuibat vicinos et affines, consulens eos, si quoquo modo matrem a periculo mortis liberare valeret. Cui quidam, qui illi Predicatori familiaris erat, valde condolens, dixit ei, "Vade cras ad publicum consistorium, quia mater tua iterum examinabitur. Tu vero sta iuxta eam; et cum magister Robertus matri tue manum imposuerit et eam de fide interrogabit, tu, quia fortior es eo, manum eius viriliter apprehende et cartulam quam in ea inveneris tolle et eam tibi reserva, et alta voce roga magistrum Robertum, ut iterum matrem tuam de fide interroget." Quod et ita factum est. Cumque ille clericus dictam cartulam de manu illius Predicatoris tulisset, matrona illa ut prius interrogata iuravit coram omnibus se nunquam illa verba audivisse nec unquam a magistro Roberto de fide interrogatam fuisse nec ei in aliquo respondisse nec quid esset heresis unquam audivisse. Filius vero eius cartulam illam omnibus ostendit, et quia arte diabolica idem Predicator per illam cartulam quos volebat decipiebat et morti tradebat. Populi vero hec audientes nitebantur eum interficere; sed raptus a clero, missus est in carcerem lapideum perpetualiter clausum. Et quia patrem et matrem et multos alios insontes velut culpabiles arte supradicta ad suam iniquitatem velandam comburi fecerat, Deus ei talem penam in presenti vita imponere decrevit, si forte vivens a malicia sua convertatur.'

[21] On priests blackmailing women in a similar way, see Baldwin, *Masters, Princes and Merchants*, I, 321–2, and II, 215 n. 53.

[22] B. Despy has re-examined both Robert's career and the melodramatic historiography devoted to him in his revisionist study, 'Les Débuts de l'Inquisition dans les anciens Pays-Bas au XIIIe siècle', *Problèmes d'histoire de christianisme: Hommage à Jean Hadot*, ed. G. Cambier (Brussels, 1980), pp. 71–104 (see esp. pp. 87–8, 93, and 103–4). Expected from Simon Tugwell is publication of his identification of Robert as the anonymous inquisitor in a story retailed in Gerard Frachet's *Vitas Fratrum*.

interrogation had at his disposal a *cartula*, whose identity is no longer precisely recoverable. Clearly in one way or another it was a text that helped in the task, perhaps a collection of legal extracts Robert had put together. Robert interrogating and his text have been distilled into a story. From the interrogation of a suspect by an inquisitor much form and procedure has dropped away – where, for example, is the taking of an oath, where a scribe recording? – and a complex set of actions has been condensed to an exchange of question and answer. Reduced to its essentials, it has gained in dramatic power. Not in view in the account of Robert's own execution of his job are his knowledge heresy – he was a former Cathar – or his experience as an inquisitor. Rather, a *cartula* has come to provide the diabolic-magical driving-power behind Robert's performance.

The preceding reconstruction follows only one path – the original text could have had other contents, such as prayers – and we are sidelining important features in the magical story and medieval magical lore, gestures, texts and spells. These two stories were rooted in debates in Languedoc and interrogations by Robert which actually took place. As they move away from these into miracle and magic, they are not moving away from historical reality, but simply towards another part of historical reality. Various past minds distilled individual occasions of the use of texts to repress heresy into stories. Through the gap between the more sober basis and the heightened miraculous or magical power possessed by the repressive texts in these stories we can see a past mental reality. Revealed in the gap is something of what people in the thirteenth century thought. If the two texts in question can stand in our discussion for the two more general genres which they represent – polemical treatises describing and attacking heresies, and the technical literature aiding inquisitors in their job – then we are being given a hint. This is how medieval people saw the active performance of both polemical tracts and (perhaps) inquisitors' handbooks in the repression of heresy.

Modern Research and this Book

The modern scholarly view of texts and repression which we have been describing has many intellectual roots, and its various contemporary manifestations have been increasing in number and intensity. Salient here are editions of polemical treatises[23] and studies of them,[24] studies of rhetoric

---

[23] For example, Salvo Burci, *Liber Suprastella*, ed. C. Bruschi, ISIME, Fonti per la Storia d'Italia, Antiquitates 15 (Rome, 2002); Peter the Venerable, *Contra Petrobrusianos Hereticos*, ed. J. Fearns, CCCM 10 (1968); *Une somme anti-Cathare: le* Liber contra Manicheos *de Durand de Huesca*, ed. C. Thouzellier, Spicilegium Sacrum Lovaniense, Études et Documents 32 (Louvain, 1964).

[24] For example, Biller, *Waldenses*, chs. 15–16; C. Bruschi, articles on Salvo Burci in *Bollettino della Società di Studi Valdesi* 179 (1997), 95–108, *Archivio Storico per le Province Parmensi* 4th s. 49 (1997), 405–27, and *Mélanges de l'École Française de*

about heresy in *exempla* and sermons,[25] editions of inquisitors' treatises,[26] together with renewed attention to the genre as a whole,[27] and editions of records of inquisitors' interrogations and sentences.[28]

The story about Robert le Bougre – first noticed and used by Charles Haskins in 1902 – was paraded by Grundmann at the very beginning of his account of heresy interrogations,[29] while *Heresy and Literacy in the Middle Ages* (1994) aired the story about texts put to ordeal by fire, providing on its cover a photograph of the representation of this in relief-work by Nicola Pisano on the tomb of St Dominic in Bologna. Both works represent important earlier

Rome: Moyen Âge 112 (2000), 149–82; D. Iogna-Prat in *Inventer l'hérésie?*, ch. 5, and n. 3 above; Lorenzo Paolini, in *Heresy and Literacy*, ch. 5; Thouzellier, *Catharisme*; M.-H. Vicaire, 'Les cathares albigeois vus par les polémistes', CaF 3 (1968), pp. 107–28.

[25] For example, Berlioz, 'Exemplum', and J. Berlioz, *Tuez-les tous Dieu reconnaîtra les siens: Le massacre de Béziers et la croisade des Albigeois vus par Césaire de Heisterbach* (Portet-sur-Garonne, 1994); for Kienzle see n. 3 above.

[26] M. D'Alatri, *L'inquisizione francescana nell'Italia centrale del Duecento, con il testo del "Liber inquisitionis" di Orvieto trascritto da Egidio Bonanno*, Bibliotheca Seraphico-Capuccina 49 (Rome, 1996); 'Un manuale inquisitoriale Vicentino', in F. Lomastro Tognato, *L'eresia a Vicenza nel Duecento: dati, problemi, fonti*, Istituto per le Ricerche di Storia Sociale e di Storia Religiosa, Fonti e Studi di Storia Veneta 12 (Vicenza, 1988), pp. 145–244; L. Paolini, *Il "De officio inquisitionis": La procedura inquisitoriale a Bologna e a Ferrara nel Trecento* (Bologna, 1976); Patschovsky, *Inquisition in Böhmen*.

[27] Parmeggiani, and T. Scharff, 'Schrift zur Kontrolle – Kontrolle der Schrift. Italienische und französische Inquisitoren-Handbücher des 13. und frühen Jahrhunderts', *DA* 52 (1996), 547–84 (both are continuing the work whose foundations were laid by Dondaine, 'Manuel', and fuller bibliography can be found in their articles); L. Paolini, 'Il modello italiano nella manualistica inquisitoriale'(forthcoming); C. Heimann, *Nicolaus Eymerich* (Münster, 2001). We are very grateful to Riccardo Parmeggiani for showing us his work before publication.

[28] Fournier, together with J. Duvernoy, *Corrections* (Toulouse, 1972), Duvernoy, 'Registre de Bernard', and J. Duvernoy, *L'inquisition en Quercy: le registre des pénitences de Pierre Cellan 1241–1242* (Castelnaud La Chapelle, 2002) – this last edition was published too late for citation in those chapters below which make use of D21; Kurze, *Quellen*; Merlo, *Eretici e inquisitori*, pp. 161–283; A. Pales-Gobilliard, *L'Inquisiteur Geoffroy d'Ablis et les Cathares du Comté de Foix (1308–1309)*, Sources d'Histoire Médiévale Publiées par l'Institut de Recherche et d'Histoire des Textes (Paris, 1984), and (forthcoming) *Le livre des sentences de l'inquisiteur Bernard Gui, 1308–1323*, Collection Sources d'Histoire Médiévale 30; Paolini, *Eresia a Bologna*; Patschovsky, *Quellen zur Böhmischen Inquisition*; *Quellen zur Geschichte der Waldenser von Freiburg im Üchtland (1399–1439)*, ed. K.U. Tremp, MGH, Quellen zur Geistesgeschichte des Mittelalters 18 (Hannover, 2000 [published 2001]). C. Bruschi, who is preparing a monograph on the interrogations contained in D21–6, *Tales of Wandering Cathars*, is collaborating with S. Sneddon and P. Biller on an edition of the records of interrogation by the inquisitors Pons of Parnac and Renous of Plassac contained in D25 and the first seventy-eight folios of D26. An edition of D21 has also been prepared by Jörg Feuchter. Note also the edition of the trial of a critic of inquisition: *Processus Bernardi Delitiosi: The Trial of Fr. Bernard Délicieux, 3 September – 8 December 1319*, ed. A. Friedlander, Transactions of the American Philosophical Society 86, Pt 1 (Philadelphia, 1996).

[29] See n. 17 above.

intellectual sources of current pre-occupation with texts and repression, on the one hand the ancient problem of inquisition trials (discussed below), and on the other hand the more recent rise of interest in literacy and heresy, manifested in Brian Stock's analysis of sects as textual communities and the international gathering of heresy historians in 1992 which resulted, again, in *Heresy and Literacy in the Middle Ages*. In the wake of this have come, for example, Thomas Scharff's pre-occupation with textuality and repression in his study of the repressive legislation of the written statutes of Italian communes, and the studies of repression in Languedoc which have come from James Given and John Arnold.[30]

This book springs from and is a part of this modern pre-occupation, sharing both its ramifications and one special area of concentration, as we shall see. The starting-point of this area of scholarship remains direct work on the texts: editing, tracking texts, identifying authors and sources, studying a particular body of texts as a genre. Both of Biller's chapters contribute to the study of the construction of the inquisitors' treatise: in chapter 7 he makes a minor addition to the sources drawn upon by the inquisitor Bernard Gui's in his discussion of Waldensian Luciferanism, and in chapter 9 he uses the language of 'finger-printing' when trying to do detective work on the origins of a description of the medieval Waldensians. Brief though it is, this is one of the most important of all medieval texts on the Waldensians: it is edited and translated in an appendix to the chapter.

In the last part of chapter 11 Anne Hudson conveys the 'researcher's story': the problems of detection in the attempt to trace the travels of letters from England to Bohemia. This follows her brilliant demonstration of how different sources constructed one and the same man differently. While Richard Wyche is a monochrome two-dimensional figure in the official texts of repression, a heretic admitting itemised errors, but a more alive and three-dimensional figure in his own writing, the two cannot be paired as false and true. For Wyche's own texts are shaped by the rules of letter-writing and the conventions of the saint's life.

In chapter 3 Jessalynn Bird engages in the fundamental task of adding to the inventory of heresy-repression texts. To a degree which has gone largely unnoticed, the Paris Masters of Peter the Chanter's circle addressed heresy. Again, insufficiently noticed, they addressed northern heresy. And – again, largely unnoticed – they anticipated the more famous later efforts by the Dominicans and Franciscans against heresy. Their works of academic theology addressed heresy, as did also their pastoral works, sermons, and aids to confession and preaching. Bird analyses the 'type' of the heretic and his mode of action found in these pastoral texts, and indicates how the purpose of *pastoralia* – instilling right faith and good morals in the laity, as protection against heresy – draws them into the corpus of texts we should designate as repressive of heresy, even if indirectly.

---

[30] Arnold, *Inquisition and Power*; Given, *Inquisition*; and Scharff, *Häretikerverfolgung*.

The book's other chapters are closely clustered, focussing on Languedo-cian records of inquisition: questions used by inquisitors, records of inter-rogation, and sentences. There has been a lot of work on these texts, in part because of their descriptive richness, in part because they form a fairly uniform set of records, and in part because of their availability. Clearly work in this *area* has been facilitated by Duvernoy's and Pales-Gobilliard's editions of two sets of interrogations, the diffusion of microfilms of the seventeenth-century copies of interrogations contained in the Doat collection, and the existence of at least two typescript transcriptions of a difficult manuscript containing depositions from 1245–6.[31] But there is more to the phenomenon than this.

The use of these sources to reconstruct the 'religious' life or broader culture and mentality of the ordinary person, famously exemplified by *Montaillou*, has had something of the uncritical attitude felicitously described by John Arnold (seeing them as 'transparent or innocent conduits of information'),[32] as critics of *Montaillou*'s author have pointed out. We noted above the antiquity of Protestant historians' criticism of the medieval sources which bear on heresy. Virtually all polemical literature directed against heresy cries out for critical comment on its distortions, while the scarcity and problematic nature of pre-inquisition sources on heresy have for decades allied themselves to enquiry along the lines of 'texts constructed heresy where there was none'. This last approach was encapsulated in the title of a recent collection of essays on the theme, *Inventer l'hérésie?*, whose question-mark elegantly warned against taking this proposition as proven rather than as a hypothesis. And in 1965 Grundmann founded modern text-criticism of inquisition hearings, and the rich tradition of enquiry and discussion which leads through many later important works: Robert Lerner's demolition of the evidence upon which the 'Sect' of the Free Spirit has been constructed (1972); Dietrich Kurze's exemplary warning about how to 'read' records of interrogations, when editing the question-list used by his inquisitor, Peter Zwicker, alongside the records of his inter-rogations in Stettin in 1392–4 (1975); Grado Merlo's discussion of inquisition in fourteenth-century Piedmont (1977); a conference and a book containing its papers dedicated to the utterance of the interrogated suspect, *La parola*

---

[31] Some American scholars have used Toulouse 609 (on which see below, ch. 9 n. 2) through a transcript made by pupils of A. P. Evans (J. H. Mundy, *Society and Government at Toulouse in the Age of the Cathars*, Pontifical Institute of Medieval Studies, Studies and Texts, 129 (Toronto, 1997), p. ix, and Pegg, *Corruption*, pp. 76 and 160 n. 73), while a transcript prepared by Jean Duvernoy has been available to some French scholars (Brenon, *Femmes cathares*, p. 389). Trial material has become available on the world-wide web, with, e.g. Nancy P. Stork providing translations of some of the interrogations of Jacques Fournier on line at sjsu.edu/depts/English/Fournier/jfournier.htm, and Jean Duvernoy announcing that he is going to make some of his transcriptions available at jean.duvernoy.free.fr.

[32] Ch. 4 below, p. 63.

all'accusato (1991); and work by Thomas Scharff addressing the inquisitor's concerns and 'truth' in his hearings.[33]

Although she addresses different genres of texts, Anne Hudson's textual-epistemological point is a leitmotiv for the fundamental concerns of this area. Good historians have always been aware of the shading into each other of source-criticism and ultimate questions of truth, and this applies particularly to the study of inquisition records. 'How *true* is what is confessed in them?' Grundmann demonstrated that records of suspects' answers contained words, phrases and whole propositions contained in the questions put by the inquisitor. We simplify here. In effect, this meant the question, 'You do believe, do you not, the proposition that x', with the record that 'John said that he believed x', where x = a complex and carefully articulated theological doctrine, identically phrased in both question and answer. In other words, there was circularity and the record produced a false account of what a person had said or had been pressed into saying in the inquisitors' words. The records of witch-craft trials of early modern Europe will have been present in most readers' minds as later analogies.

In analysing the records of confessions by Free Spirit heretics, Lerner re-applied this analysis to the records of people who appeared to have confessed such things as their freedom from the moral law after reaching a state of spiritual perfection – and the subsequent exercise of their license to indulge in indiscriminate sex – whereas in fact words from the *Ad nostrum* decree of the Council of Vienne, listing Free Spirit errors, were being put in their mouths. Lerner's was a lively and very intellectually sophisticated work, examining alongside leading questions such contributory causes as the libellous sexual-license element in the stereotype of the heretic, and 'the confessing personality'. Epistemologically, however, it was a simple exercise: explaining away, disbelieving, the source. Grundmann's earlier article will have left the reader with a more complex impression, for although much of it dealt with how far you could trust the records of inquisition hearings – how far you could or could not look *through* them – the parading of the story about Robert le Bougre will have encouraged readers to take a more complex view.

The breakthrough, however, has come through Italian historiography, to begin with Merlo. His monograph on heretics in fourteenth-century Piedmont drew upon the inquisition records of that area, some of which he edited in an appendix. These records of inquisition hearings are notoriously problematic. Not only are they repetitive and formulaic, but they also contain suspects confessing to what seems a bizarre mixture of doctrines derived

---

[33] Grundmann, 'Ketzerverhöre'; Lerner, *Free Spirit*; Kurze, *Quellen*, pp. 73–5 and 77–261; Merlo, *Eretici e inquisitori*, pp. 10–15; *La parola*; T. Scharff, 'Auf der Suche nach der "Wahrheit". Zur Befragung von verdächtigen Personen durch mittelalerlichen Inquisitoren', in *Eid und Wahrheitssuche*, ed. S. Esders and T. Scharff, Gesellschaft, Kultur und Schrift, Mediävistische Beiträge 7 (Frankfurt-am-Main, 1996), pp. 139–62; ch. 6 n. 3 below. See also the discussion of inquisitor's questions by Lothar Kolmer, cited below ch. 6 n. 3.

from different heretical sects, and the practice of sexual coupling with anyone, the person nearest to hand, when lights were extinguished at the end of meetings. In a brief but extraordinarily important introduction, Merlo summarised Grundmann's work on the source-problems of such records before turning to address the ensemble of texts which emerged from inquisition. He cut the Gordian knot, solving the problem by side-stepping it. He related different texts to their different settings and roles. Written sentences, on the one hand, were part of the publicity and propaganda campaign of repression by the official Church. They were read out publicly, with great solemnity and in the presence of many important ecclesiastical and lay personages, and alongside public preaching which listed the condemned errors and emphasized their heretical nature. This was a ritual, a performance which reinforced the Church's dominance and its sacral power. Conversely, records of interrogations were part of and coloured by the secret-police nature of inquisition. Seen in this way, the 'reliability' of records ceases to be an issue – except for someone naive enough to think that they are neutral. Read in their setting, they are simply part of that particular past historical reality.

If Merlo did not immediately influence historiography outside Italy – he has perhaps been more cited than read – we can point to one reason for this. Merlo shared a pre-occupation with Lerner. Both were addressing sources some of whose problems, like those of later witch-trials, were both obvious and stark: people confessing incredible acts. Now, the most voluminous records to survive of the high-medieval inquisition are those of Languedoc, and their most salient characteristic is this. They do not contain incredible things. Far from it. And some of them are so full of wonderfully concrete and circumstantial detail that they can seem like photographs of past reality. They do not immediately invite deconstruction.

This is misleading of course. What goes on in them is subtler and more complex, and twenty-five years after Merlo Italian historiography has supplied another historian to tackle these records. Bruschi has taken the largest series to survive from Languedoc, the records of interrogations which run from the late 1230s to the mid-1280s in the seventeenth-century Doat copies. In chapter 5 she addresses these records directly and comprehensively, analysing them (as she expressly acknowledges) within the spirit of Merlo's approach, carefully positioning their features and delineating their various filters.

Other chapters in this book show how English, American and Australian scholarship is also now focussing on this area. An Australian historian working in the United States, Mark Pegg, puts under his microscope the questions used by two inquisitors when interrogating suspects in the Lauragais in 1245–6. They were repetitive and formulaic, they structured the interrogation, and they embodied a 'consequential notion of reality and notion of truth', while at the same time their application to over 5000 suspects will have acted upon these men and women, changing (or perhaps confirming) how these people thought about things. In chapter 7 Biller also addresses questions, setting side by side a question-list for suspected followers of Waldensians written by the inquisitor Bernard Gui and the questions which were actually put. Both reflected the inquisitor's 'ideal-type' of the practices of the sect in question, an ideal-type which was – so Biller argues – deliberately adjusted when new evidence came to the inquisitor's notice. There is stark contrast between the delicacy of concern for truth shown by Bernard Gui here, and his willingness to allude to Waldensian Luciferanism. In chapter 4 Arnold, like Bruschi, takes a broader approach, situating his work within an earlier tradition which was, however, confined to source-criticism and seeing *through* the text. There is much more to be done with the texts, which he approaches through the theories of Michel Foucault and examples from the hearings of Jacques Fournier in Pamiers around 1320. Far from seeing the text as a product of concrete and material conditions, he focuses on a deeper level of the construction of language, which affects lexical choice and the structure of the questioning. Inquisitors' authoritative discourse – their language and texts – constituted a field of knowledge; this discourse *in itself* embodied power. Texts and theory have also been important to the American historian James Given, whose recent book *Inquisition and Medieval Society: Power, Discipline and Resistance in Languedoc* (1997) investigated the 'technology' of keeping records as an element of inquisitors' power. In chapter 8 he now turns to another text generated by inquisition, sentences, and in particular the nineteen passed on the Béguins by Bernard Gui. Given builds on Merlo but goes further in his depicting of the public spectacle of punishment and its role in repression, and he imports theory. Is this public theatre a demonstration of Émile Durkheim's 'collective conscience', re-affirmed on such occasions? Given cites popular criticism of the punishments, arguing that they are to be seen as part of an ideological struggle in which, in the terms of Antonio Gramsci, an alien ruling 'bloc' was attempting to impose spiritual and cultural 'hegemony' on the people of Languedoc.

A twist worthy of a 'fiction' written by Jorge Luis Borges is provided by one chapter not so far mentioned. Whereas other chapters have displayed recurring (even if varying) modern historians' concern with texts and truth, in chapter 10 Bruschi provides a preliminary version of her study of a document which results from enquiries in 1309 and 1330 into inquisitions held over the years 1284–90: enquiries which show medieval jurists concerned with texts and truth, and the subtly different criteria they applied.

Alexander Patschovsky

The giants of German historiography have cast long shadows over this introduction, which has been influenced more than anything else by Arno Borst's history of the historiography of medieval heresy and Herbert

Grundmann's articles on heresy texts, beginning with the astonishingly precocious and fundamental account of the stereotype of the heretic which he published in 1927: an article which can be seen as starting everything discussed here.[34] The apostolic-scholarly tradition has been continued by Alexander Patschovsky, who was a pupil of Grundmann and who has been the doyen of historians of heresy and inquisition for the last thirty years. The malleability of 'heresy' from one point of view – the dependence of the accusation itself on political situations and power – complements this book's pre-occupation with the construction and repression of heresy in and through texts. It is at the core of Patschovsky's forthcoming monograph *Ketzer und Politik* (*Heresy and Politics: on the Political Function of Heresy in the Middle Ages (11th–15th Centuries)*). The parallel of master and pupil upheld here applies more broadly, for just as Grundmann in 1935 permanently altered the field of study from 'heretical sects' and 'religious Orders' to 'religious movements',[35] so his pupil Patschovsky is establishing a comparably seismic shift in the early twenty-first century, as he moves the focus from heresy to the forces which led to the prosecution of 'heresy'. Crowning our book is the distillation of the arguments in his Quodlibet Lecture, in chapter 2.

[34] See n. 3 above.
[35] Grundmann, *Religiöse Bewegungen*.

The 2000 York Quodlibet Lecture

Heresy and Society
On the Political Function of Heresy
in the Medieval World[1]

Alexander Patschovsky

This paper is based on three theses:

1. that medieval society was a society dominated by endemic conflicts;
2. that heresy was a constitutive component of these conflicts and consequently fulfilled a social function;
3. that the phenomenon of medieval heresy can only be understood if it is
   regarded as a framework for the articulation of overall social processes.

There is a whole bundle of questions which are worthy of investigation
and a variety of alternative answers to them which correlate with these three
theses. For example:

– Were heresies exceptional spiritual and intellectual phenomena, completely out of keeping with their times, products of the imagination of half
  or fully demented outsiders? Or were they at most radical variants of the
  mainstream intellectual debates?
– Was heresy a phenomenon restricted to groups on the fringes of society?
  Or was it just the opposite: the form in which deviant positions within the
  social elite were polemically expressed?
– How far is it possible to speak of heresy as a minority standpoint? Is it
  simply a matter of the number of adherents? In this case heresy would be
  the ideology of a part of society incapable of achieving majority status, an
  ideology incompatible with the opinion of the majority, and, consequently, damned to persecution in a non-pluralist society. From this
  perspective heresy could then be seen pragmatically as a matter of
  actual, but not principal, historical failure. It could simply be the label
  for failed orthodoxy, and, as such, interchangeable as regards its content.

[1] I am extremely grateful to Peter Biller and his collaborators for manifold advice and
help, but above all to the Centre of Medieval Studies at the University of York for the
honour of delivering the Quodlibet Lecture of 2000 and for the opportunity, through
this, of presenting the basic outlines of a book in progress on *Heresy and Politics: on
the Political Function of Heresy in the Middle Ages (11th–15th Centuries)*, whose German
version I hope will be finished in the near future. For the English translation of the
present article I have to thank James Fearns (Konstanz).

These are only a few of many possible questions. It is immediately evident that the different answers to them lead to very different assessments of the historical significance of heresy. The following treatment is meant as a tentative but nonetheless pointed attempt to define the position of heresy as a phenomenon in the medieval world in regard to its overall social, and hence its political function.

Where am I leading you?

I

First, let me mention where I won't lead you to or what I don't want to discuss here: I won't be concerned with the classic heretical movements, such as Cathars, Waldensians and the like. Since they are rather well defined groups, they don't really produce problems in describing their place and their fate within society. The moment we get to know heretics of this kind by name and profession, we can locate them socially.This has been done, with remarkable results, for example by Le Roy Ladurie[2] for the Pyrenean village Montaillou in the time of Jacques Fournier, who later became Pope Benedict XII. Less well known even among scholars might be the results of John Hine Mundy's research on Cathar Toulouse[3] or of James B. Given on the social aspects of the repression of heresy in the entire Languedoc,[4] of Lorenzo Paolini's on Cathar Bologna,[5] of Grado Merlo's on Waldensian Piedmont,[6] and perhaps my own on pre-Hussite Bohemia.[7] All these works clearly point out that heresy was not a phenomenon of the lower strata of medieval society and thus not a sign of social tensions in a Marxist sense – between the poor and the well-to-do. On the contrary, heresy was at least in part just an indicator of the mentality of groups which were involved in a dynamic process climbing up the social ladder and which were also geographically highly mobile. Heresy, therefore, in its well defined forms could be determined socially as either indicating vertical and horizontal mobility, or just being nothing other than a usual part of society. This last point was the essential message of Le Roy Ladurie's *Montaillou*. Concerning the social

---

[2] *Montaillou* (1975). This work provoked harsh criticisms, noted and enlarged by M. Benad, *Domus und Religion in Montaillou: Katholische Kirche und Katharismus im Überlebenskampf der Familie des Pfarrers Petrus Clerici am Anfang des 14. Jahrhunderts,* Spätmittelalter und Reformation, Neue Reihe 1 (Tübingen, 1990), esp. pp. 31–6, but in my view they do not affect – in our context – the basic results of Le Roy Ladurie's remarkable study.

[3] Mundy, *Repression.*

[4] Given, *Inquisition.*

[5] Paolini, *Eresia a Bologna.*

[6] Merlo, *Eretici e inquisitori.*

[7] Patschovsky, *Inquisition in Böhmen*; Patschovsky, *Quellen zur böhmischen Inquisition*; 'Über die politische Bedeutung von Häresie und Häresieverfolgung im mittelalterlichen Böhmen', in Segl, *Anfänge der Inquisition*, pp. 235–51.

aspect of 'Geistesgeschichte', it was already pointed out long ago by my teacher Herbert Grundmann that the heretical movements of the Middle Ages had arisen out of the mainstream of medieval religious developments.[8] As a result, they don't reflect isolated phenomena, but can only be understood in a broader context, on which they themselves produce repercussions at the same time. As soon as heresies became distinguishable from the broader stream of religious thought and as such outlawed by the majority, their members were first expelled from society, and then – after having become a real threat in the opinion of the dominating groups – they were persecuted and put to death. The reasons are obvious: since society had a certain unique creed as an ideological basis for each member and as a bond for all of them, one could expect nothing but persecution of stigmatized people. In medieval times it was almost impossible that a society could be pluralistic, or even show tolerance – at least not what we associate with this word today. Only in two cases could there be a change in society at all: first, when the means of suppression didn't succeed in the end. This happened when – starting with Hussitism and ending with the Reformation – heresies became Churches. And secondly, when the evangelic creed itself increasingly lost its value; that is to say, when rationalism and agnosticism became counterparts to all religious beliefs.

II

These issues have been discussed extensively elsewhere and I won't treat them further. What really interests me in trying to determine the true place of heresy in medieval society, are not the well defined heretical groups and the way their Catholic contemporaries dealt with them, but the less clearly defined applications of the term 'heretic'.

Who, then, could be charged with heresy other than Cathars, Waldensians, Hussites and the like, or theologians like Abelard, Eckhart or Wyclif, who, by their very profession ran the risk of being declared heretics? The answer is: a lot of people! A pope like Boniface VIII or John XXII, an emperor like Frederick II or Louis the Bavarian; the rebellious cities of the Lombard League while they were struggling with this same Frederick II; the knightly Order of the Temple; defenders of the legitimacy of the Roman pope in regions of wavering obedience during the Great Schism; prominent citizens accused by their political opponents – to mention but a few. Who were the accusers? In the case of Boniface VIII we find the Colonna brothers, his deadly enemies, and, most important, King Philip the Fair of France. William of Ockham, who for years was regarded as being a heretic by the official

[8] H. Grundmann, *Religiöse Bewegungen im Mittelalter*, Historische Studien 267 (Berlin, 1935; 2nd edn, Darmstadt, 1961); English translation, Grundmann, *Religious Movements*.

Church, composed his formidable 'Dialogue' to prove the heresy of John XXII. And Louis the Bavarian inaugurated a trial, which ended with the condemnation of this 'pseudo'-pope. On the other hand he himself suffered for the rest of his life from the consequences of a judicial condemnation, which John XXII in his turn had launched against him. I needn't describe the *cause célèbre* of the Templars, nor of Frederick II, against whom his papal adversaries wielded the spiritual sword. At the same time Frederick also knew very well how to use this weapon when he equated political rebels who had offended the royal majesty with religious rebels, that is to say, heretics, who had offended the majesty of God.[9]

In their social context, most of these cases share a common pattern: while one may doubt that the accusation of heresy is convincing on dogmatic grounds – either before the throne of God or the court of the contemporary public – there can't be any doubt about the political background. But if heresy slowly became a weapon in daily political strife in the Middle Ages, this had two paradoxical consequences:

1. The dogmatic religious aspect of heresy lost its weight; it became a secondary factor, if not mere pretence, and in the end it completely lost any credit. An institution making too much use of spiritual power for secular means loses these three things: means, power, and spirit. Therefore, the threat of the accusation of heresy as the most dangerous part of the ecclesiastical penal system basically led to the dissolution of all bonds of religious authority within society, and finally of the religious creed itself.

2. But there was a second consequence as well: since the accusation of heresy lost its spiritual threat, and in the long run its dangerous consequences in daily life, it had an inflationary effect. If we watch closely the development of the definition of heresy starting with Gregory VII's famous, but practically still rather vague statement in his *Dictatus papae*:[10] 'Quod catholicus non habeatur, qui non concordat Romanae ecclesiae' ('That a person who does not agree with the Roman Church should not be held to be Catholic'), and leading to the hardly less famous wording in Boniface VIII's bull *Unam sanctam*, that obedience to the pope is essential for salvation, we cannot escape the impression that in the course of time *the* heresy par excellence had become disobedience instead of disbelief.[11] From this it follows that the

[9] This was pointed out especially by K.-V. Selge, 'Die Ketzerpolitik Friedrichs II', in *Probleme um Friedrich II.*, ed. J. Fleckenstein, Vorträge und Forschungen 16 (Sigmaringen, 1974), pp. 309–43.

[10] *Dictatus papae* xxvi, ed. E. Caspar, *Das Register Gregors VII*, 2 vols., MGH, Epistolae Selectae 2 (Berlin, 1920–23), I, 207.

[11] This thought was developped first by Y. M.-J. Congar, 'Der Platz des Papsttums in der Kirchenfrömmigkeit der Reformer des 11. Jahrhunderts', in: *Sentire ecclesiam*, ed. J. Daniélou and H. Vorgrimler (Freiburg, Basel and Vienna, 1963), pp. 196–217. For the whole development of this paradigm, see his *L'Église: de saint Augustin à l'époque moderne*, Histoire des dogmes 3, 3 (Paris, 1970), and *L'ecclésiologie du haut moyen âge: de Saint Grégoire à la désunion entre Byzance et Rome* (Paris, 1968).

meaning of the term heresy shifted from a specific distinction in the realm of thought to a general pattern of behaviour within society. It no longer showed any link to a specific creed. Consequently, 'faith', and its opposite 'heresy', had become social categories. Vague as the term heresy now had become, it was as intellectually unconvincing as socially freely applicable. So there was no reason for anybody to feel guilty on dogmatic grounds, while everybody who was on bad terms with ecclesiastical authorities could be charged with heresy.

III

But who were these authorities? Whom could one disobey in the politico-religious field? The pope and clergy, of course, the organizational structure and, according to a well established doctrine, the very substance of the Church. But lay powers, since they were the authorized protectors of the Church, could claim the same obedience as well. They did so either as the *brachium saeculare* (secular arm) of the spiritual power – Philip the Fair of France and Emperor Charles IV of Germany were masters in using these possibilities for their goals – or, if the clergy as the proper guardian of right belief and discipline proved deficient, the lay powers claimed obedience in religious matters as a subsidiary principle within Christian society. Marsilius of Padua and William of Ockham were the theoretical architects of this doctrine. And Louis the Bavarian was acting according to the outlines of their doctrine in declaring Pope John XXII a heretic.

All in all, the authorities of medieval society, being armed with the weapon 'heresy', used it as a club to discipline their opponents – mostly to curb their subordinates, and sometimes their rivals. For the historian this has two consequences:. Firstly, if we stumble across a heresy trial, especially in the late Middle Ages, we should always be aware of the political background; in many cases there is no other ground whatsoever. Secondly, if heresy became the medium for fighting out a political conflict, we are at the very core of our problem. Then, we have to ask, how can we describe a society which expressed its endemic tensions in religious terms, and how can we define heresy as one side – mostly, but not always, the losing one – in religious disputes directed by or combined with political moves?

IV

At this point it might be useful to give an example. I choose the Pataria movement in Milan in the middle of the eleventh century.[12] One might argue

---

[12] The main sources are Arnulf of Milan, *Liber gestorum recentium* iii.9–iv.3, ed. C. Zey, MGH Scriptores rerum Germanicarum in usum scholarum 67 (Hannover, 1994),

that the genuine Pataria was never depicted as a heresy in our sources. On the contrary, at least one of its leaders, Ariald, became a saint.[13] Further, whenever the term 'heresy' was used at all, it was the Patarines who branded their opponents as heretics; to be precise, as heretical simonists.[14] But that is only half the truth. The other half is that, starting from the second half of the twelfth century, the term *Patarene* was used in Upper Italy for Cathars. This fact shows that both movements seem to have had one thing in common: their opponents in the social strata. These opponents invented the term in the eleventh century and adapted it later on to apply to people who were doing basically the same things, as they saw it.

Well then, who were the Patarenes and who were their adversaries? But first, what does the word *pataria* mean?[15] This is not quite clear. Since Lodovico Muratori's time it has been generally agreed that one should understand the word as a mocking term, for example, that it may have derived from *patta*, a word in the vernacular spoken in Milan meaning rags.[16] This would clearly indicate a social meaning with defamatory character designating people of allegedly lower origin. So, is the Pataria a pauperistic movement? There were people who took this for granted.[17] But reality – as usual – is much more complex.

Let us begin our investigation into this case with the leaders of the

pp. 174–220, and Landulfus senior, *Historia Mediolanensis* iii.5–30, ed. A. Cutolo, RIS 4, part 2, pp. 85–123. Basic literature for the following passages are C. Violante, *La Pataria milanese e la riforma ecclesiastica, 1: Le premesse (1045–1057)*, Studi storici 11–13 (Rome, 1955); G. Miccoli, 'Per la storia della Pataria milanese', *BISIME* 70 (1958), 43–123, reprinted in his *Chiesa gregoriana: Ricerche sulla riforma del secolo XI*, 2nd edn (Rome, 1999), pp. 127–212); G. Cracco, 'Pataria: opus e nomen (tra verità e autorità)', *Rivista di storia della Chiesa in Italia* 28 (1974), 357–87; H. Keller, 'Pataria und Stadtverfassung, Stadtgemeinde und Reform: Mailand im "Investiturstreit"', in *Investiturstreit und Reichsverfassung*, ed. J. Fleckenstein, Vorträge und Forschungen 17 (Sigmaringen, 1973), pp. 321–50, and 'Der Übergang zur Kommune: Zur Entwicklung der italienischen Stadtverfassung im 11. Jahrhundert', in *Beiträge zum hochmittelalterlichen Städtewesen*, ed. B. Diestelkamp, Städteforschung A 11 (Cologne and Vienna, 1982), pp. 55–72.
[13] See Andreas of Strumi, *Vita sancti Arialdi*, ed. F. Baethgen, MGH Scriptores 30, 2 (Hannover, 1926–34).
[14] Arnulf of Milan iii.11, ed. Zey, pp. 180–81: '. . . asserentes omnia symoniaca. Hos tales cetera vulgalitas hyronice Patarinos appellat' ('. . . saying that all these ⟨things⟩ were symoniac. These people were called by the rest of the vulgar crowd ironically "Patarenes"').
[15] Cf. A. Frugoni, 'Due schede: "Pannosus" e "Patarinus"', *BISIME* 65 (1953), 129–35; C. Thouzellier, '"Patarins"', in her *Hérésies et hérétiques*, Storia e Letteratura. Raccolta di studi e testi 116 (Roma, 1969), pp. 204–221. But see the critical remarks of Cracco, 'Pataria', who in his turn provides an excellent abstract of the semantic history of the word.
[16] *Antiquitates Italicae Medii Aevi*, ed. L. A. Muratori, 6 vols. (Milan, 1738–42), V, 84–6, esp. 85. Cracco, 'Pataria', 360, vehemently rejected such an explanation.
[17] See e.g. E. Werner, *Pauperes Christi: Studien zu sozial-religiösen Bewegungen im Zeitalter des Reformpapsttums* (Leipzig, 1956), pp. 111–64.

movement! There were three: Ariald, who became a martyr and finally a saint, Landulf and his brother Erlembald. Ariald, who was born in the Contado of Milan, belonged to the lower nobility known as the *valvassores*. He was educated to become a cleric. And as an itinerant scholar he received a learned education which earned him some esteem even among his adversaries.[18] Landulf and Erlembald where even higher in rank. They originated from a family of *capitanei*. This was the social strata forming the higher nobility in north Italian cities. Landulf was member of the aristocratic chapter of the Milanese cathedral. His brother Erlembald was a gifted military leader.

All in all the leaders of the Pataria, at least, were definitely no humble men. This fact needn't exclude anyone from leadership of a pauperist movement or – expressed in more malevolent terms – of the mob. But who were these men's adherents who were made to believe that the clergy of Milan was rotten to the core, living only in luxury, and spending all their time hunting, fornicating, and earning money? Well, in the year 1057 these adherents were able to insitute judicial proceedings, obliging the high Milanese clergy to subscribe to an edict which enforced celibacy upon them.[19] And when this clergy tried to alter this decision, Landulf managed to make the whole Milanese community take an oath that prohibition of the clergy's fornication and simoniacal corruption should henceforth be part of the public order.[20]

The fact that a whole political community took an oath (*commune iuramentum*) is revealing enough. It shows that the Milanese Pataria was part of the broader community movement, which since the second half of the eleventh century had given rise to more or less autonomous political entities, in all the parts of Europe with flourishing cities, namely in Flanders and northern Italy. These entities were led by social groups, the members of which were not altogether newcomers in the field of politics. But they used and shared power in a way significantly different from earlier times.

What makes the difference, then? Well, basically a hierarchical structure of public power with a city-lord at the top was transformed into a sort of 'balance of power' between the ruling groups which were struggling for influence. To put it in a nutshell: a monarchical system was in principle replaced by an oligarchy. In practice the difference was not so great, because even in times of strong rulers the consent of those groups who carried out governmental decisions was necessary. Therefore, elements of a quasi

---

[18] Landulfus senior, *Historia Mediolanensis* iii.5, ed. Cutolo, p. 86: 'artis liberae magister' ('master of the [liberal] arts').

[19] Arnulf of Milan iii.10, ed. Zey, p. 179: 'pytacium de castitate servanda' ('edict about preserving chastity').

[20] Arnulf of Milan iii.11, ed. Zey, p. 180: 'Unde potestate accepta commune indicit omnibus laicis iuramentum, quasi impugnanda proponens sacrorum ordinum stupra et venales consecrationes, quod non multo post clericos etiam iurare compellit' ('Then, after taking power, he imposed a common oath on all laymen to fight against adulteries and venal consecrations of ordained people, as if it were a duty, ⟨an oath⟩ which, not long afterwards, he forced the clergy also to swear').

democratic power-sharing were implicit even in monarchic systems. This
was the case to a higher degree in an oligarchical system, which was already
by definition open to relatively big numbers of 'shareholders' in public power
in a rather democratic way.

What happened in our Milan of the Pataria, was that, besides the
archbishop and the German king as city-lords, there were three social
groups struggling for political leadership:[21] first, the aristocratic *capitanei*,
mostly representatives of the old governmental élite; secondly, the social
newcomer strata of the *valvassores*, lower nobles of free birth, but with
dependent functions (these people had successfully fought for better conditions in the early decades of the eleventh century, and since then they were
slowly mingling with the *capitanei*); and, thirdly, the so called *populus*, or *cives*
– the ordinary citizens of free status, commoners, who up to this time had no
governmental rights. But they became more and more politically potent
because of their sheer economic weight. In these circumstances the transformation of a monarchical into an oligarchical system of public power-
sharing did not mean much more than giving an institutionalized form to the
pre-existing decision-making process which evolved within a permanent
civic struggle.

Nevertheless, it is still important to note that in the pro-Pataria decision of
the Milan community of 1057 all relevant social groups were involved – some
as victims, some as victors. A victim was the old aristocratic establishment,
which had till then dominated the archiepiscopal *curia* as centre of governmental power. Its members were now stigmatized as adulterers and simo-
niacs and supporters of such people. Victors were those who tried to gain by
the communal movement. Consequently, the struggle rather quickly focused
on the appointment of the head of the archiepiscopal see in Milan as the key
to power in the religio-moral as well as in the political sphere. In the next two
decades after 1057 this resulted in nothing less than three rightly (or wrongly)
appointed archbishops acting simultaneously. As a further consequence the
pope and the German king were involved. And in the end this rather
unimportant looking incident unleashed nothing less than the so called
Investiture Contest.

When the whole Milanese community took over the anticlerical religio-
moral program of the Pataria, the communal movement became identical
with the Patarene movement. Was Milan a Patarene city, then? For some
time, yes. To be precise: Milan became Patarene and stayed Patarene as long
as the Patarene leaders were at the same time spiritual reformers and leading
protagonists of the communal movement. Nevertheless, this communal
movement had strong patriotic Milanese implications, whereas the Patarene

[21] Basic for the social structure of Milan at this time is H. Keller, *Adelsherrschaft und
städtische Gesellschaft in Oberitalien. 9. bis 12. Jahrhundert*, Bibliothek des Deutschen
Historischen Instituts in Rom 52 (Tübingen, 1979); see also G. Dilcher, *Die
Entstehung der lombardischen Stadtkommune: eine rechtsgeschichtliche Untersuchung*,
Untersuchungen zur deutschen Staats- und Rechts-Geschichte, n.s. 7 (Aalen, 1967).

spiritual movement had close relations to the reformed Roman papacy. When during the conflict with the ruling archbishop in the year 1066 the Patarene leaders asked the Roman see for support, and even received it, the majority of the Milanese populace regarded this as treachery. It is not so difficult now to understand why Ariald was killed in the riots which broke out. Later on the same reproach cost the life of Erlembald, who after his brother Landulf's death had taken over the leadership of both the Patarene and the communal movement. In 1075, when Erlembald, seeking refuge in tyrannical pressures, tried to invest a new archbishop in alliance with Rome, he and his closest adherents were killed in a violent upsurge of the populace organized again in a sworn community.[22]

Thus the beginning and the end of the Milanese Pataria were marked by sworn communities, in which the political body of a city expressed its political will. The contents of this will could at any time be, and in our case was, to a high degree religious. A certain religio-moral behaviour, or at least a particular confession of faith, became the shibboleth for certain political options. And the way this religio-moral will was expressed, became a form of politics.

V

We now have to draw the general conclusions from this specific example: at the time of the Pataria medieval society is already an inseparable *corpus mixtum* (mixed body) of secular and religious elements. We could define it as a body that was constituted as ideologically theocratic and politically profane. But we can go further: in a society, in which politics takes the shape of religion, religion inevitably becomes a matter of politics. Both spheres are so inseparably interwoven with one another, that we cannot even differentiate between subject and object, between basis and super-structure (to use Marxist terms). There is only one word which can describe the political body of the medieval European society as a whole (and it was already used in medieval literature on political theory for this purpose): that is 'Christianity', nothing else.[23]

---

[22] Arnulf of Milan iv.10, ed. Zey, p. 215: 'Unde factum est, ut simul diebus aliquot extra urbem exuentes suam sibi iurarent magna plebis cum parte iustitiam et sancti Ambrosii honorem ac dono regis accepturos sese pastorem . . .' ('Therefore it happened that a few days later they went out of the city and swore to each other, including a large part of the common people, an oath to protect their rights and the honour of St Ambrose, also swearing that they would accept a pastor by the king's gift').

[23] As an example for political theory one can take Marsilius of Padua, *Defensor pacis*, ed. R. Scholz, MGH, Fontes iuris Germanici antiqui in usum scholarum 7 (Hann-over, 1932), and as an example for political praxis the famous *Bulla aurea Karoli IV. imperatoris anno MCCCLVI promulgata*, ed. W. D. Fritz, MGH Fontes iuris Germanici

Now it is clear what heresy means in this context: the rebellious, the minor, the losing, the persecuted part – but nonetheless a constituent part of this society. Anyone who speaks about heresies as being essentially lunacies (which of course they could be, too) misses the point. One could describe medieval society as a 'persecuting society',[24] but as societies normally, and European societies always, have been ruled by dynamic forces and could be defined as conflicting entities, the question concerning medieval society is not 'Why were there conflicts and inevitably persecutions?', but 'Why, and how long were they expressed in religious terms?'

VI

As an early example of conflict within an essentially Christian social body the Pataria formed part of the greater Church reform movement of the eleventh century. This movement was able to succeed, because the lay world saw its own ends realized in what the reform defined as 'liberty of the Church', *Libertas Ecclesiae*.[25] This slogan basically comprised two goals: first, clerical autonomy from lay influence in the field of ethics according to genuine Christian traditions; and secondly, clerical independence from secular powers in the administration of ecclesiastical estates.

The first aim meant orientation towards the highest possible standards in ethics and piety provided by Christian doctrine. These standards obliged clergy and lay folk in different ways, giving the clergy by means of the Petrine doctrine the keys to salvation for everybody. This entailed high prestige, but obligation as well. A society which had become sensitive to true Christian life was highly interested in reform as a means of everyman's salvation, but at the same time also highly critical concerning the effect of reform as a means of avoiding eternal damnation. It is not difficult to discern the success of the reform movement as one root of dissent, meaning heresy. Because, inasmuch as the reform movement excited Christian society, it would prove impossible to suppress an open minded public by enforcing blind obedience to Church authorities as a primary Christian virtue.

Enforcing blind obedience proved all the more impracticable, as the second aim of Church liberty in practice inevitably led to corruption of the ethical standards which had been developed in theory. This holds especially true

antiqui in usum scholarum 11 (Weimar, 1972), where by definition the 'people' of the Empire is the 'populus Christianus'.
[24] I am referring to the influential study of Moore, *Persecuting Society*.
[25] The classical study on this subject is G. Tellenbach, *Libertas: Kirche und Weltordnung im Zeitalter des Investiturstreites*, Forschungen zur Kirchen- und Geistesgeschichte 7 (Stuttgart, 1936). See also B. Szabó-Bechstein, '"Libertas ecclesiae" vom 12. bis zur Mitte des 13. Jahrhunderts. Verbreitung und Wandel des Begriffs seit seiner Prägung durch Gregor VII.', in *Die abendländische Freiheit vom 10. zum 14. Jahrhundert*, ed. J. Fried, Vorträge und Forschungen 39 (Sigmaringen, 1991), pp. 147–75.

when we consider that since the time of Gregory VII the concept of liberty of the Church was developed in theory and practice from meaning mere autonomy of ecclesiastical estates to domination of the whole political world.

There is no need to elaborate on this further. Since the time of Gregory VII we find this incessant struggle of the later Middle Ages, which separated what had become so closely interrelated: the realm of the holy and the realm of the profane. It still took some time till Wyclif found a vigorous theoretical basis for the incompatibility of both spheres. With the partial success of the Hussite revolution this theory found its first realisation in practice. Despite these late results in theory and practice, the concept of incompatibility between the secular and the religious sphere had always been the ideological foundation of the religious movements in the high and later Middle Ages. The well-defined heretical groups as well as the not so well defined had as their common basis the postulate of a Church that was not characterized by *dominium* (lordship). If, for instance, we look at the reform proposals in the *Defensor pacis* of Marsilius of Padua, echoed in the manifestoes of Louis the Bavarian, we shall find the 'true' Roman Church organized according to the model of the Franciscan Order – to be precise, its spiritualistic branch, which means: according to the doctrine of *usus pauper* (pauperist use ⟨of all kinds of material goods⟩).[26]

To sum up this point: in a society which was at the same time as much religious as profane, where lay princes controlled spiritual life and prelates directed princely estates, where the high ethical standards of theory were in principle incompatible with daily life and practice, heresy was no exception in social life, but its natural product. It was the necessary expression of the inner contradictions of that system. In this sense, heresy is a reliable indicator for the historian: as soon as he finds traces of heresy and of its eradication, he has to cope with a society of the described type. The opposite holds true as soon as heresy becomes irrelevant. Then the type of politico-religious society must have vanished.

VII

The question is whether such a type of society ever existed. In view of the endemic character of inner-social conflicts in the Middle Ages, we would continually have to stumble over trials for heresy, if the heuristic principle which we have just been discussing had ever been effective. Nevertheless, there were quite obviously only a limited number of such trials.

As usual in all medieval social reality, the answer is rather complex.

---

[26] Marsilius of Padua, *Defensor pacis* ii.11–14, ed. Scholz, pp. 256–325; for Louis the Bavarian see e.g. the manifesto 'Gloriosus Deus', ed. J. Schwalm, MGH, Constitutiones et acta publica imperatorum et regum 6, 3 vols. (Hannover, 1914–27), I, 344–50 n. 436, esp. pp. 346–7, § 4.

1. On the one hand there were in fact many more cases of heresy, accusations of heresy, or at least threats with accusations of heresy than most historians are generally aware of. This is the case, because – as a result of our historiographical tradition – we are used to separating allegedly 'real' from what we regard as 'so-called' heresy. Consequently, in many instances we do not regard a case as being relevant for the history of heresy, especially if we are faced with forms of rather undefinable heresy, such as those I am focusing on in my present paper. The current compendia on heresy are a good example of this effect.[27]

In addition, scholars in the study of heresy sometimes tend to select their material in too narrow a way. To mention just one example: Raoul Manselli traced the development of the term *Ariana haeresis* and claimed that this term could not be found for about eighty years after the middle of the eleventh century – this means, for the period between Wazo of Liège, who supposedly reported about Manichaeans, and Henry of Lausanne, whose life as an itinerant preacher ended in heresy.[28] These eighty years almost exactly mark the age of the Church reform and the Investiture Contest. Manselli could only arrive at this conclusion, because he restricted his search for the term to those sources of heresy which are commonly looked upon as being relevant. According to him, there could not have been heretics in the original sense during the Investiture Contest, because there were no differences between the revolution of the Church and heresy. And so Manselli obviously did not feel obliged to look for the name *heretic* in a period in which by definition there could be no heresies at all.

As a matter of fact, in the period of the Investiture Contest Church reform and heresy cannot be differentiated. But the consequence of simply giving up the term *heresy* would be absolutely wrong. We only have to interpret it in the right way: heresy and its correlative catholicity are mere denominations – used *vice versa* by the opposing parties – in an overall process of social conflict. This can be seen in the existence of the term *Ariana haeresis* in sources where Manselli did not find it, because he simply was not looking for it there: for example in the genre of polemical pamphlets. In the *Libelli de lite*, edited in the MGH, the term *Ariana haeresis* turns up no less than 134 times, provided my counting is right.[29] And what is more, we can find it not only in one, but in many works, and across party lines. Dogmatically speaking, its use is totally

---

[27] It suffices to point at the by far superior example of this species from Lambert, *Medieval Heresy*, esp. pp. 3–8, where he outlines the choice he is making regarding the manifold kinds of 'heresy'.

[28] R. Manselli, 'Una designazione dell'eresia catara: "Arriana Heresis"', in his *Studi sulle eresie del secolo XII*, Studi storici 5, 2nd edn (Rome, 1975), pp. 237–46, esp. pp. 240–41.

[29] *Libelli de lite imperatorum et pontificum saeculis XI. et XII. conscripti*, ed. E. Dümmler et al., 3 vols. (Hannover, 1891–7). I am relying on a word concordance provided by Timothy Reuter which till now unfortunately only exists in one exemplar at the MGH in Munich.

unspecific. It is solely for stigmatizing the politico-religious opponent, nothing else.

So, due to the tradition of isolating the phenomenon of heresy, scholars in heresy are not utterly free from blindness in selecting their object as well as in selecting the sources. But many things could not be seen because major parts of potentially relevant materials simply have not been made accessible yet. The late Hermann Diener, scientific collaborator and vice-president of the German Historical Institute in Rome, drew our attention to one group of sources: registers of the papal penitentiary, which – starting about the middle of the fifteenth century, but with certain items even from the fourteenth century – have been preserved in large numbers. Here, in fact, all those cases should be found in which the pope had reserved to himself the right of freeing the person from the 'major' excommunication. There definitely must have been outright or at least potential heretics amongst them. And, according to Diener's observation, they seem to be listed there in consider-able numbers.[30] But no-one has collected and analysed the material so far. This is an astonishing fact, because the material should throw light upon the disciplinary effect of the instrument of excommunication. If we define excommunication as a damnation of heresy in an embryonic state, and if we further consider the notoriously inflationary use of this instrument of Church discipline, it will then become clear to what extent heresy – no matter whether embryonic or fully-grown – had been a decisive factor in medieval, or at least late medieval, political reality.

2. The previously announced complexity of my answer to the question about the true extent of the accusation of heresy does not actually lie in the fact that certain quantitative elements in this context have not yet been given their proper attention. Again the difficulty is due to a specific aspect of the convergence of the religio-spiritual with the profane-material sphere. Here I refer to an observation, which Howard Kaminsky made in his outstanding book about Simon de Cramaud with regard to the causes of the endlessly long period of the Great Schism. As the main reason he mentioned thinking 'in reified terms'.[31] When even *Spiritualia* ('spiritual ⟨things⟩') could merely indicate the material equivalent for liturgical services, we should not be surprised to find even the Papacy as an office taking on the meaning of a mere conglomerate of material claims.

---

[30] Hermann Diener made this announcement publicly in the context of a paper he gave at a conference about forgeries in the Middle Ages, organized by the Monumenta Germaniae Historica in Munich 1986, where he concentrated on forgers of papal documents (cf. H. Diener, 'Strafvollzug an der päpstlichen Kurie im 14. Jahrhundert. Aus den Registern des päpstlichen Kerkermeisters und des Großpönitentiars', in *Fälschungen im Mittelalter* 2, Schriften der MGH 33 (2) (Hann-over, 1988), pp. 607–26). He has, however, never produced details about the heretics he mentioned when he made this claim.

[31] H. Kaminsky, *Simon de Cramaud and the Great Schism* (New Brunswick NJ, 1983), pp. 9–11.

Consequently people could live with the divisibility of the Papacy without having to feel too much concern about the salvation of their own souls, the ones trustfully put into their hands, or even the ones which were separated from them by another obedience.

But – with regard to the conceptual content – if the whole religio-spiritual sphere did take on material features, then a generally spiritual term like heresy also had to take on profane connotations. Above all this means, then, that the use of the term must have been determined by the profane-material level.

If we look upon it at the political level, this fact is easily discernible. I refer here only to the trials about the thesis of tyrannicide propounded by the professor of theology Jean Petit of Paris and about the doctrine of genocide propounded by the Dominican John Falkenberg.[32] Both cases were interwoven and high on the agenda of the Council of Constance (1414–18). Both theses were advanced on behalf and for the benefit of certain political powers. One was the duke of Burgundy, John the Fearless; the other was the Teutonic Order. However, their deadly enemies – the Armagnacs and the Polish king – denounced both theses as being heretical. Since these trials for heresy were political instruments, they were fought out with theological arguments, but in the end they were settled along political lines. This actually means that there was no settlement at all, because none of the antagonists was powerful enough to push his ideas through.

So, trials against heresy were not solely carried on because of any heresy as such, but they could become the legal and theologico-argumentative place for confrontations of a completely different sort. In the course of such a trial the direction and the result were not determined by the quality of the theologico-legal arguments, but by the sheer force of the political battalions.

Consequently, the reverse also has to be true: there were no heresy trials if the political will to initiate them was lacking. To be frank, it is not that easy to prove the non-existence of something. Still I would like to substantiate this thesis with two observations.

First, whoever tries to map heresy trials according to time and space, will notice a great irregularity. Let us take Austria for example: in the Austrian region of the diocese of Passau there were at least four major campaigns against heretics between 1250 and 1400.[33] In the nearby region of the

[32] The interrelationship of both cases was outlined by H. Boockmann, *Johannes Falkenberg, der Deutsche Orden und die polnische Politik*, Veröffentlichungen des Max-Planck-Instituts für Geschichte 45 (Göttingen, 1975).

[33] Cf. H. Haupt, *Waldenserthum und Inquisition im südöstlichen Deutschland* (Freiburg-im-Breisgau, 1890); P. Segl, *Ketzer in Österreich: Untersuchungen über Häresie und Inquisition im Herzogtum Österreich im 13. und beginnenden 14. Jahrhundert*, Quellen und Forschungen aus dem Gebiet der Geschichte, n.s. 5 (Paderborn, Munich, Vienna and Zurich, 1984). For special aspects cf. P. Biller, 'Aspects of the Waldenses in the Fourteenth Century' (unpublished D.Phil. thesis, University of Oxford, 1974); Patschovsky, *Passauer Anonymus*. See also the well balanced overview by W. Maleczek, 'Die Ketzerverfolgung im österreichischen Hoch- und Spätmittelal-

archdiocese of Salzburg there was not a single trial. Why? Was that so because there were no heretics or people who could have been persecuted as heretics? This is hardly to be assumed. The decisive factor can be found in the different politics of the rulers – the Austrian dukes here and the Archbishop of Salzburg there. Even contemporaries were quite conscious of this fact. Konrad Waldhauser, a reform preacher in Bohemia in the middle of the fourteenth century, fervently complained about the god-forsaken materialistic thinking of nobles, who lacked the necessary enthusiasm for the protection of the faith and consequently for the persecution of heretics.[34]

Secondly, let us examine the world of Boccaccio and of the Italian Renaissance. People then had an outspoken contempt for the clergy. And the temper of the Quattrocento was guided by Epicurean ideals. The consequence of all that was a scarcely disguised agnosticism. We shall hardly be able to imagine that in such a world the accusation of heresy – if ever brought to the fore – could have had much significance. And, indeed, it did not. Whenever a person was accused of heresy, there were always other things involved as well.[35]

From all this, paradoxical statements follow: many more heretics had been persecuted than we have become aware of so far. And at the same time the accusation of heresy as such played a much less important role than we would have judged at first glance from the sheer number of occurrences. So,

---

ter', in *Wellen der Verfolgung in der österreichischen Geschichte*, ed. E. Zöller, H. Möcker, and B. Zimmermann (Vienna, 1986), pp. 18–39.

[34] Konrad Waldhauser, *Postilla studentium sancte Pragensis universitatis, sermo* 'Attendite a falsis prophetis' (Matthew 7. 15); cf. the extract, ed. Patschovsky, *Quellen zur böhmischen Inquisition*, pp. 125–6; cf. also F. Šimek, *Staročeské zpracování Postily studentů svaté university pražské Konráda Waldhausera* (Prague, 1947), p. 100. A similar complaint was made in thirteenth-century Austria; cf. Segl, *Ketzer in Österreich*, pp. 153–4.

[35] It does not make much sense to substantiate these general statements in detail here. However, to give an inkling of what I have in mind, see Scharff, *Häretikerverfolgung*, and H. G. Walther, 'Ziele und Mittel päpstlicher Ketzerpolitik in der Lombardei und im Kirchenstaat 1184–1252', in Segl, *Anfänge der Inquisition*, pp. 103–30; concerning the impact of heresy and high policy on Italian cities of the Trecento; on the revival of 'Epicureanism' in Italy see e.g. E. Garin, *La cultura filosofica del Rinascimento italiano*, 2nd edn (Firenze, 1979), ch. 4; access to the cause célèbre of Fra Dolcino's heretical career is provided by the study of R. Orioli, *Fra Dolcino: nascita, vita e morte di un'eresia medievale* (Novara, 1984); on the political character of Savonarola's heresy cf. the diverse publications, in the course of the celebration of the 500th anniversary of his death, edited by G. C. Garfagnini, e.g. *Savonarola: democrazia, tirannide, profezia* (Firenze, 1998), *Savonarola e la politica* (Firenze, 1997), *Savonarola e la mistica* (Firenze, 1999), *Verso Savonarola* (Firenze, 1999). It may suffice to mention the persecution of Matteo Visconti and his Quattrocento Milan by Pope John XXII, and also the persecution of 'classical' heretical sects like the Bolognese Cathars at the end of the thirteenth century (cf. Paolini, *Eresia a Bologna*), or the Piedmontese Waldensians (cf. Merlo, *Eretici e inquisitori*), with whose political character a chapter of my forthcoming book on *Heresy and Politics* deals.

both results taken together support the basic thesis of this paper: heresy is an indicator of an overall process in society, and not an isolated phenomenon.

VIII

In his dedicatory letter to Count William VIII of Montpellier Alain de Lille characterizes the heretics of his time as follows:

> The difference between the heretics of our time and those of antiquity is that the latter strove to attack our faith with the arguments of human reason, whereas the former are guided in the creation of their monstrous ideas by no form of reason whatever, be it intrinsically human or derived from God; they follow only their own headstrong desires and instincts. In former times, it is said, the various heretics of various times thought up dogmas which differed from or contradicted one another; . . . but in our times the new heretics – or should one rather say the old and aged heretics? – in the process of ageing draw together the teachings of different heresies, create one single idol from many, one single monster from many and brew one general poison from many poisonous herbs.

The quotation is taken from a work which Alain directed against the four great heretical religious groups of the Western world, the Cathars, the Waldensians, the Jews and Islam, around the year 1200.[36] Two and a half centuries later the Dominican inquisitor Heinrich Kalteisen drew on this passage, using almost the same words to describe the spiritual world of Henne Becker, an insignificant, solitary heretic from Mainz.[37] We are in the presence here of a concept of the nature of heresy which has remained stable for centuries. One is aware of certain specific features distinguishing one manifestation of heresy from another, but one also sees a universal principle operating everywhere, characterized by the metaphors of idolatry, monstrosity, and poison, which thus reduce different religious viewpoints to expressions of an alien depraved world. The cause is seen in the absence of forms of knowledge guided by reason, which have been replaced by individualistic tendencies. It is not difficult to recognize behind all this a world view which assumes that the presence of God in the world of human imagination is a

---

[36] Alain, *Contra hereticos* (PL 210, 307–8): 'qui (sc. novi haeretici) in hoc ab antiquis haereticis differunt, quod illi humanis rationibus fidem nostram expugnare conati sunt; isti vero nulla ratione humana vel divina freti ad voluntatem et voluptatem suam monstruosa confingunt. Olim vero diversi haeretici diversis temporibus diversa dogmata et adversa somniasse leguntur, . . . nostris vero temporibus, novi haeretici, imo veteres et inveterati, veterantes dogmata ex diversis haeresibus unam generalem haeresim compingunt et quasi ex diversis idolis unum idolum, ex diversis monstris unum monstrum; et quasi ex diversis venenatis herbis unum toxicum commune conficiunt'.

[37] See Grundmann, 'Ketzerverhöre', reprinted in his *Ausgewählte Aufsätze*, 3 vols., Schriften der MGH 25 (Stuttgart, 1976), I, 364–416, here pp. 415–16 with n. 104.

universal principle available to all. The path to divinely approved dogmas is illuminated by reason. If reason is lacking, fragmentation and individualisation in the formation of opinions occur, leading inevitably to isolation from God. From a philosophical point of view this is, as long as it exists, an ontological state, and as such it characterizes a quality of human existence. As a social category, a description of this state attributes to those affected the quality of outcasts, insofar as they have chosen to reject the beautiful world of God, which may be sinful and imperfect but nonetheless open to redemption, and have opted instead for a world of their own with all the conceivable negative connotations: in the words of Alain 'idolaters', that is to say, worshippers of non-entities or demons; 'monsters', that is, beings which are in principle dysfunctional; 'brewers of poisons', that is, harbingers of death, not of death as the first step to eternal life, but as the precursor of the so-called second or eternal death.

Alain, like Heinrich Kalteisen, pronounces this verdict on the heretics of his time. The comprehensive scope of Alain's work, directed against all the expressions of deviance from Christian belief virulent at the time, indicates in itself that every deviant form of thinking was seen as the negative image of the world of God. The image of the heretic, whether he was a Cathar, a Waldensian or a member of any other sect, is only a special form of the general image of religious deviance, of which Jews, pagans and Muslims are also major parts. This internal coherence of the non-catholic world is particular evident in the approach to the Muslims. On the one hand there was uncertainty as to whether they should be seen as depraved Christians, that is, heretics, or as pagan idolaters. On the other hand the term *Saracenus*, that is, Muslim, could be used for the pagan Prussians (*Pruteni*, in German: *Prutzen*) or any other heathens in the vicinity of Poland.[38] This is not so much a matter of terminological imprecision, as of an awareness that all of these forms of religious deviance were in the final analysis one and the same.

This observation can be supported by the similarity of the language used to describe all religious deviants, whether they were heretics, Jews, pagans or Muslims: they are all stupid, absurd and irrational; perfidiousness characterizes the Jews specifically, but can also be found in accounts of the heretics; arrogance, the first of the seven vices, all kinds of attachment to the world, impurity, lies, lust and excess – the list could be extended indefinitely and embellished with details, but I shall forgo this.[39] Logical coherence is not at

---

[38] Cf. the so called Treaty of Kruschwitz from 1230 between Duke Konrad of Masovia and the Teutonic Order, ed. R. Philippi, *Preußisches Urkundenbuch*, Politische Abteilung, 1, 1 (Königsberg i. Pr. 1882), pp. 58–60, no. 78: '. . . contra Prutenos et alios Sarracenos nobis conterminos . . .' ('against Prussians and other Saracens bordering on us').

[39] A sample of these can be found in A. Patschovsky, 'Feindbilder der Kirche: Juden und Ketzer im Vergleich (11.–13. Jahrhundert)', in *Juden und Christen zur Zeit der Kreuzzüge*, ed. A. Haverkamp, Vorträge und Forschungen 47 (Sigmaringen, 1998), pp. 327–57, esp. pp. 343–54.

issue when, for example, Alain reviles the Waldensians for preferring to fill their bellies rather than their heads, when they claim the right to preach.[40] One would expect just the opposite. But Alain's remarks are simply intended to brand the claim of the Waldensian preachers to be maintained by their followers as improper, as this is a prerogative of the clergy, justified by the performance of spiritual services such as preaching. And as Alain wishes to characterize the demands of the Waldensians as presumptuous and false, he reaches for the negative metaphor of devotion to the pleasures of the belly. The image as such need not be accurate. It is enough if the core of the message is right. *Belly* is simply a typical element of the metaphorical arsenal used against those who have turned their backs on God.

The social and political implications of this view of the world can easily be made out: if need be, heretics, Jews, pagans and Muslims must be eradicated, should the opportunity present itself; they should be spared at best as objects of conversion. There can be no illusions: the medieval principle of tolerance was purely opportunistic, not pluralist.[41] The history of the high and late Middle Ages could effortlessly be written as a process of increasing con- solidation in religious and legal theory and armed praxis in regard to Christian 'catholic' views on the eradication of the world they saw as deviant. Nevertheless, Hegel's famous *List der Vernunft* ('cunning of reason') has in this case too brought about very different social-psychological developments and results than might have been expected from the application of the bleak principle of the eradication of unworthy forms of existence such as the supposedly godless religious deviants. As these were numerous, sometimes powerful and even too powerful, and, therefore, not so easily silenced, the principle desiring the eradication of religious deviants was not often put into practice and the sad reality of its full destructive force was seldom realized. It seems to me much more important that the theoretical sharpness of religious exclusion led to an even more violent debate on the true catholic faith, the more seriously the participants in this game took the rules of exclusion. In this sense it was precisely the repulsive principle of religious intolerance which provided the driving force for the liveliness of the spiritual disputes.

Again: heresies and the will to exclude them are fundamental aspects of the development of the Western world and not peripheral phenomena.

IX

There is one last point I would like to mention: if, in fundamental issues of medieval society, heresy is just the other side of the coin, then we can expect

---

[40] Alain, *Contra hereticos* ii.1 (*PL* 210, 378): '. . . qui potius ut satient ventrem quam mentem, predicare presumunt'.

[41] For this view see e.g. A. Patschovsky, 'Toleranz im Mittelalter: Idee und Wirklich- keit', in *Toleranz im Mittelalter*, ed. A. Patschovsky and H. Zimmermann, Vorträge und Forschungen 45 (Sigmaringen, 1998), pp. 391–402.

that the use of the term *heretic* – and this would imply, the way of dealing with a heretical person – is not reserved to the triumphant Church militant, but is also common to its less successful opponents. And indeed, this can be proved. We might take a look at Ockham and how he judged 'his' pope, or at Wyclif with his Hussite adherents, and how – as they saw it – not only a single pope as a person, but the whole papacy as an institution became not only heretical, but downright 'antichrist'.[42] And the very moment a 'heretical' movement became dominant, the 'heretics' themselves prosecuted their enemies as heretics. An example of this is provided by the Taborites in Hussite Bohemia,[43] who extinguished both their chiliastic left wing and their Catholic opponents in the same merciless way as they themselves were or would have been extinguished, had they not been so strong, at least for some time.

*

Heresy is to be found at the basis, not at the margin, of medieval society. This forces us to approach the subject within the complex social context of its development and not in isolation. Thus, heresiology, properly understood, should be applied sociology – admittedly in a more specific sense than this term is normally used. So if we want to look closely at heresies, we inevitably have to examine the entire historical context in which the charge of heresy is made. This is especially necessary since by telling their own stories heresies inform the historian about a broader theme: that is society as such.

[42] Cf. A. Patschovsky, '"Antichrist" bei Wyclif', in *Eschatologie und Hussitismus*, ed. A. Patschovsky and F. Šmahel, Historica, series nova, suppl. 1 (Prague, 1996), pp. 83–98.
[43] Fundamental for the whole history of Hussitism and the role the Taborites played within it is F. Šmahel, *Husitská revoluce*, 4 vols. (Prague, 1993; 2nd edn, 1996). A German translation is on the way which may provide the starting point for the reception of this outstanding work in the Western world.

Texts and the Repression of Medieval Heresy

The Construction of Orthodoxy and the (De)construction of Heretical Attacks on the Eucharist in *Pastoralia* from Peter the Chanter's Circle in Paris

Jessalynn Bird

The picture that secular theologians of the twelfth and thirteenth centuries did little to combat heresy outside an academic context still prevails in otherwise outstanding surveys on heresy and histories of the inquisition and the Albigensian crusade, which portray the anti-heretical efforts of the episcopate, Paris masters and Cistercians as evolutionarily inferior ante-cedents to the friars' education, organization, and asceticism.[1] However, Peter the Chanter's circle and their Cistercian colleagues viewed academic and popular heresies as related phenomena. While policing theology as an intellectual discipline, they acted as popular preachers, judge delegates, expert witnesses, episcopal officials and *scholastici*, fostering lay devotion, defining orthodoxy, aiding bishops in applying legal and pastoral measures against heresy in Northern Europe and the Languedoc and recruiting for the Albigensian crusade. Their efforts furnished the precedents, tools, and roles used by succeeding generations of secular theologians and the friars to combat heterodoxy as many Paris-educated scholars joined the mendicant orders, shaping their educational and pastoral goals.[2]

This article will examine how heretics were represented and combated in

[1] Maisonneuve, *Études*; Dossat, *Crises*; M.-H. Vicaire, *Saint Dominic and his Times*, trans. K. Pond (New York, London and Toronto, 1964), chs. 6–7; Lambert, *Medieval Heresy*, chs. 5–6, esp. pp. 91 and 101, following Borst, *Katharer*, pp. 6–27; J. B. Russell, *Dissent and Order in the Middle Ages: The Search for Legitimate Authority* (New York and Oxford, 1992), pp. 56–7; P. H. Tibber, 'The Origins of the Scholastic Sermon, c.1130–c.1210' (unpublished D.Phil. thesis, University of Oxford, 1983/4), pp. 13–14, 19–64, 222–3. The classic treatment of the Cistercian missions in Thouzellier, *Catharisme*, is updated by Kienzle, *Cistercians*.

[2] I am writing articles on these topics. For preliminary conclusions and a fuller version of this article, see J. L. Bird, 'Heresy, Crusade and Reform in the Circle of Peter the Chanter c.1187–c.1240' (unpublished D.Phil. thesis, University of Oxford, 2001). For an English anti-heretical network, see P. Biller, 'William of Newburgh and the Cathar Mission to England', in *Life and Thought in the Northern Church, c.1100–c.1700: Essays in Honour of Claire Cross*, ed. D. Wood, SCH, Subsidia 12 (Woodbridge, 1999), pp. 11–30.

pastoralia from Peter the Chanter's circle, focusing on the *summa* (*c.* 1208–12/
13) of Robert of Courson, who served with other Paris masters as a judge
delegate and expert witness in the trials of Cathars and the Amalricians in
northern France and participated in the Albigensian crusade as papal legate
for the Fifth Crusade,[3] and the sermons (*c.* 1227–40) and priest's manual
(*c.* 1219–21) of his compatriot, Jacques de Vitry, who preached against heresy
in northern France and the Midi while recruiting crusaders with William,
archdeacon of Paris and Fulk, bishop of Toulouse, for whom he wrote the *vita*
of Mary of Oignies (*c.* 1213) as anti-heretical propaganda.[4] The *questiones* of
their colleague Stephen Langton, credited with anti-heretical preaching in
Italy,[5] the *Contra hereticos* of Alain of Lille,[6] the *Gemma ecclesiastica* of Gerald of
Wales,[7] the homilies and *Dialogus miraculorum* of Caesar of Heisterbach,[8] and
the anonymous *Contra amaurianos* will also be cited.[9]

In sermons for the laity and treatises for ecclesiastics, Jacques de Vitry and
his contemporaries depicted the heretic's *modus operandi*, portraits mirrored
in Peter of Vaux-de-Cernay's apologia for the Albigensian crusade and papal
letters urging secular leaders to intervene militarily in the Midi.[10] Exploiting
native anticlericalism, cynicism, and donatism stemming from the corruption or ignorance of the local clergy and squabbles between bishops and
burghers or noblemen over temporal jurisdiction, the heretic alienated
secular leaders and the faithful from the teaching and sacraments of
orthodox ecclesiastics, partly by contrasting the austerities of the early
Church and his own apostolic mendicancy and itinerancy to the luxurious
lives or temporal involvement of local clergymen.[11] After estranging his

[3] M. and C. Dickson, 'Le cardinal Robert de Courson: sa vie', *AHDLMA* 9 (1934), 53–
142; G. Dickson, 'The Burning of the Amalricians', *JEH* 40 (1989), 347–69; J. M. M. H.
Thijssen, 'Master Amalric and the Amalricians: Inquisitorial Procedure and the
Suppression of Heresy at the University of Paris', *Speculum* 71 (1996), 43–65; G. C.
Capelle, *Autour du décret de 1210: Amaury de Bène* (Paris, 1932).

[4] E. W. McDonnell, *The Beguines and Beghards in Medieval Culture with Special Emphasis
upon the Belgian Scene* (New Brunswick NJ, 1954), pp. 24, 28, 32 and 416; P. Funk, *Jakob
von Vitry: Leben und Werke* (Leipzig and Berlin, 1909), pp. 35–6; *H.occ.*; *VMO*. I am
preparing a translation of the *Historia occidentalis* for the University of Liverpool press.

[5] Matthew Paris, *Vita sancti Stephani archiepiscopi Cantuariensis*, in *Ungedruckte anglo-
normannische Geschichtsquellen*, ed. F. Liebermann (Strasbourg, 1879), pp. 323–39
(pp. 323–7); R. Quinto, *'Doctor Nominatissimus': Stefano Langton* (Münster, 1994),
pp. 60–1 and 68; compare Caesar, *Dialogus* v.24–5 (II, 307–9); Jacques de Vitry,
Lettres, ed. R. B. C. Huygens (Leiden, 1960), ep. 1, pp. 72–3.

[6] Biller, 'Northern Cathars and Higher Learning'; Alain, *Contra hereticos*, additional
text in Thouzellier, *Catharisme*, pp. 81–106.

[7] I shall cite Gerald, *Gemma*, which corrects the text in Gerald of Wales, *Opera*, ed. J. S.
Brewer et al., 8 vols., RS 21 (London, 1861–91), II.

[8] Caesar, *Dialogus*; Caesar of Heisterbach, *Homiliae*, ed. J. A. Coppenstein, 1 vol. in 3
pts. (Cologne, 1615); Hilka, I, III, esp. I, 6.

[9] *Contra amaurianos*.

[10] E.g. *PL* 215, 1246–7 (1207); nn. 11 and 12 below.

[11] A. Murray, 'Piety and Impiety in Thirteenth-Century Italy', in *Popular Belief and
Practice*, ed. C. J. Cuming and D. Baker, SCH 8 (Oxford, 1972), 83–106; W. L.

audience from their ecclesiastical guard-dogs, the heresiarch duped and exploited them by preaching pleasing things, mixing heretical and orthodox teaching and inserting error gradually through the warped exegesis of scriptural and patristic authorities.[12] The simple devout were attracted by the apostolic lifestyle, prayers, fasting, chastity, preaching or mutual exhortation in intimate settings, absolute poverty or communal possessions which served reformers, reforming heretics, and new religious groups as the *lingua franca* in the bid for religious legitimacy and the Paris moralists joined their Cistercian co-workers and Innocent III in consciously extending these practices in mitigated form to the laity as devout individuals or members of orthodox confraternities, the mendicant orders and various quasi-regular groups.[13]

The Paris masters' response to this perceived threat was conditioned by their ambivalent view of the laity's intellectual and devotional capabilities and the techniques they felt suited to formulate and defend an orthodox theology palatable to them. Some historians have claimed that they shunned speculative theology while urging the laity to rely on a ritually and sacramentally based salvation. The moralists' sermons, which dealt with complex doctrines, were intended for the clergy or were heavily censored for lay audiences, while the dialectic and authorities used to arrive at doctrinal conclusions presented in *pastoralia* which furnished materials and techniques for the parish priests' now largely lost catechetical homilies were omitted from indoctrinating sermons which provided a prophylactic pabulum of didactic teaching on moral and devotional issues rather than equipping

Wakefield, 'Some Unorthodox Popular Ideas of the Thirteenth Century', *Medievalia et Humanistica* n.s. 4 (1973), 25–33; M. D. Lambert, 'Catharism as a Reform Movement', in *Häresie und vorzeitige Reformation im Spätmittelalter*, ed. F. Smahel (Oldenbourg, 1998), pp. 23–39; Lambert, *Medieval Heresy*, pp. 48–9, 55–6 and 59; Grundmann, *Religious Movements*, pp. 7–30, 227–30; J. B. Russell, *Dissent and Reform in the Early Middle Ages* (Berkeley and Los Angeles, 1965); R. I. Moore, *The Origins of European Dissent* (London, 1977); Alain, *Contra hereticos* ii. 8 (385); Vaux-de-Cernay, I, 5, 12–49, §§ 5 and 12–54; n. 12 below.

[12] Sermons on Matthew 7. 15–23 typically treat this theme. See Raoul Ardent, homily no. 19, *PL* 155, 2011A; *Sermones dominicales*, pp. 699–705 (pp. 701–2); Jacques de Vitry, *Sermo ad cives et burgenses*, no. 55, in Douai, Bibliothèque municipale, MS 503, fols. 385r-388r; Jacques de Vitry, *Sermones communes et feriales*, Université de Liège, Bibliothèque générale, MS 347, fols. 146rb–147va, 148va–b; Crane, no. 155, p. 68; G. Frenken, *Die Exempla des Jakob von Vitry* (Munich, 1914), no. 94, p. 143; *Contra amaurianos*, pp. 1–2; Stephen of Bourbon, *Tractatus*, pp. 23–4, n. 3; Thouzellier, *Catharisme*, pp. 115–17 and nn. 36–7, 43 and 44; J. Longère, *Oeuvres oratoires de maîtres parisiens au XIIe siècle*, 2 vols. (Paris, 1975), I, 420–1; II, 323–4, nn. 99–100, 111–13; Caesar of Heisterbach, homily no. 37, ed. Coppenstein, III, 57–61; Hilka, I, 147–51; Caesar, *Dialogus* v.19 (I, 298–9).

[13] Nn. 11–12 above; Longère, *Oeuvres oratoires*, I, 423, II, 237; Lansing, *Power and Purity*, esp. p. 28; J. Bird, 'The Religious' Role in a Post-Fourth-Lateran World: Jacques de Vitry's *Sermones ad status* and *Historia occidentalis*', in *Medieval Monastic Preaching*, ed. C. Muessig (Leiden, Boston and Cologne, 1998), pp. 209–30 (pp. 219–27).

believers to defend their beliefs.[14] In fact, Jean-Claude Schmitt has suggested that ecclesiastics perpetuated the laity's simplicity rather than introduce uncultivated minds to complex doctrines, although council canons and sermons suggest that reformers viewed superstition, ignorance, and magic-working as fertile ground for heresy.[15]

For Innocent III and Peter the Chanter's circle assumed that the ignorance and moral failings of worldly bishops and their parochial clergy and their failure to mould their parishioners' popular religiosity through preaching enabled heresiarchs to win adherents by appealing to native cynicism or 'superstition'. They and their Cistercian and prelatial allies exhorted the diocesan clergy to preach regularly on the sacraments, the articles of the faith, the *Credo*, *Paternoster*, vices, and virtues and publicly confute heretics before they corrupted the faithful, a policy enshrined in the Fourth Lateran's mandates for preaching, annual confession and communion, and its *Credo*, carefully reformulated to counteract heretical beliefs.[16] Richard Poore, bishop of Salisbury, commanded his archdeacons to expound the Fourth Lateran's *Credo* 'soundly and in simple words' to the parish priests of their deaconate, while other bishops provided expositions of the *Credo* and the sacraments in diocesan statutes or appended manuals which priests were required to possess and use to instruct their flocks. Odo of Sully, bishop of Paris, ordered priests to counter heresy by propounding the articles of the faith with *distinctiones*, scriptural authorities and arguments according to their ability, while Jacques de Vitry portrayed his ideal preacher Fulk of Neuilly

[14] R. N. Swanson, *Religion and Devotion in Europe, c.1215–c.1515* (Cambridge, 1995), pp. 26–30, 51–4 and 63–8; Tibber, 'Origins', pp. 1–2, 13–14, 19–64, 166–72, 177–87, 222–3; d'Avray, *Preaching*, pp. 6, 20, 65 and 82–9.

[15] J.-Cl. Schmitt, 'Du Bon usage du 〈〈Credo〉〉', in *Faire Croire: Modalités de la diffusion et de la réception des messages religieux du XIIᵉ au XVᵉ siècle*, Collection de l'École Française de Rome 51 (Rome, 1981), pp. 337–61 (pp. 348–53 and 357–8); Jacques de Vitry, *Sermones ad uiduas et continentes*, nos. 69–70, Douai MS 503, fols. 425r, 427v–428v; Crane, nos. 261–9, pp. 70–2; Caesar, *Dialogus* iv.11 (I, 183); Robert of Flamborough, *Liber poenitentialis*, ed. J. J. F. Firth, PIMS, Studies and Texts 18 (Toronto, 1971), pp. 260–1 and 262–4; A. Murray, 'Religion among the Poor in Thirteenth-Century France: The Testimony of Humbert de Romans', *Traditio* 30 (1974), 285–324 (pp. 301 and 318–19); Stephen of Bourbon, *Tractatus*, §§ 327–71, pp. 274–329; Angers (1216–19), c. 105 (Pontal, I, p. 210); Albi (1230), c. 33 (Pontal, II, pp. 18 and 20).

[16] *H.occ.*, pp. 74–8, 84–6 and 182–3; Jacques de Vitry, *Sermones ad prelatos et sacerdotes*, nos. 2, 3, 4, 5 and 7; Douai, MS 503, fols. 250v–252r, 253v, 256r–v, 257r–v, 262v and 263r–v; Caesar of Heisterbach, homily no. 37, ed. Coppenstein, III, 57–61; Gerald, *Gemma* ii.35–6, 37 (pp. 259–62 and 272); Thomas of Chobham, *Summa confessorum*, ed. F. Broomfield, AMN 25 (Louvain and Paris, 1968), pp. 263–5 and 326–8; Robert of Flamborough, *Liber poenitentialis*, p. 62; Alain of Lille, *Liber poenitentialis*, ed. J. Longère, 2 vols., AMN 17–18 (Louvain and Lille, 1965), II, 19 and 167–8; Longère, *Oeuvres Oratoires*, I, 421, 424–5 and II, 325, n. 111; Thouzellier, *Catharisme*, pp. 185, 189, 191–3 and 243–4; Avignon (1209) (Mansi, XXII, 783–94); Wakefield and Evans, §§ 32 and 36, pp. 204–8 and 220–6; R. Foreville, *Latran I, II, III et Latran IV* (Paris, 1965), pp. 299–300; Baldwin, *Peter the Chanter* I, 318; nn. 66–7 below.

transmitting teaching from Peter the Chanter's classroom to his parishioners.[17] Caesar of Heisterbach recommended the discipline and excommunication of ignorant or mercenary priests who refused to combat heretics for fear of being beaten by them or deprived of tithes and offerings by their parishioners, while in a synodal sermon, Oliver of Paderborn goaded archdeacons to perform visitations and treat as heretics priests unable to explain the significance of the preposition in *credere in Deum*, rather than merely fining them.[18] Paris moralists urged prelates lacking preaching skills or life examples to appoint men who did, advice implemented by Innocent III's legates in the Midi and by Fulk, bishop of Toulouse, who supported Dominic and his followers as diocesan preachers to supplement his own pastoral and anti-heretical efforts, foreshadowing the culmination of these initiatives in Fourth Lateran's pastoral decrees and the provincial legislation inspired by them.[19]

To enable parish priests to join the dissemination of orthodoxy as confessors and preachers to their sacramental role, the Paris moralists produced *summae*, confessors' guides, sermon collections and manuals on the sacraments[20] and joined reforming bishops and Innocent III in seeking to resuscitate regional schools.[21] Orthodox *pastoralia* thus become a source, albeit a multivalent one, for the ceaseless dialectic between learned and popular belief and religiosity which resulted in the formation of a learned and popular orthodoxy and heresies.[22] For both orthodox and heterodox

---

[17] Nn. 16 above and 27 below; Paris (1208) (Pontal I, 52–93), esp. c. 84 (p. 84); *H.occ.*, pp. 94–5; Third Lateran (1179), c. 3 (*COD*, pp. 212–13); Paris (1213), Add. i.12 (Mansi, XXII, 846); Canterbury (1213–14) (*Councils & Synods* I, 23–36), esp. cs. 28–32 (I, 30–1); Montpellier (1215), c. 30 (Mansi, XXII, 954); Fourth Lateran (1215), cs. 26–7 and 30 (*COD*, pp. 247 and 249); Angers (1216–19) (Pontal, I, 138–237), esp. c. 45 (I, 166); Salisbury (1217–19) (*Councils & Synods* I, 57–96), esp. cs. 20 and 30 (I, 67–8 and 70); Trier (1228), cs. 1–7 (Mansi XXII, 25–34); Toulouse (1229), c. 45 (Mansi XXIII, 204); Albi (1230) (Pontal, II, 8–33), esp. cs. 63–4 (II, 32); Coventry and Lichfield (1224–37) (*Councils & Synods* I, 207–26); Baldwin, *Peter the Chanter* I, 32–6.

[18] Homily no. 21, ed. Coppenstein, II, 93–103; Hilka, I, 126.

[19] Nn. 17–18 above and 20 below; Vicaire, *St Dominic*, pp. 166, 171–3 and 178–80.

[20] Good introductions include L. E. Boyle, 'The Inter-Conciliar Period (1179–1215) and the Beginnings of Pastoral Manuals', in *Miscellanea Rolando Bandinelli Papa Alessandro III*, ed. F. Liotta (Siena, 1986), pp. 43–56; R. H. Rouse and M. A. Rouse, *Preachers, Florilegia and Sermons: Studies on the* Manipulus florum *of Thomas of Ireland*, PIMS, Studies and Texts 47 (Toronto, 1979), pp. 3–90; d'Avray, *Preaching*, pp. 2–7, 62–131, 159–61, 192–3 and 273–86.

[21] See Third Lateran (1179), c. 18 (*COD*, p. 220); Fourth Lateran (1215), c. 11 (*COD*, p. 240 and n. 3); Dickson, *Cardinal Robert*, p. 95; *H.occ*, pp. 89–103; P. B. Pixton, 'Pope Innocent III and the German Schools: The Impact of Canon XI of the Fourth Lateran upon Cathedral and Other Schools, 1216–1272', *Innocent III: Urbs et Orbis*, ed. A. Sommerlechner (Rome, 2002); F. Morenzoni, *Des écoles aux paroisses: Thomas de Chobham et la promotion de la prédication au début du XIIIᵉ siècle*, Études Augustiniennes 30 (Paris, 1995), 67–95.

[22] Grundmann, *Religious Movements*, pp. 230–1; G. Langmuir, *History, Religion and Antisemitism* (Berkeley, Los Angeles and Oxford, 1990), chs. 7, 9 and 10; Bernstein,

preachers were forced to grapple with the raw religiosity of their lay audiences, selectively appealing to or opposing elements of folk beliefs and practices. Reformers opposed Cathar docetism and dualism by fostering devotion to and imitation of the human and suffering Christ, and countered heretical donatism by making annual confession and communion, prayer, and attending sermons the cornerstones of the orthodox layperson's devotional life, asserting the Catholic Church's monopoly on salvific sacraments while instituting opportunities for the monitoring and formation of lay belief. Together with a quasi-monastic lifestyle of voluntary or moderated poverty and manual labor, these practices formed the orthodox rebuttal to the perceived attractions of Catharism and Waldensianism for the lay believer.[23]

The creation of a religion which addressed the laity's ritual and spiritual needs was joined by an increasing emphasis on correct belief. Chronicles and inquisitional records indicate that laypersons were interested in debating theological concepts and that the main sources of their knowledge of heresy, including attacks on the orthodox eucharist, were public anti-heretical sermons and often-informal and intimate heretical teaching.[24] Lay attendance at Sunday and feastday services was prerequisite for systematic orthodox instruction, resulting in the sabbatarian tone of the reform work of Eustace of Flay and prelates in England mirrored in councils held by Paris reformers and their allies in Northern France and the Midi.[25] Aware of women's role in Cathar and Waldensian catechization, Jacques de Vitry and other reformers targeted them as potential domestic guardians of orthodoxy for their households through the dissemination of sermons heard in church and instruction

---

'Teaching'; A. E. Bernstein, 'Esoteric Theology: William of Auxerre on the Fires of Hell and Purgatory', *Speculum* 57 (1982), 509–31, and 'Theology between Heresy and Folklore: William of Auvergne on Punishment after Death', *Studies in Medieval and Renaissance History* n.s. 5 (1982), 5–44.

[23] Nn. 13 above and 28 below; Tibber, 'Origins', pp. 165–7 and 191–2; Lambert, *Cathars*, p. 171; *VMO*, cols. 637, 640–1, 645, 647–8, 659, 660 and 664.

[24] Nn. 11–12 and 16 above; J. Arnold, 'The Preaching of the Cathars', in *Medieval Monastic Preaching*, ed. Muessig, pp. 183–205; Fredericq, I, 45 and 48–50, nos. 46, 48 and 49; Biller, 'Northern Cathars', pp. 44–5; B. Delmaire, 'Un sermon Arrageois inedit sur les ⟨⟨bougres⟩⟩ de la France (vers 1200)', *Heresis* 17 (1991), 1–15; PL 199, 1119–24; PL 204, 235–40; PL 216, 648–50 and 1210–14; Vicaire, *St Dominic*, p. 103 and p. 470, n. 40; Vaux-de-Cernay, I, 26–7, 28–9, 47–9, §§ 24, 26 and 54; Puylaurens ix (p. 52).

[25] J. L. Cate, 'The English Mission of Eustace of Flay (1200–1202)', in *Études d'histoire dédiées à la mémoire d'Henri Pirenne*, ed. F. L. Ganshof, E. Sabbe and F. Vercauteren (Brussels, 1937), pp. 67–89, and 'The Church and Market Reform in England during the Reign of Henry III', in *Medieval and Historiographical Essays in Honor of James Westfall Thompson*, ed. J. L. Cate and E. N. Anderson (Chicago, 1938), pp. 27–65; Murray, 'Religion', 299, 301–2; Pamiers (1212), c. 4 (Mansi XXII, 856); Toulouse (1219), cs. 2–4 (Mansi XXII, 1135); Canterbury (1213–14), c. 58 (*Councils & Synods* I, 35); Angers (1216–19), c. 61 (Pontal I, 176 and 178); Toulouse (1229), cs. 25–7 (Mansi XXIII, 200).

in prayers such as the *Credo, Paternoster,* and *Ave Maria.*[26] While the heretical use and gloss of the *Paternoster* led to occasional bans on vernacular translations of it and the bible, saint's lives, and theological works, the orthodox clergy did not intend for the laity to ideally view Latin prayers as an unintelligible magical mantra rather than engaging them intellectually. Jacques de Vitry's sermons to boys, adolescents, widows, and matrons provide complete line-by-line explications of the *Paternoster* and *Credo,* explaining how and why one ought to pray in church and explicating doctrines attacked by heretics, including the power of prayer for the dead, the Trinity, the indivisibility of the one true Church and the power of the sacraments.[27]

Similarly, the reformers' morally and devotionally focused penance preaching was meant to bring the layperson to the confessional, where he ideally scrutinized his motives, mental state, and doctrine while his confessor adapted the case-modelling, questions and debate practised by scholars in Paris to the negotiation, internalization, and manifestation of belief through orthopraxy and penitential and orthodox actions.[28] Realizing that outward conformity to orthodox rites could be heretically glossed or conceal ignorance, moralists urged confessors to query penitents on the articles of the faith; even priests could err on complex doctrines such as transubstantiation. Their anti-heretical sermons and handbooks for priests included authorities which the preacher or confessor could use to reinforce his audience's belief in the Trinity, incarnation, resurrection and marriage, suggesting that the Paris

[26] Jacques de Vitry, *Sermo ad coniugatos,* no. 66, Douai 503, fol. 415v; Longère, *Oeuvres oratoires,* I, 398–400; Thomas of Chobham, *Summa,* pp. 287–8 and 375; Paris (1208), c. 62 (Pontal, I, 74); Canterbury (1213–14), cs. 34–5 (*Councils & Synods* I, 31); Salisbury 1217–1219, c. 5 (*Councils & Synods* I, 61); n. 27 below.

[27] Schmitt, 'Bon usage', pp. 345 and 348–54; Swanson, *Religion,* pp. 39–40, 51, 90 and 329–38; Murray, 'Religion', 298, n. 70. Contrast Jacques de Vitry, *Sermones ad status,* nos. 68, 70 and 73, Douai MS 503, fols. 421v–422r, 425v, 426v–447r and 434r–435v; Jean Beleth, *Summa de ecclesiasticis officiis* cxvi, ed. H. Douteil, CCCM 41–41A (Turnholt, 1976), p. 218; C. A. Robson, *Maurice of Sully and the Medieval Vernacular Homily* (Oxford, 1952), pp. 82–7, §§ 2–3; nn. 3, 16 and 24 above and 33 below.

[28] Jacques provides basic instruction on penance in sermons to adolescents and the married. He decries the useless orthopraxy of a 'Renart's confession' followed by an immediate relapse and laypersons' refusal to practice self-accusation according to the clergy's categories of sins, responsibility, and circumstances. He also addresses lay concerns regarding confessors' discretion and depicts confession breaking the devil's power over the sinner (*Sermones ad status,* nos. 68 and 74, Douai MS 503, fols. 421r, 436r–v and 437v–438r; Crane, nos. 297–300, pp. 125–6). See also n. 22 above; Robert of Flamborough, *Liber Poenitentialis,* pp. 273–7; Caesar, *Dialogus* iii (I, 110–70); *Faire Croire,* pp. 67–85, 87–99 and 299–335; Paris (1208), cs. 26–39 and 73–4 (Pontal, I, 62–6, 94–6); Fourth Lateran (1215), c. 21 (*COD,* p. 245); Canterbury (1213–14), cs. 27 and 40–44 and Salisbury (1217–19), cs. 33–6, 38 and 40–5 (*Councils & Synods* I, 30, 32 and 71–5); Angers (1216–19), cs. 72, 74–5, 77–80, 82–3, 86–99, 102–4, 107–12, 114 and 120–22 (Pontal, I, 190–226); Rouen (1223), c. 9 (Mansi, XXII, 1199); Narbonne (1227), c. 7, Trier (1228), cs. 3–4 (Mansi XXIII, 28–9); Toulouse (1229), cs. 12–13 and 45 (Mansi XXIII, 196, 197 and 204); Albi (1230), cs. 39–46 (Pontal, II, 22–4).

circle envisaged the confessional as a safe context for using academic techniques to address individual doubts and disseminate doctrinal knowledge long before the Fourth Lateran's mandated annual confession.[29]

However, moral theologians remained deeply ambivalent concerning which intellectual tools were best suited for investigating theology and instructing the laity. They had condemned speculative theologians for the public and irreverent dissection of the mysteries of the faith with reason in sermons and debates, which shifted dialectic, reason, and natural observation from props and explicatory aids for a belief based on faith to the criteria for believing Christianity's essentially suprarational and supernatural mysteries. Improper use of these techniques could lead academics into error, cause their lay audiences to doubt, and furnish undercover heretics with the means of deconstructing Catholic doctrine.[30] Moreover, because the laity judged everything by the senses and appearance rather than faith, they were easily swayed by meretricious rhetoric, reasoned arguments and warped exegesis. Peter the Chanter's circle warned students and clergymen not to engage in public disputations with Jews or heretics, for the orthodox preacher could not hope to compete with heretics' teaching, which lured reprobates eager to escape penance through the doctrine of the *consolamentum*. However, they ultimately concluded that for the laity to realize that the godly-seeming heretic was a sinner and erred in faith, his teachings must be unveiled and the Catholic faith defended in debates geared more toward saving simple Christians, *credentes* and unconfirmed heretics than the obstinate heresiarch, a technique used in sermons recruiting for the Albigensian crusade as well as in debates in the Midi and sermons to faithful in Northern Europe. The preacher ought to illustrate how the heretics corrupted the scriptures, using written authorities and corporal and sensible arguments such as: if the devil created all material things, how could the holy spirit be bestowed through the laying-on of physical hands (the *consolamentum*)?[31]

For despite their misgivings, the moralists felt that they had to follow heterodox theologians in marshalling the disputational and exegetical methods used in Paris and the cathedral schools, including rational arguments, citation and interpretation of often conflicting scriptural authorities, and appeals to philosophical maxims and natural observation from Platon-

---

[29] Caesar, *Dialogus* ix.56 (II, 209–10); Gerald, *Gemma* i.9 (p. 28); Longère, *Oeuvres Oratoires* I, 424–6, II, 329 and n. 146; nn. 27 and 28 above.

[30] Jacques de Vitry, *Sermo ad scolares*, no. 15, Douai MS 503, fols. 278v–2781v, here fols. 279v–280v; *H.occ.*, p. 92; Baldwin, *Peter the Chanter*, I, 82–3 and 97–107; Fichtenau; S. C. Ferruolo, *The Origins of the University: The Schools of Paris and Their Critics, 1100–1215* (Stanford, 1985); and n. 3 above.

[31] Peter the Chanter, *Summa de sacramentis et de animae consiliis*, ed. J.-A. Dugauquier, AMN 4, 7, 11, 16 and 21 (Louvain and Lille, 1954–67), III2a, 116–18, § 193, and III2b, 377, 471, 488–91 and 542–3, §§ 319, 353 and 364; Jacques de Vitry, *Sermones feriales et communes*, Liège MS 347, fols. 146vb–148va; N. Bériou, *L'avènement des maîtres de la parole: La prédication à Paris au XIIIe siècle*, 2 vols., Etudes Augustiniennes 31–2 (Paris, 1998), I, 58–69, II, 676 and 681–2; nn. 12, 24 and 30 above and 32 and 66–7 below.

ism and the Aristotelian *libri naturales* to sway the laity and confute their opponents. However, both sides were aware that these techniques could easily be turned against them or misinterpreted by their 'rustic' audiences and often attempted to reclaim debates which had swung against them through rhetorical posturing, appealing to their life-example or the meta-phorical or visual demonstration of doctrine through miracles.[32]

Similarly, the handbooks and sermons of Paris-educated preachers, includ-ing Jacques de Vitry, Peter of Roissy, Robert of Courson, and Innocent III suggest that some reformers viewed an informed and devout laity as the best defense against heresy, although their estimate of which techniques best suited the laity and in what context complex doctrines should be introduced is occasionally ambiguous. Robert of Courson claimed that although priests must believe and understand the eucharist according to their native intelli-gence, they were not bound to academically dissect its mysteries or preach them to the laity indiscreetly. Demonstrating that Christ was present upon the altar, hidden like the sun in clouds under the outward form of the consecrated elements, they should use similar concrete proofs to move their parishioners to venerate and more fully comprehend the eucharist's effi-cacy.[33] However, because some priests led the faithful into scandal or error through sheer ignorance or heresy, Robert, Jacques, and Peter of Roissy followed Bernard of Fontcaude, Eckbert of Schönau, and Alain of Lille in their wide-ranging treatment of the doctrinal and practical difficulties intrinsic to the sacrament and inclusion of *exempla* and authorities for the information of the wavering orthodox and the confutation of heretics.[34] Jacques stressed the centrality of the eucharist to God's redemptive plan and confronted those who denied that the eucharist as performed by the Catholic Church was instituted by Christ and his apostles by citing and interpreting evidence of the eucharist's foreshadowing in the Old Testament. Although he admitted that the gospels recorded only the verbal formula necessary for transubstantiation, instituted by Christ at the Last Supper, he

---

[32] Caesar, *Dialogus* v.18, 20 and 25 (II, 296–8, 299–300 and 308–9); Vaux-de-Cernay, I, 21–31, 42–4 and 45–9, §§ 20–7, 47–8 and 51–4; Crane, no. 26, p. 9; Puylaurens ix (p. 52); Caesar of Heisterbach, homily no. 21, ed. Coppenstein, II, 93–102; Hilka, I, 133–4; Stephen of Bourbon, *Tractatus*, §§ 327–8 and 426, pp. 275–8 and 370–1; Vicaire, *St Dominic*, pp. 101–7; Thouzellier, *Catharisme*, esp. pp. 60–79 and 195–204; *Heresy and Literacy*; nn. 6, 11–12, and 16 above.

[33] Robert of Courson, *Summa* xlii.5 and 25, BnF MS Lat. 14524, fols. 160rb and 171va–vb; Jacques de Vitry, *Sermones de sanctis*, Douai MS 503, fols. 3r-4r. Written while he was responsible for educating clergymen in the diocese of Chartres, Peter's hand-book drew upon Robert of Courson's *Summa* and Alain of Lille's *Contra hereticos*. See *H.occ.*, pp. 100–1 and 289; V. L. Kennedy, 'The Handbook of Master Peter, Chancellor of Chartres', *MS* 5 (1943), 1–38.

[34] Thouzellier, *Catharisme*, pp. 51–7; Eckbert of Schönau, *Sermones contra Catharos* xi (*PL* 195, 84–94); Robert of Courson, *Summa* xliii.1, BnF MS Lat. 14524, fol. 156ra–rb; *H.occ.*, pp. 190ff; *Sermones dominicales*, pp. 334–8; Gerald, *Gemma* ii.35–7 (pp. 259–62 and 272).

claimed that the apostles had handed down the current eucharistic ritual, which fostered devotion.[35]

Cistercians and moralists also related stories of the miraculous apparition of a child or raw flesh in the eucharist and the power of the consecrated host to heal, console and sustain in contrast to the unconsecrated wafer, many drawn from the experiences of the *mulieres sanctae* of Flanders-Brabant, to rebuke the corruption or faithlessness of the celebrating priest or lay audience, to strengthen the faith of those doubting the true presence and testify to the rewards granted those celebrating or receiving the eucharist with faith and devotion. For the moralists often followed their own advice to use tangible proofs and concrete demonstrations such as *exempla*, similitudes, miracles and the imitatable lives of the saints which they felt appealed to the concrete senses of the uneducated laity without encouraging them to use reason as a barometer for belief in the mysteries of the faith.[36] Intended for anti-heretical preaching and recruiting for the Albigensian crusade in Northern Europe and the Midi, Jacques de Vitry's *Vita* of Mary of Oignies used miracles stressing the innate power and efficacy of the eucharist and the necessity of the sacraments for salvation to attract *credentes* and the wavering with a sacramentally-based worship where the comfort of the host and the emulation of an ascetic and intercessory saint replaced the abstemious perfect and the *consolamentum*.[37]

For the Paris circle was attuned to lay devotion to and concerns about the eucharist, which they selectively reinforced or repressed through use of ritual, preaching, and debate. They and their Cistercian colleagues supported the elevation of the consecrated host, which symbolized in a 'magical' and concrete gesture the concept of newly present yet concealed Christ, as did the increasingly elaborate processions which accompanied the consecrated host conveyed to the sick and dying,[38] prayers addressed in

---

[35] *H.occ.*, pp. 216–17 and 224–5; *Sermones dominicales*, pp. 334–5 and 337–8, compare Vaux-de-Cernay, I, 26–7, 28–9 and 47–9, §§ 24, 26 and 54; Puylaurens ix (p. 52); *Contra hereticos* i.60 and 62 (*PL* 210, 363–5); Robert of Courson, *Summa* xliii.8, BnF MS Lat. 14524, fols. 163ra–va; Stephen Langton, *Questiones*, Cambridge, St John's College, MS 57, fols. 207ra and 317vb–318ra; *Contra amaurianos* xii (pp. 48–51).

[36] *H.occ.*, pp. 204–9; *Sermones dominicales*, prologue, fols. 2r–4r; Jacques de Vitry, *Sermones de sanctis*, prologue, Douai MS 503, fols. 3r–4r; Jacques de Vitry, *Sermones ad status*, prologue, in Crane, unnumbered n., pp. xli–xliii; Caesar, *Dialogus* ix (II, 164–217); Hilka, III, 16–34 and 44–5; Gerald, *Gemma* i.9 and 11 (pp. 27–8 and 32–4); Robert of Courson, *Summa* xliii.24, BnF MS Lat. 14524, fols. 169va–170ra; Peter the Chanter, *Summa* I, 179–80, §§ 68–9; B. Smalley, *The Study of the Bible in the Middle Ages*, 3rd edn (Oxford, 1983), pp. 253–4; Alain de Lille, *De arte predicatoria* i (*PL* 210, 114C); *Contra hereticos* i.58 and 62 (*PL* 210, 361 and 365); J.-Th. Welter, *L'exemplum dans la littérature religieuse et didactique du moyen âge* (Paris and Toulouse, 1927), esp. pp. 66–9, 118–24.

[37] *VMO*, cols. 636–7. I am writing an article on the *vita* as anti-heretical and crusading propaganda.

[38] V. L. Kennedy, 'The Date of the Parisian Decree on the Elevation of the Host', *MS* 8 (1946), 87–96, and 'The Moment of Consecration and the Elevation of the Host', *MS*

private or during the mass to the present Christ, perpetual lights maintained before the reserved *corpus Christi*,[39] and the Corpus Christi feast,
instituted some decades after Julienne of Cornillon's original vision of 1208
during Paris reformers' and Cistercians' preaching of the Albigensian
crusade.[40] Reforming *exempla* condemning the intellectual and physical
desecration of the *corpus Christi* by Jews, heretics, or lay magic-workers
testified to the power which Christ's presence lent the consecrated host to
circumvent the natural order. Reformers also attempted to repattern the
laity's magical conception of the host after the devotion felt toward relics by
the rituals surrounding the *corpus Christi*, including an insistence upon
priestly purity and storing the consecrated host in locked pyxes or
reliquaries to protect it and demonstrate the proper priestly rather than
lay channelling of the eucharist's power; yet these measures ironically
reinforced the conflation of the magical and the holy in the popular
mind.[41] Similarly, the moralists' emphasis upon the verbal formula and

6 (1944), 121–50; Paris (1208), cs. 20, 72 and 80, and add. c. 15 (Pontal, I, 60, 78, 82 and
101); Canterbury (1213–14), cs. 17 and 45 (*Councils & Synods* I, 28–9 and 33);
Anonymous (1222–25), c. 19 (*Councils & Synods* I, 143); Coventry (1224–37), c. 3
(*Councils & Synods* I, 210); *Gemma*, I.vi., pp. 17–18; Caesar, *Dialogus* iv.65, ix.48–9 and
51 (II, 202–5 and 206).

[39] Roger of Howden, *Chronica*, ed. W. Stubbs, 4 vols., RS 51 (London, 1868–71), IV, 124;
M. Zerner-Chardavoine, 'L'abbé Gui des Vaux-de-Cernay prédicateur de croisade',
in *Les Cisterciens de Languedoc (XIIIᵉ–XIVᵉ s.)*, CaF 21 (1986), 183–204 (p. 199).

[40] John of Nivelles and John of Lirot, Jacques de Vitry's compatriots in the *cura
mulierum*, possessed ties to the leprosery of Cornillon. Julienne earned local support
for the feast from the canons and bishop of Liège, various *mulieres sanctae* and
Cistercian nuns, the monastery of Villers, and from later Paris masters involved in
preaching the Albigensian crusade and countering heresy, including Philip the
Chancellor, Guiard of Laon, and Hugh of St-Cher. Confraternities and bishops later
used the feast to counteract heretical attacks upon the eucharist. See C. Renardy, *Les
maîtres universitaires dans le diocèse de Liège: Repertoire biographique (1140–1350)* (Paris,
1981), nos. 481 and 496, pp. 361–3 and 385–7; *The Life of Juliana of Mont Cornillon*
I.ii.6–7, I.iv.20 and II.ii.6–7, trans. B. Newman (Toronto, 1988), pp. 38, 50–1 and 80–4;
VMO, col. 658; McDonnell, *Beguines*, pp. 312ff, 384–7 and 434; S. Roisin, 'L'efflor-
escence cistercienne et le courant féminin de piété au XIIIᵉ siècle', *Revue d'histoire
écclésiastique* 39 (1943), 342–78, and *L'hagiographie cistercienne dans le diocèse de Liège au
XIIIᵉ siècle* (Louvain and Brussels, 1947), pp. 178–84; M. Rubin, *Corpus Christi*
(Cambridge, 1991), pp. 164–75; C. W. Bynum, 'Women Mystics and Eucharistic
Devotion in the Thirteenth Century', *Women's Studies* 11 (1984), 179–214 (pp. 200–2),
and *Holy Feast and Holy Fast* (Berkeley, Los Angeles and London, 1987), pp. 55 and
64; Lansing, *Power*, p. 13.

[41] G. Langmuir, 'The Torture of the Body of Christ', in Waugh and Diehl, *Christendom*,
pp. 287–300; Swanson, *Religion*, pp. 100, 102, 140–1 and 182–4; Rubin, *Corpus Christi*,
pp. 44–5; Vaux-de-Cernay, I, 34, 37–8, 199–202, 205–6 and 218–19, II, 78–80, §§ 33, 40,
198–200, 203, 219 and 382; Caesar, *Dialogus* v.21, ix.6–9, 12–16, 24–5, 49 and 52 (I,
300–3, II, 171–4, 175–8, 182–3, 204–5 and 207); Hilka, III, 16–20, 28–9 and 44–5; Robert
of Courson, *Summa* xliii.15–17, fols. 166ra–va and 166vb–167rb; BL MS Royal 7.D.I,
fol. 66v; Jacques de Vitry, Sermo ad viduas et continentes no. 69, Douai MS 503, fol.
428v; Crane, no. 270, p. 113; Gerald, *Gemma* i.1, 9 (pp. 11 and 35); Canterbury (1213–
14), cs. 14–15 and 20 (*Councils & Synods* I, 27 and 29); Fourth Lateran (1215), cs. 19–20

office of the priest as the two main criteria for the mass's validity, resulting in an almost magical obsession with the perfection of the mass's verbal formula and ritual and much advice on correcting botched consecrations, stemmed from their reaction to the laity's conclusion that the masses of those who possessed concubines, sold their services, or celebrated in an irreverent, truncated, or sloppy manner were inefficacious.[42] To a lay audience with memories of non-repeatable solemn penances, the Paris circle also stressed that confession and the eucharist, particularly extreme unction, were reiterable and did not, like the *consolamentum*, depend upon the minister's unverifiable purity or require perpetual celibacy from the receiver.[43]

The *vita*'s didactic and demonstrative approach to the sacraments contrasts with the angst felt by Jacques, Peter the Chanter, Caesar of Heisterbach, and Robert of Courson regarding the intellectual dissection of the eucharistic mystery.[44] Yet Jacques and Robert supplemented scriptural authorities with logical arguments to explain when transubstantiation occurred,[45] Christ's simultaneous presence in heaven and upon the altar and in each piece of the consecrated host,[46] and the latter's retention of its appearance, taste, smell, and ability to sate.[47] These questions reflect the laity's fundamental doubts about the intangibility of Christ's presence in the host and the mechanism

---

(*COD*, p. 244); Angers (1216–19), cs. 6–28 and 44 (Pontal, I, 142–56 and 166); Salisbury (1217–19) c. 67 (*Councils & Synods*, I, 82); Canterbury (1222), c. 29 (*Councils & Synods* I, 115); Rouen (1223), c. 8 (Mansi, XXII, 1199); Albi (1230), cs. 36–7 (Pontal, II, 20 and 22); Bordeaux (1234), cs. 21–39 (Pontal, II, 54–64); Trier (1228), c. 1 (Mansi, XXIII, 27–8).

[42] Jacques de Vitry, *Sermo ad prelatos*, no. 2, Douai MS 503, fol. 252v; Robert of Courson, *Summa* xliii.15–16 and 19–24, fols. 166rb–167ra and 168rb–170rb; *H.occ.*, pp. 166–73, 218–24 and 245–6; Caesar, *Dialogus* ix.12–15, 23–4, 28–33, 53–4 and 58–61 (II, 175–7, 181–3, 186–90 and 207–15); P. B. Roberts, *Stephanus de Lingua-Tonante: Studies in the Sermons of Stephen Langton* (Toronto, 1968), p. 119; Westminster (1200), c. 1 (*Councils & Synods*, II, 1060); Paris (1213), i.2 (Mansi, XXII, 819); Canterbury (1213–14), c. 19 (*Councils & Synods*, I, 29); Bourges (1214), cs. 1–5, 8–9, 11–12 and 14 (Mansi, XXII, 931–4); Fourth Lateran (1215), c. 16 (*COD*, p. 243); Canterbury (1222) c. 11 (*Councils & Synods* I, 109); Stephen of Bourbon, *Tractatus*, § 404, p. 354; n. 16 above.

[43] J. Duvernoy, *Le Catharisme: La Religion des Cathares* (Toulouse, 1976), pp. 90, 153, 155 and 207–8; Lambert, *Medieval Heresy*, pp. 106–11 and 129–31; Vaux-de-Cernay, I, 9, § 10; *Contra hereticos* i.45–56 (*PL* 210, 351–9); Stephen Langton, *Questiones*, St John's College MS 57, fols. 178rb–179ra; Gerald, *Gemma* i.3 and 5 (pp. 12–13, and 14–16); Robert of Courson, *Summa* vi.3–6, xxvi.2 and xlv.1–2, BnF MS Lat. 14524, fols. 33ra–34va, 90va–b and 173rb–175ra; Paris (1208), cs. 46–8 (Pontal, I, 68–70); Fourth Lateran (1215), c. 22 (*COD*, pp. 245–6); Angers (1216–19), cs. 68–9 (Pontal, I, 184); Trier (1228), c. 2 (Mansi, XXIII, 27).

[44] Peter the Chanter, *Summa* I, 133, § 55.

[45] *H.occ*, pp. 224–7; n. 61 below.

[46] *H.occ*, pp. 227–9; Peter the Chanter, *Summa* I (1954), 140–1, § 56; Robert of Courson, *Summa* xliii.3–5, 7, BnF MS Lat. 14524, fols. 158vb–160ra, 162vb.

[47] *H.occ.*, pp. 229–34; Robert of Courson, *Summa* xliii.2, BnF MS Lat. 14524, fol. 157vb; *Contra hereticos* i.57–8 (*PL* 210, 360 and 362).

and efficacy of transubstantiation, doubts exploited by the Cathars, who claimed that the mass was the invention of ecclesiastics to turn a profit and that the consecrated host was no different to the bread blessed by perfects and kept with veneration by some *credentes*.[48] The pantheist Amalricians reached similar conclusions, mocking the laity's veneration of the *corpus Christi* at the moment of elevation and in processions as idolatry. The *Contra amaurianos* defended this adoration as directed toward the newly present Christ and depicted the Amalricians as insane; if Christ indwelt in all things, heretics would adore crones carrying baker's loaves.[49] Both Jacques de Vitry and Robert of Courson urged the faithful to believe that Christ's body replaced the bread's substance but remained concealed by its outward form, preventing his revelation to the unworthy and protecting the simple who would spurn raw human flesh or face heretical accusations of cannibalism. Those doubting transubstantiation's precise mechanism should consult the experts, but faith proved by tangible evidence possessed no merit. Just as the count of Poitiers tested his priests' hospitality by travelling in a tattered pilgrim's habit, so Christ concealed himself within the host to test the faithful's reception of him.[50]

Heretics also attacked the doctrine of Christ's true presence by pointing to the potential desecration of the *corpus Christi* present in the host by animals or the indevout, and to the quantity of Christ's body required for multiple masses. They interpreted the pronoun *hoc* (this) in the consecratory phrase, 'This is my body', to refer to Christ or the Church, not the bread Christ held at the last supper, and they interpreted other scriptural references to Christ's body and blood figuratively, not literally.[51] Moralists used Latin grammar and *distinctiones* to counter the last two tactics,[52] but the first two assaults led them to render Christ's inhabitation of the host comprehensible to their lay

---

[48] Y. Dossat, 'Les Cathars d'après les documents de l'inquisition', in CaF 3 (1968), 71–104 (pp. 80–1 and 87); Raoul Ardent, homily no. 19 (*PL* 155, 2011A); Rubin, *Corpus Christi*, p. 74; Caesar, *Dialogus* v.19 (I, 298–9); Frédéricq, I, 49–50, no. 49; Lambert, 'Reform Movement', pp. 31–2; Crane, no. 140, p. 62; Stephen Langton, *Questiones*, St John's College MS 57, fol. 207ra; *Contra hereticos* i.57 (*PL* 210, 359–60); nn. 11–12, 24 above.

[49] *Contra amaurianos* xi–xii (pp. 39–48); Caesar, *Dialogus* v.19 (I, 298–9).

[50] A point driven home by an *exemplum* featuring Simon de Montfort's refusal to forfeit his meritorious unsubstantiated faith by witnessing a host miracle testifying to transubstantiation in the Midi (BL MS Royal 7.D.I., fol. 67r). See *H.occ.*, pp. 209–10 and 231–4; *Sermones dominicales*, pp. 335–6; *Contra hereticos* i.57–8 (*PL* 210, 359–63); Robert of Courson, *Summa* xliii.2 and 3–5, BnF MS Lat. 14524, fols. 157vb, 158ra-160vb; Peter the Chanter, *Summa* I, 140, § 56; Hilka, III, 16; Gerald, *Gemma* i.8 (pp. 22–4); Angers (1216–19), c. 132 (Pontal, I, 234).

[51] G. Macy, *Theologies of the Eucharist in the Early Scholastic Period* (Oxford, 1984), p. 58; Lambert, 'Reform Movement', pp. 31–2; *Summa contra haereticos* xiii.1–7 (*The* Summa Contra Haereticos *Ascribed to Praepositinus of Cremona*, ed. J. N. Garvin and J. A. Corbett, Publications in Mediaeval Studies 15 (Notre Dame IN, 1958), pp. 182–4); *Contra hereticos* i.57–62 (*PL* 210, 359–65); and n. 53 below.

[52] Stephen Langton, *Questiones*, St John's College MS 57, fols. 206va–vb and 317va; *H.occ.*, pp. 225–6.

audiences' concrete frame of mind through the very dialectic and Aristotelian *libri naturales* they sought to limit in Paris, a decision they justified by Lanfranc of Bec's earlier adoption of the logical arguments, dialectic, and grammatical exegesis used in a deconstructionist manner by Berengar of Tours to defend a newly redefined orthodox eucharistic doctrine.[53]

Yet even while Jacques de Vitry and Robert of Courson used the philosophical theory of substance and accidents to explain transubstantiation, both remained uncomfortable with using reason and natural philosophy to explain a supernatural phenomenon comparable to God's creation of the world *ex nihilo*; exempt from natural law, God transformed matter just as men transformed ore into iron. However, heretics appealed to scepticism and natural observation: if mass were celebrated simultaneously upon two or more altars or Christ dwelt in each piece of the consecrated host, his presence in multiple places contradicted natural laws. Robert of Courson explained that glorified bodies could penetrate non-glorified bodies, so that Christ's resurrected body could pass through a door like sun through glass and squeeze into an unglorified host.[54] Simple images suitable for laypersons, including a gloved hand or the cloud-shrouded sun, signified his invisible indwelling. When heretics mocked transubstantiation, asking which piece of the consecrated host contained Christ's head or foot, the Chanter's circle claimed that the God-man was completely present in the host and its fragments just as an image in a mirror remained in its broken pieces.[55]

The contrast between Christ's glorified body and the host could address other doubts exploited by heretics. Surely even a mountain-sized Christ would have been consumed long ago? Was Christ dishonoured by being digested, excreted, or incorporated by unworthy recipients of the host, including animals? In order to counter these doubts and comfort the devout ill who might vomit up the host, Robert of Courson and other theologians explained that while the host's outward form was digested by any recipient, including animals, Christ's spiritual body flew directly to the worthy's minds or returned directly to heaven.[56] Moreover, the Chanter's

---

[53] *H.occ.*, p. 231; Fichtenau, pp. 228, 282–3, 284–5 and 286–93; T. J. Holopainen, *Dialectic and Theology in the Eleventh Century* (New York, Leiden and Cologne, 1996), pp. 44–118; G. Macy, 'Of Mice and Manna: *Quid Mus Sumit* as a Pastoral Question', *RTAM* 58 (1991), 157–66; idem, 'The Theological Fate of Berengar's Oath of 1059: Interpreting a Blunder Become Tradition', in *Treasures from the Storeroom: Medieval Religion and the Eucharist* (Collegeville, MN, 1999), pp. 20–35 and *Theologies*, pp. 35–43 and 46–8; *PL* 204, 235–40.

[54] *H.occ.* pp. 229–34; *Sermones dominicales*, pp. 335–6; Robert of Courson, *Summa* xliii.2, 5–6 and 16, BnF MS Lat 14524, fols. 157vb, 160vb, 161rb–vb and 167ra; Chanter, *Summa* I , 133–4 and 140, §§ 55–6.

[55] Robert of Courson, *Summa* xliii.5, BnF MS Lat. 14524, fol. 160rb; *Sermones dominicales*, p. 337; *Contra hereticos* i.58 (*PL* 210, 362); Peter the Chanter, *Summa* I, 138, 140, 167–9 and 171–2, §§ 56 and 65; *Contra amaurianos* xi (pp. 40–3).

[56] *Contra hereticos* i.57–8 (*PL* 210, 359–60 and 362–3); Vaux-de-Cernay I, 12, § 12; Lambert, *Medieval Heresy*, p. 58; Eckbert of Schönau, *Sermones contra catharos* xi (*PL* 195, 92–3); Robert of Courson, *Summa* xlii.2, 15–16, BnF MS Lat. 14524, fols.

circle interpreted Christ's words at the Last Supper, which seemed to indicate that one must eat his flesh *and* his blood to inherit eternal life, as a spiritual consumption of Christ's body and blood, present in both host and chalice, so that laity need only receive the host. However, the Waldensians, Amalricians, and Cathars used a literal interpretation of this and other verses to assault 'logical' contradictions in the orthodox doctrine of the eucharist or to argue that the laity should also receive the chalice. For example, a verse claiming that those who took the body of Christ unworthily ate and drank judgement upon themselves seemed to contradict Christ's promise above. Robert of Courson and Jacques de Vitry used a distinction to claim that it referred to the material form of the eucharist which both good and evil consume, while the original promise pertained to the spiritual power of the *corpus Christi* received only by those united to the Church and Christ. Others merely ingested the material husk to their damnation, as Jacques de Vitry and others stressed while urging potential recipients to make a full confession before communion, a message reinforced with dire tales of those striken with sudden illness or death after unworthily receiving the eucharist.[57] The Paris moralists also stressed frequency of communion, presenting the eucharist as a spiritual panacea which purged the venial sins of the living, profited those in purgatory, and strengthened against temptation.[58]

While warning priests against over-reliance upon reason and urging them to preach the basics – that Christ was physically present and the eucharist's efficacy did not hinge upon the celebrant's merit but upon his office, the consecratory formula, and its recipients' being communicate and confessed members of the Church – Jacques and Robert included dialectical and philosophical treatments of the true presence and attributed sophist questions of an ilk condemned in Paris to cynics and heretics, including these. Are only the hosts which the priest sees and intends to consecrate affected, or could hosts in another church or around the world be transformed?[59] If the bread transformed by Christ at the Last Supper had been kept by one of his disciples in a pyx, would Christ have died upon the cross and within the pyx?

157va–b, 166rb–167ra; Stephen Langton, *Questiones*, St John's College MS 57, fols. 206va–207rb; *H.occ*, pp. 226, 229–31, 234–5, 240 and 244–5; *Sermones dominicales*, p. 337; Caesar, *Dialogus* ix.10–11, 24 and 27 (II, 174–5, 176–7 and 184–5); BL MS Royal 7.D.I, fol. 65v; Gerald, *Gemma* i.9 (pp. 25–6); Macy, 'Mice and Manna', 157–66; n. 57 below.

[57] *H.occ.*, pp. 214–15, 229–35, 244; *Sermones dominicales*, pp. 336–7; Peter the Chanter, *Summa* I, 142–4, § 57; Robert of Courson, *Summa* xliii.17, BnF MS Lat. 14524, fol. 167rb-vb; *Summa contra hereticos* iii (Summa *ascribed to Praepositinus*, ed. Garvin and Corbett, pp. 181–2); *Contra amaurianos* xi (pp. 40–3); Caesar, *Dialogus* ix (II, 164–217); and nn. 12, 16 and 56 above.

[58] *Sermones dominicales*, pp. 334 and 337–8; Gerald, *Gemma* i.5–6 (pp. 14–17); Robert of Courson, *Summa* xlv.1–2, BNF MS Lat. 14524, fols. 173vb–174rb; Caesar, *Dialogus* ix; n. 23 above.

[59] *H.occ.*, pp. 240–1; Peter the Chanter, *Summa*, I, 174, § 67; Robert of Courson, *Summa* xliii.2, 7 and 24, BnF MS Lat. 14524, fols. 157va–b, 162va–b and 169va; n. 16 above.

Would he remain alive there while dead in the sepulchre?[60] Attempting to transmit scholastic techniques from Paris to the parish priest, James and Robert coached their readers in the disputational method, now properly used as a prop for theology against opponents who rejected or undermined the superior proofs of scriptural authority or where authorities were simply lacking. These discussions could be added at the priests' discretion according to the intellectual level of himself and his audience, particularly when he was forced to confront a heretic before his parishioners or to address doubts and questions in the confessional. However, heretical attacks upon the current liturgical form of the eucharist and the laity's and priesthood's fears concerning the validity of a mass where the consecration of the host or chalice had been botched also exposed divisions of opinion among moral theologians regarding the precise moment of transubstantiation as they advised priests on appropriate remedies and penances.[61]

For while decrying frivolous and doubt-provoking speculation upon the mysteries of the faith in many homiletic or pedagogical contexts, moralists nonetheless applied dialectical and philosophical techniques to them in *summae*, *pastoralia*, and sermon collections intended to furnish theologians and parish priests with ammunition to present orthodox doctrine and counter heretical error before lay audiences.[62] For example, Stephen Langton followed Prévostin of Cremona and contemporary commentators on the *Sentences* of Peter Lombard in considering speculative topics such as the creation and fall of angels and humankind and the name and nature of the trinity in addition to explanations of the *Credo* and *Paternoster*, the articles of the faith, the sacraments, and moral dilemmas. These topics were invaluable in defining, unveiling, and combatting heresies, including doubts on transubstantiation and whether Christ truly suffered and died upon the cross.[63] Jacques de Vitry's Maundy Thursday sermon, intended to prepare

---

[60] *H.occ.*, pp. 237–8; *Contra hereticos* i.57, 60 and 62 (*PL* 210, 360 and 363); Robert of Courson, *Summa* xliii.6–7, BnF MS Lat. 14524, fols. 161va–162vb; Peter the Chanter, *Summa* I, 174–7 and 180–1, §§ 67, 70; Gerald, *Gemma* i.8 (pp. 21–2).

[61] *H.occ.*, pp. 234–6 and 245–6; Hilka, III, 22–4; Caesar, *Dialogus* ix.23, 27–33, 59–60 and 65 (II, 181–2, 184–5, 186–90, 211–12 and 215-1-6); Stephen Langton, *Questiones*, St John's College MS 57, fols. 206va–b, 207ra–b and 317vb–318ra; Robert of Courson, *Summa* xliii.2–3, 8–9, BnF MS Lat. 14524, fols. 157vb–158rb and 163ra–rb; E. Dumoutet, 'La théologie de l'eucharistie à la fin du XIIᵉ siècle: le témoignage de Pierre le Chantre d'après la "Summa de sacramentis"', *AHDLMA* 18–20 (1943–5), 181–262 (pp. 227–30); Peter the Chanter, *Summa* I, 149 and 150–6, §§ 59 and 61; Gerald, *Gemma* i.8 (p. 23).

[62] Jean Châtillon called for an investigation of this paradox in 'Le mouvement théologique dans la France de Philippe Auguste', in *La France de Philippe Auguste: le temps des mutations*, ed. R. H. Bautier, Colloques internationaux du Centre National de la Recherche Scientifique 602 (Paris, 1982), pp. 881–902 (pp. 896–7); Baldwin, *Peter the Chanter* II, 68 and 70, nn. 64, 69, 72 and 81.

[63] Prévostin of Cremona, *Summa*, Vatican, Biblioteca Apostolica, MS Lat. 1147, fols. 24vb–31vb, 35rb, 43ra–45rb, 50va–56ra and 57ra–64rb; M. Colish, 'In the Footsteps of the Glossator' (paper read at the Intellectual History Seminar, Newberry Library,

laypersons and clergymen for the worthy reception or celebration of the mandatory Easter communion, recapitulated all but the most sophistical queries from his treatment of the mass in his manual for priests, which also circulated as a sermon.[64] His liturgical sermon collection exploited periods traditionally devoted to catechizing lay audiences, including major feast-days in Advent and the week before Easter, to navigate doctrinal quagmires sometimes skirted before laypersons, such as the trinity and incarnation: heretical errors provided the cognitive map to outline orthodox truth, black defined white.[65] His *sermones communes et feriales* (c. 1229–40), written for parish priests and perhaps for the Croisier order and other reformers in Flanders-Brabant, provided a primer of didactic and debating material on basic and complex doctrinal and devotional topics for the construction of sermons to counter heresy and promote orthodoxy.[66] His techniques and goals were shared by other Paris moralists and Innocent III, who designed a sermon collection for the Cistercian Arnaud Amaury to preach to the heresy-riddled province of Narbonne.[67]

In conclusion, the moralists' use of dialectical techniques and natural philosophy to counter heresy helped to rehabilitate the *libri naturales*, impacting the future shape of mendicant and secular scholastic theology. Heresy also influenced reformers' emphasis upon an incarnation-, confession- and eucharist-centred high medieval devotion supplemented by attendance at sermons and basic prayers. For despite an ambivalent regard for the laity's intellectual capacity, manifested in an increasing emphasis on doctrinal preaching and confession balanced by elitist fears concerning uneducated or unsupervised 'rustics' interpreting the scriptures, the moralists' sermons illustrate the doctrines and cult which were fast becoming the common heritage of, rather than a tool for segregation between pastor and audience via their ministry and that of their successors, the friars.[68]

Chicago, 11 March 2000); A. L. Gregory, 'Studies on the Commentaries of Stephen Langton', *AHDLMA* 5 (1930), 5–266 (pp. 22, 233–5, 255–8 and 238–41); Baldwin, *Peter the Chanter* I, 49.

[64] *Sermones dominicales*, pp. 334–9ff; *H.occ.*, p. 44.

[65] J. Bataillon, 'Approaches to the Study of Medieval Sermons', *Leeds Studies in English* n.s. 11 (1980), 19–35; *Sermones dominicales*, pp. 54–9, 67–73, 117–18 and 473–4; Vatican, Biblioteca Apostolica, MS Borghese 141, fols. 54r-56v (*marginalia* indicating reader interest); compare *Contra hereticos* i.27–34 (*PL* 210, 308–10 and 321–7); Vaux-de-Cernay I, 9–12, §§ 10–11; Fourth Lateran (1215), c. 1 (*COD*, pp. 230–1).

[66] McDonnell, *Beguines*, pp. 21–2 and 53–8; C. A. Muessig, 'The *Sermones feriales* of Jacques de Vitry: A Critical Edition', 2 vols. (unpublished Ph.D. thesis, University of Montréal, 1993/4), and 'Les sermons de Jacques de Vitry sur les cathares', in CaF 32 (1997), 69–83.

[67] *PL* 217, 309–690 (cols. 335, 344, 350, 367–72, 375–6, 389–90, 396, 408–10, 433–8, 451–60 and 469–74).

[68] d'Avray, *Preaching*, pp. 7, 11, 64–5, 95, 123–4 and 126–31. I would like to thank Peter Biller for inviting me to present this paper; both he and Gary Macy also provided invaluable offprints of their own work. I am also indebted to the queries and suggestions of audiences at York, Kalamazoo and the Newberry Library.

Inquisition, Texts and Discourse

John H. Arnold

What might it mean if, following the invitation proffered by the title to this collection of essays, we were to consider inquisitorial depositions as *texts*? The term 'text' (as preferred by literary scholars) usually presages a con-centration upon writing, rhetoric, linguistic structure – the power of language. Reading depositions as texts might therefore involve, firstly, ceasing to treat these records of apparently 'everyday language' – vernacular responses to inquisitors' questions, translated into Latin and further redacted by scribes into a third-person, past-tense account of the interrogation – as transparent or innocent conduits of information.[1] Recognizing the circum-stances which produced the records – the context of power that brought about their creation – renders problematic the more positivist desire to read 'through' the records to produce, for example, an ethnography of medieval life.[2] Although the great allure of the depositions is the access that they appear to provide to the voices of historically subaltern subjects – peasants, women, lowly clerics – it is precisely the foundations of this allure, the a priori assumption of individual voices and speaking subjects who commun-icate *through* the records, that is brought into question by reconsidering the depositions as texts. In short, to raise the issue of 'texts' is to make, once again, what has been called in various contexts the 'linguistic turn'; that is, to bring an analysis of language into historical focus.

It may appear that I am positioning past historiography here as a straw man of naive positivism, but this is not my intention. There is a long tradition of 'source criticism' surrounding depositions to which I am profoundly

---

[1] *Contra*, for example, Alexander Murray's characterization of the records as 'the nearest medieval equivalent of a tape recorder'. See A. Murray, 'Time and Money', in *The Work of Jacques Le Goff and the Challenges of Medieval History*, ed. M. Rubin (Woodbridge, 1997), pp. 3–25 (p. 7). Murray is not alone in viewing the records in this fashion: various historians have a habit of translating the third-person deposi-tions into first-person accounts, a practice rooted in a similar sense of the material.

[2] For a critique of the ethnographic project of *Montaillou* (1978), see R. Rosaldo, 'From the Door of his Tent: The Fieldworker and the Inquisitor', in *Writing Culture: the Poetics and Politics of Ethnography*, ed. J. Clifford, G. E. Marcus (Berkeley, 1986), pp. 77–97. On inquisition and ethnography, see also C. Sponsler, 'Medieval Ethnography: Fieldwork in the European Past', *Assays: Critical Approaches to Medieval and Renaissance Texts* 7 (1992), 1–30; and K. Biddick, 'The Devil's Anal Eye: Inquisitorial Optics and Ethnographic Authority', in *The Shock of Medievalism* (Durham NC, 1998), pp. 105–34.

indebted. Various authors, from Herbert Grundmann to Robert Lerner and
Grado Merlo, have raised questions and suspicions about depositions and
their use.[3] One might in fact suggest that the depositions come to us from the
Middle Ages already contextualized by critical suspicion, if we recall the
challenges that the Franciscan Bernard Délicieux mounted against Inquisition
and its documentary procedures in the early fourteenth century: Délicieux
denounced certain registers as 'false, fictitious and contrived by order of the
Dominicans' and said that if St Peter and St Paul were tried by inquisition,
even they would be found guilty.[4] And if one wishes to raise the question of
power, James Given has recently reminded us of what he calls 'the technology of documentation': the ways in which inquisitorial records functioned as
a quasi-institutional 'memory' of transgression, permitting inquisitors to use
the records in an 'analytical and activist fashion' to catch out and punish
supporters of heresy.[5]

However, it seems to me that considering depositions as texts raises
further questions than those previously addressed, questions relating not
only to trust (can we believe the evidence?) and repression (how were the
records used to aid persecution?), but to the relationship between language
itself and power: the particular *kind* of power embodied in language and the
production of meaning. As a variety of historical works, responding to
developments in literary and cultural theory, have argued in the last
twenty years, language and writing do not simply reflect power relations
but embody them. The ability to forge and disseminate an authoritative way
of talking or writing about the world affects the 'reality' of lived experience.[6]
The label of 'text' thus invites us to consider the written-ness of the records:
the language that they employ, the practices of production within which they
are embedded, and the cultural and linguistic contexts they inhabit. We could
note firstly that the depositions are in communication with other texts, most
obviously with inquisitorial manuals, and most particularly with the questions they provide. But this is not simply a case of remarking that inquisitors'
questions distort or 'frame' the material they elicit: the questions themselves
relate to pictures of heresy built up in other texts – synodal statutes, anti-
heretical polemics – and work to construct a field of knowledge within which
'heresy' is contained. For example, the oft-noted tendency of inquisitors'

[3] Grundmann, 'Ketzerverhöre'; Merlo, *Eretici e inquisitori*, esp. pp. 1–15; Lerner, *Free Spirit*. For a brief historiographical critique, see J. H. Arnold, 'The Historian as Inquisitor: The Ethics of Interrogating Subaltern Voices', *Rethinking History* 2 (1998), 379–86.
[4] Friedlander, *Hammer*, esp. p. 59.
[5] Given, *Inquisition*, p. 39.
[6] See, for example, Moore, *Persecuting Society*; D. Sabean, *Power in the Blood: Popular Culture and Village Discourse in Early Modern Germany* (Cambridge, 1984); L. Roper, *Oedipus and the Devil: Witchcraft, Sexuality and Religion in Early Modern Europe* (London, 1994); L. Gowing, *Domestic Dangers: Women, Words and Sex in Early Modern London* (Oxford, 1996).

questions to concentrate on actions rather than beliefs follows a long tradition of learned churchmen considering (with all the prejudices surrounding medieval concepts of literacy and its absence) the illiterate laity in contact with heresy.[7] One can draw a line connecting, for example, Ralph Glaber's explanation for the success, at the turn of the eleventh century, that the 'mad' peasant Leutard had in recruiting followers (because of the fact that 'rustics are prone to fall into error')[8] to the categories of heretical transgression defined by the council of Tarragona in 1242, where the label of 'believer' (*credens*) is said to only be applied to those who are 'literate and/or discerning' (*litteratus vel discretus*). The other categories – receiver (*receptator*), defender (*defensor*), supporter (*fautor*) and so on – circumvent the difficulty of ascribing 'heretical belief' to illiterate lay people by founding their definitions on actions alone.[9]

The statutes and the first inquisitorial manual, the *Ordo processus Narbonensis*, also provide procedures for the creation of the depositions, and more importantly for their production of 'truth'.[10] The manual, for example, emphasizes the need for the deponents to come 'spontaneously and penitently' ('sponte . . . et penitentes') to tell the 'pure and full truth on themselves and others' ('plenam et puram veritatem de se et aliis'). The 'truth' produced through inquisition is dependent on the presence of the inquisitors, who prompt, monitor and assess the speech of the witnesses, but the truth is authorized by the deponent, as he or she is asked to 'authenticate' their deposition by agreeing to the words of the final redaction.[11] By ascribing this degree of agency (via 'spontaneity' and 'authorship') to the deponents, the foundation of the truth-claims of inquisition is shifted from the inquisitor (although he plays a key role) to the witness; and thus the power relations involved are occluded and displaced. The depositions therefore operate as part of a larger system: they connect with a network of other texts, they are produced according to certain sets of procedures established in the statutes and inquisitorial manuals, and they form one element within a wider context of Church views, not only on heresy but the *problem* of heresy – the problem,

---

[7] On medieval concepts of literacy and illiteracy, see Clanchy, *Memory*; Stock, *Implications of Literacy*; Moore, *Persecuting Society*, pp. 135–40.

[8] Ralph Glaber, *Historiarum Libri Quinque*, ed. and trans. J. France, N. Bulst and P. Reynolds, Oxford Medieval Texts (Oxford, 1989), pp. 88–91; extract translated in Wakefield and Evans, p. 72.

[9] Mansi, XXIII, 554–5.

[10] The text of the *Ordo processus Narbonensis* is edited in *Texte zur Inquisition*, pp. 70–6; and translated in Wakefield, *Heresy, Crusade and Inquisition*, pp. 250–8. For analysis of the *Ordo* in the context of other inquisitorial manuals, see Dondaine, 'Manuel'. Note however that Dondaine's ascription of authorship has been superseded by that of Yves Dossat, who assigns the work to Bernard de Caux and Jean de St Pierre, writing in the mid-thirteenth century; see Dossat, *Crises*, p. 167.

[11] *Texte zur Inquisition*, pp. 70–2. For an analysis of 'truth' within inquisition, see T. Asad, 'Notes on Body Pain and Truth in Medieval Christian Ritual', *Economy and Society* 12 (1983), 287–327.

we might say, of the laity exceeding the rudimentary role set out for them within orthodoxy.[12] To put this in a different way, in labelling depositions as texts we might consider them as productions of a larger *discourse* concerning heresy.

The term 'discourse' is by now fairly familiar to medievalists, although perhaps most particularly in the fields of medical history and histories of sexuality and the body. Given, however, the way in which theoretical tools have a tendency to lose their analytical focus when they slip into more common usage, it is worth exploring for a moment what we might mean by this term, and what implications it might carry for our consideration of depositional texts. There are a variety of ways in which people have used and theorized the term 'discourse', from a fairly loose sense of a 'shared language' to the rigid and Marxian 'Ideological State Apparatuses' proposed by Louis Althusser. Predominantly, however, the term is linked to the French theorist Michel Foucault.[13]

A discourse, for Foucault, indicates a particular set of linguistic and symbolic practices that lays claim to coherence and authority, and in so doing, constructs a particular arrangement of the world: a field of knowledge, a group of privileged subjects who possess that knowledge, a range of objects which can be arranged and distributed within that knowledge, and a set of mechanisms that claim to guarantee the production of 'truth' within the particular discourse. The example of a specific discourse to which his analysis returned on several occasions was that of medicine: where a field of language and practices (medical vocabulary and procedures) produce and position various subject positions (doctors and patients), authorized by a 'will to truth' behind which lurks the exercise of power (the advancement of medical science).[14] In analysing discourse in this way, Foucault tries to unmask what is 'taken for granted' or left unsaid within any particular cultural context, and to suggest that where we note the strongest claims to the production of 'truth', we must be most watchful for covert operations of power.[15] In short, therefore, Foucault tries to expand the boundaries of our

---

[12] On the changes in ecclesiastical attitudes towards the laity between the twelfth and thirteenth centuries, see for example A. Vauchez, *The Laity in the Middle Ages: Religious Beliefs and Devotional Practices*, trans. D. E. Bornstein (Notre Dame IN, 1993), esp. pp. 85–106.

[13] For an overview of discourse, see D. MacDonell, *Theories of Discourse: An Introduction* (Oxford, 1986).

[14] See M. Foucault, *Madness and Civilisation*, trans. R. Howard (New York, 1965); *The Birth of the Clinic*, trans. A. M. Sheridan (London, 1973); *The Archaeology of Knowledge*, trans. A. M. Sheridan (London, 1972).

[15] 'Power', for Foucault, is another word with a particular nuance: rather than considering the overt operation of *force* or *repression*, 'power' is taken to indicate the more covert and consensual arrangement of reality into a particular shape, including the intrinsic power-relations between different people and institutions. See, for example, M. Foucault, 'Truth and Power', in *Power/Knowledge: Selected Interviews and Other Writings 1972–1977*, trans. and ed. C. Gordon et al. (New York, 1980), pp. 109–33.

suspicions; something that, it seems to me, should temperamentally suit most historians, even if they also have an innate suspicion of technical vocabulary or 'jargon'.

The nuances of Foucault's thoughts on language and power changed and developed over his substantial body of writing, and hence I am unwilling to attempt a further exegesis of what he 'really' or 'essentially' meant. However, given his own playful and undogmatic relationship to the theoretical tools he developed, we might feel free to focus on one of the clearest expositions of discourse that he provided, set out in a lecture originally delivered in 1970 under the title 'The Orders of Discourse'.[16] In this piece, Foucault – emphasizing however that the relative tidiness of his description was intended only heuristically – suggests three groups of 'procedures' by which discourse is ordered, each 'procedure' containing further subsets of systems and mechanisms. The first procedure is that of 'systems of exclusion': forbidden speech, the division between the speech of the mad and the sane, and what he calls the 'will to truth', which we might understand as the grounds or mechanisms accepted as necessary for successfully establishing a claim to be speaking the truth within a particular historical or cultural moment. These systems of exclusion function from the 'exterior' of discourse, patrolling its boundaries. The second group of procedures are however 'internal': systems of classification and distribution, that function (Foucault suggests) to control elements of 'chance' within language. Foucault talks here in particular of the idea of a 'discipline', for example the academic discipline of history: the discipline allows the formulation of new propositions (such as thinking about depositions as 'texts'), but demands that they be made and unified around a particular domain of objects (in this case, historical documents rather than, say, biological cells), arranging them in a particular way, using a particular set of methods, rules and techniques 'proper' to that discipline (including, for example, the footnotes appending this article and the academic tone of voice I am currently employing).

The third group of procedures are what Foucault calls 'the rarefaction . . . of the speaking subject': who is allowed to speak, when, under what circumstances. The most obvious mechanism here is ritual: the condition, action and position adopted, say, by the parish priest when consecrating the Host; or, closer to the area considered by this collection, by the *perfectus* when performing the *consolamentum*. One can consider here also, as a more submerged procedure, what Foucault calls 'doctrine'. Doctrine operates by linking together a particular set of language and actions with a particular, but diffuse, group of people. However, Foucault suggests, doctrine's linking of language and individual 'puts in question both the statement and the speaking subject, the one by the other'. That is, doctrine always involves mechanisms for checking whether the one who is speaking is allowed to participate within the particular discourse, by seeing if they are part of that

[16] M. Foucault, 'Orders of Discourse', *Social Science Information* 10 (1971), 7–30.

discursive community; and conversely, doctrine examines the *content* of the speech of the speaking subjects, to see whether they are still speaking within 'doctrinal truth' – and where necessary excludes and rejects those who are not. However, as Foucault argues, 'heresy and orthodoxy do not derive from a fanatical exaggeration of the doctrinal mechanism, but rather belong fundamentally to them'.[17] That is, doctrine – and we might here start to read 'religion' for doctrine – depends upon policing a resistance or acceptance of a particular discourse. Without this policing, doctrine – religion – does not exist.[18]

This tripartite map of discourse is, as Foucault notes, too neat and abstract in its divisions: each of these groups of procedures overlap and intertwine, and particular discourses may place more emphasis on certain procedures rather than employ them all. Nonetheless, Foucault's map gives us a particular way of looking again at inquisition and depositional texts. If we consider the history of inquisition in Languedoc in the thirteenth and early fourteenth centuries, we can, I would suggest, see the development of a particular 'inquisitorial' discourse. The conciliar statutes, and the *Ordo processus Narbonensis*, set out what might be described as a 'discipline' for the study, identification and policing of heretics. The statutes – particularly, as noted above, the council of Tarragona in 1242 – map out a system of categorization for heretical transgression, dividing those tried into *hereticus, credens, fautor, occultator* and so on.[19] They establish a system for distributing people within these categories, based overwhelmingly on the extent and quality of the actions they had performed, and assign penances that represent their categorized identities to the populace at large. They outline a mechanism for the production of 'truth' within inquisitorial discourse, a mechanism that begins fairly simply with the careful but blunt questions on actions, times, places, and contexts of heretical support; but which increasingly, over the course of the thirteenth century, places greater weight on the 'truth' produced by personal confession, understood as the revelation of an interior 'truth' uncovered or brought forth through the inquisitorial context. This 'truth' is authorized by the agency ascribed to the subject confessing, as the deponent is in various ways positioned as autonomous, even within the coercive context of inquisition: consider, here, the way in which various

---

[17] Foucault, 'Orders of Discourse', p. 64.

[18] For an interesting analysis of the role of power in the creation of religion, see T. Asad, 'Anthropological Conceptions of Religion: Reflections on Geertz', *Man* 18 (1983), 237–59.

[19] The Council of Tarragona in 1242 establishes eleven categories of heretical transgression, drawing on a vocabulary partly established by earlier councils, but supplying a much greater sense of definition and process than prior legislation. Although the council was primarily concerned with the prosecution of Waldensian heretics, it was influential on inquisitorial procedure in general, not least because of the presence at Tarragona of Raymond de Peñafort, a pre-eminent authority on canon law in the period. For background and analysis of the councils, see Maisonneuve, *Études*, pp. 283–307.

deponents are said to have 'spontaneously' confessed, although having been imprisoned for some time prior to their interrogation.[20] Overall then, one might say that inquisition develops a particular field of *knowledge* about heresy: the divisions between types of heresy, the conduct expected by those in contact with heresy, the framing theories of heretical transmission. Embedded in, and constructed by, that field of knowledge are the 'knowing subjects' – the inquisitors – and the objects of their study – the deponents. The knowledge constructed within inquisitorial discourse carries – as with every discipline – assumptions about the distribution of elements, theories of causation, modes of interpretation, that are particular to its historical and political context. The depositional texts that survive for the historian's study are, therefore, both products of and elements within this inquisitorial discourse.[21] To make, therefore, an obvious point: inquisitorial knowledge is not the same as 'our' knowledge. Or rather, we must be especially wary of the seduction of inquisitorial knowledge, as operations of power – the arrangement of reality into a particular, inquisitorial, shape – are covered over by a concurrent reassurance that this knowledge is a production of 'truth'.

If we wish to return to the textual nature of the depositions, we might ask, then, what is 'taken for granted' or left unsaid within inquisitorial discourse. If we look to the inquisitorial depositions of the mid thirteenth century, we can see how the selection and textual presentation of inquisitors' questions and deponents' answers work to produce a particular picture of heresy, and lay contact with heresy. The discursive construction and representation of a certain kind of agency on the part of the deponents – an agency, as noted above, that works to legitimate the 'truth' produced within inquisition – works at the textual level to emphasize the 'freedom' of the deponents' speech, minimizing in certain ways the inquisitorial presence. Inquisitors' questions are usually only clearly visible when the answer received is negative; for example, 'Asked if he had ever believed the heretics to be good men, or gave or sent [anything to them], or led or received [them], or received peace from the heretics or from their book or made a pact with anyone not to reveal heresy, or was present at the *apparellamentum* or the

---

[20] For example, Raymond Garrigue of Puylaurens was imprisoned after his first interview, in which he had denied all knowledge of heresy. Three more interrogations took place, with the witness in prison between each. Finally, having been imprisoned for a year and a day (as the record carefully notes) he 'spontaneously' ('sponte') confessed. See D26, fols. 291r–292v; and for other examples fols. 102v, 112v–113r, 131v; D25, fol. 320r.

[21] It is worth noting, briefly, that I am not suggesting that 'text' and 'discourse' are synonymous. Space forbids a full discussion of the relationship, but we might note firstly that a Foucauldian notion of discourse includes practices – such as the disciplinary mechanism of confession and penance – that are not purely linguistic but also bodily; and that, as I will further explore below, the depositional texts speak within inquisitorial discourse, but may also be read for traces of other discursive practices.

consolamentum of the heretics, he said no.'[22] However, most examples are less comprehensive, and betray less of the mechanisms working to structure the text. With the guide of the interrogatory provided by the *Ordo processus Narbonensis*, it is not difficult to guess at the questions hiding behind many inquisitorial statements: when, for example, at the beginning of his deposition a witness 'said that he saw at Cabaret, at the time of the war, Guiraud Abit, bishop of the heretics, and many other heretics, living publicly there in their houses and frequently preaching, both in the streets and in their houses', it is not difficult to divine that the witness was asked something like 'when and where did you first see heretics, what did they do, and what contact did you have with them?'[23] However, other elements in the depositions that might at first appear to be specific details provided spontaneously by the witness may in fact also have been prompted by the presence of questions, revealed only on the rare occasions when those questions are made prominent by a negative response. For example, one deponent, recounting a dying Cathar adherent receiving the *consolamentum*, was asked how much money the sick man left as a bequest to the heretics, replying that he did not know.[24] This strongly suggests that on the more frequent occasions when deponents state the amount of a bequest, they are not spontaneously recalling a detail that impressed them as important, but responding to an area of inquisitorial interest. Another common detail – again one that might be read as a tiny element of verisimilitude – is prompted by the inquisitors: 'Asked if he and the aforesaid others adored the heretics there . . . or ate with them there *at the same table* or [ate] bread blessed by them, he said no'.[25] Eating 'at the same table', it would appear, was not a detail supplied by the deponents' unfettered memories, but had some import for the inquisitors – possibly indicating closeness, companionship, and hence 'belief' of a particular nature. The details of the rituals described by deponents are also affected by inquisitorial questions. Another deponent, eating with the heretics, was asked 'if at the first bite or sip [the heretics] said "bless"', indicating that this detail, found frequently elsewhere in the registers, was prompted by inquisitors. Another ritual, the greeting and petitioning of heretics labelled 'adoration' by inquisitors, is similarly affected: a deponent was asked if he said anything after the final *benedicite* - that is, whether he continued with the formula identified elsewhere in the records,

---

[22] D22, fol. 75v, 'requisitus si credidit unquam haereticos esse bonos homines, vel dedit, vel misit, vel duxit, vel receptavit, vel recepit pacem ab haereticis vel a libro eorum, vel fecit condictum cum aliquo de non revelando haeresim, vel interfuit apparellamento vel consolamento haereticorum, dixit quod non'.

[23] D23, fols. 233v–234r, 'apud Cabaretum, tempore guerrae, vidit ibi Guiraldum Abith, episcopum haereticorum, et alios multos haereticos qui publice stabant ibi in domibus suis et praedicabant frequenter tam in viis quam in domibus . . .'.

[24] D23, fols. 86v–87r.

[25] D24, fol. 13v, 'interrogatus si ipse testis et alii supradicti adoraverunt ibi dictos haereticos vel comederunt ibi cum eis in eadem mensa vel de pane benedicto ab eis, dixit quod non'.

'bless me and pray God to lead me to a good end'.[26] Another deponent greeting heretics was asked 'if he the witness and the aforesaid others bent their knees in front of the said heretics more often than once, or said "bless", or added anything else'.[27] Elsewhere we find deponents asked to specify in whose house a certain *consolamentum* was performed, similarly in whose house another deponent met heretics, and most comprehensively, whether a deponent thought the heretics were 'good men'.[28]

Now, this is not to suggest that the occasional presence of these questions indicates that all of these details – including calling Cathar *perfecti* 'good men' – were inquisitorial inventions. Obviously inquisitors could expand and refine their questions, and the details they sought, as they gained further information from previous depositions. However, it nonetheless indicates that the way in which inquisitors shaped the material could be happening at a profound and somewhat concealed level; and that the pattern of 'knowledge' they produced and reproduced on the Cathar heresy had a strong tendency to militate against recognising nuance and heterogeneity in the lay relationship to heresy. What underlies this process of 'flattening out' the myriad individual relationships between laity and *perfecti* is, I would suggest, the assumption that the *illitterati* – the laity – could not engage in 'belief' in any complex fashion. The questions asked by inquisitors, and hence the 'knowledge' that they produce about heresy, focus upon actions simply because (in the mid-thirteenth century) they did not see any further meaningful grounds on which one would identify 'belief'. For example, the records display an extraordinary lack of interest in the details of what heretics preached, and absolutely no interest in what deponents *thought* about what heretics preached. The inquisitors only wished to know who had been present at the preaching. When asked about 'belief', deponents are required simply to place themselves on one side or other of the line separating the inquisitorial binary division of orthodoxy and heresy; to respond, we might say, to the resistance or acceptance of doctrine. In the earlier records, deponents who admit to belief most frequently say that they 'believed in the heretics from the year of discretion [that is, most probably, since they were twelve or fourteen years old] such that they believed that if they died within the sect they would be saved', and, by implication, quit that belief when abjuring heresy at the conclusion to their deposition.[29] 'Belief' as constructed

---

[26] D23, fol. 222v.

[27] D24, fol. 12v, 'si ipse testis et alii supradicti pluries quam semel flexerunt genua sua coram dictis haereticis vel dixerunt "benedicite" vel aliquid aliud adiecerunt'.

[28] D24, fols. 53r, 177v, 122v.

[29] In the records from the later thirteenth century – recorded primarily in Doat 25 and 26 – the termination of 'belief' at this point is stated much more explicitly. For example, from the deposition of Bernard Benedict: 'he had remained in love and belief in the heretics for thirty years or more, but he had relinquished it in the preceding year, namely in that week in which he began to confess' ('in amore et credentia haereticorum steterat triginta annis et amplius, sed eam reliquerat anno precedenti, videlicet illa septimana in qua incepit confiteri'); D26, fol. 311v.

here is not an interiorized process, but a much more straightforward matter of allegiance. The 'agency' ascribed to deponents is thus of a very limited kind: sufficient to authorize, as 'spontaneous', the words that they produced under interrogation, but with regard to their relationship to faith (whether orthodox or heterodox) essentially circumscribed by their illiterate nature.

But what of the later depositions, the records of the Fournier inquisition in the early fourteenth century? Surely, in the fascinating detail supplied in those rich sources, we see the communication, through the texts, of individual thoughts, feelings and fears? It is certainly true that inquisitorial texts change drastically between the thirteenth and early fourteenth centuries, and given more space it would be interesting to consider *why* they changed – why inquisitorial discourse found space, in the early fourteenth century, for that which it could not hear or would not record in the mid-thirteenth century. But even if we set that question aside for now, considering the later depositions as texts continues to raise further problems as to how we view their engaging testimony. Let us therefore conclude by considering one particular deposition from the Fournier register, to investigate how it is shaped and produced by inquisitorial discourse, and to consider what that discourse continued to 'take for granted' in its production of a particular picture of reality.

The deposition I would like to analyse is that of Guillaume Austatz, *bayle* of Ornolac.[30] Seven witnesses gave testimony against Guillaume between 11 May and 28 July 1320. It is probable that the accusations of the initial witness, Galharda Rous, first brought Guillaume to the attention of the inquisitors. She attested firstly that, about four years previously, when talking with Austatz in her house about God and the Resurrection, Guillaume had argued that when a body died, the soul would re-enter another body of a new-born child, and by way of proof, had suggested that 'if every human soul was received back into the particular body in which it had been, and every soul had its own body, when the world has existed for many years, all the world would be filled with souls, such that, as he said, one could not fit them into the space between Toulouse and the village of Mérens' because, although souls are small in size, there have been so many people alive. Galharda further attested that, having asked Guillaume in his position as *bayle* to help her recover some money stolen from her, and he having refused, she had told him that she would pray to the Blessed Mary for a miracle to recover her money and to avenge her on the robbers. Guillaume, however, had said to her that the Blessed Mary did not have the power to do this, and would not avenge her, because Mary could not kill men or cause death. Finally, Galharda attested that she had heard from Alazaïs Monier that after the death of Alazaïs's four sons, Guillaume had spoken to Alazaïs, and told

---

[30] Austatz may be familiar to readers from his appearances in *Montaillou*, where bits of his deposition are used in fragmented form across a number of chapters. See *Montaillou* (1978), pp. 22, 69, 206, 210, 241, 303, 317 and 335–6.

her not to grieve, since she was young and could have more children, and the souls of her dead sons would enter the bodies of the new infants.[31]

The subsequent witnesses (Alazaïs herself amongst them) repeated variations on these accusations, along with further matters concerning Austatz. The picture they provided of Guillaume was of a man who had said and done things that raised a strong suspicion of heresy: a man who had uttered a number of dubious beliefs about souls and the afterlife, who had denied the power of the Virgin Mary to intercede in this world, who was said to have practised usury when he was living in Lordat, who did not take communion and who ate meat during Lent, who had spoken against the execution of the Waldensian heretic Raymond *de Costa* (saying that it would have been better if they had burnt Bishop Fournier), who had said that priests could not demand a specific amount for oblations and that rich men could not enter heaven, and who was a man who came from 'heretical kin' ('genus hereticalis').[32] Guillaume, it would appear, was clearly implicated in heresy. To what degree, however, does this picture depend upon the constructions of inquisitorial discourse? In what ways might the inquisitorial production of this text work to construct a *particular* image of Guillaume, silencing or displacing other possible readings?

Guillaume himself was first questioned on 15 and 16 July 1320, and was subsequently arrested, being brought forth from prison for questioning on six further occasions between 11 August and 1 September, before a final session on 3 September to confirm his confession. On 7 March 1321 he was sentenced to imprisonment. Eight years later this was commuted to wearing the yellow crosses of infamy that indicated his past transgressions. It is interesting to note the comparative harshness of Guillaume's sentence. Although he was arguably connected with the Cathar heresy (having heard various Cathar tenets of faith, including the transmigration of souls, from his mother), according to both his own confession and the evidence of his accusers he had never actually met a Cathar *perfectus*.[33] If we want to understand the severity with which Guillaume was punished, we have to look beyond actions and consider the role that inquisitorial discourse played in constructing him as a threat, as someone whose speech and deeds required policing and punishment.

The short vignettes given by the witnesses of Guillaume's transgressions formed the basis for the inquisitors' opening summary of the accusation against him on 15 July 1320. Fournier told him that it was said that he had asserted that each human soul did not possess its own body, but migrated

---

[31] Fournier I, 191–3.

[32] The witnesses' statements are presented in Fournier I, 191–9.

[33] Guillaume admitted that he had met and spoken with Raymond Sabatier, his brother-in-law, but prior to Sabatier's heretication; and similarly had met Pierre Autier, but before he left for Lombardy to become a *perfectus*. Guillaume persistently denied believing that one could be saved through the Cathar faith, or supporting them at all. See Fournier I, 205 and 207.

from body to body upon death; that souls were not saved or punished according to how they had conducted themselves when alive; that Raymond *de Costa* was a good Christian and had taught the truth; and that the Church did not have the power to set the amount offered as oblations. And because of these things he was 'thus, moreover, defamed of being a believer, aider and receiver of the Manichaean heretics' ('sic eciam infamatus quod hereticorum manicheorum fuerit credens, fautor et receptator') and of their sect.[34] Guillaume denied the charges, but was not believed and was thus held for further questioning.

The presence, in this first interrogation, of the terms *credens, fautor* and *receptator* reminds us of the inquisitorial framework of knowledge: these are terms drawn from the transgressional categories defined by the council of Tarragona back in 1242. Note that to this point in the text, the witnesses against Guillaume had not actually reported anything specifically that indicated aiding or 'receiving' Manichaean – that is, Cathar – heretics.[35] He had apparently spoken up in favour of Raymond *de Costa*; but this heretic was, remember, a Waldensian. Despite these initial complications, the inquisitorial framework of knowledge was from the start working to construct Guillaume in a particular way, to position him within preconceived patterns about heresy and its workings.

Another element of suspicion was the fact that Guillaume came from 'heretical kin' ('genus hereticalis'): Galharda Rous said that both his mother and sister had died in Carcassonne prison on account of heresy, and that his brother-in-law was a heretical fugitive. We should note, however, that this familial contextualization of Guillaume was prompted by the inquisitor, who specifically asked Galharda (and another witness, Alazaïs Monier) whether Guillaume came from a *genus hereticalis*.[36] Although the theme of connecting family and heresy has been popular with modern historians of Catharism, its meaning for the inquisitors should give us pause. What is implied, exactly, by the idea of a *genus hereticalis*? We glimpse here, I suspect, an underlying assumption of inquisitorial discourse about one of the routes by which heresy was transmitted: possibly through family teaching, but perhaps also simply through intimate personal contact. It is of course perfectly possible that family context affected people's attitudes towards heresy; and Guillaume's mother, by his own admission, played some kind of role in the formation of Guillaume's thoughts about souls and the afterlife. But we should take care over whether we wish to adopt this tenet of inquisitorial 'knowledge' as our own. What the concept of a *genus hereticalis* essentially does is to defer the problematic question of 'belief' – how it is transmitted, why people come to hold and accept certain tenets – outside the frame of

[34] Fournier I, 200.
[35] Being a 'receiver' usually meant accepting heretics into one's house and providing them with hospitality; being a *fautor* implied more diffuse supportive actions, such as sending things to them, having contact with them in general, and so on.
[36] Fournier I, 192 and 194.

enquiry. Reading other inquisitorial depositions, it is clear a family connection with heresy did not automatically indicate allegiance or belief on the part of all family members.[37] Where we find, in the depositions from the thirteenth century, deponents in contact with heretics who were also kin, the meaning of that connection remains something of a mystery: were they in contact because the relatives were heretics (and believers in heresy because brought up that way)? Or were they in contact with them because they were family? The idea of 'heretical kin' takes for granted certain underlying assumptions – or, perhaps, leaves unexpressed the troubling complexities of the negotiation of 'belief'.

Another element of inquisitoria 'knowledge' is the way in which it orders and distributes 'belief'. As noted above, the inquisitor's initial interrogation of Guillaume opened with a summary of his transgressive statements. These were further extracted, in his second interrogation, into seven heretical 'articles', where Guillaume's statements on the soul and other matters are positioned as erroneous theological propositions.[38] The details recorded elsewhere in the text allow us to contrast Guillaume's words on souls with the 'articles' produced by the inquisitor. Where the inquisitor questioned Guillaume on articles such as whether the soul had its own ('propria') body, whether the soul left one body and entered another upon death, whether the soul would be resurrected and reassume flesh and bone and so on, elsewhere we find that Guillaume's statements were rather more complex and somewhat contradictory. On the transmigration of souls, he admitted telling either Bartholomée d'Urs or Alazaïs Monier, on the death of her son, that God would either put the soul of her lost son into a new child when she conceived or that his soul would be in a good place. Questioned further on what he had meant by this, Guillaume emphasized that he had spoken to comfort the woman, and that what he had really meant (although he admitted that 'the said words did not signify this', 'dicta verba hec non significent') was that she would receive consolation from having another child.[39] Regardless of what Guillaume 'actually' believed about transmigration (if, in fact, one can legitimately even frame 'belief' in such a way), he presents the meaning of his words as dictated by context ('for comfort') in a way that inquisitorial discourse could not accept. Furthermore, given some of the other statements alleged by the witnesses, Guillaume seemed to have some contradictory beliefs about the soul: how, for example, does one square transmigration with the belief that the rich could not enter the kingdom of heaven? Or that all souls would have to pass through Purgatory before reaching heaven?[40] On the question of the Resurrection, Guillaume provides

---

[37] See, e.g., the deposition of Arnaud Sicre. Arnaud's family was disinherited because of its support for heresy, but his response was to blame the Cathars, and to act as an inquisitorial spy against them. Fournier II, 20–81.

[38] Fournier I, 201.

[39] Fournier I, 202.

[40] Fournier I, 197–9 and 207–8.

another contextualization for his thoughts and doubts: he confessed that about six or seven years previously, he had been at the cemetery of the church in Ornolac when they were digging a new grave. As they dug, old bones were turned up and brought to the surface, and seeing these bones Guillaume had said to those present, "'It is said that the souls of the dead return in the same flesh and bones as those in which they once were . . . And how is it possible that the soul that was formerly in these bones can return there?", speaking questioningly.'[41] We gain a certain, rather complex, picture of Guillaume's beliefs from the detail of the text – that he had a variety of thoughts and doubts about souls and what happened to them after death, thoughts that were heavily affected by the context within which he uttered them – that is transmuted by inquisitorial discourse into a clear, abstract set of heretical propositions.

What we are noting here is the *production* of heresy. This is not to claim that Guillaume was 'innocent' of the faults alleged against him, but that the way in which Guillaume's various statements are repositioned by inquisitorial discourse as 'heresy' – as opposed to, say, confusion or doubt – involves the operation of a certain kind of productive power. Looking back to the statements of the witnesses, we can see a field of speech and behaviour is mapped out by inquisition as suitable for policing, which in turn tacitly constructs a 'right' way of behaving. Guillaume is suspected because of things that he had said, but also because of things he had *not* said and done: that he had not taken communion, that he had not fasted during Lent. Most intriguing is the evidence of Alazaïs de Bordes, who told Fournier that on a certain day she had been supposed to cross the river Ariège but was scared to do so, and so had taken shelter 'totally stupefied and afraid' ('tota stupefacta et timida') in Guillaume's house. He had asked her why she was scared, and she indicated that she was afraid that she might drown, to which he had said 'why were you afraid, when it would have mattered as much for you to die here as elsewhere?'('Quare timuisti, tantum valuisset tibi mori ibi quam alibi?') She replied that she did not want to die without making confession and doing the other things that a good Christian should; and 'the said Guillaume was silent, and gave no response to these words' ('dictus Guillelmus tacuit, et nullum ad hec verba dedit responsum').[42] As this silence becomes coded as suspicious, the field of power is extended: not only to cover specific heretical 'articles', but the 'right' way of behaving as a 'good Christian'. It is worth noting, similarly, how two of the witnesses, when reporting Guillaume's statements on other matters, also find themselves briefly under the inquisitorial eye, asked why they did not report these words earlier, or why they did not reprimand Guillaume when he first said

[41] Fournier I, 206, '"Dicitur quod anime hominum defunctorum revertuntur in eisdem carnibus et ossibus in quibus fuerant . . . et quomodo potest esse quod in istis ossibus revertatur anime [sic] que primo fuit in eis?", interrogative loquendo.'
[42] Fournier I, 196.

them.[43] Heresy becomes a matter not only of what you do, but of what you fail to do.

In analysing how 'heresy' and transgression are constructed and categorized in the records surrounding Guillaume Austatz, I have also been attempting to point to details which might permit us other ways of reading him beyond the inquisitorial; other ways, that is, of considering Guillaume outside the category of 'heretical believer'. Against this analytical move, it might fairly be objected that Guillaume himself, after his initial interrogations, finally admitted that his belief in the transmigration of souls came from the Cathars: specifically, that his mother (who had been in contact with the *perfecti*) had reported to him various beliefs told to her by Pierre Autier, and Guillaume had 'stayed in perfect belief' ('stetit in credencia perfecta') that what Autier had said about souls transmigrating was true for two or three years, and that he was in this belief when he spoke to Alazaïs Monier and the other women about their dead children. This is so, but it is worth considering for a moment another element of the records' textuality: their production of *narrative*. There are two, intimately intertwined, narratives in Guillaume's deposition. One is a narrative of revelation: how Guillaume's words on souls are positioned and repositioned, until at the end of his third interrogation, he admits that he had heard the beliefs of the Cathar *perfectus* Pierre Autier on the topic. The other is a narrative of discipline: how Guillaume twists and turns under the inquisitorial gaze, until brought in his sixth and seventh interrogations to admit his fault, abjure heresy, and repeat the words of orthodox authority and obedience. Together, these form the requisite contours of confession: the revelation of a hidden truth, and the 'recognition' by the subject confessing of his fault and subsequent submission to legitimate authority.

These narratives form an essential, textual, element in inquisitorial discourse: they seek to control the elements of 'chance' (or, we might say, 'detail') in Austatz's speech, and to locate him firmly within the categorized schema of transgression. However, if we go back over those details of what Guillaume said, this delineated identity becomes harder to sustain. Here, for example, is what Guillaume said in his third interrogation about the words on transmigration that he had heard from Autier, via his mother:

> He began to doubt if it was true, that which his aforesaid mother had said to him on the aforesaid [heretical] articles, and sometimes it seemed to him that it was true, and at other times the contrary, but, as he said, for two or three years, as it seems to him, he stayed in perfect belief that it was true . . .[44]

---

[43] Fournier I, 191–8.

[44] Fournier I, 205, 'ipse incepit dubitare si verum esset illud, quod predicta mater eius dixerat sibi super predictis articulis, et aliquando videbatur ei quod verum esset, aliquando contrarium, sed, ut dixit, per duos vel tres annos, ut sibi videtur, stetit in credencia perfecta quod verum esset illud . . .'.

The tensions implicit in this sentence ('sometimes it seemed . . . other times the contrary' versus 'in perfect belief') are amplified in Guillaume's fourth interrogation, when he is brought to explain yet again what he thought about souls (having just recounted his tale of witnessing the fresh grave being dug):

> Asked if he ever believed that human bodies could not rise again, he said yes, for virtually the whole day, because he said the aforesaid words [on seeing the bones dug up], but, as he said, he did not believe this at other times, so far as *possibility* is concerned; but, as he said, for virtually two years after he had heard from his mother, amongst other things, that the said Pierre Autier, heretic, had said to her that human bodies would not rise again, he was in doubt and doubted whether there would be resurrection of the dead or not; and sometimes he was being drawn to one side, and at another time to the other; and, as he said, some times he believed that there would be no resurrection . . . although he did not believe this completely, he sometimes stayed in the contrary belief, because he had heard it preached thus in church, and moreover because Guillaume d'Alzinhac, priest of Carbonne, who sometimes stayed in his mother's house at Lordat, had said to him that there would be future resurrection of dead men and women – he [Alzinhac] had taught him when he was a young boy and living with his mother at Lordat.[45]

Inquisition works to provoke these elements of detail in order – via narrative – to contain them. Guillaume is allowed to have his say (confusing and confused as it was) on his beliefs in order that he be brought to discipline and repentance. In his last interrogation (prior to his final sentencing) he was asked if he had ever previously confessed the heresies he had held. He said not, 'because he used not to believe, as he said, that he had sinned in believing the aforesaid and in persisting in them; but now, as he said, he recognized that he had gravely erred in believing the aforesaid errors' and begged for absolution, promising obedience to the inquisitor.[46] The complexities of Guillaume's beliefs, or perhaps we might say his relationship to belief,

---

[45] Fournier I, 206, 'Interrogatus si aliquando credidit quod non possent corpora humana resurgere, dixit quod sic, per illam diem quasi totam, quia predicta verba dixit, sed, ut dixit, hoc non credidit alio tempore, quantum est de possibili, sed, ut dixit, quasi per duos annos, postquam audiverat a matre sua, inter cetera, quod dictus Petrus Auterii hereticus dixerat ei quod humana corpora non resurgerent, ipse stetit in dubio et dubitavit si resurrectio hominum mortuorum esset vel non, et aliquando trahebatur ad consenciendum uni parti, alia vice alteri, et, ut dixit, aliquando credidit quod non esset resurrectio . . . licet non totaliter hoc crederet, aliquando stabat in credencia contraria, quia sic audiverat in ecclesia predicari, et etiam quia Guillelmus de Alzinhaco, presbiter de Carbona, qui aliquando stetit in domo matris sue apud Lordatum dixerat ei quod resurrectio esset futura hominum et mulierum defunctorum, qui instruxerat eum dum iuvenis erat, et morabatur cum matre sua apud Lordatum.'

[46] Fournier I, 211–12, 'quia non credebat, ut dixit, se peccasse predicta credendo et in dicta perseverando, sed nunc, ut dixit, recognoscit se graviter deliquisse predictos errores credendo'.

are displayed but then rendered safe; the confessional narrative produces closure, fixing Guillaume into the assigned identity of confessing, penitent subject. The inquisitorial text provides space for Guillaume's recontextualizations of his speech precisely in order to lead him, through the repetitions of further questioning, to a disavowal of these words and to a recitation of inquisitorial language: that by the end of his deposition, Guillaume must confess his beliefs and doubts *as errors*, and abjure them, seeking absolution from inquisitorial power. We have here a prime example of what Foucault means by the strategies that discourse uses to control the element of chance within the possibilities of language. The speech of the deponent is brought forth in order to classify and order it within the domain constructed by the inquisitorial eye of power.

In viewing depositional texts as elements within discourse, are we then in danger of presenting a pessimistic view of the sources? Is this, as some critics of Foucault would have it, a picture of discourse and power that overwhelms all possibility of struggle, resistance or escape?[47] I think not. Foucault himself was quite clear, at the end of his career, that he had never suggested that resistance was impossible or futile – only that it was inescapably bound up with the relationships of power found throughout human society.[48] Thus, if we view Guillaume's tactical attempts to respond to the charges against him (by recontextualizing what he had said, by withholding certain information and so on) as a form of resistance, we must also recognize that it is this resistance that allows inquisitorial discourse to extend its field of power, by policing these areas of speech and belief.

However, as these heterogeneous elements of speech – the confusions and doubts and complexities that Guillaume expresses – are displayed to us through the text, there remains a possibility of producing a reading of the deponent that differs from the inquisitorial view. To label Guillaume a 'Cathar believer' surely erases the nuances of his confession.[49] In fact,

---

[47] See, for example, L. Patterson, 'Historical Criticism and the Claims of Humanism', in *Negotiating the Past: The Historical Understanding of Medieval Literature* (Madison WI, 1987), pp. 41–74.

[48] See for example M. Foucault, 'The Ethic of Care for the Self as a Practice of Freedom', in *The Final Foucault*, ed. J. Bernauer and D. Rasmussen (Cambridge MA, 1988), pp. 1–20.

[49] Guillaume's support for the Waldensian, Raymond *de Costa*, further complicates the matter. It is equally difficult to label him a Waldensian 'believer', as although Guillaume clearly spoke out against *de Costa*'s execution, his motives were somewhat complex. He admitted in his own confession saying that it would have been better if the bishop of Pamiers (that is, Fournier himself) had been burnt instead of the Waldensian, but emphasized that he meant by this, not that the bishop was in fact a heretic, but that if the bishop was burnt, the Sabartès would be freed from the tithe on sheep (*carnalages*) that they had been contesting with the bishop (various deponents in the Fournier register express similar resentment against this tax). Guillaume further emphasized that he did not see at the time how Raymond *de Costa* could be a heretic, 'when he believed in God, the blessed Mary, and all the saints, and the seven articles of faith' ('cum crederet Deum, beatam Mariam, et

according to Guillaume's testimony, even his mother (the one actually in contact with Pierre Autier) had a more complex relationship with the Cathar faith: when he asked her if she believed what Autier had said about the soul and salvation, 'she said that she neither believed nor disbelieved' ('respondit quod nec credebat nec discredebat').[50] Such a simple equivocation explodes the implicit binary opposition of inquisitorial logic, the demand that doctrine makes to either accept or reject its call. Which is as much as to say that if depositional texts are the products of inquisitorial discourse, they also contain *other* kinds of language – other discourses within which deponents speak, traces of which are also available to historical analysis. But that remains a project for another time and place.[51]

omnes sanctos, et septem articulos fidei'). That is, it would seem, his support for the Waldensian did not necessarily indicate a support for Waldensianism itself. See Fournier I, 208–10.

[50] Fournier I, 204.

[51] Such an analysis is attempted in Arnold, *Inquisition and Power*, along with a more extensive discussion of inquisition, power, subjectivity and discourse. My thanks to Peter Biller, Caterina Bruschi and all the participants of the conference for their comments and insights on heresy and texts; and to my colleagues Mark Knights and Simon Middleton for their suggestions and reactions to a draft of this article.

'Magna diligentia est habenda per inquisitorem':[1] Precautions before Reading Doat 21–26

Caterina Bruschi

Heritage

It might seem *naive*, perhaps superficial, but I still think that a historian's first attitude towards primary sources is curiosity. Furthermore, if we are talking about heresy and inquisition, curiosity drives us to get hold of words, dialogues, in an ultimate effort to shore up fragments of those lives that are so quickly forgotten, so easily moulded into statistics and theories, so often just used as means to substantiate our statements.

Names and stories are not enough: inquisition trials remain perhaps one of the few types of sources which allow us to hear people's voices.

The 1960s and 1970s saw the development of a new historiographical trend, which aimed at a new and critical approach to trial sources. However important, source-criticism had been too often either ignored or carried out too superficially. For it was easier and more profitable to regard the trial depositions in one's hands simply as repositories of information, and of evidence which could be picked out quickly to support a theory or attest a fact.

It was Herbert Grundmann, in his 'Ketzerverhöre',[2] who cast doubt on this way of reading heresy trials. After him both Robert Lerner and Grado Giovanni Merlo underlined and emphasized the importance of a method of interpretation which took careful note of the frame of reference of the text, and the cultural milieu within which the text was structured and its protagonist's 'actors' lived. Both of them adopted precautionary measures appropriate to each particular trial situation: Lerner to the so-called 'heresy of the Free Spirit',[3] Merlo to the inquiries of Piedmont in the fourteenth century.[4]

---

[1] This phrase is taken from D32, containing an extraordinary enquiry about some of the D26 depositions (see below ch. 10, p. 215). On the pope's orders, some *doctores* analysed and deconstructed the whole document, trying to ascertain its degree of reliability. As the final sentence led in almost all cases to a condemnation, the consistency of the inquiry had to be proved in a reliable way.

[2] Grundmann, 'Ketzerverhöre'.

[3] Lerner, *Free Spirit*.

[4] Merlo, *Eretici e inquisitori*. Later on he reaffirmed his position, leaving out of consideration any inquisitorial concern for searching for the truth and for the sincere

While our discussion builds upon these earlier developments in criticism, we should note, however, that these approaches were developed by historians who were confronting unusual difficulties. Their sources conformed heretics to other rejected or marginal groups, emphasising their libertine sexual activities and doing this within very rigid and repetitive frameworks and language. Overall these records pose a stark and simple problem for the reader – to believe their contents or not[5] – and they are far removed from the more ordinary-seeming material and subtler problems of the heresy trials of Languedoc.

When we approach a particular source the inheritance of these historians encourages us to be careful, not just thinking in terms of 'filters' when viewing the text, but also defining a series of concerns which need to be listed every time. While these are no more than the obvious tools for a correct and fair textual interpretation, they produce what Merlo, in particular, called 'a paradox'. Though the tools were produced because of the problem of credibility, their sustained application leads to the replacement of credibility as *the* fundamental theme. The fundamental theme now becomes the reasons and dynamics of the supply of information in these sources themselves.[6]

Just one year before Merlo's words, Carlo Ginzburg was reinforcing this line with the publication of his famous *The Cheese and the Worms*, which rapidly became a classic and not just among heresy scholars. The whole story of the miller Menochio, living in late fifteenth century northern Italy, was itself proof of evidence: his life and thoughts were the core of Ginzburg's interest, and the voice of this semi-literate miller was being heard for the first time, giving the pages a strong sense of vitality and authenticity. Moreover, Ginzburg's work pointed to the crucial importance of looking at the relationship between literacy and popular culture in any record of interrogation like this. Interlocking approaches – as Ginzburg suggested – should include linguistic analysis, narratology, and keeping an eye on modern communication theory (but is it possible to separate these three?). Ginzburg claimed that 'the fact that many of Menochio's utterances cannot be reduced to familiar themes permits us to perceive a previously untapped level of popular beliefs, of obscure peasant's mythologies',[7] a substratum of common peasants' knowledge. Although his work slightly differs from my analysis, focussed as it is mainly on written culture, it provides us with useful tips about methods of reading depositions.

contrition of the suspects ('La coercizione all'ortodossia: comunicazione e imposizione di un messaggio religioso egemonico (Sec. XIII–XIV)', *Società e Storia* 10 (1980), 803–23).

[5] According to a recent contribution by J.-L. Biget ('"Les Albigeois": Rémarques sur une dénomination', in *Inventer l'hérésie?*, pp. 219–55), these accusations are not a feature of the 'late' sources, but rather a reflection of the typical Cistercian fears, also present in early sources, from the Third Lateran Council onwards (1179).

[6] Merlo, *Eretici e inquisitori*, p. 13.

[7] C. Ginzburg, *The Cheese and the Worms: The Cosmos of a Sixteenth-Century Miller* (London, 1980), p. xix; the original Italian edition was published in 1976.

Following this path and when reviewing Le Roi Ladurie's *Montaillou*,[8] Natalie Zemon Davis underlined the importance of linguistic filters in popular narration. In order to reach a deep understanding of narratological problems, a strong awareness of language and its dynamics is needed.

A heavy inheritance comes from these scholars: they set up the *pars destruens* ('destructive part') of innovative textual criticism, providing a strong basis for the method that I aim to pursue. It seems to me that it is now time for the corresponding *pars construens* ('constructive part'): it is now time, that is, to give direction to the considerable amount of data emerging from the filters.

On the whole, we are facing a process of memory construction, a building-up of an ideal image of a trial, shaped both by the deponent and the inquisitor.[9] I am not striving to discover a 'truth' after trying to strip the 'filters' from the depositions: my starting-point is a text in its whole, constructed with a very concrete goal, recorded with techniques and features (that are themselves dependent on several practical and subjective features), and built up by both the actors in this performance. I am very aware that in the end I myself am a builder, resetting and producing another constructed text about the same 'stories'. Further, this text has to be read not just as a literary product: it records the lives, deaths, plots, suffering and feelings of people who really were brought to trial, gave their testimony and for this were condemned.

At the centre of my interest are volumes 21–6 of the Doat Collection, relating to the Toulouse area and containing mainly trial depositions of Cathars and Waldensians from 1237 to 1289.[10] Internal features, contents, actors, area and time are variables within each of them. Internal and external characteristics differ quite strongly, with each volume displaying a distinctive and unique pattern that requires in turn its own individual and unique method of reading. Doat material has usually not been regarded in such a way, because at first sight it does not present the clearly manipulated evidence of other trial records, such as those that preoccupied Grundmann and the others. It sounds so plain and clear in its rhapsodic rhythm and development – it is sometimes even quite boring – that one can easily forget the precautions needed when reading it.[11]

My general line is that the original dialogue between inquisitors and

[8] N. Z. Davis, 'Les conteurs de Montaillou ⟨note critique⟩', *Annales: économies, sociétés, civilisations* 34 (1979), 61–73; *Montaillou* (1975).
[9] The theme of 'construction' is still an up-to-date topic: two of the most recent works on heresy are based upon it – Given, *Inquisition*, and *Inventer l'hérésie'*.
[10] See the account of the Doat collection in C. Molinier, *L'Inquisition dans le Midi de la France au XIII et XIV siècle* (Paris, 1880) pp. 34–40.
[11] See for textual analysis in general Stock, *Implications of Literacy*; B. Stock, *Listening for the Text: On the Uses of Past* (Baltimore and London, 1990); and Clanchy, *Memory*. See also I. Illich, *In the Vineyard of the Text* (Chicago IL, 1993); *Medieval Text and Contemporary Readers*, ed. L. A. Finke and M. B. Shichtman (Ithaca and London, 1987).

witnesses has been modified several times: first of all by the witness, then by a series of selections, dissections, and voluntary omissions carried out by the inquisitors and notaries. I shall therefore begin by listing and describing the 'filters' through which we should look at the confessions: I shall call them 'tools'. Linked to this approach are the 'two "truths"' that the actors, inquisitor and deponent, give life to. Fragments of the deponent's 'truth' are visible. I shall call them 'objects' and give examples, calling them 'surplus features': that is, what – though filtered – appear to be genuine and authentic pieces of the original deposition. All the time it is necessary to keep in mind how – as has been said above – a first selection took place during the trial itself, while a second is the result of the recording process. Their modes and criteria throw light on the 'building method' employed and chosen by the parties. Going down this path I hope to arrive at an understanding of the aims of all who took a part in shaping the record: and, further, what the message is – conscious or unconscious – that the final stage of the register conveys to modern readers.

Tools: 'Filters'

What impressed me most when first browsing through the volumes was tremendous variation in the methods of recording. Some of the registers are lively, narrative and intriguing, while others are totally formulaic, mechanical and repetitive. How many things contributed to this differentiation? External conditions relating to the course of the trial and the deliberate will of each of the two parties could have driven the inquiry and its registration to the stage we now read. At the same time there is pressure which comes from the survival among modern historians of a rather old-fashioned notion of these features, which creates a fixed and still image of the trial: a discourse led by only one conductor – the inquisitor – towards the alteration and functional use of the original deposition.

Filters depending on the enquiry: number
Most confessions were collected during the so-called 'periods of grace', when a mitigation of punishment was granted by the inquisitors to those who voluntarily confessed or gave testimony on matters of heresy.[12] Nearly six

---

[12] The *literature* on procedure is quite wide. An overview of inquisitorial manuals about procedure can be found in Molinier, 'Rapport', pp. 158–206, and Dondaine, 'Manuel'; see now Parmeggiani. According to Dondaine's lists, the earliest manuals are the *Consultatio* of Pierre d'Albalat known as the *Directorium* of Raymond of Peñafort (1242), the *Ordo processus Narbonensis* (probably 1248/9), and the *Explicatio super officio Inquisitionis* (1262–77). On *fluctuation* in procedure, J. Paul, 'La procédure inquisitoriale à Carcassonne au milieu du XIII siècle', CaF 29 (1994), 361–96. This shows day-to-day variations in *formule*, following the notaries' notes. On *evolution* of procedure after the 'crisis', Dossat, *Crises*, from p. 195. On *defence*, W. Ullmann, 'The

thousand witnesses are recorded by MS Toulouse 609[13] – it is easy to imagine crowds of people waiting for their turn to give their deposition, outside the inquisitor's residence: plots, agreements, common lines of defence could have been set up by them.[14] They sometimes had to face days far away from home, long impatient waiting, expense, and probably fear. Bernard Barre from Sorèze has a little argument with some fellow villagers, wanting to persuade him not to accuse them during his hearing. Finding him reluctant they come up with an old proverb, 'Men catch oxen by their horns, and peasants by their tongues.[15] Again, in Toulouse 609 Pons Stephen gives evidence of agreements on a common line of defence:

> He said that when brother W. Arnaldi was carrying out an inquisition, Raymond of Auriac said to him the witness – in the presence of Raymond Hugh, knight of Aiguesvives, in the diocese of Carcassonne – that when questioned by the inquisitors one should answer 'not yet' to everything. In fact all the men of Auriac had agreed among themselves to give such an answer in front of the inquisitors. And then he the witness replied to Raymond of Auriac that there was no way he would say 'not yet' to the said inquisitors. Instead, he would tell them the whole truth on everything he knew about heresy.[16]

Defence of the Accused in the Medieval Inquisition', in *Law and Jurisdiction in the Middle Ages*, ed. G. Garnett (London, 1988), pp. 481–9; *La parola*. Examples on registers are J.-M. Vidal, 'Le tribunal d'Inquisition de Pamiers. Notice sur le régistre de l'évêque Jacques Fournier', *Annales de St-Louis-des-Français* 8, I (Oct. 1903), 377–435; Duvernoy, 'Registre de Bernard'. See also H. A. Kelly, 'Inquisition and the Prosecution of Heresy: Misconceptions and Abuses', *Church History* 58 (1989), 439–51. On *tempus gratie*, see A. P. Evans, 'Hunting Subversion in the Middle Ages', *Speculum* 33 (1958), 1–22. An example of the importance of number in interrogations, is in N. Eymerich and F. Peña, *Le manuel de l'Inquisiteur*, selected and trans. L. Sala-Molins (Paris and The Hague, 1973), ch. 30, pp. 142–3.

[13] Toulouse 609. It contains the depositions of the 1245–6 inquiry held by Bernard of Caux and Jean of St Pierre; see ch. 6 below. Another striking example is that of the period 1245–6, when Bernard of Caux was working in the Toulouse area (partly included in D22 and D24), quoted in Y. Dossat, 'Une figure d'Inquisiteur: Bernard de Caux', CaF 6 (1971), 153–72.

[14] Ullmann, 'The Defence'.

[15] D25, fol. 296v: 'Bovem capit homo per cornu, et rusticum per linguam.' See P. Biller, 'Heresy and Literacy: Earlier History of the Theme', in *Heresy and Literacy*, pp. 1–18 (p. 9). The author refers to J. W. Hassell, *Middle French Proverbs, Sentences and Proverbial Phrases*, Subsidia Medievalia 12 (Toronto, 1982), p. 55, n. B118, 'On prend le boeuf par la corne et l'homme par la parole' (earliest French attestation 1463), and p. 130, n. H50, 'On prende l'homme par la langue'; see also *Proverbes français antérieurs au XV siècle*, ed. J. Morawski (Paris, 1925), no. 225, p. 9 ('Bele parole fet fol lié') and no. 1588, p. 58 ('Par les cornes loye on les buefz').

[16] 'Dixit quod cum frater W. Arnaldi faceret inquisitionem Ramundus de Auriaco dixit ipsi testi, presente Ramundo Hugone milite de Aquis Vivis diocesis Carcassonensi, quod quando inquireretur ab inquisitoribus ad omnia responderet eis "no⟨n⟩dum", quia sic condixerant inter se omnes homines de Auriaco de dicta responsione cum essent coram dictis inquisitoribus; et tunc ipse testis respondit Ramundo de Auriaco quod [n]ullo modo diceret "no⟨n⟩dum" inquisitoribus

Undoubtedly, the higher the number of deponents, the shorter and drier the records. Pressure of numbers produced rapid summary proceedings that could have taken weeks in other circumstances. This is the first filter, arising from practical conditions, that could strongly affect the 'factual truth' as it is commonly understood: a powerful and insidious filter, imposing the aim of concision on the record and thereby perhaps limiting and abbreviating the 'ideal' deposition, 'ideal' as commonly held. This first filter can also mislead and distort modern historians' perspectives.

Filters depending on the enquiry: grilles

While the written record may be shaped by such practical conditions, at the same time it presupposes a pattern of questions – not all taken down, and those that are not necessarily completely. These questions themselves in turn depend on several elements connected to the inquiry: the nature and number of clues, the tracks followed by the investigation, the presence or absence of previous depositions, the inquisitor's and notary's knowledge of technical and theoretical matters, and the stage of development of both canon and civil law.[17] Besides these elements no doubt each inquisitor and notary carried with them their own personal experience, the particular aim of the investigation and the reasons why they brought the witness to trial. In a dialogue there is what we might call the 'psychology of exchange' – anticipating each other's views, for example – and there is deliberate intention: trying to produce a desired result, such as escaping the charge, hiding friends or finding someone guilty. I strongly believe that intrinsic in any dialogue is each party's tendency to drive the other party's reactions and hence the path of the discussion itself.

The final result of this various and multiform process of construction is represented by six volumes differing from each other in their structural features but also – and more importantly – in their methodology of interrogation. Whereas the focus is sometimes on relationships between the deponents, some other interrogations concentrate on heretical beliefs, on preaching activity or ways and modes of the ritual of *hereticatio* (administering the Cathar *consolamentum*). Some are particularly centred on the activities and movements of the Cathar hierarchy, while others' curiosity is directed towards the everyday life of the common 'believers'. Only through a thorough confrontation of the volumes *in toto* can one understand how the different filters affect the construction of truth. For instance, the structural grid of the interrogation becomes much more visible to the reader when the

prefatis, immo diceret eis plenariam veritatem de hiis que noverat de heresi.' This is quoted in W. L. Wakefield, 'Heretics and Inquisitors: The Case of Auriac and Cambiac', *Journal of Medieval History* 12 (1986), 225–37 (p. 229).
[17] Quite often, in fact, the questions proposed correspond exactly to the conciliar canons, see Merlo, *Eretici e inquisitori* and Grundmann, 'Ketzerverhöre'; on 'literary' *topoi*, Lerner, *Free Spirit*, pp. 20–5; more extensively Given, *Inquisition*, pp. 24–51, on the 'technology of documentation'.

same episode is seen recurring in different depositions or registers. The case of the massacre of Avignonet offers the most remarkable example. The Doat volumes provide 'multiple versions' of this obscure page of history, differently shaped by different deponents, questions, situations and roles. Even here, the modern historian can do no more than gauge the personalisation of a story, measure the angle of one human being's perspective on the facts: in the end, objectivity is always hidden in an onlooker's eyes.

Filters depending on the process of recording: procedure

To judge from first appearances, the main feature slowing down and limiting the natural flow of narration is the formulaic mode found in the written record. Whenever applied to the extreme, the text becomes no more than a series of confirmations (or denials) of accusations and questions. One senses a broken rhythm, characterised by short and monotonous sentences, giving a strong impression of a form – a form to be filled in only with 'yes', 'no', and 'I don't know'.

Listing the stages of the interrogation can help in figuring out this element.[18] Even in only its simplest form it contains filters. First, there was questioning of the witness, where the questions could be based on the contents of previous depositions (for example, in the case of a suspect of heresy, accusations brought against her or him in the depositions of other witnesses). Or simply on a question-list spelled out in an inquisitors' manual, 'When did you first see heretics? Where? With whom?', and so on: a grille of questions. This dialogue was held in Provençal. Secondly, the notary wrote a first draft – in Latin – and re-read it aloud to the witness, this time in Provençal. The latter was free to approve or modify the text, and only later on did the notary proceed to the definitive registration, again, in Latin. This last stage is what appears written on the parchment of the manuscript, undeniably differing from the first deposition, if one assumes that for each of the phases selections, misunderstandings and mistakes will have occurred. Even though the final version had to be ratified, it was always possible that the witness was unable – or did not want – to remember every previous statement, or which version of the facts he gave to the notary, or more simply did not think it necessary to dwell upon details, fearing to bore and annoy the inquisitor.

Filters depending on the process of recording: translation

Viewed from a distance, problems related to language – many of them common to the genre of records of interrogations under any legal system – lie on the *surface* of our written texts. However, the variety of translations within the confessions, the linguistic competence of the officials, and the requirement of complete interchangeability of Provençal and Latin are

---

[18] See, for example, *Ordo processus Narbonensis*, in *Texte zur Inquisition*, pp. 70–6 (p. 71). More specific is Vidal, 'Le tribunal', p. 387.

language problems as well, and ones which also existed at a deeper level of the texts, constituting – that is to say, structuring and producing – them in a fundamental way.[19] We must not neglect the fact that such a complex structure of translations required a body of quite highly skilled notaries, and that whenever the tribunal lacked such competence a rigid series of formulas and questions could have been very convenient. In addition to this, the more complex the structure and grille of questions, the longer the notary's job, particularly in the case of a non-expert, non-skilled or stupid one. Sometimes, therefore, a very formulaic and strict text may be a symptom of deficient officials at work.

Filters depending on the process of recording: competence

Composing the written record involved selection. Impossible to measure, given the total absence of notes taken during the audition, selection aimed at the deletion of elements, digressions, names, particulars and phrases that were evaluated as superfluous, useless or even inconvenient. Nor could the notes have been taken down word for word. As a consequence, the criteria underlying our records were mostly applied by the notary. Although subordinated to the inquisitor's authority, the notary was trained in law, and able to assess and evaluate the relevant *loca* (important passages) of the confession.[20] His prominent role during the hearing is attested by Peter Ferreol of Trébons, at his third and last retractation. After abjuring and receiving a *penitentia arbitraria* (arbitrary[21] penance), he bluntly claims that in the record of the previous hearings the notary only wrote part of what he said. 'He omitted to declare this, because he forgot – as he said in his first confession – and also because the notary who at the time received his confession did not care to write anything apart from what he confessed he had committed before the "time of peace".'[22]

At least a couple more filters are identified by Peter's words. First, the notary uses a chronological criterion to select from the confession: a boundary of time dividing what is worthwhile from what is superfluous. The notary 'non curavit', 'he did not take care' to record what follows the 'tempus pacis', imposing a strong barrier on our comprehension of the sequence of facts. He nevertheless seems to trust the deponent, and to leave him free to carry out his own selection. What has already been filtered

---

[19] In a wider sense, inquisitors used Provençal as an 'exchange-language', and Latin as a 'codification-language'.
[20] See W. L. Wakefield, 'Les assistants des inquisiteurs témoins des confessions dans le manuscrit 609', *Heresis* 20 (1993), 57–65. As far as I know, MS Clermont-Ferrand 160 is the only example of a record of notes taken by a notary. The case comes from the Carcassonne inquisition (1249–58). On its features, see J. Paul, 'La procédure'.
[21] = 'Variable, according to the discretion of the person who imposes it'.
[22] D26, fol. 64r: 'Omisit dicere propter oblivionem sicut dicit in prima confessione sua, et quia notarius qui tunc recepit confessionem suam non curavit scribere nisi ea que confitebatur commisisse citra tempus pacis.'

by Peter himself in his previous confessions is recorded, while further questions are omitted and the enquiry is not taken further. One can read his attitude as that of a busy official who is in a hurry, and is now hearing somebody who has already appeared before the court. Knowing his previous depositions the notary evaluates as important only the last part of Peter's confession. Essentially, what he does is to cut.

A very similar attitude emerges in the deposition of Baretges, wife of Peter Grimoardi, when recalling a confession completely deleted from the records. 'Her confession was not written, because the inquisitors did not want to record it'.[23] Whether this is a note from the inquisitor, interpreting some sort of reluctance in Baretges' words, or Baretges' own statement, whether true or false, this phrase is considered worth recording. Later on, Bernard Gui suggests in his manual:

> However, it is not expedient for all questions[24] to be written down, but only those which reach more plausibly the substance or the essence of a fact, and those which seem to express truth the most. In fact, if in some deposition one finds such an abundance of questions, another deposition containing fewer questions could seem diminished ⟨in value⟩.[25] Furthermore, it is rather difficult to find any congruity in the inquiry when so many interrogations are recorded – a matter for awareness and precaution.[26]

It is worth noting Gui's criteria for a fair record: *substantia facti* (the substance of a fact), *natura facti* (the essence of a fact), *veritas* (truth), some sort of 'balance' of the depositions within the same enquiry/register, and finally *concordia* (congruity) among them.

Filters depending on narration

Further interesting filters depend on the dynamics of narration. Such filters are the only ones arising from the words and will of the deponent. Only when deposing in front of the judge does he or she have the opportunity to modify the construction of the record. Although important, confessing just what one wants to be known is not the only way to influence the text. Approving or denying the text submitted by the notary is another, powerful one, especially given that the main objective of inquisitorial records is to list, file and

---

[23] D22, fol. 43v: 'confessio sua non fuit scripta quia inquisitores noluerunt scribere confessionem ejus'.

[24] Here the Latin *interrogatio* seems to mean one act of questioning, together with the reply.

[25] *diminuta*: Wakefield and Evans translate as 'too brief', Mollat as 'tronquée'.

[26] 'Non tamen expedit quod omnes interrogationes scribantur, set tantum ille que magis verisimiliter tangunt substantiam vel naturam facti, et que magis videntur exprimere veritatem. Si enim in aliqua depositione inveniretur tanta interrogationum multitudo, alia depositio pauciores continens posset diminuta videri, et etiam cum tot interrogationibus conscriptis in processu vix posset concordia in depositionibus testium inveniri, quod considerandum est et precavendum': Gui, *M*, p. 32.

preserve. Such intervention by the deponent is one of the determinants of the text in its essence and during its formation.

However many digressions may have come from a deponent, there are few in the record[27] – few because they will have been seen as redundant and pointless to record, though to the modern reader they are of more significance. Only a comparison between different depositions within one enquiry can highlight what goes beyond the 'set pattern', the main line followed by that specific questionnaire. The highlighted part can be read as an accused person's construction. Here we are going further down the path of Ginzburg's 'untapped level' of narration. In classifying these 'surpluses' I shall begin with filters that depend strictly on the narrative process itself, moving then to a freer reading of the depositions. Finally, I shall try and sketch the general characteristics of the 'surplus'.

Awareness of the characteristics of storytelling in popular culture is a prerequisite for my enquiry – here I simply refer the reader to Natalie Davis's discussion of them.[28] Without altering the peculiarity and value of each deposition, my aim has been to identify where and to what extent the discourse was driven and constrained into a literate, pre-shaped grille. Not merely 'physically' in a trial context, but rather during the definitive recording of dialogues.[29]

Filters depending on narration: linguistic level
The cultural 'transposition of language' onto a new cultural level – from popular to literate, and/or the other way round – undoubtedly generated further filters in the deposition. Whenever a translation, a summary, or a record, was required by the procedure, the notary had to reshape the deponent's words into a new language. This process did not just translate the words, it substantiated the record with a new terminology, at once more technical and revealing a different, more refined perception of the semantic value of the words. Far from judging its level, I aim here to underline the problem of 'cultural opposition'. Whatever the deponents' socio-cultural level, the linguistic technicalities of a functional record suppressed and reshaped the semantics of depositions. Many a time a highly literate inquisitor had to face a peasant, and even when he did not, a complete uniformity of background can never be assumed. This element of 'cultural opposition' is a further thing either side could take advantage of, or instead perceive as a limit to understanding the other. Not just a question of variation of content, it is more a matter of a forcing of language. Evidence of cultural non-uniformity provoked in both parties a self-censorship and a shifting of

---

[27] Although cautious and manipulative, even Eymerich's manual sets a limit. It states that it is never fruitful to interrupt the suspects while confessing since they could feel like going back to their stubborn silence (*Le manuel de l'Inquisiteur*, p. 10).

[28] N. Z. Davis, *The return of Martin Guerre* (Cambridge MA and London, 1983), p. 3.

[29] See also J. Fentress and C. Wickham, *Social Memory* (Oxford, 1992), chs. 1, 3 and 4.

language towards unusual significance. The same mechanism works when speaking different languages, or talking to people belonging to different cultural levels: people aim at simplifying syntax and words when wanting to clarify, and tend to complicate them when wanting to hide.

Should we then deduce that richness in detail is proportional to the deponent's desire to distract the interrogator? Not always. Another element has to be considered: popular narrative schemes are strongly based on the use of digression and detail.[30]

Filters depending on narration: will

Another feature to be taken into account is the will of the deponent. Putting aside the pressures of the questioning, we must remember the obvious, namely that the deponent confessed what he/she wished to be known.[31] Scholars and the media tend to deny any degree of agency, and rather produce a predominantly stereotypical picture: a witness, petrified and completely non-reactive in front of the sadistic minister of the repressive power.[32] Reconsideration is needed of these sorts of images, which derive only in part from historical evidence and more from preconceived ideas and emotions about the inquisition. The Doat accounts – even at a first glance – do not display people as particularly passive or as impotent victims deprived of opportunity to defend and justify their behaviour. This is not to claim that the deponents had equal weight in shaping the dialogue, nor that inquisitorial tribunals were friendly or harmless. To escape was often the goal; horrible,

---

[30] A recent talk with Grado Merlo convinced me of the fact that – as he claims – 'heretical behaviour is determinative of heretics' image, and a distinction between popular and literate culture is sometimes quite reductive'. I have in fact talked – and shall do again – about 'popular narration', ascribing such a definition both to peasant and literate confessions, albeit in different measure. Furthermore, in my perspective 'popular narrative' is a more evident feature than the literate discourse, being farther away from the 'grilles' of *doctores*, and more likely to be instinctive in one who is under psychological pressure, and therefore suitable for a confession. See also N. Z. Davis, *Fiction in the Archives: Pardon Tales and their Tellers in Sixteenth-Century France* (Stanford, 1987), esp. p. 18, and n. 43. P. Friedmann, talking about texts *on* peasants, claims, '(. . .) images of peasants did not form an uncontested or "hegemonic" discourse that serenely justified how peasants were treated. Historians reading literary sources are often tempted to reduce them to ideological statements at the expense of their specificity as essentially imaginative works. . . .) doctrinaire though such texts may be, they possess an individuality, seriousness, and inner tension that resists ideological simplification.' (*Images of the Medieval Peasant* (Stanford, 1999), p. 4).

[31] 'Le plus souvent, ce sont eux qui organisent leur récit à leur manière et sans interruption'; Davis, 'Les conteurs', p. 70.

[32] The influence of media culture, guilty of both a banalization and a sensationalization of sources and historical events, is a worrying and increasing phenomenon. The pressure of the market – both on publishers and on universities (the courses *must* present the required 'appeal' to new students) – erodes serious research and imports morbid curiosity. Inquisition and heresy 'sell' to the extent to which they stress the mystery and fascination of perversion and sadism.

unforgettable episodes affected life in southern France. Rather, I am trying to underline how wrong it is for the historian always to give life to this same stereotype, encouraging the assumption that the same 'emotional reactions' are always found among the deponents. In fact, analysis of the depositions shows that any attempt to reconstruct the emotional impact of the 'inquisitorial performance' on a single individual relies on a far too high number of variables for it to be clearly understood.

How resilient are the witnesses? To what extent can their role be defined as 'active' in the construction of the text? The well-known case of the notary William Tron from Tarascon throws some light on the question.[33] As a miserly, disliked and bitter man, William provokes a strong reaction from the people he has harmed in the past. Previous colleagues and enemies plan to accuse him – falsely – of heresy, in order to have him imprisoned, and thus bring about his collapse. Setting up an elaborate net of cross-testimonies, accusations and clues, they manage to make the powerful criminal law of both the lay and inquisitorial power work to their own purposes. Jacques Fournier, in charge of the enquiry, discovers and destroys the plot.

Should we then suggest that in each case people had varying perceptions of danger, that the levels of fear and risk were always different? Yes. Proof is the fact that some of the Doat registers are filled with retractations. Apart from the reasons for the alteration (perhaps force), this implies in the witness a specific degree of agency in hiding some of the facts in the first instance. While realizing the dangers connected to an official hearing, he/she decides to take the risk that the inquisitor, unhappy with the first deposition, may feel the need to go further, asking more.

Filters depending on copying

Let us step forward to 1663–9, when Monsieur Jean de Doat, supported by a team of copyists and proof-readers, was appointed to preserve and reproduce all the relevant documents and manuscripts kept in the archives of the south of France. The volumes resulting from this large-scale conservation project are copies of the lost registers and still represent the largest and most complete source of information on Catharism. Their selection, transcription, correction, copying, and assemblage followed mainly Doat's personal criteria, but they also depended on the accessibility of the documents, the collaboration of wardens and archivists – often suspicious and hostile to the operation – and the availability of copyists able to read Latin and to transcribe it decently. On these matters, in fact, Doat himself had much to complain, when reporting to the finance inspector in Paris.[34]

---

[33] J. B. Given, 'Factional Politics in a Medieval Society: A Case-Study from Fourteenth-Century Foix', *Journal of Medieval History* 14 (1988), 233–50. See also Given, *Inquisition*, pp. 156–63.

[34] H. Omont, 'La Collection Doat à la Bibliothèque Nationale: Documents sur les recherches de Doat', *Bibliothèque de l'École des Chartes* 77 (1916), 286–336. See also

What concerns us here are the further filters supplied to the text first of all by the overall chronological sequence of the volumes (itself probably dependent on the steps followed by Doat's mission) and secondly by the selection and sequence of depositions within each volume. Thus, not only the thirteenth but also the seventeenth century constructed grids. Great care is needed in examining the range of filters produced during this 'second birth' of the registers.

Charles Molinier provided a detailed inventory.[35] From vols. 21 to 37 Doat's team collected and transcribed the following documents:

— sentences of condemnation, papal letters, official decrees of the lay authority, public oaths, excerpts from the trial interrogations, council decrees, statutes and privileges, safe-conducts, catalogues of sentences (D21);
— interrogation abstracts and depositions (D22–28);
— transcription of Gui's *Practica*, letters, sentences and general actions of the Inquisition (D29–30);
— abstracts of Carcassonne trials (D31);
— abstracts of heretics' beliefs and trials from 1265 to 1636 (D32–5);
— letters, bulls and *formulae* (D36);
— thirteenth-century fragments of anti-heretical treatises: Raniero Sacconi's *Summa*, Stephen of Bourbon's *De septem donis*, and the *Disputatio inter catholicum et patarinum hereticum* (D37).

The architecture of the collection mirrors that of the archives, which probably contained much larger holdings, together with normative texts, sentences, and manuals. Moreover, the material had been catalogued on territorial criteria. Inquisitorial enquiries too related to one specific diocese, area, or town: and so both the first and second 'births' of the registers were based on a geographical principle. According to Doat's letters, his team moved from town to town, following his instructions, chasing after documents, archives, archivists, and therefore reproducing the same pattern of the parochial and municipal collections. Modern readers inherit two kinds of filters from this double process of assemblage: a selection of material, and a quite high percentage of risk of misunderstanding and mistakes arising from both copyists' incompetence and the numerous steps in the procedure of reproduction. Nevertheless still transparent and visible through the Doat copy are the historical memory of the investigation – the records and its geographical pattern – and the inquisitor's library, his knowledge and instruments.

Dossat, *Crises*, pp. 37–55, on the archival contents of the Dominican convents in Toulouse and Carcassonne.
[35] Molinier, *L'Inquisition dans le Midi*.

Objects: 'Surplus'. Defining Features

What is left, after stripping all the listed filters one by one? After analysis through these lenses, how much of a deposition still maintains the distinctive features of living speech? Paradoxically, it is in the most rigid and repetitive registers that what was not necessarily required by the interrogation is most immediately recognisable. In the midst of utter dryness, a particular bright-ness shines out. This is the part which is most attractive to us.[36] Purely for practical purposes I decided to catalogue these fragments, filing them into new boxes. Here, where I am acting as a 'memory builder', I am very much aware that my own reconstruction may falsify the overall perspective: but I believe every cognitive process is a reconstitution in itself. What exceeds our filters I have further listed in categories of what I call 'surplus'. Here follows a selection of the most indicative examples. It is – once again – arbitrary. As in a philological operation, the last – or first? – tool is one's own *divinatio*: intuition of what is probable.

Food, tools, portraits

As Cathar faith required the complete abstinence from all food deriving from sexual intercourse,[37] the range of alimentary products allowed in a Cathar community was very limited. Consequently, questions relating to food were favoured by the inquisitors, for their clear evidential bearing on heterodoxy. Very often food is among the very first questions addressed to the deponent, 'if you ate together, what kind of food did you prepare?' Together with a series of quite standardised answers, it is sometimes possible to find unusual details about recipes or typical food. The *credentes'* favourite meal seems to be simple vegetables, fish, bread, but more than once this bread is specified as a *fogacia*, a flat loaf baked without yeast, often served with the main courses. Bona *de Podio* prepared for a Cathar guest 'an eel or fish pudding'.[38] Bernard *de Ravat* offers the famous heretic Esclarmonde 'a pipe full of (= measure of) wine'.[39] Women's confessions are sometimes more accurate on details of clothing; a distinction of fabrics and dressing items can be a means of establishing memories within the registers, showing how precisely the deponent recalls the facts. The same function can be ascribed to the words

---

[36] Arno Borst, although convinced that 'Wir sehen hier nur das den Inquisitoren vertraute Bild des Tatbestandes Ketzerei', admitted that 'nur, wenn die Vernom-menen redselig und die Vernehmenden schreibfreudig sind, entrollen sich Sitten-bilder, die für die Ketzergeschichte von Wert sind' (Borst, *Katharer*, p. 25).

[37] Sacconi's famous statement, recently questioned by B. Hamilton, suspecting the Cathars of having a major concern about souls reincarnated into animal bodies. B. Hamilton, 'The Cathars and Christian Perfection', in *Essays in Honour of Gordon Leff*, pp. 5–23 (pp. 21–2).

[38] D25, fol. 84r: 'unum pastillum piscium seu anguillarum'.

[39] D24, fol. 259r: 'quandam canam plenam vini'.

of a dialogue, the physical description, the confession of feelings. Philippa, the wife of Peter Roger of Mirepoix, remembers how her grandmother, the famous Marquesia, several times gave her 'shirts, veils, gloves and other clothes to be worn';[40] Bona of *Podio* gives the account of her guest's clothes as 'a coat and a blue serge hood ⟨lined?⟩ with white fur'.[41] Tools and machines, by preference, crop up in men's accounts, as for example 'a certain wheeled instrument in which fire is normally put' (fire-throwing weapon?),[42] or 'an oven to bake bread', made by the heretics for Faure *parator* (cloth-finisher?).[43]

Physical descriptions impress the modern reader. They aimed originally at concrete visualisation of characters, and the vivid images they produce are typical of oral recording and popular storytelling techniques. Their presence demonstrates how – even under extreme psychological pressure – cultural patterns and narratological schemes tend to be reproduced and faithfully preserved, with no great alteration of the deponent's view of reality and scale of values. The range goes from simple physical description to the depiction of a scene or a role.

William *de Tureta* portrays the people who came to a Cathar *consolamentum*: a young man 'rather fat and rosy-cheeked', 'a dark and tall woman', others 'well-dressed, one of whom was rather podgy, another pale and skinny'.[44] During a theological dispute between a Franciscan teacher of the *Studium* in Toulouse and a heretic, the latter refers to a biblical character specified no more precisely than the one 'who howled while singing';[45] Bernard *de Camone*, a priest, recalls among the participants in a Cathar ceremony a man 'called Annel *de Bugeria*, who could swim and stay under water for a long time';[46] Joan, daughter of Ysarn *de Pas*, remembers a woman, Guillelme Salamone, 'who was scabby'.[47] Berbegueira likes details: her confession is full of them. She apparently suffers from arthritis, since, in front of a Cathar *hereticus* 'she the witness could not bow bending her knees, except with great difficulty';[48] then, later on, she refuses to go and honour the same man in the upper room of a friend's house because 'she did not dare to attempt the stairs'.[49] But once she meets a *perfectus*, she depicts him in the most vivid and

---

[40] D24, fol. 199v: 'camisias, savenas, cirotecas, et alias res aptas ad portandum'.
[41] D25, fol. 84v: 'unum supertunicale et unum caputium cum pellibus blanchis de sarga blava'.
[42] D26, fol. 297r: 'quoddam instrumentum cum rotis in quo solet poni ignis'.
[43] D24, fol. 190v: 'unum furnum ad decoquendum panem'.
[44] D26, fols. 84v and 93r: 'satis pinguis et coloratus', 'quadam mulier longa et bruna', others 'bene induti quorum unus erat satis pinguis, et alius macillentus'.
[45] D22, fol. 91r: 'qui ululabat cantando'.
[46] D26, fol. 301v: 'qui vocabatur Annel de Bugeria piscator, qui diu sciebat natare et stare sub aqua'.
[47] D23, fol. 286r: 'que erat scabiosa'.
[48] D24, fol. 136v: 'non poterat dicta testis inclinari flexis genibus, nisi cum maxima difficultate'.
[49] D24, fol. 138v: 'non fuit ausa committere se scalis'.

concise description I have ever came across, 'They went into the room to see the said heretic, like a monster who was sitting there on his throne, still as a log'.[50]

Beliefs[51]

Among the main features of D22 is an interest in beliefs, myths and doctrine. Several depositions, in response to a very succinct series of questions, focus on these matters, sometimes widening the description to direct reporting of phrases and conversations – dare one say, 'truthful' reporting?

A clear example of realism is given by the nine depositions in the case of Peter Garcia (1247).[52] The voluntary deponents, mainly Franciscans, declare that they have secretly witnessed a six-months debate between Peter and his brother William Garcia, listening from the floor boards above the room in which the two met, right below the roof. The words recorded and related to the inquisitors are nearly the same: not so similar that we are led to assume lexical standardization by the recorder, not too different, and sometimes enriched with new details. It is a case of – supposedly – animated invective against anti-Cathar repression, which would have Peter declaring, 'that no way should justice be done through condemning someone to death, and that an [inquisition] official was a murderer if, in judging someone as heretic, he then killed him (. . .), and that all the preachers of the cross [crusade] are murderers, and that the cross which they preach is nothing more than a little piece of leather ⟨stitched⟩ on a shoulder'.[53] Virtually the same statements are reported by other witnesses, and in one case we are provided with further specification about the 'cross', which becomes 'nothing more than a piece of leather on a shoulder, or a piece of string, with which to tie one's hair'.[54] Nevertheless, the beliefs Peter refers to are standardised topics of the Cathar rhetorical sermon and preaching: marriage equals prostitution, the unworthiness of the Catholic clergy, the validity of some of the Scriptures, the non-divinity of Christ. The high level of this disputation, although intrinsically interesting, is not relevant to us, either in language and contents, and its evident *topoi* preclude assessment of the reliability of the record.

A completely different way of talking is shown in the deposition of

[50] D24, fol. 137v: 'Intraverunt ad videndum dictum hereticum tanquam monstrum qui sedebat ibi in sella sua tanquam truncus immobilis.'
[51] This clashes with Duvernoy's statement, 'L'élément réligieux, où penitential, disparaît donc largement derrière l'élément juridique et procédurier. Aussi bien la "credentia", la croyance de l'accusé, n'éveille-t-elle guère la curiosité de d'Inquisiteur' ('Bernard de Caux', p. 8).
[52] D22, fols. 88r–107r.
[53] D22, fol. 90v: 'quod nullo modo est facienda iusticia aliquem condemnando ad mortem, et quod officialis erat homicida in iudicando aliquem esse hereticum, si postea interficeretur (. . .), et quod predicatores crucis sunt omnes homicide et quod crux qua predicatur nihil aliud est nisi parum de pellia super humerum'.
[54] D22, fol. 93r: 'nisi parum de pellia super humerum, idem cordula cum qua ligantur capilli'.

William Feraut, reporting the words of the well-known William Fabre. The whole testimony deals with beliefs, and the genuineness of the account is strikingly evident from both content and lexicon:

> He heard W. Fabri *de Podio Hermer* saying (. . .) that when God saw his kingdom impoverished through the fall of the evil ones, he asked the bystanders, 'does any of you wish to be my son, and me to be his father?', and as nobody answered, Christ who was God's *bailli* (official), answered him, 'I want to be your son, and I shall go wherever you send me', and then God sent Christ as his son in the world to preach God's name, and this is how Christ came ⟨to the world⟩.[55]

And, further on, 'Item, he said that he heard W. Audebert claiming that the heretics say that oxen and horses ploughed and carried hay and worked in heaven as on earth'.[56]

Usually we impute to inquisitors any recurrences of the same *topoi*, stylistic elements and accusations. Interestingly, quite a few of these recurrences can be ascribed to the heretics. Rhetorical accusations against clergy and the religious are reported, as well as stereotypical lines of debate, as in the case of Peter *de Noya*:

> Item, he said that he heard heretics' preaching several times errors about visible things: that God did not create them, that the sacred host was not the body of Christ, and that even if it was as big as a large mountain, it would already have been eaten'.[57]

Again, here are the words of R[aymond] of Rodolos, who 'heard Aymeric *de Na Regina* saying that God had not entered the blessed Virgin, but rather had come as a shadow in her, and that God did not establish the mass, but the cardinals and clergy did so, for the love of substantial offerings'.[58]

The interaction and cross-fertilization of Cathar preaching discourse and peasant images sometimes produces rather vivid images. According to a deponent, the wife of Artaud Bos declared,

---

[55] D22, fol. 26r: 'Audivit W. Fabri *de Podio Hermer* dicentem (. . .) quod cum Deus videret depauperatum regnum suum propter casum malignorum quesivit a circumstantibus, "vult aliquis esse filium meum, et quod ego sim pater eius?" et cum nullus responderet, Christus qui erat baiulus Dei respondit Deo, "ego volo esse filius tuus et ibo quocumque me miseris", et tunc Deus tanquam filium suum misit Christum in mundum predicare nomen Dei, et ita venit Christus.'

[56] D22, fol. 26v: 'Item dicit quod audivit a W. Audebert quod heretici dicunt quod boves et roncini arabant et trahebant finum et laborabant in celo sicut et in terra.'

[57] D22, fol. 29r: 'item dixit quod audivit predicationes hereticorum pluries de erroribus de visibilibus quod Deus ea non fecerat, de hostia sacrata quod non erat corpus Christi, et si esset ita magnum sicut mons grandis, iam comestum esset.'

[58] D22, fol. 31v: 'audivit Aymericum *de Na Regina* dicentem quod Deus non venerat in beata Virgine, sed obumbraverat se ibi tamen, et quod Deus non statuit missam, sed cardinales et clerici amore magnarum oblationum'.

That the devil had made man with clay, and asked God to put a soul in him, and God replied to the devil, 'he will be stronger than me and you if you make him with clay, therefore make him with sea sand!', and the devil created man with sea sand, and God said, 'this is good: in fact he is not too strong, and not too weak', and [God] put a soul in him.[59]

Discourses interlace and influence each other. To what extent did preaching develop into a 'lower level' explanation of the Scriptures? Was it a phenomenon to be ascribed just to Cathar/heretical preaching, or to orthodox as well? Is this simplification – lowering to the level of the everyday – something which has to be seen as a reduction brought about by the deponent operating within his/her own cultural frame of reference? Or should it rather be considered as an automatic reaction to the *hearing* itself, in a manner and to a degree which are impossible to measure? Is it an instinctive 'switch' from one communicative level to another (i.e. a sort of 'automatized translation' of linguistic level)? Should we assume a higher recurrence of this mechanism arising from the secrecy of most Cathar mythology, which – unlike Catholic preaching – had to be selected and mainly hidden from the common *credentes*?[60]

Provençal[61]

Among the variety of 'surplus' features, phrases in vernacular are probably the most evident. The Doat volumes record quotations from poems in Provençal, excerpts from a translation of the Bible and particularly short phrases of direct speech, which maintain their genuine and authentic character. Arising from a notary's deficient skill in translating into Latin, or from his deliberate decision to leave these fragments in Provençal, or for other reasons, these excerpts can be considered the only authentic remains of the original interrogation dialogue. Although differing in nuance, volumes 22, 24 and 25 contain most of this evidence. Where we find a slighter degree of 'construction' in some of these depositions and unusual attention to speech being shown by the officials, there is usually a higher concentration of data.

The range of phrases in Provençal goes from interjections – normally broadly local – to lively and animated dialogues, fragments of prayers, old sayings, and quotes from texts that we may not have but which we can see were codified in that language.[62] The considerable significance of this

[59] D22, fol. 32r: 'quod diabolus fecit hominem de terra argila, et dixit Deo quod mitteret animam in hominem, et Deus dixit diabolo, "fortior erit me et te, si de argila fiat, sed fac eum de limo maris!" et fecit diabolus hominem de limo maris, et Deus dixit, "iste est bonus: non est enim nimis fortis nec nimis debilis", et misit Deus animam in hominem'.
[60] See again Ginzburg, *The Cheese and the Worms*.
[61] I am extremely grateful to Professor Peter Ricketts and Dr Shelagh Sneddon for translating the most intricate passages for me.
[62] See G. G. Merlo, 'Sulla cultura religiosa dei primi Valdesi', in *Identità valdesi*, pp. 71–92; see *Heresy and literacy*, esp. P. Biller, 'The Cathars of Languedoc and

bilingual structure, where we find it, is that it provides an open window into the trial scene and its original development.

With the sole exception of D24, fol. 231v, all the following passages are taken from D25 and D26. This is because volume 25 displays a high interest in particulars, with the redactor choosing to leave them as they were actually stated, while D26, although quite similar in character, adds rather a lot in direct speech.

Notable is the dialogue occurred during a Cathar *hereticatio*, when the *filius minor* says, 'Pregatz ne aquest pro home quen pregue Dieu', and the ill man replies, 'Senher, pregatz en Dieu'; the *filius maior* then carries on, 'Dieu nesia pregatz.' Far from standardized and ritualistic formulas, a believer is reported to have expressed his thoughts about the afterlife, 'Si ego morior in die veneris, perduz so, si passa lo di vendres, eu so sals.'[63] More obviously, there is literal citation of the *incipits* of vernacular texts whose possession, quotation or use provoked suspicion, such as the satire written by the (Catholic) Guiot de Provins, who ended his days as a Clunicac monk,[64] 'About the stinking and terrible world',[65] or a book of auguries, 'If you wish to know what is *cofres*'.[66] Again, translations of the Bible assume a high significance here, both in the incrimination of the suspect, and in that they provide specific and 'internal' information to the inquisitor, 'That no one should ascend to heaven except the Son of the Virgin who came down from heaven',[67] 'Today you will be with me in Paradise.'[68]

The requirements of an enquiry and of the consequent possible incrimination of the suspects make the recording of vernacular rather an obvious and functional option in some cases. Although the liturgical, textual and homiletic clusters, within which the use of the vernacular was in itself suspicious, were therefore immediate areas for enquiry, there would seem to be less point in looking for the vernacular in other cases. However, abstracts of poems and invectives were also important. The literal recording of pieces of satire intended, in fact, to be invectives against the Roman Church and its ministers, could be sufficient to incriminate a suspect.

Dossat already identified an excerpt from a *sirventes* ascribed to Guilhem Figueira, which in Doat runs thus, 'To make a sirventes in this key which

Written Materials', pp. 61–82, and L. Paolini, 'Italian Catharism and Written Culture', pp. 83–103.

[63] D25, fol. 171r: 'If I die on a Friday, I shall be lost [damned], if Friday can pass, I am saved.'
[64] Merlo quotes some of these passages in *Identità valdesi*, pp. 90–1.
[65] D25, fol. 201r: 'Del segle puent et terible'. Compare *Les oeuvres de Guiot de Provins, poète lyrique et satirique*, ed. J. Orr (Manchester, 1915), p. 10: 'Du siecle puant et orible'.
[66] D25, fol. 273v: 'Si vols saber que ez cofres'. I have left untranslated this last word, which may be a technical term.
[67] D25, fol. 199v: 'Que degus no poja [*MS has* 'poia'] al cel mas lo fil de la Verge qui del cel dechendet.'
[68] D25, fol. 199v: 'Hoi seras ab mi en Paradis.'

pleases me . . . [one line from the original is missing here] and I know without doubt that I shall attract ill-will from (in the original poem it is 'dels = about') the false deceitful people of Rome, the head of decadence where all good decays.'[69] Equally important for the personal involvement of the two suspects is this dialogue taking place after the massacre of Avignonet in 1242. Walking together, William Fabri, who was among the conspirators, asks his friend Stephen, 'Would you like to hear some good verses (coblas), or a good *sirventes*?', and carries on, 'Brother William Arnaldi "the cuckold" is cuckolded and broken!' To whom Stephen replies, 'These coblas are so good that the . . . [?] text *or* parchment is cut.'[70] Finally, one can feel the original flavour of living speech in the instinctive response of the man, waiting for his hearing, to his potential accusers and neighbours, 'Good man, for the days of your life, do not do any harm to your neighbours!'[71]

Although it would be fair to say that these quotations are no more than a tiny fraction of the totality of the depositions, what is important here is the opportunity they provide to investigate why and how the original speech has passed through the filters. Vernacular evidence – although driven by the inquisitor's questions – is the only authentic survival of the first act of the 'deposition performance'.

Feelings

The 'surplus' – lying beyond the functional schemes of the deposition – is often what we might call the 'affective feature'. Remarks about feelings or personal involvement are a symptom of 'openness' of the text for its modern readers. We can imagine an individual – either acting freely or under psychological compulsion – eventually providing *us* with something beyond the ordinary and common standardized answers. Whatever the hidden intention of the questioned, the scarcity of such evidence speaks for itself: nearly all of even the most 'free' interrogations lack personal comments on feelings or intimate matters. The unusual tone of personal involvement that is displayed in some depositions could simply be eloquent characterisation of someone's connections with heretical communities and individuals, but it could also be an attempt to justify someone's absence or presence on the scene, diverting the inquisitor's attention to other things.

---

[69] D25, fol. 199r: 'Du sirventes far en est so que magensa et sai ses doptar que naurai malvolensa dels fals de manples de Roma que ez caps de la chaensa que dechai tots bes.' It is mentioned by Dossat, 'Vaudois méridionaux', p. 222 and n. 61; on Figueira, see also CaF 4, 1969, pp. 136–7.

[70] D22, fol. 11v: 'Vultis audire bonas coblas vel unum bonum sirventes?' 'Frater W. Arnaldi Cogot es escogotatz, et pesxiatz!' 'Sic bone sunt iste coble cocula [*or* cocu la] carta es trencada.' The translation and meaning of this last sentence are uncertain. The modern colloquial English catch-phrase 'so sharp he cuts himself' might possibly approach the flavour of the original – suggesting 'These coblas are so sharp they cut the parchment.'

[71] D25, fol. 296v: 'Pros hom vos a votz dias, no fassatz mal a vostres besins!'

Because uncommon and not required by the series of questions, its presence in the records is a clear sign of the deliberate choice of the official to put it into writing. With most of this type of evidence, we should assume that the words were actually said, and that the emotions they expressed were true or plausible.

Within a long deposition and the usual lists of names and reports of meetings, the rare occurrences of emotions are gifts to us: gifts of human presence and healthy reminders. In the deconstruction of texts we are led to towards treating them as abstractions, objects to be sectioned with mathematical precision. But the trials and depositions talk to us about and pass on to us the life and death of real individuals.

Bertrand of Alamans, probably a *nuncius*, is allegedly implored by a couple of parents to act as a go-between with their daughter. He is to go and talk to her, now a heretic, to convince her to go back to her father. Bertrand agrees, he arranges a meeting for the three of them, during which the parents ask her 'at all costs to give up the sect'. The daughter refuses to betray her new beliefs, and the parents have to back down and accept the new unwanted situation.[72]

A few folios below the inquisitor allows Raymond Aiffre space to display sentiments of brotherhood and love. He and a sibling are called to the deathbed of a third brother, who asked for the Cathar baptism. After the ceremony is completed, they do not feel like going and honouring the *perfecti*, as commonly required by the ritual, 'because of grief for their brother'.[73] Later, Raymond confesses his feelings for a Cathar woman, widow of one of his friends. 'Veziada, the wife of the late Peter Carracier, was heretic at the time, and he the witness loved her passionately.'[74]

Way beyond the impact of the interrogation on an individual, there is another kind of psychological pressure which is visible in these accounts of feelings. In a Cathar's life the ideal conclusion of the soul's earthly pilgrimage is the moment of the *consolamentum*, in which, through the purging of all the imperfections of human nature, the soul regains its lost purity and is prepared for the following, higher stage of its life. Both as a collective and personal experience, such a moment would be of the highest emotional significance. As Cathars, and as human beings Raymond *de Miravalle* and his brother avoided their father's *hereticatio* 'as, because of ⟨their⟩ lament and grief for his the witness's father's death, they fled the house'.[75] Another witness recalls the moving image of a woman at a heretication, 'Algaia, wife

---

[72] D23, fols. 67r–v: 'quod modis omnibus desereret dictam sectam et rediret ad domum patris sui'.

[73] D23, fol. 83r: 'propter dolorem dicti fratris'.

[74] D23, fol. 84v: 'Veziada, uxor quondam Petri Carracier, tunc temporis erat heretica, et ipse testis adamavit eam.'

[75] D23, fol. 234v: 'quia propter planctum et dolorem de morte patris ipsius testis erant a domo excussi'.

of the late Pons *de Villanova*, who was crying profusely'.[76] Again in relation to a Cathar *consolamentum*, D25 records this remarkable account of a grieving woman. 'He the witness and Raymond Petri, entered the house of the aforesaid ill man, and as he just died, his sister Ermessendis was hitting her cheeks with her hands, not daring to cry out until the heretics had gone a long way away.'[77]

Stories

In the textual structure as a whole, the narrative pieces suddenly change the rhythm of the writing, interlacing it with dialogues, as in the popular manner of recounting. Wider fragments of stories are mostly included in D22 and D24, the registers relating – not by chance – to the cases of Avignonet and Montségur, in which the purpose of leaving long depositions was to provide the most extensive survey of the facts. The political weight and importance of these two cases both allowed and recommended a freer inquiry and partly explains the higher percentage of direct speech. As already pointed out, if a high number of deponents caused a restriction of narrative freedom, the contrary applied here. Given the significance of the circumstances, a relative latitude was accorded to the deponents, as the inquisitor limited the questionnaire to four or five major points. The deeper the questioning, the larger gaps in the grille or sieve.

The incidence of anecdotic features in a deposition is the best litmus test of the text adhering to the 'narrative level' of the deponents. Anecdotes and details in storytelling belong to and are recognised by the textual community,[78] they can also substantiate chronological references external to the official time-counting techniques, and they are a mental code of everyday popular stories.

The massacre of Dominican inquisitors at Avignonet in 1242 is a well-known and dark episode in the opposition to the Catholic Church and its ministers in Languedoc. Six long depositions provide us with a detailed report of the murder of William Arnaldi and his servants, providing an account that is memorable not just because they are six different points of view, but mainly because each story-teller maintains his own character and style within the deposition. The inquisitor's interrogatory, based on four or five questions, 'formats' very genuine and convincing reports, entangled with direct speeches, dialogues, descriptions. The same grille of questions submitted to all the deponents guarantees an unvarying recording style. The

---

[76] D24, fol. 105v: 'domina Algaia, uxor tunc Poncii de Villanova, que flebat mirabiliter.'

[77] D25, fols. 253v–254r: 'Raymundus Petri et ipse testis [Peter Pictavin] accesserunt ad domum predicti infirmi, ubi cum iam obisset Ermessendis soror eius percussiebat genas suas cum palmis, non audens clamare donec heretici supradicti longe se absentassent.' Peter Biller drew my attention to this passage.

[78] The concept of 'textual community' comes from the works of Brian Stock, among them *Listening for the Text*.

chronological boundaries go from the plot to the last events related to the massacre. The *questions* relate to identity and links between the conspirators, and to practical details of the attack itself, which were enormously relevant to its reconstruction. Despite the obvious and assumed reduction and summarising of the depositions, the individuality springing out of them is striking and impressive. We shall use it as a device to support our 'theory of filters'.

Emphasis on pictorial details characterises Peter Vignol's deposition. He meets the vociferous group of conspirators on their way back home, he recounts their clothes stained with blood, their rude and coarse language. One can 'see' this grotesque-looking parade, riding their stolen horses and carrying precious items taken from the inquisitor's trunks. Some of them, walking along the path, dressed as Dominican friars, were shouting,

> He the witness (. . .) heard from the above-mentioned [men] that they had killed brother William Arnaldi and his companions at Avignonet, and then William *de Plainha*, who had brought letters, led along some black horse which he had taken from the brothers themselves, or from their companions. Among the servants there were some wearing the scapulars of the said brother Preachers who had been killed. They were approaching and shouting, saying, 'Tell Peter Roger and Raymond of Péreille to come and hear the sermon of brother William Arnaldi!'[79]

Alzeu *de Massabrac*, displays a completely different perspective. Left outside Avignonet, he had the task of controlling the entrance to the village. He therefore meets the group of conspirators leaving the scene of the murder, and remembers a list of people and spoils stolen from the inquisitor's residence.[80] Alzeu is able to describe by whom and with which weapon each person was killed: a sword, a club, a hatchet, even a crossbow. His personal selection of the elements in the story insistently highlights weapons and macabre details. He refers to an astonishing dialogue between two of the conspirators:

> Item, Peter Roger asked John Acermat, 'Where is the cup?', and John Acermat replied to him, 'It's broken', and Peter Roger said, 'Why did not you bring it [with you]? If I had it, I'd make a golden band in it, and always

---

[79] D22, fols. 257v–258r: 'Ipse testis audivit dici a predictis quod interfecerant fratrem Guillelmum Arnaldi et socios eius apud Avinionetum, et tunc Guillelmus de Plainha qui aportaverat litteras adduxit quendam palafredum nigrum quem habuerat de fratribus vel de sociis suis, inter quos servientes erant aliqui qui portabant induta scapularia dictorum fratrum predicatorum qui fuerant interfecti, clamantes in adventu et dicentes, "dicatis Petro Rogerii et Raimundo de Perella quod veniant ad audiendum sermonem fratris Guillelmi Arnaldi!"'

[80] Such abundance of detail has to be seen in the light of (but not explained away by) the fact that possession of stolen objects makes the individual liable for prosecution (see W. Ullmann, 'Reflection on Medieval Torture', in *Law and Jurisdiction*, ed. Garnett, pp. 123–37).

drink from it!' Asked about which cup he meant, he replied [that it was] the cup of brother William Arnaldi's skull.[81]

Yet, the most complete and vigorous account is recorded in the deposition of Imbert of Sales, the only deponent to report striking details about the massacre itself. He was there when some people smashed the heavy portal of the building, and killed two servants with hatchets, on the stairs to the main hall. He remembers details about the slaughter and saw the bodies of the two murdered friars, their servants and wardens. He remembers some of the murderers taking pride in the event, shouting and laughing. A staggered and scared attitude emerges through his words, while he confesses the horrible facts.

They reached the hall of the Count of Toulouse, where the brother inquisitors were lying, and smashing the portal they went in, and killed brother William Arnaldi and Stephen, the inquisitors, and their fellows, and the servants. Yet, he the witness remained outside, and Arnaud Roger said to him, 'Imbert, why did you not go where the others are? Maybe, in fact, they will seizing stuff from there, stuff [earlier taken] from heretics, or something else.' And then he the witness replied to him, 'Sir, where shall I go? I don't know where to go.' And then two men from Avignonet said to him, 'We'll take you there.' Having heard this he the witness, and all the foot-soldiers who had come to the castle of Avignonet, together with those two men from Avignonet, reached the highest point in the castle, and when they were there, they found the brother inquisitors and their fellows killed (. . .) [and those who were there] were stealing the things and clothes and books belonging to the inquisitors, and they were [MS: were not] smashing the chests. And then he the witness got a pyx of 'gingerite',[82] and more than ten pence for the transportation of the objects which he and some others had from there. He the witness also added that he heard that Raymond d'Alfaro, who then was wearing a long, white pourpoint robe, was boasting that he had hit the brother inquisitors with a wooden club while saying, 'Be well! Be well!'[83]

[81] D22, fols. 286v–287r: 'Item Petrus Rogerius quesivit a Iohanne Acermat dicens, "Ubi est copa?" et Iohannes Acermat dixit ei, "Fracta est", et Petrus Rogerii dixit, "Quare non aportasti eam? Nam si haberem eam, facerem in ea cuiculum [*mistake for* circulum?] aureum, et semper biberem in ea!". Interrogatus de qua copa dixit, repondit quod de cupa capitis fratris Guillelmi Arnaldi.'

[82] I use a neologism, 'gingerite', for *Zinziberacum* - seemingly a derivative of *zingiber/i*, 'ginger' – which I have been unable to find in any dictionary of medieval Latin. My conjecture is that it was a word for some metal alloy, and is here used to signify metal of little value.

[83] D24, fols. 163v–164v: 'Venerunt ad salam Comitis Tholosani ubi fratres inquisitores iacebant, et frangentes hostium intraverunt et interfecerunt fratrem Guillelmum Arnaldum et Stephanum inquisitores, et socios eorum, et familiam. Tamen ipse testis remansit extra, et Arnaudus Rogerii dixit eidem testi, "Imberte, quare non accedistis vos ad locum ubi sunt alii? Nam forte hereticis inde raubam vel aliquid aliud occupabunt". Et tunc ipse testis dixit eidem, "Domine, quo ibo? Nescio quo eam". Et tunc duo homines de Avinioneto dixerunt eidem testi, "Nos ducemus vos illuc",

Construction Method, Aims: Some Preliminary Conclusions

Undoubtedly there is a direct consequential link between the assumption of 'what a trial is' and the method of registration chosen by the inquisitor/official. Through the analysis of each single register historians can gain a clear overview of the different 'ideal types' of trial displayed there. Through the study of structural differences, one can discern each 'ideal type' of interrogation.

D21 is probably the most uneven of the five registers. Alongside depositions, it brings together a wide range of normative material such as pontifical and conciliar decrees, letters and suchlike. Therefore one needs a preliminary selection, isolating only the interrogation records for comparison. Even at a first glance, it appears that the inquisitor tends here to propose a series of four or five main *capitula* (questions), which he had previously prepared, about the events he aims at reconstructing. His main task is to ascertain the suspect's guilt, thus he bases his question-list on previous depositions, accusations, and all the data he has gathered against a particular individual. Two features emerge vividly from D21. Private and public preaching of heretical beliefs seems to be quite a usual matter for the deponents, while at the same time the Catharism they depict is a familiar and everyday one. It is openly lived and free from fear of delation, completely rooted in the social – more than political – structure of the villages. The criterion followed in assembling the textual *corpus* of the volume shows us that we are dealing with an early period of anti-heretical activities. The fact that such a varied *corpus* represents all the notary needed for his activity (records, norms, manuals) implies that the enquiry procedure was not yet sufficiently internalized and automatic.

Focus on the narrative component is the essence of D22. Formulality is slight, witnesses are few, freedom of speech is accorded to all. Behind it a wider grille of more varied questions has to be assumed. Such a 'free' scheme allows historians to read a vast amount of data on heretical beliefs, and to find a lot of evidence about connections between the higher heretical hierarchy, the nobles, and the local political environment. The impression here is of an uncommon religious commitment, with an enquiry directed towards both organization and wider organizational dynamics.

> et hoc audito ipse testis et omnes servientes pedites qui venerant in Castrum de Avinioneto simul cum illis duobus hominibus de Avinioneto ascenderunt in caput castri, et quando fuerunt ibi, invenerunt fratres inquisitores et socios eorum et familiam interfectos . . . [and those who were there] non [sic] occupabant res et raubas et libros inquisitorum et frangebant arca [sic]. Et tunc ipse testis habuit inde unam pixidem de zinziberaco, et ultra decem denarios pro portatione rerum, quas cum aliis quibusdam inde habuit. Adiecit etiam ipse testis se audivisse tunc quod Raimundus Dalfaro qui portabat tunc perpunctum album longum, iactabat se quod ipse cum quadam clava lignea percussit in fratres inquisitores, et dicebat, "Ta be! Esta be!"'

Given the mostly rigid and formulaic nature of D23, it is possible to assume a *tempus gratie* (period of grace) behind it. This volume is pertinent to the 'stereotypical image of trial' handed down by historians. We cannot find any case of retractation in it, which suggests a relatively moderate use of imprisonment. Many of the depositions, in fact, end laconically with the formula 'the witness declares that he/she does not know any further information regarding heresy and heretics'.

D25 and D26, on the contrary, are extraordinarily rich sources of details and information. I analyse them together mainly because one is the continuation of the other. The deposition of Peter de Beauville is recorded partly in D25, continuing and concluding in D26.[84] Although the reason for this is unknown – we cannot determine with chronological precision the stages of its copying – we can assume that the scribes were ordered to continue the copying of one register into the following volume, perhaps because of tight finance and the strict deadlines of the project. Was 'optimization' of resources, therefore, behind this link between the two registers? Despite the links, there is substantial difference in the method of registration. While most of D26 is based upon a more rigid and regular frame of questions, D25 is filled with anecdotes, details, dialogues, and names. In a careful reading this appears to be a less restrictive and schematic interrogation, which leaves the defendants freer to organize their own version of facts. It is thanks to structural discrepancies that one is able to define the purpose of the enquiries. Most of D26 shows particular interest in connections between nobles, clergyman, notaries and politicians, while in D25 the questions focus on women, peasants, life in the villages, even on little children connected to Catharism and their familial relationships.

This quick and schematic distinction of 'ways of recording' helps to define the structure of our texts. Different recording techniques correspond to a multiform range of typologies in the registers. My goal has been to create precautionary tools, in order to give each register its unique reading 'key'. It can be discouraging to know that the range of precautions and filters is virtually endless, fluid and changeable over time. Nevertheless, in the certainty of the ultimate hopelessness of the search for Truth, I have tried to bring to light some textual frames, then to isolate a series of objects which exceed these frames. Conscious of the value of the 'text' in itself, I have aimed at a strict analysis of 'textual tools', and only at a second stage at reading further.

Interrogations and their records attest the presence of two Truths, inseparably entwined in the text. The 'textual building' the inquisitors wanted to shape – knowingly or not – is not my task to establish here. One could suppose – as past scholars did – a 'top-down' thrust modifying the original

[84] D25, fol. 297r–D26, fol. 2r. Together with D25, the first seventy-eight folios of D26 continue with interrogations from 1273–9, while the remainder of D26 contains interrogations of 1284–5 and 1288–9.

dialogue: the inquisitors, driving the discourse into a set path of questions, are therefore the only responsible agents of a 'factually incorrect' registration. The need to justify their persecutory anxiety required a proof of how strongly dissidence was threatening the unity of the true Church. I am more and more convinced that such an attitude would have needed a complete and objective knowledge of the social/political/cultural context in its totality, a conscious awareness of the inquisition's own role within it, together with a sharp evaluation of the risks and responsibilities related to it: an external overview we could hardly ascribe to anyone! Furthermore, such an interpretation would imply that the inquisitors had a profound perception of their own capacity to influence the registration, and complete awareness of possessing a 'portion' (or a 'whole') of the Truth. Here not only our common sense but also a serious reading of the depositions should make us wary. The will to drive the dialogue, to select the facts, has to be ascribed to the heretics as well as to the inquisitors. The assumption of ignorance, unconsciousness, stupidity and powerlessness does not do them justice.[85] They were actors – in every respect – in this sharp dialogic fight between the parties.

To moderate the biases attributed to the churchmen, historians should keep in mind that the registers themselves were a tool meant for internal use only. Their promotional and publicist value was virtually non-existent outside the trial context, even when they had some circulation beyond the inquisitor's possession of them.[86] A more balanced approach is required. We

---

[85] Different is the view expressed by Given, when talking about an 'inert and pliant mass, waiting passively to be shaped by their [the inquisitors'] techniques' ('Inquisitors', p. 357).

[86] The old scholarly debate about the 'nature' of inquisitorial registers is still an up-to-date topic: historians argue whether they were an instrument of public manipulation by and promotion of the inquisitorial institution, or rather public records of the inquisitorial activity, often acting as a 'protection' against over-subjective application of the norms. What Merlo described as the 'public role' of the inquisitorial texts (*Eretici e inquisitori*, pp. 11–12), cannot be ascribed to our sources: rather, it is a strong feature of the *sentences* and *sermons* pronounced during the open declaration of allegations and penances. The judicial connotation of trial records was clearly and deeply investigated by Lorenzo Paolini in his *Introduction* to the edition of the *Acta Sancti Officii Bononie ab anno 1291 usque ad annum 1310*, ed. L. Paolini and R. Orioli, 3 vols., ISIME, Fonti per la Storia d'Italia 106 (Rome, 1982–4) (pp. xiii–xxxiii), which has been too quickly forgotten. It is my impression that although conciliar prescriptions and a precise set of papal norms tried to discipline the praxis of interrogations, it is the confused and indecisive *application* of the law that puzzles historians. If it is true that canonists could not limit/control the subjective interpretation of the norm, the historiographical analysis of juridical science and analysis of its practical effects should consequently be considered as different enterprises. There is evidence that some inquisitors themselves, in fact, after or during their assignment, were submitted to trial for having read too personally the prescribed norms, or for having been too slack in their application. It is the historian's duty, however, to determine some 'average-feature' in these sources, and it seems quite clear to me that on average the registers were intended to be a tool for investigation and record, despite the fact that some sort of access to them

need to discard the monolithic image of a repressive structure of power, opposed to an unarmed group of believers that – we should never forget – was able to hold that structure in check for decades. Very different is my impression of the depositions, especially when we find a series of long retractations within them.

The aim of reading with 'precautions' is to find tools for comprehension. Most of the textually-constitutive differences in the registers have a reason to be analysed only in relation to the purposes of each single inquiry. Each situation, inquisitor, officer, witness, imposed a personal approach and a different method on the running of any particular interrogation. This is why, in the end, the elements of similarity in the volumes are few.

Stepping back to a 'general' reading of the sources, we need to note that the functional nature of trial accounts is underlined by a further element. As we remarked earlier, these records follow a geographical criterion.[87] As is well known, the medieval Inquisition in southern France was a fragmentary (although well structured) institution, whose officers, responsible for different enquiries, were mostly unconnected to each other. There is no evidence of any concerted action, or of a common strategy of action. The pope or his legates, whenever urged by the situation, sent one or two inquisitors to the main centre in the area in question, in an attempt to restore control and establish back the Church power. Their main task consisted in a detailed enquiry, to be equipped with special and exceptional powers, in strict collaboration with the lay government. That is why these special papal legates mainly needed to record as accurately as they could facts and names.[88]

One last example helps to underline the contemporary perception of written material, together with the 'surprising' reaction of the deponents. The implication for us? A warning to approach the concepts of fear and risk with care. Saving one's life – or, even more importantly, one's patrimony – induced the witnesses to display extraordinary opposition to the churchmen. Since this reaction follows unknown and individual patterns of perception, regrettably it remains unmeasurable.

Our story is about the theft of the Carcassonne registers. According to the depositions, in 1282 two Cathar *perfecti* together with members of the lay government of the town agreed to find a way to 'bravely defend themselves against the inquisitors, as it was necessary.'[89] Perceiving the inquisitors' presence as a threat to their freedom and an interference, they initially tried to propose a range of solutions to stop the vigorous activity of the

---

was also provided to the accused, in order to provide an opportunity to defend their position.

[87] As shown – although with a different purpose – in Given, *Inquisition*, pp. 35–6.

[88] See Dossat, *Crises*, p. 195. The situation in Italy was different, as has been shown by L. Paolini in his remarkable study, 'Il modello italiano nella manualistica inquisitoriale' (forthcoming).

[89] D26, fol. 270v: 'viriliter se defenderent contra inquisitores, quia necessarium erat'. Several confessions are recorded here; see D26, fols. 195v–275v.

officials. Among these, one was to choose some representatives who would go to Rome and submit their official complaints to the pope, or – even better – to send a delegation to those citizens who had already confessed and accused others, in order to persuade them to retract their accusations. Another was to present a formal petition to the inquisitors themselves, asking them to take pity and be merciful with the followers and sympathisers of the alternative church. The group did eventually cast aside all these plans, and arrived at a more radical solution: to steal 'all the inquisition's books relating to this land, that is the Carcassonne region, in which the confessions are recorded'.[90] Although the precise wording may have been superimposed, it carefully underlines the importance of the episode and shows much of the way in which the fact had been perceived.

First, the feeling that *this* written material is hostile and dangerous does not depend on the false nature of accusations, or on the adulteration of confessions. The registers are dangerous *as registers*, a threaten to the citizens' freedom of worship. They are a written proof of guilt, and therefore indisputable evidence of illicit connections and linkages. People, then, do not fear their being twisted and counterfeit, but the danger to freedom constituted by their very existence. Evidence of this can be found in the choice of books to be stolen. The dangerous ones are the records of trial interrogations ('the books containing the depositions of witnesses who gave testimony about the fact of inquisition into heresy')[91], and not – as perhaps we would expect – the sentences, as the last acts of the trials and strictly linked to punishment and repression.

The high degree of danger ascribed to these particular books and records suggests further thoughts. The citizens did reckon that to steal them meant to stop inquisitorial activities, at last putting an end to the inquiries threatening the tranquillity of the city. We need to go far beyond a simple and reductive correlation between theft and liberty, with its consequent identification of a quasi-totemic destruction of the evidence with the intent to regain freedom. It is much more interesting to pursue the perception the contemporaries had of a deep bond between liberty and the writing/conservation of the records. In this way we move further, beyond the recently analysed connection between punishment and freedom.[92]

The bond to which I refer represents also – in my view – an evident symptom of a different perception of 'community'. If looked at from the citizens' point of view, in fact, inquisitorial activity violates the boundaries and territory of a community of residents, villagers, relatives, structured both on a territorial and a familial basis. However, 'community' as understood by

[90] D26, fol. 211v: 'omnes libros inquisitionis qui pertinent ad terram istam, scilicet de Carcassesio, in quibus sunt scripte confessiones'.
[91] D26, fol. 262r: 'libros depositionum testium qui deposuerunt super facto inquisitionis heresis'. We would expect here 'super facto heresis', not 'super facto inquisitionis heresis'.
[92] Different is the approach in Given, *Inquisition*.

Caterina Bruschi

the ecclesiastical power is a synonym for Christianity, diocese, parish district, a totally divergent concept, whose ideological assumptions rely on a sub-stantially doctrine-based frame of reference, a 'religious set' of principles and laws. In the light of these different approaches, every action by either party clashes with the opposite party's frame of thought and collective percep-tion.[93]

Eventually the citizens of Carcassonne, together with their noble chiefs, some Cathars and knights, got in touch with Bernard Agasse, a well-known *scriptor librorum* (book writer), and asked him to put his knowledge at the disposal of their 'mole', one of the inquisitors' servants. Together, they would certainly find the right books and remove them from the shelves – for the servant, an illiterate, would not be able to recognize the titles and the handwriting on the covers. Bernard met the 'conspirators' more than once to reach a satisfactory agreement. He raised questions about his recompense, which he thought inadequate in relation to the high risks he was going to undertake in the enterprise.

What is my conclusion, after this 'deconstruction' of the records? I have the strong impression that the dialogical conflict between the two parties was much more even, a more 'balanced' affair than has often been thought. The two parties' worlds, languages, aims, beliefs and realities inevitably clashed, and shaped both the dialogue itself and its recording. Unfortunately, their fundamental opposition, far from providing historians with a simple path leading in one interpretative direction only, has given rise to the record of a much more involved and astonishingly complex conflict. Its true under-standing requires meticulous and renewed textual analysis. In the end, all of this has left me with more questions than answers, and with insatiable curiosity about one thing above all others. Was it behaviour that shaped the accusations, or rather the accusation that 'framed' behaviour?

---

[93] See the fundamental Waugh and Diehl, *Christendom.*

Questions About Questions: Toulouse 609 and the Great Inquisition of 1245–6

Mark Pegg

'Did you believe the heretics to be "good men"?' the Dominican inquisitor Joan de Sant-Peire questioned the noble Auriac widow Alazaïs den Pata on Monday, 26 June 1246, 'or adore them, or give them anything, or send them anything, or receive them, or get the peace from the heretics, or from a book of theirs, or participate in the *aparelhamen* or the *consolamen* of the heretics?' Alazaïs den Pata's response, after such a spiel, was a brusque 'No'.[1] Such a cascade of questions, in one tumbling combination or another, and always driven by a concern for what an individual might have done rather than what he or she might have thought, were recited almost six thousand times between May 1245 and August 1246 when Joan de Sant-Peire and his Dominican *socius* Bernart de Caux summoned all men over fourteen and all women over twelve from the Lauragais (a fertile plain between the Ariège and Agout rivers) to the cloister of the abbey-basilica of Saint-Sernin in Toulouse. These questions framed, structured, and shaped the way in which the two friar-inquisitors understood, interpreted, and so judged the confessions heard and transcribed at Saint-Sernin. This cumulative quizzing, and the rigorously consequential model of reality it embodied, not to mention the notion of truth it articulated, profoundly transformed (or finally confirmed) how the men and women of the Lauragais thought about themselves, each other, and heresy. All attempts at understanding the great inquisition into heretical depravity of Bernart de Caux and Joan de Sant-Peire, and so the thousands of testimonies surviving as manuscript 609 in the Bibliothèque municipale of Toulouse, must begin with some questions about questions.[2]

---

[1] Toulouse 609, fol. 95r: 'Requisita si credidit unquam hereticos esse bonos homines, vel adoravit, vel dedit, vel misit, vel receptavit, vel recepit pacem ab hereticis vel a libro eorum, vel interfuit apparelhamento vel consolamento hereticorum. Dixit quod non.' This essay condenses, refines, and occasionally expands, some of the arguments made in Pegg, *Corruption*, esp. pp. 45–51.

[2] The original parchment leaves of Bernart de Caux and Joan de Sant-Peire's inquisition are lost. Indeed, only a handful of parchment fragments still exist of any inquisitorial *originalia* from the middle of the thirteenth century, and most of these scraps of skin were found in the bindings of seventeenth-century books. Two other Dominican inquisitors, Guilhem Bernart de Dax and Renaud de Chartres, had the Lauragais testimonies copied onto paper sometime after October 1258, though no

Questions, though potentially ambiguous, are very culturally specific
predictions about knowledge, about inductive practice, in that they
exemplify generally accepted notions of truth, commonly valid rules of
inference, habitually accepted methods of deduction. Answers justify a set
of questions because they complete their sense, their function, their particular
purpose. Questions and answers, like inductive habits deriving from precise
evidence and deductive techniques framed by general assumptions, get
confirmed, derive validity, from being brought into agreement with each
other. Questions get amended, dropped, and reworded, if they yield answers
(and inferences) that individuals and communities are reluctant to understand, are unwilling to accept. Answers (and inferences) get rejected if they
violate questions that individuals and communities are, at the very least,
reluctant to amend and, at the extreme, willing to resist. The questions
utilized at Saint-Sernin, in and of themselves, justified the deductive
methods, the principles of analysis, the system of classification, by which
Bernart de Caux and Joan de Sant-Peire formulated the past, present and the
future of heresy in the Lauragais. This does not mean that the two friar-
inquisitors already knew what they would hear, or read, at Saint-Sernin, just
that all testimonies would be judged, and in a large part shaped, by what this
analytic formula was expected to yield. The process of justifying the choice of
particular questions, which the two friar-inquisitors not only had to do for
themselves but also for those they interrogated, was a delicate exercise in
making mutual adjustments between what was asked and what was inferred.
The ability to select the right questions was as much a test of Bernart de Caux
and Joan de Sant-Peire, in their search for truth about heresy, as giving the
right answers was a test of those being interrogated, in their ability to confess,
or conceal, this truth.[3]

---

later than August 1263. This copy has dwelt in the Bibliothèque municipale of
Toulouse since 1790. This paper manuscript is now catalogued as Toulouse 609. It
consists of 260 folios, though only 254 are paginated, with each leaf measuring 291
millimetres high and 236 millimetres wide. A startling fact about Toulouse 609, and
one that can never be forgotten, is that it is only two books, five and four, arranged in
that order, out of an estimated ten that Bernart de Caux and Joan de Sant-Peire
originally compiled. There is also some uncertainty about how many testimonies
Toulouse 609 actually contains. This vagueness is due to witnesses being referred to
by different names in different places throughout the manuscript. Consequently,
Dossat, *Crises*, p. 232, gives the figure of 5471; Douais, *Documents*, I, cliii, has 5600;
C. Molinier, *L'Inquisition dans le Midi de la France au XIIIe et au XIVe siecle: étude sur les
sources de son histoire* (Paris, 1880), p. 190, argued for somewhere between 8000 and
10,000; R. Abels and E. Harrison, 'The Participation of Women in Languedocian
Catharism', *MS* 61 (1979), 215–51 (p. 220), counted 5604; W. Wakefield, 'Inquisitor's
Assistants: Witnesses to Confessions in Manuscript 609', *Heresis* 20 (1993), 57–65
(p. 57), opts for 5600; Given, *Inquisition*, p. 39, decided on 5518; and Pegg, *Corruption*,
p. 169 n. 52, accepts Dossat's figure. More detailed palaeographic discussions of
Toulouse 609 are in Dossat, *Crises*, pp. 56–86, and Pegg, *Corruption*, pp. 20–7, 151–60.
[3] On the questions used by medieval inquisitors, and some of the problems this causes
in using inquisitorial registers, see the helpful comments of Grundmann, 'Ketzer-

On Thursday, 1 June 1245, in a wonderful reversal of the questions that Joan de Sant-Peire would throw at Alazaïs den Pata almost a year later, the squire Izarn Niger from Issel recited this breathless swirl of innocence to Bernart de Caux, 'I never saw heretics except caught, nor believed, nor adored, nor gave, nor sent, nor received, nor led, nor caused to be led, nor heard the preaching of them.'[4] Answers like this, recorded many times in Toulouse 609, spliced together with the less frequent transcription of a friar-inquisitor (or an assistant) actually interrogating a person, allow for an inventory of the questions used by Bernart de Caux and Joan de Sant-Peire at Saint-Sernin. It also allow for the specific place of a particular question, the point when this was asked and not that, to be discerned in the overall structuring of interrogations and testimonies. This script can be further edited by employing the *formula interrogatorii* that the two Dominicans set forth in the small pamphlet they composed about inquisitorial method two years after their Lauragais inquiries. This deceptively simple book, one of the earliest (if not the first) inquisitorial manuals, and known as the *Processus inquisitionis*, was very much a *mémoire* on the questions tried, tested, and confirmed at Saint-Sernin.[5]

verhöre'; G. Merlo, *Eretici e inquisitori*, pp. 11–15; Dossat, *Crises*, pp. 239–40; L. Kolmer, *Ad Capiendas Vulpes: Die Ketzerbekämpfung in Süd-frankreich in der ersten Hälfte des 13. Jahrhunderts und die Ausbildung des Inquisitionsverfahrens*, Pariser Historische Studien 19 (Bonn, 1982), pp. 92–5, 97, 159, 171–5, 182–5, 204; and Given, *Inquisition*, pp. 44–57. See also the thoughtful discussions about questions, deduction, induction, and classification by M. Douglas, 'Rightness of Categories', in *How Classification Works: Nelson Goodman among the Social Sciences*, ed. M. Douglas and D. Hull (Edinburgh, 1992), pp. 239–71, esp. pp. 258–9; S. K. Langer, *Philosophy in a New Key: A Study in the Symbolism of Reason, Rite, and Art*, 3rd edn (Cambridge MA, 1979), esp. pp. 3–9; and N. Jardin, *The Scenes of Inquiry: On the Reality of Questions in the Sciences* (Oxford, 1991). Now, see N. Goodman, 'The New Riddle of Induction', in his *Fact, Fiction, and Forecast*, 4th edn (Cambridge MA, 1983), pp. 59–83; N. Goodman and C. Elgin, *Reconceptions in Philosophy & Other Arts & Sciences* (Indianapolis and Cambridge, 1988), p. 446; and the collected (philosophical) essays on the problem of 'grue' put forward in Goodman's 'The New Riddle of Induction' in *Grue! The New Riddle of Induction*, ed. D. Stalker (Chicago and La Salle, 1994), esp. I. Hacking, 'Entrenchment', pp. 193–224.

[4] Toulouse 609, fol. 127v: '. . . dixit quod nunquam vidit hereticos nisi captos, nec credidit, nec adoravit, nec dedit, nec misit, nec recepit, nec duxit, nec duci fecit, nec eorum predicationem audivit'.

[5] Y. Dossat, 'Le plus ancien manuel de l'inquisition méridionale: le *Processus inquisitionis* (1248–1249)', *Bulletin philologique et historique (jusqu'à 1715), années 1948–1949–1950* (1952), pp. 33–7, and Dossat, *Crises*, p. 167. Dondaine, by contrast, in 'Manuel', argued that the *Processus*, which is number two in his list of manuals, was the work of the inquisitors of Narbonne, the Dominicans Guilhem Raimon and Peire Durant. Kolmer, *Ad Capiendas Vulpes*, pp. 198–203, accepted Dondaine's attribution of the *Processus*. Dossat convincingly demonstrated this judgement to be mistaken. Wakefield, *Heresy, Crusade and Inquisition*, p. 250, also accepts that the *Processus* was written by Bernart de Caux and Joan de Sant-Peire. Cf. Given, *Inquisition*, p. 45, where he attributes the *Processus* to no particular inquisitor, though he does emphasis that it was the earliest manual. A. Tardif edited the

All testimonies began with a person first abjuring heresy and then taking an oath that he or she would 'tell the full and exact truth about oneself and about others, living and dead, in the matter of the fact or crime of heresy [that is, the heresy of the good men and the good women] or Waldensianism'.[6] After these words were recited, 'Did you see a heretic [a good man or a good woman] or a Waldensian?' was, invariably, the first question. The answer, 'No', might end the inquisition there and then. 'Yes', however, immediately led to other queries. 'If so, then where and when, how often and with whom, and who were the others present?' 'Did you listen to the preaching or exhortation of heretics?' 'Did you give heretics lodging or arrange shelter for them?' 'Did you lead heretics from place to place or otherwise consort with them or arrange for them to be guided or escorted?' 'Did you eat or drink with the heretics or eat bread blessed by them?' 'Did you give or send anything to the heretics?' 'Did you act as the financial agent [*questor*] or messenger [*nuncius*] or assistant [*minister*] of the heretics?' 'Did you hold any deposit or anything for a heretic?' 'Did you receive the peace from a heretic's book, mouth, shoulder, or elbow?' 'Did you adore a heretic or bow your head or genuflect and say "bless us" before the heretics?' 'Did you participate, or were you present at their *consolamen* and *aparelhamen* [*consolamentum* or *apparellamentum* in Latin]?' 'Did you ever confess to another inquisitor?'[7] 'Did you believe the heretics to be good men and women, to have a good faith, to be truthful, to be the friends of God?' 'Did you hear, or do you know, the errors of the heretics?' 'Did you hear them say that God had not made all visible things, that there was no salvation in baptism, that marriage was worthless, that the Host was not the body of Christ, and that the flesh would never be resurrected?'[8] 'If you did believe these errors, and also believed the heretics to be good, then how long have you persisted in these beliefs?' 'And when did you first begin to believe in the heretics and their errors?' 'Did you leave the sect of the heretics?' 'How long ago did you leave and did you ever see the heretics

---

Processus inquisitionis (from MS 53 at the Biblioteca Universitaria de Madrid) in Tardif, *Processus* (translated in Wakefield, *Heresy, Crusade and Inquisition*, pp. 250–58). Ramon de Peñafort had already written a guide for inquisitors in the kingdom of Aragon around 1242, and though he sets out an approach for making inquiries into heresy, his manual lacks the tone of experience pervading the *Processus* and reads more like the handbook of an early thirteenth century confessor than an inquisitor. Nevertheless, Bernart de Caux and Joan de Sant-Peire had probably read Ramon de Peñafort's pamphlet before writing their own manual. On Ramon de Peñafort's manual, see Dondaine, 'Manuel', 96–7. Douais edited the manual in his *Inquisition*, pp. 275–88.

[6] Tardif, *Processus*, p. 672. In Toulouse 609, e.g., see the beginning of Pons de Beauteville's testimony on 16 June 1246 at fol. 129r, '. . . requisitus de veritate dicenda de se et de aliis, tam vivis quam mortuis, super crimine heresis et valdesie, testis juratus, dixit quod . . .'.

[7] Tardif, *Processus*, p. 672.

[8] E.g. Raimon Bru's response to these questions at Toulouse 609, fol. 130v.

after this time?'[9] 'Did you ever agree to keep silent about all these things?' 'Did you ever hide the truth?' usually concluded the interrogation.

All these questions, with their distinct rhythm and investigative precision, lead to the intriguing and far from whimsical problem of why bother with questions at all in the search for heresy – a point which Arnaut del Faget and Guilhem Vezat, cowherds from Maurens, actually stressed for Bernart de Caux in their testimonies of Tuesday, 16 January 1246. Three years earlier, these two cowherds had come across a couple of unknown men in the woods around Maurens and immediately 'knew in their hearts' that these strangers were heretics.[10] Certainly, by the middle of the thirteenth century it was no great feat to suspect two anonymous men in a Lauragais wood of being *bons omes*, and for such suspicions to be more often than not correct, but that is to miss the lesson here, which is that Bernart de Caux and Joan de Sant-Peire would never have hunted for the good men, the good women, and their believers, through heartfelt knowledge, through intuition, alone. Neither did the two friar-inquisitors rely upon demonic or heavenly revelations, such as miracles, to discern a good man in the way that Dominic Guzman was said to have done in the Lauragais only a few decades earlier. Once, during a sermon against the *boni homines* that the founder of the Dominicans was preaching at Fanjeaux, a grotesque and intolerably smelly cat leapt into the congregation and identified a heretic.[11] By the time this anecdote was told to Étienne de Bourbon by the Dominican Romeu de Llivia, sometime around 1261, complete faith in miraculous clues, like putting too much trust in an intuitive truth, merely demonstrated that one did not know how to go about investigating the origins of anything.[12]

Wondrous evidence can help and be the sign of a saint, just as a lucky guess can work for a cowherd, but their conflation of cause and effect, so that the past history of a present crime never had to be explained, were both judgements about the world without the necessity of having to understand the world being judged. To forego tracing great waves back to small ripples, to ignore the continuity of evil in a gift much given, simply left all the whys and wherefores of heresy, all the work of detecting heretics, and so all the work of punishing them, up to God. Which is exactly what the fiery Cistercian abbot Arnaud Amalric apparently did when Béziers was captured in 1209 during the first year of the Albigensian Crusade. The crusaders had a

---

[9] E.g. Toulouse 609, fol. 120r, for the testimony of Peire Jouglar where the question was written into the confession: 'Requisitus si, postquam dimisit sectam here-ticorum, vidit hereticos, dixit quod plures vidit stantes apud La Besseda.'

[10] Toulouse 609, fol. 117v, where Arnaut del Faget says about himself and Guilhem Vezat: '. . . et perpenderunt in animo suo quod heretici erant'.

[11] Stephen of Bourbon, *Tractatus*, pp. 34–5.

[12] Guillaume d'Auvergne in his *De Universo* – *Opera Omnia* (Paris, 1674; repr. Frankfurt, 1963), p. 1055 – written around 1235, clearly stated this persuasive thirteenth-century forensic notion. On the related problem of defining and under-standing the causes of medieval wonder, see C. W. Bynum, 'Wonder', *AHR* 102 (1997), 1–26, esp. pp. 7–11.

problem about how one could precisely distinguish Catholic from heretic, the good from the bad, amongst the people of Béziers. 'Kill them!' was Arnaud Amalric's judicious solution. 'Truly,' the legate concluded, 'the Lord will know his own.'[13] Whether this anecdote about Arnaud Amalric is true or not, and all we have is the word of Caesarius of Heisterbach to go by, it still evokes an approach virtually unthinkable for two Dominican inquisitors in the middle of the thirteenth century. To Bernart de Caux and Joan de Sant-Peire, there was nothing inherently miraculous or demonic about why heretics did what they did. Heretical thoughts and habits were not to be explained by reference to anything outside the usual course of nature. So, like any human whose motives were less than supernatural, less than holy, a heretic could be, indeed had to be, judged and punished through profane procedures.[14]

In this way, the inquisition at Saint-Sernin, as a procedure for discovering the truth about heresy, was markedly different from the judicial ordeal. Fire and water as reliable tools in judging veracity, though not the only methods of proof before the thirteenth century, were certainly the specific practices which men like Bernart de Caux and Joan de Sant-Peire knew themselves to be abandoning in their need to collect truthful and systematic evidence (especially after canon eighteen of the Fourth Lateran Council in 1215 explicitly stated that clergy could not participate in the ordeal).[15] The legal plumbing behind the ordeal was, relatively speaking, simple and well-hidden, whereas the investigative formula adopted at Saint-Sernin could not help but reveal much of its legal and moral structure. The basic inquisitorial design used at Saint-Sernin was, therefore, very similar to the Roman-inspired and canon-regulated *ordo iudiciarius*. These rules of procedure, built upon written and oral evidence, had been developing since the middle of the twelfth century and all ecclesiastical courts (and many secular) had adopted them by the thirteenth.[16] If the ordeal may be characterized as

---

[13] Caesar, *Dialogus* v.21 (I, 302). See also Berlioz, *'Exemplum'*.

[14] E.g. Caesar, *Dialogus* x.1 (II, 217), where he had this to say about miracles and nature: 'Novicius: Quid est miraculum? Monachus: Miraculum dicimus quicquid fit contra solitum cursum naturae, unde miramur' ('Novice: What is a miracle? Monk: We call a "miracle" anything which happens contrary to the usual course of nature, at which we wonder').

[15] W. Davies and P. Fouracre, 'Conclusion', in *The Settlement of Disputes in Early Medieval Europe*, ed. W. Davies and P. Fouracre (Cambridge, 1986), pp. 207–40, strongly argue against assuming simplistic notions of proof, procedure, and truth in the centuries before the twelfth and thirteenth; and K. Pennington, *The Prince and the Law, 1200–1600: Sovereignty and Rights in the Western Legal Tradition* (Berkeley, 1993), pp. 132–5. A. García y García, *Constitutiones Concilii quarti Lateranensis una cum commentariis glossatorum*, Monumenta iuris canonici, Series A, Corpus glossatorum 2 (Vatican, 1981), pp. 66–8, and Mansi, XXII, 1006–10.

[16] On the *ordo iudiciarius*, see esp. L. Fowler-Magerl, *Ordo iudiciorum vel ordo iudiciarius: Begriff und Literaturgattung* (Frankfurt-am-Main, 1984), and Pennington, *The Prince and the Law*, pp. 135–64.

letting God be the judge of a person's guilt or innocence, so that the evidence which caused a man or a woman to be accused in the first place was either confirmed or dismissed through divine judgement, then the ordeal was a style of judging which no ordinary person could ever truly imitate.[17] Inquisitorial method, on the other hand, was a system made to be imitated.

In this very human investigative schema, able to be taught, copied, and adapted, the back-and-forth progression towards knowledge about heresy articulated in the questions of Bernart de Caux and Joan de Sant-Peire clearly resembled the linear step-by-step *quaestio disputata* studied by Dominicans and Franciscans in thirteenth-century Paris.[18] Indeed, as a *studium generale* had been established near Saint-Sernin as a requirement of the 1229 treaty of Meaux-Paris, with Parisian masters of theology and philosophy specifically dispatched to train local mendicants in the fight against the heretical *boni homines*, such intellectual techniques were taught at Toulouse.[19] Scholars endeavoured to ask the right questions, within the constraints of a consciously stylized dialogue form, in their Aristotelian processions to the truth.[20] Nevertheless, despite this similarity to what was learnt in the *studia*

---

[17] On the judicial ordeal, see J. Baldwin, 'The Intellectual Preparation for the Canon of 1215 against Ordeals', *Speculum* 36 (1961), 613–36, and 'The Crisis of the Ordeal: Literature, Law, and Religion around 1200', *Journal of Medieval and Renaissance Studies* 24 (1994), 327–53; P. Brown, 'Society and the Supernatural: A Medieval Change', in *Society and the Holy in Late Antiquity* (Berkeley and Los Angeles, 1982), pp. 302–32; D. Barthélemy, 'Présence de l'aveu dans le déroulement des ordalies (IXème-XIVème) siècles', in *L'Aveu: Antiquité et moyen-âge*, Collection de l'École Française de Rome 88 (Rome, 1986), pp. 315–40; R. Bartlett, *Trial by Fire and Water: The Medieval Judicial Ordeal* (Oxford, 1986), pp. 4–12, esp. pp. 42–3 for his criticism of Brown and p. 142 for his emphasis on the ordeal used for judging 'invisible' crimes like heresy before 1200; Pennington, *The Prince and the Law*, pp. 132–4, for his criticism of Bartlett; and T. Head, 'Saints, Heretics, and Fire: Finding Meaning through the Ordeal', in *Monks and Nuns, Saints and Outcasts. Religion in Medieval Society: Essays in Honor of Lester K. Little*, ed. S. Farmer and B. Rosenwein (Ithaca, 2000), pp. 220–35.

[18] A. Kenny and J. Pinborg, 'Medieval Philosophical Literature', in *The Cambridge History of Later Medieval Philosoph: From the Rediscovery of Aristotle to the Disintegration of Scholasticism 1100–1600*, ed. N. Kretzmann, A. Kenny and J. Pinborg (Cambridge, 1990), pp. 26–9.

[19] The *studium* of Toulouse was, after a remarkable grant of Pope Gregory IX in 1233, considered equal in all privileges with Paris, including the provision that any student awarded the *licentia docendi* in Toulouse could freely *regere ubique*, that is, teach wherever they chose without any further examinations. On the Toulouse *universitas* of masters and scholars, see Y. Dossat, 'Université et Inquisition à Toulouse: la fondation du Collège Saint-Raimond (1250)', in *Actes du 95e Congrès national des Sociétés savantes, Reims, 1970*, Section de philologie et d'histoire jusqu'à 1610 1 (Paris, 1975), pp. 227–38, esp. pp. 227–30; M.-H. Vicaire and H. Gilles, 'Rôle de l'université de Toulouse dans l'effacement du catharisme', CaF 20 (1985), 257–76; and P. Nardi, 'Relations with Authority', in *A History of the University in Europe*, ed. H. de Ridder-Symoens (Cambridge, 1992–), I, 89, 94.

[20] On the dialogue form in the Middle Ages, see P. von Moos, 'Literatur und bildungsgeschichtliche Aspekte der Dialogform im lateinischen Mittelalter. Der

of Paris and Toulouse, a dialectic as practised by mendicant *litterati* was not
the paradigm copied at Saint-Sernin. The Lauragais interrogations were only
spoken dialogues in so much as they involved someone asking questions and
someone giving answers, and though this resemblance is important, especially the stylization of the quizzing tempo and the resulting answers, the
ability to question the questioner did not really exist.

Now, although the twenty-first canon of the Fourth Lateran Council called
upon Christians to truthfully confess all their sins once a year to a priest,
alone and not in public, it would be wrong to see the early confessional and
the early inquisition as possessing so close an affinity that medieval men and
women might confuse the two procedures or imagine them to be one and the
same thing.[21] Certainly, all confessions were meant to be uttered, to be heard,
to be the result of questions asked and answers given, yet the very act of
immediately recording testimonies makes the friar-inquisitor different from
the priest-confessor – though, it has to be admitted, an early itinerant friar-
inquisitor in the Lauragais such as the Dominican Guilhem Arnaut did not
always bother to record the testimonies he heard.[22] In any case, and this is
perhaps more crucial, confessing to a friar-inquisitor, or even to a friar-
enquêteur of Louis IX or Alphonse de Poiters, was probably more of a
common experience for someone living in the Lauragais in the middle of
the thirteenth century than confession to a priest which, since the council of
Toulouse in 1229, was meant to be three times a year (Easter, Pentecost, and
Christmas).[23] Still, the great inquisition of Bernart de Caux and Joan de Sant-

Dialogus Ratii des Eberhard von Ypern zwischen theologischer *Disputatio* und
Scholaren-Komödie', in *Tradition und Wertung: Festschrift für Franz Brunhölzl zum
65. Geburtstag*, ed. G. Bernt, F. Rädle and G. Silagi (Sigmaringen, 1989), pp. 165–209,
and his 'Rhetorik, Dialektik und *civilis scientia* im Hochmittelalter', in *Dialektik und
Rhetorik im früheren und hohen Mittelalter: Rezeption, Überlieferung und gesellschaftliche
Wirkung antiker Gelehrsamkeit vornehmlich im 9. und 12. Jahrhundert*, ed. J. Fried
(Munich, 1997), pp. 133–56.

[21] *COD*, p. 245. On confession, see M. Mansfield, *The Humiliation of Sinners: Public
Penance in Thirteenth-Century France* (Ithaca, 1995), pp. 66–8, and esp. pp. 76–7 for her
word of warning about confusing the early confessional and the early inquisition;
A. Murray, 'Confession as an Historical Source in the Thirteenth Century', in *The
Writing of History in the Middle Ages: Essays Presented to Richard William Southern*, ed.
R. H. C. Davis and J. M. Wallace-Hadrill (Oxford, 1981), pp. 275–322; A. Murray,
'Confession before 1215', *Transactions of the Royal Historical Society* 6th s. 3 (1993), 51–
81; and Bernstein, 'Teaching'.

[22] According to na Baretges in a testimony given to Bernart de Caux on Thursday,
16 February 1245, in Doat 22, fol. 43v: 'Requisita si scivit quando frater W. Arnaldi et
socius ejus venerunt apud Castrum Sarracenum pro inquisitione (. . .) Dixit tamen
quod confessio sua non fuit scripta, quia inquisitores noluerunt scribere confessionem ejus' ('Asked whether she knew when friar Guilhem Arnaut and his fellow
friar came to Castelsarrasin to do an inquisition (. . .) She said instead that her
confession had not been written, because the inquisitors did not want to').

[23] The same caution should also be extended to confession and inquisition manuals –
in that the techniques recommended for an inquisitor should never be read into the
role of a confessor. Cf. A. Cazenave, 'Aveu et contrition: Manuels de confesseurs et

Peire was something of an experiment in which the practice of confession, in and of itself, as the only form of *penitentia* (penance) necessary to be a Christian, was tried and tested.

In the middle of the thirteenth century, as God the Judge finally became Christ the Saviour, as he truly became more 'human' and his servants more 'divine', as all sorts of men and women undertook the *imitatio Christi*, as professing religion (and so heresy) became an act more defined by the law than by liturgy, as confessing became one of the most important ways of realizing what it meant to be a Christian, men like Bernart de Caux and Joan de Sant-Peire could trust themselves, and be trusted by others, to judge innocence and guilt.[24] The judicial ordeal expected no individual confession, no testimonial about a life lived over the years, no scribal record for reading and reflection.[25] The ordeal asked only one question, that being whether an accused person was guilty or innocent, and it was a query put to God. The friar-inquisitors, through carefully formulating questions, all of which were clearly earth-bound rather than heaven-sent, allowed the causes of heresy to be just as carefully formulated. The right questions allowed the inquisitors to accumulate answers about individual lives, to stockpile evidence about past deeds, and, more importantly, it allowed them to discover the truth without having to rely upon heartfelt insight or wondrous miracles.[26]

Eighty years after the great Lauragais inquisition, the Dominican Bernard Gui in his *Practica inquisitionis heretice pravitatis* – a long inquisitorial manual full of learned advice and a surprisingly sly wit – while repeating the questions used by Bernart de Caux and Joan de Sant-Peire, focussed his interrogatory method much more upon what a suspected heretic thought and not upon what he or she might have done. Significantly, while *heresis* only

interrogatoires d'Inquisition en Languedoc et en Catalogne', in *La piété populaire au Moyen Age: Actes du 99e Congrès national des sociétés savantes, Besançon, 1974, Philologie et histoire jusqu'à 1610* 1 (Paris, 1977), pp. 333–49. The decree of the Council of Toulouse (1229), is in Mansi, XXIIII, 197.

[24] On *imitatio Christi* (imitation of Christ), see G. Constable, *Three Studies in Medieval Religious and Social Thought: The Interpretation of Mary, The Ideal of the Imitation of Christ, The Orders of Society* (Cambridge, 1995), pp. 143–248. On professing religion, see J. Van Engen, 'Professing Religion: From Liturgy to Law', *Viator* 29 (1998), 323–43.

[25] Cf. J. Baldwin, 'From the Ordeal to Confession: In Search of Lay Religion in Early Thirteenth Century France', in *Handling Sin: Confession in the Middle Ages*, York Studies in Medieval Theology 2, ed. P. Biller and A. J. Minnis (York, 1998), pp. 191–209.

[26] Cf. L. A. Smoller's analysis of questions and investigative procedures in her 'Defining Boundaries of the Natural in Fifteenth-Century Brittany: The Inquest into the Miracles of Saint Vincent Ferrer (d. 1419)', *Viator* 28 (1997), 333–59. Also, on the asking of questions in other cultures, particularly in a legal context, see E. Lunbeck, *The Psychiatric Persuasion: Knowledge, Gender, and Power in Modern America* (Princeton NJ, 1994), esp. pp. 133–44; R. French, *The Golden Yoke: The Legal Cosmology of Buddhist Tibet* (Ithaca, 1995); and J. D. Spence, *Treason by the Book* (New York, 2001).

meant the good men and the good women to Bernart de Caux and Joan de Sant-Peire, the word meant a great deal more to Bernard Gui when he was inquisitor in Toulouse from 1307 to 1324. The *boni homines* as 'Manichaeans' were now one of five major heretical sects: the Waldensians, the Béguins, the pseudo-apostles, and 'Jews who have been converted to the faith of Christ and return to the vomit of Judaism'.[27] These various heresies demanded equally various investigative techniques, because as 'different and specific medicines exist for particular diseases, so neither is the same method of questioning, investigation, and examination to be employed for all heretics'.[28] Bernard Gui also felt it expedient to preface his Manichee-detecting questions with a description of the way of life, the customs, and the behaviour of the dualists.[29] Bernart de Caux and Joan de Sant-Peire never implied in the *Processus inquisitionis* or in their great inquisition that one needed to undertake secondary reading in heresy in order to know what to look for, in order to understand a clue, in the way that Bernard Gui did.

The questions at Saint-Sernin appear to be conspicuously unconcerned with theories, histories, and genealogies about the origins of the heresy of the good men and the good women. No one ever asked at Saint-Sernin, and no one ever confessed, about Manicheans, Bogomils, acquaintances from the Balkans, or transient Byzantine heretical holy men drifting into the Lauragais (and then out of it).[30] Bernart de Caux and Joan de Sant-Peire were certainly

---

[27] Gui, *P*, p. 237: . . . conversorum ex Judeis ad fidem Christi qui redeunt ad vomitum Judaysmi . . .'.

[28] Wakefield and Evans, p. 378; Gui, *P*, 236–7: 'pocius singulorum diverse sunt et singule medicine, sic nec ad omnes hereticos diversarum sectarum idem modus interrogandi, inquirendi et examinandi est servandus'.

[29] Gui, *P*, esp. pp. 237–9 ('De erroribus Manicheorum moderni temporis') and 239–41 ('De modo et ritu vivendi ipsorum Manicheorum'). On Bernard Gui's methods as an inquisitor, see Pales-Gobillard, 'Gui Inquisiteur'; Paul, 'Mentalité'; Given, 'Inquisitor at Work', pp. 207–32; and Given, *Inquisition*, pp. 44–51.

[30] Good, as well as nuanced, summaries of the evidence (and scholarship) for missionary and doctrinal connections between the *bons omes* and the Bogomils, are G. Rottenwöhrer, *Der Katharismus*, 4 vols. (Bad Honnef, 1982–93), III: *Die Herkunft der Katharer nach Theologie und Geschichte*, 74–114, 570–1; Fichtenau, pp. 70–126; B. Hamilton, 'Wisdom from the East: the Reception by the Cathars of Eastern Dualist Texts', in *Heresy and Literacy*, pp. 38–60; and Lambert, *Cathars*, pp. 29–59; J. and B. Hamilton's *Christian Dualist Heresies in the Byzantine World c. 650–c. 1450* (Manchester, 1998) is a remarkable collection of translated sources on dualism and has a useful 'Historical Introduction', pp. 1–55; and M. Barber, *The Cathars: Dualist Heretics in Languedoc in the High Middle Ages* (Harlow, 2000), 6–33. A visit by the supposed Bogomil bishop of Constantinople, *papa* Nicetas, to Saint-Félix-de-Caraman in the Lauragais happened in 1167. The document that records Nicetas' journey is lost and only exists as an appendix to Guillaume Besse's *Histoire des ducs, marquis et comtes de Narbonne, autrement appellez Princes des Goths, Ducs de Septimanie, et Marquis de Gothie. Dedié à Monseigneur l'Archevesque Duc de Narbonne* (Paris, 1660), pp. 483–6. This document, given to Besse by 'M. Caseneuue, Prebendier au Chapitre de l'Eglisle de Sainct Estienne de Tolose, en l'an 1652' (p. 483), is probably (at best) a mid-thirteenth century forgery by some *bons omes* or

aware of their heresiology, that should never be doubted, if for no other reason than that the *studium* at Toulouse was certainly teaching it, while Dominicans, Franciscans, priests, monks, and bishops, were certainly preaching it.[31] Obviously, the questions about belief asked at the end of an

crezens (and which undoubtedly ended up surviving in an inquisitorial archive) rather than a seventeenth-century forgery. B. Hamilton, 'The Cathar Council of S. Félix Reconsidered', *AFP* 48 (1978), 23–53, is generally assumed to have proven the validity of Besse's appendix – I remain, despite the subtlety of Hamilton's argument, unconvinced. In support of Hamilton, e.g., P. Jimenez, 'Relire la Charte de Niquinta – 1) Origine et problématique de la Charte', *Heresis* 22 (1994), 1–26, and 'Relire la Charte de Niquinta – 2) Sens et portée de la Charte', *Heresis* 23 (1994), 1–28; Lambert, *Cathars*, pp. 45–59. Cf. Y. Dossat, 'À propos du concile cathare de Saint-Félix: les Milingues', *CaF* 3 (1968), 201–4, where it is argued that Besse's document was a seventeenth-century forgery (and probably forged by Besse). It has also been argued that Bogomil dualism was secretly carried back by crusaders returning from twelfth-century *Outremer*. On such heretical transmissions from the Levant, see C. Thouzellier 'Hérésie et croisade au XIIe siècle', *RHE* 49 (1954), 855–72, who was the first to strongly suggest the importation of dualist beliefs by returning crusaders. Along similar lines to Thouzellier, Karl Heisig, 'Ein gnostische Sekte im abendländischen Mittelalter', *Zeitschrift für Religions und Geistesgeschichte* 16 (1964), 271–4, suggested that crusaders brought ancient Gnostic practices back from the East to the Rhineland.

[31] E.g. Toulouse 609, fol. 18v, where Raimon de Quiders from Mas-Saintes-Puelles, testified, '. . . sed non audivit eos dicentes errores (. . .) sed audivit clericos exprimentes errores quos heretici dicent' ('. . . but he did not hear them pronouncing errors (. . .) Instead, he heard priests reporting the errors said by the heretics'). Or, Toulouse 609, fol. 235v, where Izarn Boquer of Lavaur noted that he knew about the heretical idea that God did not make visible things because the bishop of Toulouse preached it. Indeed, swearing that one knew what the heretics taught only because a priest, a mendicant, or the bishop of Toulouse, had described them was sometimes a falsehood behind which a *crezen* hoped to hide. Guilhem de Castilho, a knight from Gardouch attempted this in his first testimony on Monday, 8 May 1245, Toulouse 609, fol. 110r – he was, however, called back the next day and, though he said his memory was a bit hazy, he now recalled having heard some heretical errors when the good man Guilhem de Solier give a sermon twenty-five years earlier in a house before an audience of twenty people. Two years after the Lauragais inquisition, Bernart de Caux and Joan de Sant-Peire were again at Saint-Sernin from Thursday, 22 August to Tuesday, 10 December 1247, and during this time they heard testimonies from four Franciscans about what they had overheard a certain Peire Garcias say about the dualist cosmology of the *boni homines*. The two friar-inquisitors did not use the *formula interrogatorii* of their great inquisition, or of their manual, with the four Franciscans. Indeed, the friar-inquisitors seem to have asked no methodical questions of the Friars Minor at all, except for some points of clarification. These testimonies also reveal that Bernart de Caux and Joan de Sant-Peire could easily have asked very different questions in their Lauragais interrogations, easily concentrating on ideas rather than habits. The two Dominicans during their great inquisition heard nothing that even came close to what the four Franciscans told them about the heretical dualist thoughts of Peire Garcias. Douais edited all the testimonies concerning Peire Garcias – originally in Doat 22, fols. 89–106 – in his *Documents*, II, 90–114. Cf. Lansing, *Power and Purity*, pp. 87–8, where these testimonies are used too easily, too unreflectively, and so inappropriately, to explain what an early thirteenth century Italian heretic might have thought.

interrogation were ideas that any thirteenth-century intellectual knew to be dualistic and so heretical, like the Devil making the world or the Host not being the body of Christ but, much more important than this, was the fact that all of the questions of Bernart de Caux and Joan de Sant-Peire, especially when taken together, resonate with a rigorous and powerful anti-dualism.[32] It was this inescapably rigid aspect of the Saint-Sernin questions – a quality that also permeated the canons of the Fourth Lateran Council and something reiterated in all the lesser ecclesiastical councils of Languedoc – that tied them to the rigidly inescapable heresiology of the thirteenth century that saw the potential for dualism everywhere and in everything.

A related heresiological and investigative problem, and one easily ignored, is that an interrogation at Saint-Sernin may have opened with a reference to the Waldensians but the questions, and the testimonies, were actually rather uninterested in the followers of Vaudès. There was no separate set of questions for the Waldensians, as Bernard Gui listed in his *Practica*, and what was asked at Saint-Sernin quite explicitly focused on 'the good men who are called heretics', *boni homines qui vocantur heretici*, as Artau d'En Artigad from Avignonet succinctly worded it in his testimony on Monday, 6 November 1245.[33] The Waldensians, though mentioned in a handful of testimonies and understood to be heretical, functioned in the Saint-Sernin questions, for the friar-inquisitors and those being interrogated, as a confessional aid for specifying behaviour, beliefs, memories, and relationships only dealing with the good men and good women.[34]

---

[32] See the observations about anti-dualism and Dominican learning in J. Coleman, *Ancient and Medieval Memories: Studies in the Reconstruction of the Past* (Cambridge, 1992), pp. 422–4.

[33] Toulouse 609, fol. 135r. The *Processus inquisitionis* – Tardif, *Processus*, p. 672 – had these few extra questions about whether a person 'was present at a Waldensian Lord's Supper, had confessed sins to them, had accepted penance or learned anything from them'. In Toulouse 609 no questions were ever asked on these issues and no testimony ever mentioned them.

[34] A remarkable (and rare) confession about the Waldensians was that of the elderly Michel Verger, Toulouse 609, fol. 136r, who recollected on Friday, 15 December 1245, for Bernart de Caux, Arnaut Auriol, the prior of Saint-Sernin, and Guassias, priest of Roquecézière, that in 1221 at Avignonet, 'Valdenses persequebantur dictos hereticos, et multociens fecit [ipse testis] helemosinam dictis Valdensibus, quando querebant hostiatim amore dei; et quia ecclesia sustinebat tunc dictos Valdenses, et erant cum clericis in ipsa ecclesia cantantes et legentes, credebat eos esse bonos homines' ('the Waldensians persecuted the said heretics, and many a time [he the witness] gave alms to the said Waldensians, when they were begging door to door for the love of God, and since at that time the church was supporting the said Waldensians, and they were with the clergy in the church itself singing and reading, he thought they were good men'). Interestingly, Puylaurens, in his *Chronique*, p. 24, composed less than a decade after the inquisition at Saint-Sernin, lamented that ignorant Lauragais priests had once allowed the Waldensians of Lyon to publicly preach against the 'Manichaeans'. On Michel Verger, see Mundy, *Repression*, p. 8, and Pegg, *Corruption*, pp. 84 and 96. On the Waldensians, see Thouzellier, *Catharisme*; the collected essays in Biller, *Waldenses*; and Audisio, *Dissent*, pp. 1–39.

Bernart de Caux and Joan de Sant-Peire may have focused on habits, actions, and relations, rather than ideas, thoughts, and philosophies, but they never assumed that one or the other existed, or could exist, in isolation. This anti-dualistic formula for truth, where thoughts and habits, meanings and things, bodies and souls, were understood to be in agreement with each other was, in a very real sense, rehearsed, verified, and entrenched, through the questions used at Saint-Sernin. Truth, 'the conformity of meaning with things', was how the Dominican Thomas Aquinas, thinking and writing in the middle years of the thirteenth century, characterized this slippery prize his fellow friars were attempting to grasp as inquisitors.[35] As such, the questions used by Bernart de Caux and Joan de Sant-Peire, though occasion-ally making for some dull and repetitive reading in Toulouse 609, reveal the forensic model that the two friar-inquisitors not only had about what made individuals into heretics and believers in heretics, but also what actually made them men and women. Instead of a person existing as a separate entity before coming into contact with other people, a man or a woman to the friar-inquisitors only existed as an individual through the relationships they had, or were anticipated to have, with other people.

The inquisition at Saint-Sernin, by necessity, if it were to have any purpose at all, could not simply question a village here and a hamlet there, as Bernard Gui or Jacques Fournier would later do, it had to question all *castra* within a specified area, all men and women, no exceptions, young or old, pregnant or leprous, noble or servile, 'even of those who insist they know nothing about other people and have committed no crime', because not to do so would be to think of individuals and their communities as having the ability to separate themselves from the context, from the complicity, of others.[36] On the contrary, what made individual men and women, what revealed the thousands of lives they had lived and would go on to live, were their innumerable relationships with other men and women. Further, this schema had a surprisingly precise sense of the distances that relationships classified as heretical or not could travel, could survive before breaking down. Geographically speaking, the world catalogued at Saint-Sernin was rarely larger than that travelled from Toulouse in, say, two or three days; sometimes longer journeys were mentioned but the questions at Saint-Sernin, and the testimonies recorded in manuscript 609, never focussed upon these trips or places. This was not a statement about how localized the horizons of men and women in the Lauragais were, these people did move

---

[35] Thomas Aquinas, *Summa contra Gentiles* i.59: 'Cum enim veritas intellectus sit adaequatio intellectus et rei, secundum quod intellectus dicit esse quos est vel non esse quod non est . . .'. E. Serene, 'Demonstrative Science', in *Cambridge History of Later Medieval Philosophy*, p. 504, translates this passage about truth as '. . . the conformity of the understanding with reality, such that the understanding says that what is the case is so, and that what is not is not'. See also Coleman, *Ancient and Medieval Memories*, pp. 422–64.

[36] Tardif, *Processus*, p. 673.

around, quite a lot in fact, not only in the Lauragais but out of it.[37] Instead, it was an empirical observation by Bernart de Caux and Jean de Sant-Peire about how far their notion of relationships in the past, the present, and the future could physically go before they dissipated, before they became difficult to trace, and so something to be investigated by a very different set of questions.

Another aspect of the investigative model used at Saint-Sernin, and something that relates specifically to why some people remembered things from well in their past, is that though the friar-inquisitors' definition of individuality depended upon perceived continuities of relations through time, there was no temporal limit placed upon the repetition of habits classified as heretical. A relationship with a heretic from, say, 1205, even if it never happened again, could still be the cause of something yet to occur. No one could ever divorce him or herself from the old habits and the anticipated relationships that made them – even in death, as the inquisition sought out the graves of good men, good women, and their sympathizers.[38] No relationship, action, or thought, could ever be contingent or accidental. There could be no separation of cause and effect in the confessed narrative of an individual life. It was a vision where no one received the benefit of a doubt and where women, for instance, were not seen as any more susceptible to heresy than men. The universe of Saint-Sernin, at least for those years of questioning, was decidedly deterministic. Coincidence, and it occurs in many testimonies, was the only way of breaking the friar-inquisitors' deductive method.[39] As observers, readers, listeners, interrogators, and finally judges, everything was implicated in everything else to Bernart de Caux and Joan de Saint-Peire.

In the questions asked at Saint-Sernin were the very principles of analysis by which the past, present, and the future of heresy in the Lauragais were formulated. These questions, by demanding a particular style of truth be understood even by those who wished to resist it, through making individuals think about certain continuities in their lives, forever changed the way in which thousands of men and women saw, felt, and understood not only heresy in their lives but also their very existence in the world. Questions, indeed, even questions about questions, have their historical meanings as much as anything else, and though this basic point is all too often ignored, to

---

[37] Pegg, *Corruption*, esp. pp. 42–3 and 118–19.

[38] Tardif, *Processus*, p. 677. On the friar-inquisitors and *bayles* systematically seeking out the graves of heretics for burning, see Guilhem Pelhisson, *Chronique (1229–1244) suivie du récit des troubles d'Albi (1234)*, ed. and trans. J. Duvernoy, Sources d'histoire médiévale 25 (Paris, 1994) pp. 56–7. On the burial of heretics, see W. Wakefield, 'Burial of Heretics in the Middle Ages', *Heresis* 5 (1985), 29–32, and Pegg, *Corruption*, esp. pp. 110–11.

[39] E.g. the use of coincidence as an attempt to demonstrate innocence was used by Peire Alaman of Mas-Saintes-Puelles, Toulouse 609, fol. 13r, and Bernart de Quiders, the lord of Mas-Saintes-Puelles, Toulouse 609, fol. 18r. These two testimonies are discussed in Pegg, *Corruption*, pp. 124–5.

do so in the case of the great inquisition of Bernart de Caux and Joan de Sant-Peire would render the thousands of testimonies they heard, transcribed, and which survive in manuscript 609, as nothing more than confession after confession of incoherent memories and line after line of essentially meaningless answers.

Why no Food?
Waldensian Followers in Bernard Gui's
Practica inquisitionis and *culpe*

Peter Biller

Reading Bernard Gui's sentences[1] on followers of the Cathars can make us feel hungry. There is Jeanne of Sainte-Foy of Toulouse preparing a fish-pie,[2] Sybil Bernard of Bouillac using bread, water, cabbage and herbs to prepare a sauce,[3] Dominic Durand carrying a dish of rice and almonds,[4] and Bernarda of Toulouse taking a piece of salmon to be prepared and put into bread.[5] And thirsty. Gerald of Artigues received the Cathars Peter and James Autier in his house, but his wine was not good enough, and so Gerald 'went out looking for better and clearer wine than he had in the house'.[6]

Through another of Gui's sentences we read a physical detail about a Waldensian preacher called Christian, that he was 'a big and fat man'.[7] If we

---

[1] 'Sentences': strictly speaking, many of these were *culpe*; see the discussion below. On Gui, see *SOPMA* I, pp. 205–26, and IV, pp. 50–1; CaF 16 (1981); B. Guenée, *Between Church and State: The Lives of Four French Prelates in the Late Middle Ages*, trans. A. Goldhammer (Chicago and London, 1991), pp. 37–70; and A.-M. Lamarrigue, *Bernard Gui (1261–1331): un historien et sa méthode*, Études d'Histoire Médiévale 5 (Paris and Geneva, 2000). See further on Gui as a writer n. 34 below.

On the *Liber sententiarum* see A. Pales-Gobilliard, 'Pénalités inquisitoriales au XIVᵉ siècle', *Crises et réformes dans l'Église de la réforme Grégorienne à la préréforme* (Paris, 1991), pp. 143–54, and Given, *Inquisition*, chs.1 and 3. Pales-Gobilliard has finished preparing her re-edition, which is to appear as *Le livre des sentences de l'inquisiteur Bernard Gui, 1308–1323*, Collection Sources d'Histoire Mdivale 30. This study has been prepared using Limborch's 1692 edition, which follows the spelling of the manuscript and is a remarkably accurate transcription. It should be noted that Limborch transposed the position of the three indexes or tables (names of places, list of sermons, index of persons under places, which were at the beginning of the manuscript (BL MS Add. 4697, fols. 7ra–10r) to the end of his edition (Gui, *Ls*, pp. 395–415)); cf. Given, *Inquisition*, p. 35.

[2] Gui, *Ls*, p. 69, 'pastillum de piscibus'. Jeanne is mentioned by Brenon, *Femmes cathares*, p. 335.

[3] Gui, *Ls*, p. 67.

[4] Gui, *Ls*, p. 56.

[5] Gui, *Ls*, p. 192.

[6] Gui, *Ls*, p. 59, 'ipse portavit eis panem et vinum, et quesivit pro eis melius et clarius vinum quam esset illud quod habebat in hospicio suo'. Gerald is mentioned by Given, *Inquisition*, p. 56.

[7] Gui, *Ls*, pp. 377–8, 'hominem magnum et pinguem'. Christian is discussed further in

think he must have needed a lot of feeding, this thought reminds us that although we get extravagant details about the menus of the Cathar Good Men, we never get to know the menus of fat Christian's or other Waldensians' meals. The reason is obvious. Cathar Good Men were distinguished among other things by what they refused to eat, while the Waldensians were not. See here the crisp contrast in Gui's *Practica*:[8]

De modo et ritu vivendi ipsorum Manicheorum	*De modo vivendi Valdensium*
Item, numquam comedunt carnes nec etiam tangunt eas, nec caseum nec ova . . .	Item, Valdenses communiter comedunt et bibunt cibos communes.
On the way and rite of living of these Manichees	*On the way of living of the Waldensians*
Item, they never eat meats nor even touch them, nor cheese, nor eggs . . .	Item, the Waldensians generally eat and drink ordinary foods.

Consequently people who were questioned by inquisitors about Cathars were asked about food, while those questioned about Waldensians were not.
    While there is no puzzle here, there is a salutary reminder. Modern

my 'Fat Christian and Old Peter: Ideals and Compromises among the Medieval Waldensians', in *Pragmatic Utopias: Ideals and Communities, 1200–1630*, ed. R. Horrox and S. Rees Jones (Cambridge, 2001), pp. 174–87.

[8] Gui, *P* V.i.2 and V.ii.5, pp. 240 and 248; Gui, *M*, pp. 18 and 50; Wakefield and Evans, pp. 381 and 392. On the *Practica*, see Dondaine, 'Manuel', pp. 115–17, and Pales-Gobilliard, 'Gui Inquisiteur', pp. 253–64. Five medieval manuscripts of the *Practica* are listed in *SOPMA* I, 222, together with a copy in two seventeenth-century manuscripts (D29–30). These are described more fully by Michel Mollat in Gui, *M*, pp. xxv–xxix. Two further medieval manuscripts are listed in *SOPMA* IV, 51, and to these should be added Stadtbibliothek Soest, MS 14b, fols. 101vb–104vb; see B. Michael, *Die mittelalterlichen Handschriften der Wissenschaftlichen Stadtbibliothek Soest* (Wiesbaden, 1990), pp. 102–6, describing the manuscript (of *c*. 1410–15), from west Germany, possibly Cologne, containing the introduction and ch. 5 of the fifth part of the *Practica*. Twenty-nine formulae from the *Practica* were copied into a Bohemian inquisitor's handbook of *c*. 1330 contained in Wolfenbüttel, MS Helmstedt 331, discovered by Patschovsky and edited by him in *Inquisition in Böhmen* – see the list in p. 9 n. 28.
    The only complete edition is that by Canon Célestin Douais (Gui, *P*), a transcription of Toulouse, Bibliothèque municipale, MS 387, made with occasional reference to Toulouse, Bibliothèque municipale, MS 388. Though equipped with an index, this edition has virtually no apparatus.
    The fifth part of the *Practica* was edited by Mollat, 'd'après les meilleurs manuscrits' (Gui, *M*), with a parallel French translation. Mollat identified many of Gui's borrowings from some earlier sources, notably Stephen of Bourbon's *Tractatus de variis materiis predicabilibus*, and the *De inquisitione hereticorum* attributed to David of Augsburg; see Mollat's account of the sources, Gui, *M*, pp. xviii–xxv. Mollat did not identify all of Gui's borrowings from these sources, and he only made slight inroads into the large task of identifying sources and parallels in Gui's *culpe* and sentences.
    The fifth part, in Mollat's edition, was translated into English (Wakefield and Evans, pp. 375–445), with much useful additional annotation (pp. 754–67).

scholars analyse a world of inquisitors receiving set answers to set questions, a world closed to the intrusion of testimony about the real world. If we see splendidly detailed evidence about the material world as far removed from this closed world, we need to think again. In the real past both Cathars and Waldensians ate food, but what survives in the texts – on the one hand a blank with regard to the food that kept the fat Waldensian going, and on the other hand a rich feast of Cathar food – has been brought about by the presence or absence of inquisitor's questions about food. This introduces my theme, Waldensian followers as they were seen through Bernard Gui's eyes and texts. In practice this means Waldensian followers on the one hand in what remains from Bernard's inquisition of them, and on the other hand in Bernard's description of them in the inquisitor's manual he wrote, the *Practica inquisitionis*.

Questions to Waldensian Believers

Let us first adjust our view to Bernard's, by recapitulating the general principles which he enunciated in the fourth part of the *Practica*, which is a treatise on the office of inquisition.[9] The aim of inquisition is the destruction of heresy. The destruction of heresy is brought about through the destruction of heretics. This is only achieved through the true conversion of heretics or their physical burning. This applies to both full heretics, 'perfect' heretics, and those non-full ('imperfect') heretics who share the faith of the 'perfect' heretics but not the rites and observances of their form of life, the 'believers'.[10]

Assessing who the latter are is an urgent practical matter, something which occupied the largest part of an inquisitor's activity, and Bernard's treatise, which was an adaptation of an earlier treatise on the same theme, went to

---

[9] Here Gui adapts a previous treatise, the *De auctoritate et forma inquisitionis*, written between 1280 and 1288–92 (Mollat, *Manuel*, pp. xvii–xviii, and Dondaine, 'Manuel', 113–17). This section is studied in Paul, 'Mentalité'.

[10] Gui, *P* IV.iii.2, p. 218: 'Sciendum est itaque quod hereticorum quidam dicuntur heretici "perfecti", quidam vero "imperfecti". Dicuntur autem "perfecti" heretici illi qui fidem et vitam hereticorum professi sunt secundum ritum suum eamque tenent seu servant et aliis dogmatizant; "imperfecti" autem heretici dicuntur illi qui fidem hereticorum quidem habent, set vitam ipsorum quantum ad ritus et observantias eorumdem non servant; et isti proprie "credentes" hereticorum appellantur et sic heretici judicantur.' ('It is therefore necessary to know that some heretics are called "perfect", some instead "non-perfect". Called "perfect" heretics are those who have professed the faith and way of life of the heretics according to their rite, and hold and observe ⟨this way of life⟩ and teach ⟨this faith⟩ to others. Called "non-perfect" heretics are those who do indeed have the faith of the heretics, but – as far as rites and observances are concerned – do not follow their way of life. These last are properly termed "believers" of heretics, and thus are judged to be heretics.')

Henceforth 'believer' is released from its quotation marks, while I continue to use it to mean 'believer', as defined by inquisitors.

town on this. What acts or deeds can be used, asks Bernard's treatise, to
assess someone as a believer? The treatise distinguishes between acts which
are certain signs and those which are probable signs, which, even if they are
on their own not proving signs, nevertheless if found together at the same
time constitute very strong proof.[11] Bernard's treatise includes extracts from
previous legal consultations, and most prominent here is the subtle discussion in the consultation of Guy Foulques.[12] The heart of man is high and
inscrutable, *altum et inscrutabile*, wrote Guy. There is a clear preference for
actus et opera, actions, external signs: not, clearly, because these authors
ignored the human heart, but because such signs were more accessible and
measurable. There was discussion of what signs counted. Suppose someone
visits, a heretic, provides gift or guidance, or does similar things in which
nothing is shown to have been expressed about heretical rite? I do not believe
these things mean that a person should be regarded as a believer, wrote Guy
Foulques, although some have written the contrary. All these things can
happen through ordinary affection, intercession of friends or for money.
Signs should be certain, and the inquisitor should not take as proofs those
signs which can be explained otherwise. The fact of hearing a heretic's
sermon once and not returning to hear a sermon again is not a sign. Bernard's
treatise concludes with enumeration of the qualities required of the good
inquisitor, fervour, constancy, and alertness when dealing with things that
are in doubt. He should not easily believe everything that is plausible, for it is
not the case that everything that is plausible is true, and he should not
obstinately disbelieve what is implausible, because often something that
seemed implausible has turned out to be true.[13]

There is an impressive tradition of thought and reflectiveness here. It has
its apparent counterpart in those things which are so distinctive in the fifth
part of Bernard's *Practica*, and which constitute in their systematicness such a
decisive step forward from previous inquisitors' manuals.[14] There each sect in
turn is given a careful description which embraces its history, its cult, its

---

[11] Gui, *P* IV.iii.2, p. 222: 'Est autem sciendum quod culpe seu actus vel opera ex quibus
possunt judicari talia facientes esse credentes hereticorum dupliciter distinguen-
dum, quia hujusmodi culpe quedam sunt certe et vehementer cogentes, quedam
autem sunt probabiles, que, et⟨si⟩ singule non probent, tamen simul collecte faciunt
validissimum argumentum.' ('It is therefore necessary to know that one should
distinguish in two ways the offences, acts or deeds the perpetrators of which are
thereby adjudged to be "believers" of heretics, for among these offences some are
sure and strongly compelling, some others are possible. And even if these latter are
not individually compelling, taken all together they form very powerful evidence.')
[12] Gui, *P* IV.iii.2, pp. 223–4, ultimately copying Gui Foulques [Clement IV], *Consultatio*,
qu. 9, *De credentibus hæreticorum*, ed. C. Carena, *Tractatus de officio sanctissimae
inquisitionis et modo procedendi in causis fidei . . . his accesserunt quindecim quaestiones
ad Inquisitores D. Guidonis Fulcodii* (Cremona, 1681), pp. 459–60.
[13] Gui, *P* IV.iii.2, p. 233, 'sit vigilans inter dubia, ut non facile omne verisimile credat,
quia non omne tale semper est verum; nec oppositum pertinaciter discredat, quia
sepe invenitur esse verum quod non verisimile videatur'.
[14] Dondaine, 'Manuel', p. 117.

distinctive way of life and its beliefs, and each of the descriptions of
individual sects is equipped, therefore, with a highly developed *special* list
of questions to be put to the believers of the particular group in question,
with continuing emphasis on external actions as signs. In his introduction
Gui discriminated further, envisaging the general application of the interrogatory that was appropriate to a sect, and then the further moulding of this
interrogatory to this or that individual. Using a medical analogy (that there is
not one medicine for all diseases but rather individual diseases with their
individual medicines), he wrote that, similarly, one should not follow a single
mode of interrogating, questioning and examining all the heretics of various
sects, 'but rather one should employ an individual and particular mode for
each person, in most cases' ('set ad singulos, ut in pluribus, singularis et
proprius est habendus').[15] I said 'apparent counterpart': is the intellectual
finesse, which is held up as a model in the treatise on the office of inquisition,
also to be found in the construction of these question-lists, and in Bernard's
and his assistants' use of these question-lists when interrogating people?

Let us look at Bernard's section on the Waldensians in the fifth part of the
Practica, where eight descriptive and more literary chapters (discussed in
section 2 below) conclude with a ninth chapter which is an inquisitor's form:
a question-list for believers of the Waldensians. This begins with a question
about whether the person under interrogation had seen them, and, if so,
when, where and with whom, and who the Waldensians were, that is to say,
what their names were. It continues with a question about whether the
person had heard them, and goes on to such questions as eating at the same
table, praying with them according to their rite, confessing sins to them and
receiving penance and absolution, giving them anything or receiving anything from them, acting as their guides, and knowing others who believed
them and gave them lodging. It is a tick-list of the signs that a person was a
Waldensian believer, with some preference for accessible and measurable
external actions, and no provision for enquiry about inner matters.

There is one immediate problem when we turn to the use of such a
question-list. Let us recall the sequence of documents produced by inquisitors, numbering them. When acting as inquisitors, Bernard and his assistants
will have had such a question-list [1] in their hands or heads, using its
questions when interrogating suspects.[16]

At this time they produced another text, a record of the question and
answer session [2]. This was in Latin. It will have given only abbreviated
versions of the questions, and much of the time it will have simply left them
to be inferred from the reply. So, for example, a witness was asked when she
first saw the Waldensians, and she replied that she first saw them two years
ago. Here the written record will only show the reply. This reply – 'She said

---

[15] Gui, *P* V, p. 237; Gui, *M*, p. 8; Wakefield and Evans, p. 378.
[16] In my discussion of inquisitions which have left traces in the *Liber sententiarum*, I do
not distinguish between Bernard and his assistants and *locum-tenentes*.

that she first saw Waldensians two years ago' – is not preceded in the written record by the question 'She was asked when she first the Waldensians'. The question is omitted in the first instance for the sake of brevity and economy, not for any devious reason.

Then, at a later stage, Bernard and his assistants made from this written record a 'summary and abridged extract concerning *culpe*, in which the essence of the confession is completely dealt with, insofar as it bears upon the guilt (*culpa*) of the person in question' [3].[17] In this last phrase the word *culpa* denotes the overall guilt of a person, but the various guilty acts committed by the one person are *culpe*, plural. In Gui's *Practica* nomenclature slides, with 'brevis extractio culparum' ('brief extract of ⟨items⟩ of guilt') becoming *culpa*, a word which now comes to denote the text itself.[18]

This *culpa*, the text containing the extract, was then used for the consideration of penalties. It was read in the vernacular to the deponent, and it was turned into the second person singular to be read out in public ('You, Agnes, from Toulouse, as it appears in your confession did such and such') as part of the formal act of sentencing [4].

Our problem is that, while Bernard's question-list [1] and many of his *culpe* [3] and *culpe*-cum-sentences [4] survive, text [2] does not.[19] And it is this which would have been most useful to us when asking how the question-list was applied.

Not all is hopeless. We can infer much of text [2], and we can do this with reasonable certainty. This is in part because words remain the same, as we shall see. It is also because we can take a couple of sentences [4] on Waldensian followers which were copied into Bernard's *Liber inquisitionis* and set them beside the earlier record of interrogation [2], which had been carried out not, for once, by Bernard Gui, but by Jacques Fournier. In these we can use a comparison of [2] and [4] as a control. This control suggests that conjecturally reconstructing [2] from [3] and [4] is sound.

What we see, first of all, is a series of texts which vary in their length, detail and individuation. The question-list is short, and constitutes an ideal-type of the mainly external acts of an unnamed follower [1]. A single named follower is then the centre of a rather long text, which contains first a preamble noting persons present, including the deponent, the date and the taking of an oath, and then goes on to include many details and names in the quite long answers of the deponent [2], in answer to questions. While remaining an individual the deponent is then contracted in the *culpa* [3], which omits many

---

[17] Gui, *P* iii.1 (p. 83), 'extractione summaria et compendiosa de culpis, in qua complete tangitur substantia confessionis cujuslibet persone quantum ad culpam illius de qua agitur'. In the same section (p. 84) it is called a 'brief extract' (*brevis extractio*).

[18] Gui, *P* iii.1 (pp. 84–5); in Gui, *Ls*, see e.g. p. 252, for *Culpa relapsi* (*Culpa* of a relapsed person) as the rubric to such a text.

[19] We know from Dossat, *Crises*, p. 40, that a volume once existed which probably contained both such interrogations and sentences, entitled *Processus et sententie contra Valdenses a Bernardo Guidonis*.

of the names and details to which he or she attested, and the sentence [4] in turn may contract the items of the *culpa* to one general charge. From one point of view these are the same text, contracted and expanded, pushed in and pulled out at each stage like a concertina. The ratio between [2] and [4] could be five to two: the record of Jacques Fournier's interrogations of two Waldensian followers is around 10,000 words, while material extracted from this record and reconstituted as a sentence on these two is about 1800 words.[20] The *culpa* [3] of a priest who was a Waldensian follower is over twice the length of his sentence of condemnation [4], which reduced the items to the statement that he had confessed committing things in the sect.[21]

Bernard Gui's *culpe* of Waldensians and sentences on them are very repetitive and formulaic. They suggest that his interrogations of Waldensian followers stuck more to set formulae than his interrogations of Cathars, while both – *culpe* of Waldensians and Cathars and sentences on them – suggest a man who was less inquisitive and more concerned with speed and efficiency than Jacques Fournier. Let us probe deeper with two examples, beginning with an elementary one.

First, Bernard Gui asked both Cathar and Waldensian believers about hearing. 'Did they ever hear them?'[22]

Interrogatoria ad credentes de secta Manicheorum	*Interrogatoria specialia ad illos de secta Valdensium*
si audivit predicationem, et de hiis que dicebant et docebant	si unquam audivit predicationem aut doctrinam seu *admonitiones* aut verba ipsorum

Interrogatory for believers from the sect of the Manichees	*Special interrogatory for those of the sect of the Waldensians*
if he heard preaching, and about those things which they said and taught	if he ever heard their preaching or teaching or admonitions or words

A Cathar believer was asked if he heard *predicatio*, and what the Cathars said and taught, *dicebant et docebant*.[23] While a Waldensian believer was also asked whether he heard *predicatio* and *doctrina*, there was an additional category: 'did he hear *admonitiones aut verba*?' Here *admonitio* meant moral teaching. A Cathar follower was not asked about *admonitiones*.

The difference we notice here takes us in two directions. In the *culpe* and the sentences, the presence and absence of key elements in these questions

[20] Fournier, I, 508–32, and Gui, *Ls*, pp. 288–91.
[21] Gui, *Ls*, pp. 252–4 (*culpa*) and 254–5 (sentence). The ratio is about five to two, the *culpa* about 1100 words, the sentence about 460.
[22] Gui, *P* V.i.5 and V.ii.9, pp. 242 and 256; Gui, *M*, pp. 28 and 76; Wakefield and Evans, pp. 385 and 402.
[23] I am using 'he' rather than 's/he' or the gender-free singular 'they' when translating third person singular Latin verbs, even though these were themselves gender-free. Repeated use of 's/he' would insidiously and mistakenly attribute a general gender-free outlook to inquisitors, and the use of 'they' could sometimes veil a distinction between plural and singular.

acts like the presence or absence of questions about food. On the one hand, the question about *admonitiones* was applied, and elicited a great amount about not only distinctive Waldensian points – not swearing or killing – but many other *moralia*. The result is a lot of explicit testimony about Waldensians trying to get their followers to behave better. Do good. Do not do evil. Do not lie.[24] Do not do unto others what you would not have done to yourself.[25] And so on. On the other hand there is not a single instance that I can find where a Cathar urges a follower not to do evil, not to lie, not to steal, or not to harm other people.[26]

These questions also take us in another direction. The question-list seems to have been based on two ideas in the inquisitor's mind, a positive and a negative: Waldensians were pre-occupied with moral behaviour and Cathars were not interested. In the second case, the lack of questions about preaching *moralia* did not encourage Cathar followers to remember passing moral comments which Cathar Good Men may sometimes have made, however inconsistently. The negative leads to no enquiry, and therefore possible distortion by omission. The result? *Perhaps* Catharism is going to seem a little bit simpler and more consistent than it was.

What of the positive, the inquisitor's idea of Waldensian interest in preaching *moralia*? I should make it clear here that my own feeling is that the idea was based on good and honest observation, simplifying probably more varied behaviour. But that is not the main point, which is that, by the time such an idea got to the question-list and dictated the questions to be asked, it was like a Weberian 'ideal-type'. Our initial suspicion must be that, when the question-list was applied, its select questions and the answers they elicited must have tended to reinforce the 'ideal-types' while excluding anything which might modify them and taking them a little further away from reality. Must have tended or might have? Or might have but did not?

My next example suggests 'might have but did not'. It concerns the Waldensian mode of praying. The question-list contains the following questions about prayer:[27]

> item, si ante prandium vel post et ante cenam vel post vidit eos orantes et
> de modo orandi et standi in oratione; item, si ipse oravit cum eis vel vidit
> alios orantes et quos et ubi et quando, et de hiis que dicunt orando.

---

[24] See, for example, Gui, *Ls*, p. 223, 'non . . . mentiretur'; p. 344, 'non faceret nec diceret malum'; 'facerent bonum et caverent a malo'; p. 356, 'non faceret nec diceret malum, et quod non mentiretur'; p. 358, 'non faceret nec diceret malum'; p. 359, 'facerent bonum et caverent a malo, et non mentirentur'; p. 366, 'non facerent malum'.

[25] Gui, *Ls*, p. 367, 'non faceret nec diceret malum, nec faceret alicui quod nollet sibi fieri'.

[26] This and some apparent exceptions are discussed in my 'Cathar Peace-Making', in *Christianity and Community in the West: Essays for John Bossy*, ed. S. Ditchfield (Aldershot, 2001), pp. 1–23.

[27] Gui, *P* V.ii.9, p. 256, Gui, *M*, p. 78, and Wakefield and Evans, p. 402.

(item, if he saw them praying before or after dinner or before or after supper, and about the mode of praying and position during prayer; item, if he prayed with them or saw others praying and who and where and when, and about those things which they say when praying.)

Here are statements reproduced in *culpe* and based on depositions containing answers to (approximately) similar questions, which I give deliberately out of sequence, earliest, latest, and then in between (1) (3) (2).

First, in a *culpa* based on a confession of 1312:[28]

(1) Item, oravit cum Valdensibus ante prandium et post, flexis genibus inclinatus super bancam, secundum modum et ritum orandi ipsorum.

(Item, he prayed with the Waldensians, before and after supper, on bended knees bowing over a bench, according to their rite and mode of praying.)

Based on a confession of 1322:[29]

(3) post prandium et post cenam ipsa cum aliis personis quas nominat oraverunt cum dicto Valdensi secundum modum orandi Valdensium, videlicet flexis genibus, inclinata super bancam, dicendo pluries *Pater Noster*.

(after dinner and after supper, together with other persons whom she names, she prayed with the said Waldensian according to the mode of praying of the Waldensians, that is to say, on bended knees, bowing over a bench, saying the *Our Father* many times.)

Based on a confession of 1320:[30]

(2) post cenam oraverunt super quandam cayssiam flexis genibus secundum modum ipsorum, et ipse oravit cum eis, et steterunt in dicta oracione tam diu quod potuerunt dixisse LXXX vel C vicibus oracionem *Pater Noster*.

(after supper they prayed, ⟨leaning⟩ over some chest on bended knees, according to their mode, and he prayed with them, and they stayed in the said praying for so long that they could have said the prayer *Our Father* eighty or one hundred times.)

The question which lay behind (1) was probably that specified in the Practica's interrogatory, but without 'de hiis que dicunt orando', 'about those things which they say when praying'. Thus, here in 1312, a question, which was put to a follower about praying, elicited an answer in which he confessed to praying in the Waldensian manner, kneeling in some way on a bench. In 1322 a question put to a follower elicited the same reply, but now there is an additional detail: saying the *Pater Noster* many times (3). In 1320 (2) when the question was put to a follower a lot of additional information came through,

[28] Gui, *Ls*, pp. 239–40.
[29] Gui, *Ls*, p. 357 (1322).
[30] Gui, *Ls*, p. 355 (1320).

about the period of praying being so long that one could have said the *Our Father* many times.

Two of these statements (1) and (3), are very formulaic, and they are repeated. The shortest statement (1) is found most often, in virtually identically wording, especially in confessions from 1309–12, while (3), with its additional detail, is found several times, again with virtually identical wording, but this time mostly in confessions from a later period, 1320–2.[31] One hypothesis to explain what was happening goes like this. First, the question which Gui and/or his assistants put in the early years was very short, like the question specified in the *Practica*'s interrogatory, but without 'de hiis que dicunt orando', 'about those things which they say when praying'. Then, by around 1320–2 the inquisitor Bernard and/or his assistants have added to the question: 'and did you say the *Pater Noster* many times?' Why would they have done this? In a few cases believers who, when answering the question, had been volunteering many additional details about the mode of prayer, heavily underlining large numbers of *Pater Nosters* – as in the example quoted above, where time passed in praying would have enabled eighty or one hundred to be said.[32] In other words, Bernard and/ or his assistants noticed depositions like the one from which this *culpa* was extracted, and they then sensitively adapted the detail of their 'ideal-type' question to accommodate the new evidence they were hearing.

The dates of confessions – indicated in my footnotes – show that not everything neatly fits this schema. There are many further possibilities which the hypothesis does not cover. For example, there could have been differences in the questions employed by inquisitors acting at the same time, Gui on the one hand and an assistant on the other. There could have been a third type of question about mode of praying, one which went on to ask how long praying lasted. And the recording of one formula could have been contaminated by memory of another – a scribe could have imprinted a more detailed later formula onto a briefer earlier formula when writing in 1322 and summarizing a confession of 1312. All this means, however, is that the hypothesis I have put forward, which cannot be modified or developed

---

[31] Close repetitions of (1) – 1309: Gui, *Ls*, p. 216; 1311: pp. 222, 224, 225, 227, 233, 235, 236 (bis), 237, 239, 239–40, 242, 247 and 376; 1312: pp. 217, 223 (bis), 225, 226 (bis), 227, 231, 233, 234 (bis), 235, 236, 237–8, 238 (bis), 239, 240 (bis), and 241 (bis); 1314: p. 231; 1316: pp. 224 and 237; 1317: p. 224; 1320: pp. 345, 352–3, 354, 355 and 373.
    Close repetitions of (3) – 1320: pp. 353, 358 and 367; 1322: pp. 356 and 357. See also p. 375 (confession of 1312, a summary of which is being copied in 1322), and p. 376 (confession of 1316, a summary of which is being copied in 1322).

[32] Other examples of (2) – 1315: Gui, *Ls*, p. 241 ('stando ibi diu', 'staying there for a long time'); 1316: p. 369 ('stando ibi per unam magnam pausam', 'staying there for a great interval'); 1320: p. 368 '(tam diu quod potuerunt dixisse x vicibus oracionem Pater Noster', 'staying there so long they could have said the Our Father ten times') and p. 369 ('stando ibidem diu', 'staying there for a long time'). See also p. 351 ('diu stantes ibidem', 'staying a long time there'), a confession of 1312, a summary of which is being copied in 1321.

much because the evidence is too thin, must necessarily be too simple to cover such complex possibilities. It does not derogate from the principal suggestion: one element in this complex past was an inquisitor's, or several inquisitors', conscious development of the question put to followers, deliberately and delicately tailoring it to make it fit Waldensian practice more precisely.

Description of the Waldensians

While this interrogatory – the list of questions to be put to Waldensian followers – formed the last of nine chapters devoted to the Waldensians in the fifth part of the *Practica*, the previous eight chapters dealt with the history of the Waldensians (ch. 1), their names (ch. 2), their errors (ch. 3), their rite of celebrating mass (ch. 4), their way of life (ch. 5), their way of teaching (ch. 6), and finally the artifices and deceptions they use when examined and the sophistries of their statements (chs. 7–8).

We cross from one genre to another as we move back from this question-list to these earlier chapters: from an inquisitor's tool to history and description; from a formulary to literature. This is underlined by part of the apparatus in the edition through which we usually access the fifth part of the *Practica*, that of Michel Mollat, who printed in italics sections where Bernard Gui copied verbatim and also adapted previous sources.[33] Such indication of dependence on previous literary sources is absent from the question-list in chapter 9, but is present in all of the first eight chapters. For example, when writing his account of the origin and history of the Waldenses, Gui copied out large parts of the treatise on preaching written by the Dominican Stephen of Bourbon, who died around 1261, and when providing an account of the deceits adopted by the Waldensians he copied a lot from the mysterious treatise on inquisition which was once attributed to David of Augsburg.

Although Mollat's annotations miss many of the sources or analogues of Gui's text, they are useful in themselves, and their underlining of this generic contrast between different parts of the *Practica* is a timely reminder of a different Bernard Gui, a man of broad learning and a writer in various genres. Here we are helped by the magnificent general picture of Gui which was presented by Bernard Guenée in 1987. Guenée sketched for us the Gui who was a book-lover, building a library in the convent at Toulouse; the Gui who was a careful historian, leaving copies of his works in various convents, with blank spaces at various points for filling in; and the Gui who was a scholar, noticing discrepancies between various texts.[34] I turn now to the

---

[33] See n. 8 above.

[34] See n. 1 above. In Lamarrigue's study of Gui as a historian, *Bernard Gui*, see the descriptions of him compiling and combining sources (ch. 7), reducing and abbreviating them (ch. 8), and comparing and criticizing them (ch. 9).

picture given of Waldensian history and way of life by Gui the writer and
historian – as well as Gui the inquisitor.

Let us investigate Gui by looking more closely at three passages in these
chapters, beginning with early Waldensian history in chapter 1 and, within
this, the description of the early stage in the movement when Valdes was
attracting both men and women as followers and sending them out to preach.
Here we begin by juxtaposing and reading at the same time Stephen of
Bourbon on this and Bernard Gui.[35]

Stephen of Bourbon	Bernard Gui
Waldensis . . . officium apostolorum usurpavit et presumpsit, evangelia et ea que corde retinuerat *per vicos et plateas* [Song of Songs 3. 2] predicando, multos homines et mulieres ad idem faciendo et se convocando, firmans eis evangelia. Quos eciam per villas circumjacentes mittebat ad predicandum, vilissimorum quorumcunque officiorum. Qui eciam, tam homines quam mulieres, idiote et illiterati, per villas discurrentes et domos penetrantes et in plateis predicantes et eciam in ecclesiis, ad idem alios provocabant.	Valdesius seu Valdensis . . . sectatores . . . apostolorum sibi officium usurparunt et presumentes per vicos et plateas evangelium predicare; dictusque Valdesius seu Valdensis multos homines utriusque sexus viros et mulieres ad similem presumptionem complices sibi fecit ipsosque ad predicandum tanquam discipulos emittebat. Qui, cum essent ydiote et illiterati, per villas discurrentes et domos penetrantes, tam viri quam etiam mulieres, in plateis ac etiam in ecclesiis, viri maxime, predicantes multos errores circumquaque diffuderunt.
(Valdens . . . usurped and presumed the office of the apostles, preaching 'in the streets and the broad ways' the gospels and those things he had learnt by heart, calling to himself many men and women to do the same, strengthening the gospels in them. These ⟨people, who were⟩ of the vilest possible occupations, he also sent off to preach in the neighbouring villages. These ⟨people⟩ also, both men and women, idiots and illiterate, wandering through villages and entering homes and preaching in the broad ways and even in churches, encouraged others to do the same.)	(Valdes or Valdens . . . ⟨his⟩ followers usurped to themselves the office of the apostles, presuming to preach the gospel 'in the streets and the broad ways'. And the said Valdes or Valdens made many persons of both sexes, men and women, his accomplices in a similar presumption, and sent them out to preach as disciples. These, although they were idiots and illiterate, wandering through villages and entering homes, both men and women, preaching – especially the men – in the broad ways and even in churches, spread many errors all around.)

We are comparing a text written before 1261 by a Dominican who had
talked to people who had talked to Valdes, with a text written in the early
fourteenth century which recycles the mid-thirteenth century text. How is
Gui altering his source? Whereas in the mid-thirteenth century account
Valdes took upon himself an office and instructed his followers to imitate,
in the text produced seventy years or so later Valdes and the followers are
conflated into a group of persons, plural, who do this. The base occupations
of the followers disappear, as do the neighbouring villages. Here it seems that
Gui is nodding benignly towards the passing of time. These omissions in his
version of the narrative parallel a more general erosion: by now, one hundred
and fifty years had passed since the story took place.

---

[35] Stephen of Bourbon, *Tractatus*, pp. 291–2, and Patschovsky and Selge, p. 16; Gui, *P* V.ii.1, p. 244, Gui, *M*, pp. 34 and 36, and Wakefield and Evans, p. 387.

Gui was not so happy with the form of the founder's name as he found it in his source. Evidently Gui – Gui the scholarly historian – had come across another form elsewhere. Unwilling to jettison either form, Gui states both – *Valdesius seu Valdensis* – displaying a concern with precise and various naming which we shall discuss at the end of this paper.

Gui's most dramatic addition to the early history of the Waldensians comes, however, during his taking over of Stephen's repeated underlining of women. Gui has it both ways, in that he is again unwilling to jettison what he found in his source, 'both men and women', while he is again concerned to juxtapose this with something else, in this case a radical qualification: 'mostly men'. From where did this come?

When Gui turned to past history, extending from the origins to the mid-thirteenth century, he will have found the *mulieres Valdenses*, the Waldensian Sisters, writ large.[36] Early inquisitors had been much struck by the Waldensian Sisters, and there is a lot of material on them in Peter Sellan's *culpe* for Waldensians in Quercy in 1241–2 and in the inquisition forms of a Languedocian inquisitors' handbook whose latest document is dated 1265. But material closer to Gui in date will have told him a different story. In the more recent description of the Waldensians in the *De vita et actibus*, he will have found women playing a very restricted role, and he will have found this also in his experience as an inquisitor. The followers he questioned named about fifty 'perfect' or full Waldensians: all men. As far as we can tell from the *culpe*, it was only when questioning a Waldensian Brother called Stephen Porcherii in 1314 that Gui was told about a full Waldensian female heretic, a *mulier* or *soror* Waldensis, called Raimonde of Castres.[37] Fifty men, one woman: unlike mid-thirteenth century Dominicans, Gui will have thought of Waldensian Sisters as small beer, a tiny phenomenon. When inserting his qualification, then, *viri maxime*, 'mostly men', Gui seems to have been consciously reshaping early Waldensian history to make it fit more with recent and contemporary reality as he saw it.

The next passage occurs in chapter 5, *On the way of Life of the Waldensians, De modo vivendi Valdensium*.[38] In the middle of this chapter there is a description of the hard, practical financial and administrative core of the movement. Believers and friends give money, and the collections are sent upwards. Every year there are one or two general assemblies, 'chapters-general'. At these the senior person organizes and disposes things, including the sending out of Waldensians to various parts and regions to hear confessions and receive alms, and he also 'hears and receives an account of money collected and expended' ('audit et recipit rationem de collectis et de expensis factis').

We cannot do what we did with Gui's account of Waldensian history: we

---

[36] For the following paragraph, see Biller, *Waldenses*, ch. 8, esp. pp. 128–45.
[37] Gui, *Ls*, p. 201.
[38] Gui, *P* V.ii.5, p. 249; Gui, *M*, pp. 50 and 52; and Wakefield and Evans, p. 393.

cannot juxtapose this with a text whose precise verbal parallels establish exactly what Gui's source was and how he was adapting it. However, we can get a very good idea of how Gui knew this. Gui's *culpe* show that he had interrogated various full Waldensians, any one of whom could have given him this material. Near to these men was a former priest called John Philiberti who had been on intimate terms with the Waldensian Brothers and had been invited to join them. As I argue in chapter 9 below, one of Philiberti's four confessions to inquisitors between 1283 and 1319 may have been the Burgundian confession which was transformed into an anonymous descrip-tion of the Waldensians called the *De vita et actibus*. This text also describes chapters, the sending out of Waldensians to particular regions, and the handling of money at the chapters, it conforms in many details with other Burgundian Waldensian material found in Gui's *culpe* and sentences, and it is likely to have been one of Gui's sources. There are two conjectures here, neither of which I can prove, but if Gui was not using Philiberti and the *De vita et actibus*, he was using very similar sources. Even though these sources cannot be definitively identified, it is clear that Gui was concerned to obtain good information about Waldensian finance and administration and to report it soberly.

It is worth bearing this in mind: that Gui is matter of fact and without prejudice when writing about such matters as organisation and money. This acts as a control when we turn to lurid stuff. I am alluding here to the famous passage on Luciferanism which is to be found at the end of Gui's fourth chapter on the Waldensians.[39] Gui's editor Mollat drew attention to one of Gui's possible literary sources here, the *De inquisitione hereticorum* attributed to David of Augsburg, but rather surprisingly did not notice Gui's use of Stephen of Bourbon.[40] Let us begin with these two earlier texts which Gui read, placing after them Gui's own statements.

Stephen of Bourbon[41]

Item, cum ego inquirerem in comitatu For-isiensi de hereticis [a tale follows about the appearance of a black dog] . . .
Item, quasi simile accidit in Alvernia, ubi multi fuerunt capti apud Sanctum Porcia-num et deducti apud Claremontem ubi convocaverat me episcopus ejusdem loci, dominus Hugo de Turre. Quedam mulier, capta in quibusdam maleficiis, accusavit plures et illos qui capti detinebantur,

Item, when I was enquiring about heretics in the county of Forez [tale about black dog] . . .
Item, a more or less similar thing happened in the Auvergne, where many were taken prisoner at Saint-Pourçain and taken to Clermont, where the bishop of this place, lord Hugues de la Tour, had summoned me. A certain woman, seized ⟨while engaged⟩ in certain sorceries, accused many and those who were being held captive

[39] Amidst the abundant literature on this topic, outstanding and fundamental are the articles by Patschovsky cited in n. 48 below.
[40] Gui, *M*, pp. 48–9 n. 1.
[41] Stephen of Bourbon, *Tractatus*, pp. 322–3.

[1] dicens quod magistram quamdam ⟨habuerat⟩ que eam frequenter duxerat ad quemdam locum subterraneam, ubi conveniebat multitudo hominum et mulierum cum luminibus torticiorum et candelarum, circumdantes quamdam cufam plenam aqua que erat in medio, in cujus medio erat hasta affixa; et magister eorum adjurabat Luciferum per barbam suam et per potenciam quod veniret ad eos, et per multa alia; ad quam adjuracionem
[2] descendebat catus teterrimus per lanceam,
[3] et aqua cum cauda, vadens in circuitu, omnes aspergebat,
[4] et luminaria omnia extinguebat; quo facto, quilibet eorum accipiebat illum vel illam qui ei primo occurrebat, et cum eo turpiter admiscebatur. Propter hoc dicti homines erant capti, qui hec omnia negabant, licet dicta mulier diceret eos ibi sepe vidisse convenisse.

[1] saying that she had a certain mistress who had frequently taken her to a certain underground place, where a multitude of men and women would come together with lights of torches and candles, handing round a cup full of water which was in the middle, in the middle of which a spear had been fastened. And their master would adjure Lucifer by his beard and by his power and by many other things to come to them. At this adjuration
[2] a very dark cat would come down by the spear,
[3] and going around it would sprinkle water on everyone with its tail,
[4] and it would extinguish all the lights. When this was done, every man among them would seize the first man or woman who reached him, and mix shamefully with him ⟨or her⟩. On account of this the said people were seized, ⟨and⟩ they denied all these things, although the said woman said she had often seen them meet there.

De inquisitione hereticorum[42]

Noctibus autem maxime huiusmodi conventicula frequentant . . . Quod autem, ut [1] *dicitur*, osculentur ibi catos vel ranas vel videant dyabolum, vel extinctis lucernis pariter fornicentur, non puto istius secte, nel aliquod horum intellexi ab illis, quibus fidem adhiberem.

Moreover, they frequent assemblies of this sort, mostly at night-time . . . However, that they kiss cats or frogs there or see the devil, or fornicate together after the lights have been extinguished, as [1] *is said*, I do not reckon to be of this sect, nor have I truly learnt any of these things from those in whom I would place trust.

Bernard Gui[43]

. . .credentibus suis clamculo in suis conventiculis dogmatizant. . . . Sciendum quoque est quod predicta secta multa alios errores ab olim habuit et tenuit, et adhuc in aliquibus partibus habere [1] *dicitur* in secreto, sicut . . . et [4] de mixto abhominabili in tenebris faciendo quilibet cum qualibet indistincte et [2] de apparitione cati et [3] aspersione cum cauda et de quibusdam aliis que in summulis super hoc conscriptis latius continentur.

. . in their assemblies they dogmatize to their believers in secret. . . . It should also be known that the aforesaid sect formerly had and holds many other errors, and in some areas [1] *it is said* still to hold ⟨them⟩ them in secret, such as . . . [4] ⟨the error⟩ about abominable mixing in the darkness, any man doing with any woman indiscriminately, and [2] about the apparition of the cat and [3] the sprinkling with the tail and about certain other things which are contained more extensively in the tracts written on this ⟨matter⟩.

When reading this part of the *De inquisitione hereticorum*, much of whose other parts Gui copied on other matters, he was coming across one uncontroversial point, the secrecy in which Waldensians met. This appears also in his own text, rooted in either the *De inquisitione hereticorum* or Gui's own

---

[42] *De inquisitione hereticorum* X, pp. 210–11; *EFV*, p. 160.
[43] Gui, *P* V.ii.5, p. 248; Gui, *M*, p. 48; and Wakefield and Evans, p. 392.

interrogations, or both. He also came across Luciferan allegations, heavily summarized and reported as rumours – *dicitur*, 'it is said'. And he met this earlier author's statement of his own belief, that this applied to another sect, not to the Waldensians.

As we saw, when writing Waldensian history Gui had already used the earlier French Dominican Stephen of Bourbon. After reading Stephen on heresy, Bernard had to move forwards only a few folios in order to arrive at the next section, on the invocation of demons. There he found the earlier Dominican reminiscing about his experience when acting as inquisitor among heretics. A woman had described the apparition of a cat, aspersion with a tail, putting the lights out and indiscriminate sexual coupling. Stephen described not only her allegation but what followed. Stephen reports that the men arrested on account of her confession denied everything. A reader *could* see some reserve in Stephen, in the sequence of woman's confession, men's arrest, and men's denial, and the absence of any comment by Stephen himself.

Gui deliberately omitted the denial found in the *De inquisitione hereticorum*. But he let some reserve stand, however, and he establishes distance between his own manual and this material. *Dicitur* is retained. He alludes to rather than describes the material, in a style which is reminiscent of the extreme compression of the *De inquisitione hereticorum*. And he tells the reader to go off to the special little tracts, *summule*, which contain more about such stuff.[44]

Let us stand back from this, and set it in middle distance. First of all, writers of inquisitorial treatises were capable of making trenchant and utterly clear statements on this topic. We have seen this a few decades earlier than Gui, in the *De inquisitione hereticorum*, and we see it again seventy years later. Writing a polemical treatise against the Waldenses in 1395, a German inquisitor raised Luciferanism again. Unlike Gui, the German had questioned Waldensians about this, and had received a denial. Rather to our surprise, in a treatise in which he used very unpleasant language about the Waldensians, this inquisitor forcefully repeated the denial.[45]

Set against these examples, Gui's position seems clear: standing on the fence, trying to have his cake and eat it. What was going on in his mind? To begin with, he was reading. If there was the negative in the *De inquisitione hereticorum*, there was also some positive material in Stephen of Bourbon, a man whose life had impressed itself on Gui's mind, for it is only through Gui's obituary that we have any external biographical details about Stephen. To some degree, Gui may have been behaving as we have seen him else-

---

[44] I take 'this' – *hoc* in *summulis super hoc conscriptis* – to mean Luciferanism, sex and associated material, and the *summule* to be little tracts in which the association of this material and heresy could be found. It could also mean Waldensian errors in general, in which case *summule* refers to other treatises dealing with the Waldensians, such as the *De inquisitione hereticorum*. The latter is Mollat's suggestion, Gui, *M*, p. xix.

[45] Biller, *Waldenses*, p. 279.

where, pedantically taking note of differences between sources, and showing reluctance completely to discard either of them.

What of the Gui who lived in the world, working both as an inquisitor in Languedoc and travelling extensively on high Church affairs? There is no sign of Gui encountering material like this in his own interrogations in Languedoc, nor is there any trace of him questioning Waldensians about it. It runs utterly counter to his presentation of Waldensians as moralizers.

We need to stand back here, taking a longer view, looking beyond Languedoc and recalling two general developments, first in the long and complex history of the Church's fundamental views of the morality of Waldensian heretics. Let us take as examples the passing presence of Waldensians in the writings of two Franciscans. The earlier is the great Tuscan preacher Servasanto of Faenza (died around 1300), the text a sermon on learning:[46]

> Multi enim fuerunt viri sanctissimi, qui propter defectum scientiae facti sunt haeretici. Exemplum de Pauperibus de Lugduno, qui fuerunt prius boni, et ab Ecclesia dilecti; dum tamen ex simplicitate haeresim praedicare coepissent, corrigi renuerunt, et se in suis haeresibus confirmaverunt.

> (For there have been many very holy men who have become heretics because of lack of learning. Example in the Poor of Lyons, who were first of all good and loved by the Church, though in the course of time through simplicity they began to preach heresy, refused to be corrected, and strengthened themselves in their heresies.)

The later Franciscan was Guiraud d'Ot, who was to become Minister General of his Order three years later. The occasion is the academic exercise of lecturing on the sentences of Peter the Lombard, and the setting is the lecture-halls of Paris in 1326. By this date scholars like Guiraud are importing their reading of Aristotle's *Politics* into the discussion of marriage in the fourth book of the sentences:[47]

> Item, Ari⟨stotele⟩s .2. Polit⟨i⟩ce recitat quod fuit opinio Platonis quod mulieres deberent esse communes, moderno autem tempore est heresis aliquorum vocatorum 'Valdencium', qui certis temporibus congregant se ita quod sunt ad unam partem et mulieres ad aliam partem, et extinctis tunc luminibus commiscent se, et istud vocant 'mixtum'.

> (Item, in the second ⟨book⟩ of the *Politics* Aristotle says that it was Plato's opinion that wives should be ⟨held in⟩ common, in modern times, however, ⟨this⟩ is the heresy of some people who are called 'Waldensians'. At certain

---

[46] In Bonaventure, *Opera omnia*, ed. A. C. Peltier, 15 vols. (Paris, 1864–71), XIV, 87–8; on the mistaken attribution to Bonaventure of sermons printed here by Servasanto, see L. Oliger, 'Servasanto da Faenza O.F.M. e il suo "Liber de virtutibus et vitiis"', in *Miscellanea Francesco Ehrle* I, Studi e Testi 37 (Rome, 1924), 148–89 (p. 167).

[47] BnF MS Lat. 3068, fol. 58vb. On such use of the *Politics*, see my *The Measure of Multitude: Population in Medieval Thought* (Oxford, 2000), pp. 50–2.

times these come together in such a fashion that the ⟨men⟩ are on one side and the women on the other side and then, with the lights put out, they mix together, and they call this the 'mixed'.)

Although the Waldensians were heretics preaching heresies in the earlier text, there is no disguising the moral warmth in the depiction of men who had once been *boni* and *dilecti* by the Church. Thirty or forty years later they figure in an academic lecture in Paris, casually alluded to as *the* upholders and practitioners of indiscriminate nocturnal sexual coupling. Neither of these Franciscans are known to have had dealings with Waldensians, neither of them were inquisitorial writers, and this is what makes them so much more useful as witnesses to general change. The decades around 1300 had seen a seismic shift in the moral view of Waldensians.

While the association of heresy with sex and Luciferanism was old, there was an extraordinary acceleration in the years after 1300 both in the presence of this material and the appearance of an association precisely with Waldensians. Orgiastic stories, Luciferanism and Waldensians appeared in a report of an inquisition in Krems in 1315 and also in trials in Schweidnitz in the same year – the latter in material discovered and edited by Alexander Patschovsky – and Guiraud d'Ot's passing reference in Paris shows just how far this material had spread in the following decade.[48]

Now, these years were precisely the middle years of Gui's professional life, and the years in which the *Practica* was beginning to take shape. Gui could have heard of this material at Dominican chapters, at the papal court, or perhaps when travelling over the Alps to Turin in 1317. At the length of a little over 1000 words the report of the inquisition in Krems was a *summula*, and is therefore a candidate for being one of those (various) *summule* on the matter to which Gui referred his readers.[49] This, then, is my second suggestion, that when Gui was writing these lines he had in mind both the silence of his own inquisitorial practice and the strength of reports being produced in these years, especially about Germanophone Waldensians. Although in familiar fashion he allowed both to influence his text, in this case he gave more weight to what he read in Stephen of Bourbon and what he may have heard from northern Europe. And in so doing he himself contributed to the darkening of opinion in these years.

We see Gui carefully constructing and perhaps sometimes adapting in the light of new evidence an 'ideal type' of the external signs of Waldensians. He then interrogates and produces texts, in which Waldensian followers'

[48] A. Patschovsky, 'Waldenserverfolgung in Schweidnitz', *DA* 36 (1980), 137–76 (pp. 154–5); 'Zur Ketzerverfolgung Konrads von Marburg', *DA* 37 (1981), 641–93 (from p. 651).
[49] Where scholastic authors use the plural 'some say' (*aliqui dicunt*), we can sometimes see that one individual is being generalized: a third person equivalent, as it were, of the royal 'we'. The plural in *summule* could be a similar generalisation of one, and it could also refer to the plurality of copies of a singular *summula*.

appearance is an odd mix of the ideal-type and their individual reality. Gui's views dominated. They 'constructed', if we prefer to put it this way, the language and themes of the texts in which the Waldensians have left their traces.

When we read critically the records of trials one of the first elements in the filter which we notice is language: the inquisitor's language, interposing a veil or a pane of frosted glass between us and the ordinary individual, Occitan-speaking, whose testimony appears to be recorded. The deponent's vernacular has been translated into Latin, her or his actions have acquired Inspector Plod's terminology, and her or his key-words have been translated into the key-words of a Latin-literate inquisitor. *Bona fena* (Good Woman), has become *heretica*, the grammatically female version of a Latin word from a thesaurus of words with precise etymologies and theological and canon-legal meaning in the mind of a highly educated Catholic cleric. Broadly speaking I think we should analyse inquisition texts in this way. But it is precisely language and naming which is given a remarkable twist by one of Gui's interests.

Gui's interest in Valdes's name was part of his general interest in language and naming. The preamble to Gui's question-list distinguishes between what 'we' call them and the terms they use among themselves:[50]

> appellamus 'Valdenses' seu 'Pauperes de Lugduno'; ipsi autem in⟨ter⟩ se vocant se 'Fratres' seu 'Pauperes Christi'.

> (We call them 'Waldensians' or the 'Poor of Lyons', they however among themselves call themselves 'Brothers' or the 'Poor of Christ'.)

As a result, Gui's *culpe* are littered with such distinctions. I conclude here with the testimony of the believer Andrew Garini, who came from a strong Waldensian family. His parents William and Helys were both believers, as were also two brothers and two sisters of Andrew (several of whom married into strong Waldensian families), while a third brother, Huguet Garini, became a 'full' Waldensian, and after capture was burnt to death at Avignon. Andrew appeared and confessed in 1320, recounting his instruction about Waldensians by his parents around 1320, and retailing to the inquisitor what he heard about them:[51]

> ipsi vocabant se 'Fratres', et gentes appellabant eos 'Pauperes de Lugduno', et inquisitores hereticorum persequebantur eos et faciebant conburi, et vocabant eos 'Valdenses'.

> (They called themselves 'Brothers'; ordinary people called them 'the Poor Men of Lyons', and inquisitors, who persecuted them and had them burnt, called them 'Waldenses'.)

---

[50] Gui, *P* V.ii.9, p. 256; Gui, *M*, p. 76; and Wakefield and Evans, p. 402.
[51] Gui, *Ls*, p. 369.

The question or questions put to Andrew Garini were the inquisitor's, and Garini's responses were translated and extracted from the Latin record of depositions for entry into a *culpa*. Despite all this, what is left in the text is a very multi-dimensional picture. Waldensians are named and seen in differ-ent ways, according to the different angles of view of different groups, inquisitors themselves are set in middle distance, and an expression of bitterness and hostility survives.

Here, finally, is an extraordinary paradox. It is the mind of Bernard Gui, and/or the minds of his assistants, which, in a certain sense, produces and constructs this text. But the text indicates three different ways of seeing things, only one of which was that of the inquisitor.

The Béguins in Bernard Gui's
Liber sententiarum

James Given

Words – both spoken and written – and their control were central to the work of the medieval inquisitors of heretical depravity. Mastery of the spoken word was essential to the task of interrogating suspected heretics, a mastery that was needed both to penetrate suspects' verbal screen of denials and half-truths and to avoid leading the simple into confessing errors that they did not really believe. To this aspect of their work, the authors of inquisitorial manuals, such as Bernard Gui and Nicholas Eymerich, gave much attention, detailing the ruses that suspects might employ to avoid revealing the truth and the techniques that a clever inquisitor could use to unravel their webs of deceit and arrive at a truth that those under interrogation would prefer to keep hidden.[1] The composition of written texts – summaries of interrogations, registers of sentences, etc. – was also central to the endeavors of the inquisitors. These written texts not only constituted a legal record of the proceedings against heretics and their sympathizers, they were also used, through the building of dossiers against suspects, as an active means by which to produce truth.[2]

'Truth', of course, should be understood as meaning that which the inquisitors wished to be true. As critics, both medieval and modern, have pointed out, the inquisitors often produced testimony that was both less and more than a bare recital of objective fact.[3] In the hands of unscrupulous or unskillful inquisitors their potent tools could be used to shape the often inchoate ideas and statements, often orthodox, of suspects into avowals of heretical belief.[4] More recently, inspired by Foucauldian ideas about the capacity of 'discourse' to create domains of power, scholars have tried to sketch how the very process of interrogation predicated those subjected to it

---

[1] See Gui, *P*, pp. 235–93, and N. Eymerich, *Directorium inquisitorum Fr. Nicholai Eymerici ordinis Praedicatorum, cum commentariis Francisci Pegnae sacrae theologiae ac iuris utriusque doctoris* (Venice, 1595), pp. 430–5.

[2] On this see, Given, *Inquisition*, pp. 24–51, and Given, 'Inquisitors'.

[3] For the career of one of the most notable medieval critics of the inquisition, see Friedlander, *Hammer*.

[4] Grundmann, 'Ketzerverhöre', and Lerner, *Free Spirit*.

as 'confessing subjects', autonomous, individualized transgressors required to acknowledge their errors.[5]

For the most part historians have tried to use the inquisitors' records to recover the words of the heretics themselves. The sources have been mined to discover what heretics believed and practiced. In reality what we possess and can read today are not the words of the heretics, but the words of the inquisitors. In this essay I will examine one set of these words, those recorded in Bernard Gui's *Liber sententiarum*, and show how they were part of a complex mechanism for the production of power. I will also touch on how those words could be reinterpreted and reshaped so as to undermine that very power.

To illustrate how this phenomenon worked, I will focus on the sentences of one particular type of heretic, the Béguins. The Béguins, members of the Franciscan Third Order, were followers of the Spiritual Franciscans.[6] They adhered to a rigid interpretation of the meaning and role of poverty in St Francis' rule, regarded the Franciscans who had been burned at Marseilles in 1318 as martyrs, revered the Languedocian friar Pierre Jean Olivi as a great teacher and saint,[7] and looked on Pope John XXII as the mystical antichrist.

Compared to other types of heretics, they do not play a major role in Bernard Gui's *Liber sententiarum*. Of the 637 individuals who appear in the register, only nineteen (three per cent) were punished for this particular heresy. However, the sentences of these nineteen Béguins are quite interesting. For one thing, they show us how the inquisitors went about constructing a new heresy, since the Béguins had until the second decade of the fourteenth century been good Catholics, attached, as members of the Franciscan Third Order, to one of the most attractive and dynamic religious movements of the thirteenth century.

But first we need to clarify the contents of Bernard Gui's register. The *Liber sententiarum* is by far the largest register of inquisitorial sentences to have survived from the Middle Ages.[8] Its history has also been a curious one. Sometime in the seventeenth century the *Liber* was acquired, possibly by an Englishman of radical Protestant opinions, and taken to England. It found its way into the hands of a Dutchman, Philip van Limborch, who transcribed it

[5] Arnold, *Inquisition and Power*.
[6] On these heretics, see R. Manselli, *Spirituali e Beghini in Provenza*, SStor 31–4 (Rome, 1959). This work has been translated into French by J. Duvernoy, *Spirituels et Béguins du Midi* (Toulouse, 1989).
[7] On Olivi, see the works of D. Burr, *Olivi and Franciscan Poverty: The Origins of the Usus Pauper Controversy* (Philadelphia, 1989), and 'The Persecution of Peter Olivi', *Transactions of the American Philosophical Society* n.s. 66 pt 5 (Philadelphia, 1976), and *Olivi's Peaceable Kingdom: A Reading of the Apocalypse Commentary* (Philadelphia, 1993).
[8] The manuscript original of the *Liber* is BL MS Add. 4697. It has been printed as an appendix to P. van Limborch, *Historia inquisitions, cui subjungitur Liber sententiarum inquisitionis Tholosanae ab anno Christi MCCCVII ad annum MCCCXXIII* (Amsterdam, 1692).

and published it in 1692 as an appendix to his history of the inquisition. Thereafter the manuscript seemed to disappear. Scholars assumed that it had been lost or destroyed. But in the 1970s it was rediscovered in the British Library, where it had been safely residing for several centuries.[9]

The *Liber* contains 907 different 'acts', recorded between 3 March 1308 and 19 June 1323, relating to individuals convicted of heresy (see Table 1).[10] In 633 of these acts Gui imposed some form of penance or punishment on an individual. Of these, 544 (85.9%) were imposed on people who were alive at the time and 89 (14.1%) on deceased individuals. The other 274 acts consisted of the commutation of a previously imposed penance into a lesser penalty. The 907 acts in the register relate to only 637 individuals,[11] some of whom appeared up to three times in the register.

Gui's sentences were generally imposed during grand and impressive ceremonies, known as *sermones generales* ('general sermons'). On 23 April 1312, for example, Gui processed some 208 people. This was the largest number of people he dealt with in any *sermo generalis*. But it was not uncommon for him to sentence scores of people at a time. On 25 May 1309 he sentenced 91 people; on 5 April 1310, 110; on 7 March 1316, 74; on 30 September 1319, 160; and on 12 September 1322, 152.

What goals did an inquisitor like Gui hope to attain through these public and impressive *sermones generales*? Unfortunately, the inquisitors rarely engaged in a self-conscious exposition of the purposes of their system of punishment. If one leafs through Gui's manual of inquisitorial procedure, the *Practica inquisitionis*, one finds only scattered comments about the meanings of the punishments he imposed. Uppermost in Gui's mind was the repressive

---

[9] M. A. E. Nickson, 'Locke and the Inquisition of Toulouse', *British Museum Quarterly* 36 (1971–2), 83–92. In general, Limborch's edition is a very good one, faithfully reproducing the readings of the original manuscript. See J. Duvernoy, 'L'Édition par Philippe de Limborch des sentences de l'inquisition de Toulouse', *Heresis* 12 (1989), 5–12. My own examination of a microfilm of the register bears out Duvernoy's conclusions.

[10] For a fuller discussion of Gui's register, see Given, 'Inquisitor at Work'.

[11] Most of the individuals recorded in the register had been tried and condemned by Gui. Some, however, had not. Some were individuals who had been given penances by other inquisitors which Gui, acting as their successor in office, commuted at a later date. Some were individuals who had been tried primarily by other inquisitors. According to the reforms instituted by Pope Clement V at the council of Vienne (1311–12), inquisitors and local bishops were for certain matters required to act together. Therefore some of the sentences in the *Liber* relate to people who were tried primarily by Jacques Fournier, bishop of Pamiers. One person, the notorious Franciscan Bernard Délicieux, was tried by a specially appointed papal commission. But since Bernard had been very active in leading opposition to the inquisitors, Gui made certain to record his sentence. The register also contains two other, 'collective' sentences, a 'reconciliation' with the community of the *castrum* of Cordes, and an order for the destruction of copies of the Talmud confiscated from Languedocian Jews.

Table 1 Acts recorded in Bernard Gui's register

Sentences imposed	Number	Percentage
Pilgrimages	17	2.7%
Simple crosses	79	12.5%
Double crosses	57	9.0%
One year prison term	1	0.2%
Perpetual imprisonment, normal regime	268	42.3%
Perpetual imprisonment, normal regime and house destroyed	8	1.3%
Perpetual imprisonment, strict regime	31	4.9%
Burned alive	41	6.5%
Deceased, but would have been imprisoned if alive	17	2.7%
Deceased, but would have been burned if alive	3	0.5%
Burned posthumously	52	8.2%
Burned posthumously; house destroyed	14	2.2%
Remains to be exhumed	3	0.5%
Condemned *in absentia*	40	6.3%
Ordered on crusade	1	0.2%
Reserved for other judgment	1	0.2%
Total	633	100.2%
Commutations of previously imposed sentences		
	139	50.7%
Released from prison, to wear crosses		
Allowed to lay aside crosses	135	49.3%
Total	274	100.0%
Grand Total	907	

Source: Gui, *Ls*.
Note: Percentages of 'Sentences imposed' sum to more than 100 because of rounding.

and destructive aspect of the inquisition's work. In his discussion of the way in which the tasks of the inquisition should be carried out, he has this to say:

> Concerning the order of proceeding, it is to be remembered that the method of any procedure is governed by its end. The end of the office of the inquisition is the destruction of heresy; this cannot be destroyed unless heretics are destroyed. Moreover, these cannot be destroyed unless their receivers, supporters, and defenders are destroyed . . . Heretics are destroyed in a double fashion: first, when they are converted from heresy to the true, Catholic faith . . .; secondly, when they are surrendered to the secular jurisdiction to be corporally burned.[12]

[12] Gui, *P*, pp. 217–18, 'Circa ordinem itaque agendorum, sciendum est quod ordo cujuslibet rei sumitur per respectum ad finem. Finis autem officii inquisitionis est, ut heresis destruatur, que destrui non potest nisi heretici destruantur, qui etiam destrui non possunt nisi destruantur receptatores, fautores et defensores eorum . . .

Although Gui does not give us much guidance, we need not abandon all hope of understanding the rationales that governed his system of punishment. Sociologists have given much thought to the phenomenon of punishment and it is instructive to reflect on how Gui's work relates to this body of interpretation. One of the most influential understandings of punishment has been that advanced by Emile Durkheim. He argued that the force that holds together a simple society, one that does not have a complex division of labor, is the *conscience collective*, a shared universe of moral values regarded as sacred. A crime violates this sacred order. It shocks and dismays 'healthy' consciences. The result is a passionate call from the outraged public for vengeance. Through the act of punishing the offender, the members of a society reaffirm their group solidarity and restore the sacred moral order.[13]

This model, attractive as it may seem, does not fit Gui's work. Clearly many people in Languedoc clamoured for the punishment of heretics and their sympathizers. Nevertheless, the penalties the inquisitors inflicted cannot be understood simply as the inevitable consequences of an offended *conscience collective*, for there was no unified, monolithic *conscience collective* in medieval Languedoc. Indeed, the inquisition existed precisely because the collective consciousness of medieval Languedoc was contested terrain. The Catholic Church and its opponents were engaged in a desperate struggle over the moral constitution of society, a contest that turned on such issues as the relation of the divine to the mundane, the spirit to the flesh, and divine authority to worldly power. Some Languedocians may have hated and loathed those punished by the inquisitors as enemies of God and everything decent, but others saw them as martyrs and saints.

It makes more sense to think of the inquisitors' punishments within a Gramscian problematic, as part of a struggle to impose a cultural and spiritual hegemony on the people of Languedoc, to win their active assent to the myths that justified the existing distribution of power and authority.[14] Gui may not have been the agent of an outraged collective consciousness, but he was the agent of an outraged ruling bloc. In punishing heretics he was not applying sanctions for violating a non-existent *conscience collective*, he was striving to create such a collective consciousness. He sought to impose the Church's moral order on a social formation many of whose members were actively opposed to its vision of the right ordering of the world and mankind's relation to the divine.

To accomplish this end, Gui acted as though his penitential system was a species of theatre. The imposition of punishment was a performance in which

---

Destruuntur autem heretici duppliciter, uno modo cum ad veram catholicam fidem convertuntur . . .; alio modo quando relicti seculari juditio corporaliter concremantur.'

[13] See, in general, E. Durkheim, *Moral Education: A Study in the Theory and Application of the Sociology of Education*, trans. E. K. Wilson and H. Schnurer (New York, 1961).

[14] A. Gramsci, *Selections from the Prison Notebooks of Antonio Gramsci*, ed. and trans. Q. Hoare and G. N. Smith (New York, 1971), pp. 12–14, 244.

the Church's official version of correct spiritual order was acted out in a grandiose and impressive public fashion. The subjects of this performance were as much the members of the audience as they were the people whom the inquisitors sentenced.

To enhance the propaganda effects of these general sermons, Gui took care to arrange for impressive and well-attended ceremonies. Once a sufficient number of trials had been concluded, Gui set the date for the sermon on a feast day and summoned the people to attend. The sermon itself was held at a local church or other place suitable for a large gathering.[15]

When the appointed day arrived, the inquisitor, true to his Dominican vocation, began the proceedings with a sermon. He then received oaths from royal officials, town consuls, and other individuals possessing temporal jurisdiction, all of whom swore to aid the inquisitors in persecuting heretics and their sympathizers. Before the inquisitor imposed sentences on those who had been found guilty, he commuted the penances of people who had previously been condemned. The message that this action conveyed was that the Church was a truly merciful and compassionate mother.

Gui then turned to those who had been newly condemned. The inquisitor had previously had drawn up a list of the *culpe*, or faults, of each of those to be sentenced. These lists specified the nature of the condemned's involvement with heresy. Although composed in Latin, the *culpe* were read out in the vernacular. Not only did this performance justify the punishments imposed by the inquisitors, it also reinforced and restated the nature of orthodoxy. By specifying exactly what illegitimate belief and practice were, the *culpe* firmly circumscribed the sphere of legitimate, orthodox belief and practice. In effect, the reading of these lists of faults was a pedagogic tool. Those in attendance should have gone away from the day's proceedings with no doubt as to what was, and was not, acceptable belief.

Once the *culpe* had been read, those to be sentenced abjured their heresies and swore to obey the Church and the inquisitors. Gui then lifted the excommunication they had incurred as a result of their heretical acts. Finally, he proceeded to the imposition of sentences. These were proclaimed first in Latin and then in the vernacular. Gui's practice was to have these read out in a particular order. First he imposed penitential pilgrimages, next the wearing of crosses, and, third, perpetual imprisonment.

He then turned to dealing with people who were deceased. The names of those individuals who would have been imprisoned had they lived were announced. As punishment for their errors, their property was confiscated. Then came sentences ordering the 'simple' exhumation of those who had been guilty of heretical dealings but had not confessed during their lifetime. The next group Gui sentenced were those who had received the Cathar *consolamentum* on their deathbeds or who had been demonstrated to have

---

[15] At Toulouse most sentences were imposed at the cathedral of St-Etienne.

died impenitent. The remains of these individuals were not merely exhumed but also burned.

Gui then returned to the living. First he declared excommunicated those who had fled his jurisdiction. And then he imposed the most draconian sentence in his arsenal, relaxation to the secular arm, which meant death at the stake. The first to be sent to the flames were individuals who had relapsed, that is, people who had previously admitted and abjured their errors only to return to them. These people, even if penitent, were handed over to the secular authorities for execution. The next group sent to the fire were the elite members of the various heretical sects, Cathar Good Men, Waldensian priests, etc. who refused to recant their errors.[16]

If need be, the inquisitor then excommunicated those fugitives who had refused to answer his citations and fled, but who had not received a definitive sentence terminating their process. Finally, he decreed the destruction of those houses where individuals had received the Cathar *consolamentum*.[17]

Many of Gui's punishments had a highly public, theatrical character. The destruction of houses and their conversion into garbage dumps were intended as perpetual reminders of the fate that awaited heretics. False witnesses who had sought to entrap the innocent with concocted denunciations were, before being imprisoned, exhibited on scaffolds with red tongues affixed to their clothing. Most of those who repented of their heresies and sought reconciliation with the Church did not have to endure such intense public humiliation; but the punishments they received were nevertheless eminently public and even more protracted. The yellow crosses affixed to the clothing of many penitents were a concrete, constantly visible sign of both the high cost of involvement with heresy and the merciful nature of the Church. And the penitents trudging the roads of western Europe on their compulsory pilgrimages were a dramatic reminder, even to those outside Languedoc, of the ever present danger of heresy.

The most memorable punishment, and that most laden with terror and meaning, was, of course, the burning of relapsed or unrepentant heretics. Sentences to the stake, however, were relatively rare. Gui imposed these capital sentences on eleven occasions. The largest number he consigned to the flames at a single time were the seventeen Cathars executed on 5 April 1310. All told Gui sent forty-one people to the stake. Less striking than the burning of the living, but still dramatic, were the sentences executed on the cadavers of the deceased. Gui ordered the exhumation and burning of sixty-six cadavers.[18]

---

[16] Gui also envisaged sending to the stake a group composed of those who had confessed, recanted their testimony, and despite their guilt having been proved by other means, contumaciously persisted in maintaining their innocence. In practice, he seems never to have sentenced such people himself.

[17] Gui's description of a *sermo generalis* is in Gui, *P*, pp. 82–6.

[18] On three occasions Gui ordered the exhumation, but not the burning, of the corpses of those people convicted of involvement with heresy.

If we compare the sentences imposed on the various types of heretics, we can see that the Béguins were treated with unusual severity (see Table 2). A larger proportion of the people condemned for this heresy were sent to the stake than for any other heresy. Four, or 21.1%, suffered this fate. By contrast, only 7.8% of the Waldensians and 6.4% of the Cathars were burned.[19]

Béguins were also more likely to be sentenced to periods of imprisonment. Over two-thirds, thirteen in all (68.4%), were immured. Once again, Cathars and Waldensians received less rigorous treatment. Of the 469 Cathars in Gui's register, a little over half, 249 (53.1%) were imprisoned, while only thirty-six of the eighty-nine Waldensians (40.4%) received a similar punishment. The lighter penalties inflicted by the inquisitors also show variation with respect to the different types of heresy. As might be expected, only one Béguin (5.3% of the total) was sentenced to wear crosses. Waldensians and Cathars received this type of penalty more frequently, in about equal proportions, with 21.3% of Waldensians and 22.8% of Cathars being sentenced to wear these badges of infamy. No Béguin received the lightest possible penalty, the requirement to perform only a number of penitential pilgrimages, whereas 7.8% of the Waldensians and 2.1% of the condemned Cathars did.

Clearly the Béguins were treated more rigorously than other heretics. To an extent, Catharism and Waldensianism can be regarded as 'normal' heresies in Languedoc.[20] The inquisitors had had long experience with them. By the beginning of the fourteenth century, Catharism was also a sect in full decline, on the brink of extinction. Waldensianism would have greater staying power; but its followers were relatively few and were for the most part confined to limited geographical areas in Languedoc.

The heresy of the Béguins, however, was new. Indeed, until John XXII decided to settle the disputes over poverty in the Franciscan order, the Béguins had been regarded as orthodox. Moreover, the heresy had grown up in the very heart of the Church. And, as Gui emphasized in his sentences, it was a heresy that fundamentally threatened authority within the Church itself.

The crucial element in Gui's depiction of the Béguins as heretics was their attitude toward ecclesiastical authority. This is illustrated very clearly in the sentence by which Gui sent two Béguins, Pierre Hospital of Montpellier and Pierre Guiraud of Gignac, to the stake on 12 September 1322.[21] This is a very unusual sentence in Gui's register. For the most part his sentences, like those of other inquisitors, consist of a list of false beliefs and practices to which the condemned have confessed. The heretical status of these acts is assumed, or

[19] If we consider only those people who were alive at the time they were sentenced for either Catharism, Waldensianism, or Béguinism, we find that 7.6% of the Cathars (30 of 393), 8.4% of the Waldensians (7 of 83), and 21.1% of the Béguins (4 of 19) were burned alive.

[20] Good introductions to these heresies in Lambert, *Cathars*, and Audisio, *Dissent*.

[21] Gui, *Ls*, pp. 391–2.

Table 2 Individuals and their penalties broken down by type of heresy

Penalty	Cathars	Waldensians	Béguins	Other
Pilgrimages	10	7	0	0
	2.1%	7.8%	0.0%	0.0%
Crosses	107	19	1	7
	22.7%	21.1%	5.3%	31.8%
Prison	249	36	13	9
	52.9%	40.0%	68.4%	40.9%
Deceased but would have been imprisoned	16	1	0	0
	3.4%	1.1%	0.0%	0.0%
Burned alive	30	7	4	0
	6.4%	7.8%	21.1%	0.0%
Deceased but would have been burned	3	0	0	0
	0.6%	0.0%	0.0%	0.0%
Burned posthumously	58	6	0	2
	12.3%	6.7%	0.0%	9.1%
Remains exhumed	3	0	0	0
	0.6%	0.0%	0.0%	0.0%
Other	19	15	3	4
	4.0%	16.7%	15.8%	18.2%
Total	471	90	19	22

Source: Gui, *Ls*.
Note: The unit of analysis in this table is the individual, not the sentence. Since some individuals received more than one sentence, they are counted more than once in this table. Therefore, column totals sum to figures greater than those shown and percentages sum to more than 100%.

simply proclaimed. But in this particular sentence Gui actually sets about constructing an argument against the views of the Béguins. It is therefore worth considering in some detail what he has to say.

The heart of the issue, as it appears in the sentence, is the refusal of the Béguins to acknowledge the full dimensions of papal authority. Hospital and Guiraud, like the other Béguins, denied that the pope, as the vicar of Christ, could 'declare, alter, interpret, or moderate' the rule of the order of St Francis. For the Béguins, the rule of St Francis had the same evangelical status as the four gospels. Hospital and Guiraud asserted that the 'rule is the gospel of Christ, and those who in their understanding or practice fall away from it are widely separated from the faith and gospel of Christ'.[22] Therefore, just as the pope did not have the right to alter the gospels, so he did not have the right to interpret or alter the rule of St Francis. If he did, as John XXII had done, the members of the Franciscan order were not bound to obey his decrees or interpretations of the rule.

[22] Gui, *Ls*, p. 391, 'potestatem Romani pontificis . . . declarandi ac interpretandi et moderandi regulam beati Francisci'; 'regula evangelium Christi est, et qui in ejus intellectu seu observacione deficiunt procul a fide et Christi evangelio separantur'.

In replying to this line of reasoning, Gui made two principal arguments. The first was that, in denying that the pope could amend the Franciscan rule, the Béguins had put themselves outside the Church. Since the popes were the vicars of Christ, whose authority descended from St Peter, prince of the apostles, any Christian who refused to submit to his authority was guilty of the sin of paganism.

In addition to appealing to the plenitude of papal power, Gui also attacked the assertion that Francis' rule had evangelical status. To proclaim the evangelical status of his rule was, as Gui noted, tantamount either to postulating the existence of five gospels instead of four, or to abrogating the four existing gospels in favour of a new gospel, that of St Francis. This was not only impious and inimical to the faith, but irrational. Of course, Gui observed, the papacy does not have the authority to change or correct the gospels, but only submits itself to its most pleasant yoke. However, the rule of St Francis is not equivalent to the gospels, but merely a laudable and outstanding form of the spiritual life, confirmed and approved by the popes and, like all rules, subject to change by those same popes.

Thus it is heresy to defend and venerate as martyrs and saints those Franciscans and Béguins who have been burned for refusing to obey the pope. Moreover, in asserting that those bishops and ministers of the Church who have persecuted the Béguins have deprived themselves of all power to pass judgments or perform the sacraments, Hospital and Guiraud are guilty of Donatism. They have also erred in defending the doctrines of the Franciscan theologian, Pierre Jean Olivi, concerning the apocalypse. Despite the fact that many of Olivi's opinions have been found heretical by a commission of theologians, Hospital and Guiraud refuse to be bound by the Church's condemnation of these doctrines. They have also subscribed to various fantasies about what they believe to be the approaching end of the world, fantasies which are at once heretical, insane, and 'fabulosa' ('incredible'). Finally, in seeing the Roman Church as the great whore of Babylon described in the Apocalypse, they are manifestly schismatic.

The sentences of the other seventeen Béguins do not present such argued reasons for their condemnation, but their contents echo the sentence of Hospital and Guiraud. For example, the special evangelical status of St Francis's rule reappears in the sentences of Guillaume Ruffi of Cintegabelle and Raimond Juliani of Mazères. They are both portrayed as stating that the rule of St Francis was the same as the rule that Christ had imposed on his apostles. To act against it was thus to act against the gospel of Christ. Just as the pope cannot add to or diminish the gospel, so he cannot add to or diminish the rule of St Francis.[23] Raimond *de Buxo* of Belpech asserted that Francis' order was more perfect than any other, and that God had promised that it would endure until the end of the world.[24]

---

[23] Gui, *Ls*, pp. 315 and 302.
[24] Gui, *Ls*, p. 299.

The other Béguins enlarged on the limitations of papal power. Raimond *de Buxo* stated that the pope could not dispense from vows of poverty or chastity. If he did grant such dispensation to someone who subsequently married, any children produced by that union would be illegitimate.[25] Pierre Tort of Montréal believed that the pope could not dispense from any vows of chastity or virginity, even in a case where a great evil could be avoided or a great good, such as converting a kingdom to Christianity or ending a war, could be accomplished. He recognized only one exception to this rule: if there remained only three people in the world, one of whom was the pope, and the other two a man and a woman who had taken vows of chastity, then the pope could grant them dispensation from their vows lest the human race die out.[26]

The Donatist aspect of Béguin belief appears in several sentences. Raimond de Buxo asserted that if Pope John XXII had been correctly informed by the inquisitors as to the deeds of the Béguins and had knowingly acquiesced in their punishment, he had become a heretic.[27] Pierre Gastaudi of Belpech stated that from the moment that John XXII had decreed that the Franciscans owned property in common he had lost the powers that belonged to his office. He could not bind or loose, excommunicate or absolve; he could not make prelates, nor could he administer the sacraments of the Church, except baptism and the consecration of the host, although no good Catholic should receive these sacraments from him. John's actions had rendered the office of the papacy vacant, and unless he desisted from his purpose, the cardinals were free to proceed to the election of another pope.[28]

Another theme that frequently appears in the sentences of the Béguins is the conviction that the Apocalypse was at hand. Raimond *de Buxo* had read in Olivi's *Postilla* on the Apocalypse that the great whore of Babylon, dressed in gold, sitting on a beast with seven heads and ten horns, and holding in her hand a golden cup, was the Roman Church, which persecuted those spiritual men who wished to adhere to the poverty of Christ by following the rule of St Francis. Just as the synagogue had been destroyed because it had crucified Christ, so this carnal church would be destroyed. He also believed that St Francis was the angel depicted in the Book of Revelations whose face was like the sun and who held an open book in his hand. To St Francis there had been revealed the truth of the life of Christ.[29]

Several Béguins believed that Pope John XXII was the mystical antichrist who was preparing the way for the great Antichrist,[30] who was already alive.[31] Indeed, Maria *de Serra* of Cintegabelle asserted that the Antichrist was

---

[25] Gui, *Ls*, pp. 298–9.
[26] Gui, *Ls*, p. 328.
[27] Gui, *Ls*, p. 300.
[28] Gui, *Ls*, p. 323.
[29] Gui, *Ls*, pp. 298 and 301.
[30] Gui, *Ls*, pp. 304 and 312.
[31] Gui, *Ls*, pp. 309 and 330.

already more than twenty years old. She believed that he would be a member of the Franciscans, and would appear at first with the semblance of sanctity and perfection.[32]

A curious element, however, appears in the case of Guillaume Ruffi of Cintegabelle, who went to the stake as a relapsed heretic on 12 September 1322.[33] Among other things, he had induced two women to lie naked with him in bed, by telling them that to embrace, kiss, and touch one another 'dishonestly' without having intercourse was a very great good work. Whether or not Guillaume actually believed this is not altogether clear from his list of *culpe*. Yet he had reported to Gui that it was commonly said among the Béguins that there were in Italy Fraticelli and other 'men of penitence' ('homines de penitencia') who believed that no-one could claim to be perfect unless he lay naked in bed with a woman.[34]

This practice is clearly an echo of that attributed to the heretics known to Gui as the Pseudo-Apostles, that is, the followers of Gerard Segarelli and Dolcino of Novara.[35] Although only Guillaume Ruffi seems to have shared this particular aspect of Apostolic belief, there were strong parallels between the Béguins and the Pseudo-Apostles. Both movements were devoted to the idea of poverty, both grew up in the shadow of the Franciscans (although Gerard Segarelli, the founder of the Apostles, was thought unworthy of admission to the Franciscan order), both came to believe that their members constituted the true, spiritual Church, as opposed to the carnal Church that persecuted them, and both expected the imminent arrival of the Apocalypse. Dolcino, in fact, inspired by dreams of the end, conducted an armed struggle for two years from the mountains of northern Italy, until he was captured in 1307 and sent to the stake.[36] The similarity of belief and a connection in Gui's mind may help explain the severity that he displayed toward the Béguins.

Now, let us turn from examining how Gui tried to portray the Béguins as heretics to the question of how his audience received his performance. Many of those present at the *sermones generales* interpreted the day's events in ways that would have pleased Gui and his fellow inquisitors.

After observing how the condemned behaved, some witnesses went home

[32] Gui, *Ls*, p. 319.
[33] Gui, *Ls*, p. 381.
[34] Gui, *Ls*, pp. 382–3.
[35] On these see G. G. Merlo, 'Il problema di fra Dolcino negli ultimi vent'anni', *Bollettino storico-bibliografico subalpino* 72 (1974), 701–8, and 'Salimbene e gli apostolici', *Società e Storia* 39 (1988), 3–21, and R. Orioli, *L'Eresia a Bologna fra XIII e XIV secolo: II, L'eresia dolciniana*, SStor 93–6 (Rome, 1975), and *Venit perfidus heresiarcha: il movimento apostolico-dolciniano dal 1260 al 1307*, SStor 193–6 (Rome, 1988), and G. Leff, *Heresy in the Later Middle Ages*, 2 vols. (Manchester, 1967), I, 191–5. Gui himself sentenced only a single Pseudo-Apostle, Pedro of Lugo; Gui, *Ls*, pp. 360–1.
[36] See *Historia fratris Dulcini heresiarche di anonimo sincrono e De secta illorum qui se dicunt esse de ordine Apostolorum di Bernardo Gui*, ed. A. Segarizzi, 2nd edn, RIS 9, part 5. Gui himself discussed these events in his life of Pope Clement V, in E. Baluze, *Vitae paparum Avenionensium*, 2 vols. (Paris, 1693), I, 66–7.

convinced of the correctness of the inquisitors' actions. Pierre Tort of Montréal, for example, made a habit of attending the executions of Béguins. How they died determined his view of their orthodoxy. Because the Béguins he had seen executed at Béziers conducted themselves well, he believed them to be martyrs and saints. Concerning the Béguins who had been burned at Narbonne, as well as those executed at Capestang and Lunel, however, he was uncertain as to whether or not they were saved, since he had not been present. Those burned at Narbonne and Pézenas he believed to be heretics, since they had borne their punishment badly and said many unpleasant things to the inquisitor and the assembled bishops.[37]

The conclusions drawn by those who attended one of these ceremonies were not, however, always those the inquisitors intended.[38] After listening to the inquisitor's sermon, hearing the *culpe* and sentences read, and watching how the condemned conducted themselves, many people were convinced that the heretics were right and the inquisitors wrong. For example, Pierre Espeyre-en-Dieu, a weaver of Narbonne, was present at the cemetery of St Felix in Narbonne when two Béguins were burned. Before they were executed, a friar named Bernard Maurini preached a sermon on the subject of their condemnation. Evidently he tried to portray the condemned as pig-headed men who were dying for no good reason. At one point he proclaimed, 'These men wish to be burned for barley and for the colour brown; these . . . men are very badly informed.'[39] When Pierre heard these words, he thought to himself that it was a great evil to put good men to death for nothing more than this. He left the cemetery convinced that the Béguins had been treated unjustly.[40]

Pierre was not the only one to come away from a *sermo* feeling that the inquisitors had acted contrary to justice. Bernard Durban of Lodève was present when his sister Esclarmonde, together with several other Béguins, was burned at Lunel. When her sentence was announced, he could not clearly hear what was said because of the noise of the crowd; but he later learned that she had asked that her confession be read out, a request that the

---

[37] Gui, *Ls*, p. 328.

[38] A later inquisitor, Nicolas Eymerich, was aware that those about to receive their penances might not behave as expected. In his *Directorium* he noted that some penitents, if not fully converted, might take advantage of their appearance before the crowd to deny the truth of the statements in their *culpe*; *Directorium*, p. 504.

[39] D28, fols. 250r–v: 'Item, quando frater Maduis, et P⟨etrus⟩ de Fraxino fuerant condemnati in cimiterio sancti Felicis Narbonae, ipse loquens interfuit. Et a longe audivit frater [*sic*] Bernardum Maurini tunc praedicantem. Et inter caetera ab eo intellexit haec verba, "Pour ordi, et pour brun se voulent lassar cremar; aqueste gent . . . sont bien mal estrut . . ."' ('Item, when brother Maduis and P⟨eter⟩ de *Fraxino* had been condemned in the cemetery of St Félix de Narbonne, he the speaker was present. And from a distance he heard brother Bernard Maurini who was then preaching. And among the other things he understood that he said these words, "...").

[40] D28, fols. 249v–250v.

inquisitors refused. Mulling this over, Bernard came to have grave doubts about whether his sister had been justly punished.[41]

How the condemned endured the flames was closely observed. The fortitude displayed by some could make a very favorable impression. Bérenger Jaoul, who attended the execution of some Béguins at Lodève, was impressed by the manner of their death. He later told one Maneta Rosa that they had endured their punishment patiently, neither crying out, nor even uttering a single word. All in all, he said, it had been 'a most beautiful thing to see'.[42]

This perception of the Béguins as martyrs often led to a macabre scramble for the grizzly remains of their charred corpses. The inquisitors were curiously uninterested in or incapable of policing the execution grounds. Perhaps the fact that they technically did not carry out executions, but entrusted them to secular authorities, played a role in this lackadaisical attitude. Once heretics had been executed, onlookers were free to treat the remains rather as they pleased. For example, the morning after a number of Béguins were burned at Lunel a crowd descended on the place of execution. Several of the charred corpses were still relatively intact. Martin Alegre of Clermont-l'Hérault, together with some others, found Esclarmonde Durban's cadaver. They pulled it apart, putting the pieces into sacks. Martin himself made off with a hunk that he thought was either a heart or a kidney.[43]

The pieces of bone and flesh scavenged from execution sites were venerated as holy relics. Bérengère, wife of Guillaume Dominique Veirerii of Narbonne, carried around in a purse a small bone of one of the Béguins burned at Narbonne.[44] Some people were very assiduous in acquiring such relics. Raimond de Niaux of Cintegabelle and his wife Bernarde, both condemned to the *mur* (prison) in July 1322, managed to build up a respectable collection, including an assortment of bones and ashes of Béguins burned at Béziers and Lunel. They also acquired a piece of the wood to which either Brother Maduis or Brother Pierre de Frayssenet had been bound when executed. These objects were kept in a pyx, which was stored in Bernarde's chest. From time to time they took these relics out and kissed them. Their trove of sacred treasures was, however, modest compared to the cache they had seen in an unnamed person's house in Narbonne. This individual had acquired the complete head of a woman burned at Lunel, to which was still attached part of the neck, shoulders, and chest, as well as parts of the shins and some other bits.[45]

These grizzly stories demonstrate, if nothing else, the inadequacy of a

---

[41] D28, fol. 12v.

[42] '. . .pulcherimum [*sic*] erat hoc videre'; D27, fols. 81r–v.

[43] D28, fols. 16r–v. The piece of Esclarmonde that Martin made off with was possibly the heart seen at Clermont-l'Hérault by Bernard Peirotas, a priest of Lodève, who was condemned in July of 1323; D28, fol. 22r.

[44] D28, fols. 121r–122r.

[45] Gui, *Ls*, pp. 310–14.

Durkheimian interpretation of inquisitorial punishments. The penalties handed down by the inquisitors were not an expression of an outraged collective consciousness; rather they were a weapon in an on-going, and hotly contested, ideological struggle. The inquisitors, while ostensibly punishing infractions of a universal and unchanging moral order, were actually trying to impose the sectional moral vision of a dominant elite on an often recalcitrant social formation. Their punishments had as much to do with theatre and propaganda as they did with justice.

Fingerprinting an Anonymous Description of the Waldensians

Peter Biller

There are just a few texts from the whole of the Middle Ages that attempted to describe the Waldensians as a whole movement. The last one came from a very cultivated man who was one of the last of the medieval Waldensian Brothers, Georges Morel, in a letter he wrote to Swiss reformers in 1530.[1] One earlier notable text was an anonymous account of the Waldensians, connected in some way with the massive inquisitions of German-speaking Waldensians around 1400,[2] while another yet earlier one was the description contained in the fifth part of Bernard Gui's *Practica* (completed 1323–4).

Most mysterious among these is the *De vita et actibus . . . Pauperum de Lugduno*, 'On the way of life and activities . . .of the Poor of Lyons'. Its six numbered sections address in turn the definition and names of different strata in the group, beliefs, the religious form of life of the 'hospices', the annual general chapters, the rite of profession whereby someone became a full Waldensian, and the Waldensians' pastorate among their followers. Although only about 1750 words long, the *De vita* stands out among these descriptions for the glittering precision and close familiarity of the picture it paints. But we do not know when and where it was written and how it originated. As a consequence, it has been difficult for historians to make use of it.

Earlier Study

Before addressing these questions I am going to summarize earlier work on the text, beginning with manuscripts and editions. In 1888 Charles Molinier

---

[1] V. Vinay, *Le confessioni di fede dei Valdesi riformati*, Collana della Facoltà Valdese di Teologia 12 (Turin, 1975), pp. 36–51 (see esp. pp. 36–45); the most recent discussion is E. Cameron, *Waldenses: Rejections of Holy Church in Medieval Europe* (Oxford, 2000), pp. 212–16.

[2] J. J. I. von Döllinger, *Beiträge zur Sektengeschichte des Mittelalters*, 2 vols. (Munich, 1890), II, 367–9; see also Patschovsky, *Quellen zur Böhmischen Inquisition*, p. 29 n. 55, the list of editions and manuscripts in my 'Aspects of the Waldenses in the Fourteenth Century' (unpublished D.Phil. thesis, University of Oxford, 1974), pp. 366–7, and n. 53 below.

described a manuscript which contained a copy made in 1600, in Milan, Ambrosiana MS A.129 inf., fols. 182r–187r.[3] In 1890 Ignaz von Döllinger published the *De vita* using a Vatican manuscript, Vat. Lat. MS 2648, fols. 71va–72vb, and in his customary fashion making many errors in transcription,[4] while Wilhelm Preger produced a superior edition from the same manuscript.[5] In 1906 Célestin Douais described another manuscript, Dôle, Bibliothèque Municipale, MS 109, which contains the *De vita* at fols. 32r–34r, and he printed the beginning, with its chapter titles, and in 1926 this manuscript was given a longer description by Guillaume Mollat.[6] A fragment in a Rome manuscript (Archivio generalizio O.P., MS II 63), which consists of only eight-one words from the beginning of the *De vita*, was published by Gottfried Opitz in the late 1930s.[7] In 1947 Antoine Dondaine brought these previous studies together, describing the Dôle and Vatican manuscripts more elaborately.[8] Grado Merlo has referred to the existence of an unpublished typescript study produced in 1983 by R. Long and held in the library of the Department of History of the University of Turin.[9] Finally, from Giovanni Gonnet, who had written a note on the *De vita* in 1967, there came in 1998 a posthumous anthology of texts on the medieval Waldensians, which contains a re-publication of Preger's edition of the text, together with a part-paraphrase part-commentary in French.[10]

References to the *De vita* have also been made in passing in many articles and monographs dealing more generally with the medieval Waldensians, some of which I shall mention while summarizing earlier suggestions about the text's provenance, beginning with Dondaine. After listing manuscripts and describing two of them – I repeat the essentials in the next paragraph below – Dondaine suggested a probable date for the *De vita*: late thirteenth or early fourteenth century.[11] And he conjectured that it originated in Germany.

[3] Molinier, 'Rapport', 176–81, with details about the *De vita* at 180–1.
[4] Döllinger, *Beiträge*, II, 92–7.
[5] W. Preger, 'Über die Verfassung der französischen Waldesier in der älteren Zeit', *ABAW* 19 (1890), 641–711 (pp. 708–11).
[6] Douais, *Inquisition*, pp. 353–6 (the *De vita* at p. 354); Mollat, *M*, p. xxix.
[7] G. Opitz, 'Uber zwei Codices zum Inquisitionsprozess. Cod. Cas.1730 und Cod. des Archivio generalizio dei Domenicani II 63', *Quellen und Forschungen aus italienischen Archiven und Bibliotheken* 28 (1937/8), 106; Opitz comments on the manuscript (script of the fourteenth century, and the whole not later than 1350, 'Ich glaube') on pp. 79–81, and his formal description and excerpts begins on p. 100; the beginning of *De vita* is given on p. 106.
[8] Dondaine, 'Manuel', 125–8, 130–40 (on the Dôle manuscript), 130, 154–67 (on the Vatican manuscript), 183–4 on the *De vita*.
[9] G. G. Merlo, *Valdesi e valdismi medievali: itinerari e proposte di ricerca* (Turin, 1984), p. 11 n. 17, and *Identità valdesi*, p. 44 n. 48.
[10] G. Gonnet, *Le confessioni di fede Valdesi prima della Riforma*, Collana della Facoltà Valdese di Teologia (Turin, 1967), pp. 9 and 104–6; *Enchiridion Fontium Valdensium*, ed. G. Gonnet, 2 vols., Collana della Facoltà Valdese di Teologia, Roma, unnumbered and 22 (Torre Pellice and Turin, 1958–98), II, 177–87.
[11] See n. 8 above.

His views were followed by Giovanni Gonnet (1967, 1998) and Pierette Paravy (1993).[12] Amedeo Molnár (1974) wrote of the text as 'constructed on the basis of depositions from a German follower of the Waldensians'.[13] In his 1981 survey of earlier scholarship, Martin Schneider accepted the German hypothesis, but preferred an earlier date, suggesting the mid-thirteenth century as correlating with the *De vita*'s account of Waldensianism.[14] The German theory is not mentioned by either Grado Merlo (1991) or Euan Cameron (2000). The latter sees the *De vita* as a 'controversial text, of uncertain date and provenance', and both follow Schneider in preferring an earlier date: 'certainly before the end of the thirteenth century' (Merlo), and 'a date no later than the middle of the thirteenth century' (Cameron).[15]

The German hypothesis has not swayed everyone. In a study of Waldensians in Burgundy and Gascony (1974), which made much use of *culpe* and sentences in Bernard Gui's *Liber sententiarum* and Jacques Fournier's interrogation of the Waldensian Raimon de la Côte, Jean Duvernoy commented that the *De vita* describes the Waldensian mission precisely as it is encountered in these inquisition materials.[16] Unaware then of Duvernoy's comment, I also remarked on the parallels between the *De vita* and Bernard Gui's *Liber sententiarum* and *Practica*, in an article (1994) which included a note from a romance vernacular philologist, John N. Green, on one word of Occitan origin contained in the *De vita*; when reprinting this in 2001 I added further argument against a German origin.[17] These preliminary comments are much modified and extended in the study of the text which follows here. Appended is an edition and translation.

---

[12] See n. 10 above; P. Paravy, *De la chrétienté romaine à la réforme en Dauphiné: évêques, fidèles et déviants (vers 1340 – vers 1530)*, Collection de l'École Française de Rome 183, 2 vols. (Rome, 1993), II, 927.

[13] A. Molnár, *Storia dei Valdesi dalle origini all'adesione alla Riforma (1176–1532)* (Turin, 1974), p. 83: 'ricostruito sulla base delle deposizioni di un "amico" valdese tedesco'.

[14] M. Schneider, *Europäisches Waldensertum im 13. und 14. Jahrhundert*, Arbeiten zur Kirchengeschichte 51 (Berlin and New York, 1981), pp. 140–2.

[15] Merlo, *Identità valdesi*, p. 43 n. 47 ('sicuramente anteriore alla fine del XIII secolo', changing the opinion he expressed earlier in his *Eretici e inquisitori*, p. 42 ('della fine del secolo XIII o dell'inizio del secolo XIV'); Cameron, *Waldenses: Rejections of Holy Church*, pp. 73 n. 13 and 74 n. 20.

[16] J. Duvernoy, 'L'unité du valdéisme en France à la fin du XIIIe siècle (Bourgogne, Sillon rhodanien, Gascogne)', *Valdo e il valdismo medievale*, Bollettino della Società di Studi Valdesi 136 (1974), 73–83 (p. 78 and n. 27).

[17] P. Biller and J. N. Green, 'Appendice: argent allemand et hérésie médiévale', *Entre idéal et réalité: Actes du Colloque international. Finances et religion du Moyen-Age à l'époque contemporaine*, ed. M. Aubrun, G. Audisio, B. Dompnier and A. Gueslin, Institut d'Etudes du Massif Central, Centre d'Histoire des Entreprises et des Communautés, Collection 'Prestige' 5 (Clermont-Ferrand, 1994), pp. 49–56; reprinted in Biller, *Waldenses*, pp. 225–31, together with additional material, pp. 299–300.

German Origin and an Early Date

The general character of the manuscripts analysed by Dondaine did not point in any particular or positive way towards Germany. However, the *De vita* mentions countries – Germany is mentioned three times, Lombardy twice, *Provincia* once.[18] The reasoning seems to be that frequency indicates Germany. The argument seems questionable, not only because the numbers are so small and the majority so slight, but also because it is not self-evident that the author of a text which sets out to describe things internationally is most likely to refer most often to his or her own country. The opposite may be more likely. Here it is instructive to look at the compilation by the Anonymous of Passau, *c.* 1266, which is of indubitable Austro-German origin. This bears on Germanophone Waldensians, with two references to their relations with Lombardy. The first warrants comparison with the *De vita*.[19]

Anonymous of Passau	*De vita*
Item, peregrinantur et ita Lombardiam intrantes visitant episcopos suos [*in another recension, the first phrase runs:* ipsi se fingunt peregrinari]	Ad quod concilium veniunt tres vel 4^{or} heretici perfecti de Almania habentes secum aliquem clericum vel alium interpretatorem, et fingunt se aliquo modo se velle apostolorum Petri et Pauli limina visitare.
(Item, they travel like pilgrims [*or* they pretend to go on pilgrimage], and thus entering Lombardy they visit their bishops)	(Three or four perfect heretics come to this council, bringing together with them a cleric or another interpreter, and they pretend in some way to be wanting to visit the holy places of the apostles Peter and Paul.)

The other is a question, intended to be put to Germanophone Waldensians: 'An umquam collectam fecerint ad mittendum fratribus in Lombardia?' ('Did they ever make a collection to be sent to the Brothers in Lombardy?').[20]

In the Anonymous of Passau the verbs and the dative in *fratribus* all indicate motion *to* somewhere: go on pilgrimage; enter Lombardy; send to the Brothers in Lombardy. By contrast, the *De* vita's verbs, *ab*, *de* and the ablative are all *from* somewhere: 'come from Germany', 'is brought from Germany' ('veniunt . . . de', 'apportatur de'). In the sentences quoted from the Anonymous of Passau and in the immediately surrounding prose, there is no reference to Germany. The work is very Austrian or German – its author or compiler born in Upper or Lower Austria, and probably a Dominican, his experience one of inquisition of Germanophone Waldensians – but he has no

---

[18] References are to the text of the *De vita* printed below, here *De vita* iii, iv.

[19] Anonymous of Passau, ed. J. Gretser, *Maxima Bibliotheca Veterum Patrum*, ed. M. de la Bigne, 28 vols. (Lyons and Geneva, 1677–1707), XXV, 266c; M.A.E. Nickson, 'The "Pseudo-Reinerius" Treatise, the Final Stage of a Thirteenth-Century Work on Heresy from the Diocese of Passau', *AHDLMA* 62 (1967), 255–314 (p. 302).

[20] Patschovsky, *Passauer Anonymus*, p. 67. Repeated in an inquisitor's handbook of the first half of the fourteenth century, Patschovsky, *Inquisition in Böhmen*, p. 103.

need to insist on this.[21] He is inside Austria/Germany, looking out, and what he mentions is the country which he sees outside, namely Lombardy.

The analogy suggests an author in the *De vita* who refers more to Germany precisely because he is outside Germany. From his viewpoint – in southern France *or* Italy, and he does not spell this out because he and his early readers know this – he is looking at Waldensianism in several countries, and when looking *outside* his country he is struck by several things about Waldensians in Germany. And he writes of people or money as *coming* or *being brought out of* Germany ('de Almania').

What of the dating so far suggested? Dondaine established much about the other contents and the dates of the four manuscripts in which the *De vita* is extant. All four are anthologies of formulae and tracts or treatises for inquisitors. The Ambrosian manuscript is a copy, made in Rome in 1600 by a Vatican Library scriptor, of a parchment manuscript re-copied in 1491 from its own exemplar in the library of the Dominican convent and monastery of Santa Maria-sopra-Minerva. Its prototype is likely to be not later than *c*. 1350, and it is adapted to the needs of inquisitors in northern Italy; Dondaine suggested that the prototype could be the Dominican Archive manuscript described by Opitz, whose script was fourteenth century and, in Opitz's belief, from around 1350. The latest dated text within the Vatican anthology is *c*. 1330, and it is another example of an Italian collection. Mollat suggested that the Dôle manuscript, copied in 1455, belonged to the Dominican convent of Saint-Cloud (Jura).[22] In turn, this was based on a manuscript of an inquisitor's anthology which was almost certainly once in the archives of the Dominicans in Toulouse. Its chronologically latest texts are by Bernard Gui – including his *Practica inquisitionis* – and it represents an example of the sort of anthology in use in Languedoc between *c*. 1320 and *c*. 1350. Though the manuscripts do not provide a very precise terminus, they clearly suggest that we should be looking before *c*. 1350, and perhaps no later than *c*. 1330.

Before this period – but how long before? Suggestions have been made on the basis of the *De vita*'s contents. Cameron points to its description of features which were characteristic of early Waldensianism – Waldensians wearing perforated footwear and living part-sedentary lives in 'hospices'. These will have fallen away as serious persecution got going, and the *De vita*, therefore, dates from before 1250. This suggestion is useful in focussing our minds, but we need to ask how securely we can date the *De Vita* thus, by correlating its contents with stages characteristic of particular periods.

Women preached and taught among the early Waldensians: *culpe* on followers drawn up by the inquisitor Peter Sellan (1241–2) have many examples.[23] But, while we can still find a Waldensian Sister in Bernard Gui's inquisition records around 1300, there is no trace of her having been

---

[21] See on him Patschovsky, *Passauer Anonymus*, pp. 146–50.
[22] Mollat, *M*, xxix.
[23] Biller, *Waldenses*, pp. 139–42.

pastorally active. This can be juxtaposed to the *De Vita*: there are Sisters, but they are not pastorally active.

We can follow a line of references to Waldensian 'hospices', from relatively early times to Bernard Gui, one of whose *culpe*, as we shall see later, refers to them. The references to a 'house of the Waldensians' ('domus Valdensium') are quite common in the *culpe* of those followers who appeared before Peter Sellan, and they proceed alongside three *culpe* on women who confessed to having rented houses, in one case for two years, to the 'Waldensian Women' ('mulieres Valdenses').[24] In another set of depositions, a woman confessed to having lived a religious life with three named 'Waldensian Women' in Castelnaudary for three or four years.[25] While at this early and open stage, there were houses of Sisters, separate from those of the Waldensian Brothers, it is clear that the *De vita*'s description of Brothers living with Sisters whom they pretend are their wives or sisters, for the sake of secrecy, comes from a later stage. If clandestinity adopted because of persecution is usable in this way, for relatively later dating, then we should also note the guise of pilgrims adopted by Waldensians travelling to general chapters that is noted in the *De Vita*.

We can also follow a line of references to the wearing of sandals up to the time of Bernard Gui.[26] Three followers who had appeared in front of the inquisitor Peter Sellan had made or repaired sandals for the Waldensians.[27] That the period of concealment which followed this went together with the continued possession of sandals can be seen from a sentence on a female follower from the 1230s, which specifies that Waldensians had been 'hiding' ('latentes') in her house with their books and sandals.[28] At this later stage we must presume that sandals were only occasionally worn – at the time of reception and on occasions of assured safety? – and that most of the time the Waldensians were clothed and shod in a safely unremarkable way. Followers from different Waldensians groups still referred to them as 'the sandal-shod' ('sandaliati') when talking to the inquisitor Anselm of Alessandria, whose 'note-book' treatise rests on an inquisitor's career which stretched from 1267 to 1279.[29] In Bernard Gui's *Practica* (completed 1323–4) wearing sandals is why one name for the Waldensians is 'sandal-wearers' ('Insabbatati'). But it is a thing of once upon a time: 'formerly' ('olim') they wore sandals.[30] Here are the chronological boundaries. Sandal-wearing is described in the present tense, as current, between 1267 and 1279, whereas by 1323–4, it was described in the past tense, a disused practice, but one which is still remembered, at least in an inquisitor's mind and text.

---

[24] D21, fols. 219r, 221v, 228r–v.
[25] See p. 193 below and n. 112.
[26] Patschovsky and Selge, p. 59 and n. 8.
[27] D21 fols. 203r, 215r and 261v.
[28] Patschovsky and Selge, p. 59.
[29] Dondaine, 'Manuel', pp. 318–19.
[30] Gui, *P* V.ii.2 (p. 245), and *M* (pp. 37–9).

This method does not point to a date before 1250, and there are further weaknesses in dating the *De Vita* in this way. This or that feature is in the first instance characteristic not of a particular stage in Waldensianism but of the generalisations and simplifications of modern historians when conjecturally reconstructing successive stages in Waldensianism. None of these reconstructions have the complexity, variation, paradox and detail of whatever Waldensian reality actually was. They exclude different possibilities in the development of Waldensianism. Sedentary life in *secret* religious 'hospices' may have been possible for longer than is usually suggested, and distinctive sandals may have been worn only at the rite of ordination or only within the religious houses. A Waldensian told the inquisitor Jacques Fournier (1320) that the Waldensians bore the pastoral staff not materially but spiritually, applying this also to other material insignia. Similarly, the Brothers may have been seen for a long time by their followers as 'sandal-shod' spiritually, even though they were no longer seen actually wearing sandals.[31]

Further, we need to bear in mind more complex possibilities in the memory and the presentation of material to inquisitors. Take for example the *culpa* which survives on the Waldensian follower Peter Aymoni in Bernard Gui's *Liber sententiarum*. Peter had received Waldensian Brothers and he and his wife had prayed together with them according to their rite for much of their lives. Now, if Peter had described the Waldensian Brothers as he *first* learnt about them? Or as he knew them just before his confession, forty-five years later?[32] Nearly half a century later, sticking to what he learnt as a youth, he might have been a fossil, and antiquated in his views. The same could apply to someone giving the evidence upon which the *De vita* is based.[33]

Broad Fingerprinting of the *De vita*

The principle involved in trying to date *De vita* by its contents is self-evidently reasonable, since comparison is ultimately our only resource. However, we can diminish the possibilities of error if we try to avoid the mediation through modern historians' reconstruction of stages in Waldensianism, and instead look at the surface details of texts. Although there was some continuity there was also variation, through time and place, in the questions the inquisitors put, in the material they chose, in the details whose percolation into depositions their questions encouraged, and in the language they used. Consequently the texts they produced also vary in detail and wording, having as it were their distinct fingerprints. How do the fingerprints of the *De vita* and other groups of inquisition material compare?

---

[31] Fournier, I, 57.
[32] Gui, *Ls*, pp. 352–3.
[33] See p. 178 below for another possibility suggested by Caterina Bruschi.

I list here these groups, holding one in reserve. They are the *culpe* surviving from the inquisitorial activity of Peter Sellan (1241–2) in Quercy;[34] the depositions of Waldensians in the 1245–6 enquiries of Bernard of Caux and John of St Pierre in the Toulousain;[35] the inquisitorial formulae from an inquisitor's anthology-handbook (collection of formulae, of which the last dated one is 1265) – originally from Languedoc, but adapted for use in Lombardy;[36] the descriptions of Waldensians and list of questions to be put to a Waldensian in the Anonymous of Passau's compilation, *c.* 1266;[37] the slightly later treatise of the Pseudo-David of Augsburg, whose authorship and region have never been ascertained;[38] and interrogations by Jacques Fournier in Pamiers in 1319–20.[39] If we press hard on the terminus provided by the manuscripts, we look also at the depositions by Piedmontese Waldensians interrogated by Alberto de Castellario at Giaveno in 1335,[40] and at the fragments of depositions in Bohemia in front of Gallus of Neuhaus between 1335 and *c.* 1353–5.[41]

There are some overlaps, as one would expect, between any one of these and the *De vita* - most with the depositions in front of Jacques Fournier – but nowhere is there really marked, extensive and detailed thematic and semantic parallelism. However, when the *De Vita* is juxtaposed with two other texts which I omitted from my list – the *culpe* and sentences (1309–22) in Bernard Gui's *Liber sententiarum*[42] and the formal description of Waldensianism in Part 5 of his *Practica* – this parallelism is found.[43] The fingerprints are not identical: but they are very close.

Before summarizing the parallels, I must make some caveats. There are countless and complex overlaps and inter-connections between Gui's questions, his *culpe*, his sentences, and the description of the Waldensians in his *Practica*. The *Practica* itself is sometimes a mosaic of earlier texts, and its vocabulary, therefore, resembles archaeological strata of various dates. The role of the *De vita* as one of these sources is discussed later. Finally, there is a statistical element to what follows, which most of the time establishes that the

---

[34] These appear in D21, fols. 143r–310v, *passim*. Material on Waldensians in other D volumes is rare: D22, fols. 30r, 71r–v and 77v; D23, fols. 118r and 139r; D24, fols. 133r–v and 281r; D25, fols. 9v–10v and 195v–200v.
[35] Toulouse 609, fols. 96r–v, 136r, 157r, 234v and 248r–252v.
[36] Formulae from this relating to French Waldensians are edited in Patschovsky and Selge, pp. 55–69.
[37] Parts of this are edited in Patschovsky and Selge, pp. 70–103 (the collection included also the texts on pp. 19–43), and on earlier editions see Patschovsky, *Passauer Anonymus*, ch. 1.
[38] See the survey of the problem of this text in Schneider, *Europäisches Waldenserthum*, pp. 142–5.
[39] Fournier, I, 40–127, 508–32.
[40] Edited by Merlo, *Eretici e inquisitori*, pp. 161–255.
[41] Patschovsky, *Quellen zur Böhmischen Inquisition*, pp. 175–255.
[42] On this, see ch. 7 above, n. 1.
[43] Gui, *P* V.ii.1–68 (pp. 244–52), and *M* (pp. 34–64); Wakefield and Evans, pp. 386–97.

De vita shares more with these texts than with others, not that it shares nothing with others.

Comparison starts with the words used for the Waldensians themselves, words which are not unique to these texts. All three of them spell out that the members of the group as a whole were called the *Pauperes de Lugduno*, the Poor of Lyons, and that the male Waldensians were called Brothers, *fratres*.[44]

De vita	*Liber sententiarum*	*Practica*
se dicunt 'Pauperes Christi' seu 'Pauperes de Lugduno'. . . .homines . . . recipiuntur et 'fratres' . . . nuncupantur	vocabantur 'Pauperes de Lugduno', et ipsi inter se vocabant se 'fratres'	communiter vocant se 'fratres' et dicunt se esse 'Pauperes Christi' seu 'Pauperes de Lugduno'
(they say they ⟨are⟩ the 'Poor of Christ' or 'Poor of Lyons' . . . men . . . are received . . . and they are named 'Brothers')	(they were called the 'Poor of Lyons', and among themselves they called themselves 'Brothers')	(generally they call themselves 'Brothers' and they say that they are the 'Poor of Christ' or the 'Poor of Lyons')

Perfectus in the sense of a 'full' heretic as opposed to a follower was not often used in texts about Waldensians, but it was used in all three of these texts and also in the *De inquisitione hereticorum* of the Pseudo-David of Augsburg. I provide the examples when returning to this later. Two of the texts also generalize Waldensian usage for the names of followers:[45]

De vita	*Liber sententiarum*
de secta hereticorum predictorum . . . alii 'amici' eorundem et 'credentes'	scivit quod ipsi inter se vocant se 'fratres', et sic vocabant eos 'amici' et 'credentes' ipsorum
(among the sect of the aforesaid heretics . . .the others are called their 'friends' and 'believers')	(she knew that they among themselves called themselves 'Brothers', and thus they called them [= followers like the witness and her husband] their 'friends' and 'believers')

One semantic oddity in the *De vita* occurs in repeated pairings of two words: *qualiter . . . profitentur seu consolentur*, 'how they profess or are consoled', *professio eorum . . .consolandus*, 'their profession . . . the one who is to be consoled'.[46] *Profiteri*, 'to profess', and *professio*, 'profession', are clearly being used to mean 'to take vows' and become a Waldensian, and 'the taking of such vows', using vocabulary standard for the monastic profession of vows.[47] What is peculiar is the equivalence with 'to be consoled'. A commonplace was the use of this verb in depositions about the receiving of the Cathar *consolamentum*. For example: 'et tunc fuit hereticata, consolata et recepta, et ab

---

[44] *De vita* i; Gui, *Ls*, p. 217; Gui, *P* V.ii.5 (p. 249) and *M* (p. 52). A high proportion of the *culpe* on Waldensian followers includes the detail: Gui, *Ls*, pp. 221, 222, 223, 224, 226, 227, 234, 242, 339, 343, 354, 356, 357, 358, 359, 367, 368 and 369; see pp. 353 and 367 for less formulaic examples.

[45] *De vita* i; Gui, *Ls*, p. 222.

[46] *De vita* rubric of v.

[47] See the second meaning of *professio* listed in J. Niermeyer, *Mediae Latinitatis Lexicon Minus* (Leiden, 1976), p. 859.

eis secundum modum et ritum hereticorum' ('and then she was hereticated, consoled and received, and by them according to the heretics' rite').[48] There is no equivalent of this in other texts on the Waldensians, although there are scattered traces of the word *consolamentum* being used to denote the Eucharist in Bohemia (1335) and in Piedmont in 1387.[49] However, there is a comparable semantic oddity in Bernard Gui's texts, where the Waldensians' hearing of confessions is frequently found, and described in conventional vocabulary: 'confessiones talium audiunt et absolvunt et penitentiam injungunt' ('they hear the confessions of these [their followers] and absolve them and impose penance').[50] The *Practica* and the *Liber sententiarum* also contain a sentence in which a gloss follows a reference to Waldensian confession, absolution and penance: 'quam vocant "melioramentum"' ('which they call the "melior-amentum"').[51] *Melioramentum* was one of the words conventionally used to describe the Cathar rite of adoration. There is an analogy between these two cases, the uses of *consolari* for Waldensian profession and *melioramentum* for Waldensian confession. Both Bernard Gui and the *De vita* display a similar readiness to borrow a term from Catharism and apply it to a Waldensian ritual.[52]

There is greater closeness, though not identity, when the *De vita* and Gui describe formal Waldensian meetings. The *Practica* and *De vita* both describe the Waldensian council, held once or twice a year:[53]

De vita	*Practica*
semel in anno in quadragesima celebrant concilium vel capitulum generale . . . ordinat . . .de	singulis annis tenent aut celebrant unum vel duo capitula generalia . . . ordinatur de . . .
(once a year during Lent they celebrate a Council or General Chapter . . . he ordains about . . .)	(every year they hold or celebrate one or two General Chapters . . . it is ordained about . . .)

Some of the wording is the same: *celebrant, capitulum generale, ordinat* or *ordinatur*. Both texts have the Waldensians coming to the General Chapter in disguise, though not the same: they pretend to be travelling pilgrims in the *De vita*, while in the *Practica* they are like merchants when gathered in a

---

[48] D25, fol. 50v.
[49] See Patschovsky, *Quellen zur Böhmischen Inquisition*, p. 236 lines 6–7 and the appended note.
[50] Gui, *P* V.ii.3 (p. 246) and *M* (p. 42).
[51] Gui, *Ls*, p. 263; Gui, *P* iii.34 (p. 133); *De vita* iv.
[52] In her *culpa* one Waldensian follower is recorded as referring to a Waldensian as 'de illis bonis hominibus' (Gui, *Ls*, p. 241) – 'one of these good men', in a moral sense? Or, 'one of these "Good Men"', where 'Good Men' was a name? If she was calling Waldensians 'The Good Men', a term used for Cathars, this was another example of contamination of Cathar vocabulary.
[53] Gui, *P* V.ii.5 (p. 249) and *M* (p. 50). The terms 'council or chapter', 'concilium seu capitulum', also appear in the *Vita et conversatio*, emanating from Germanophone areas around 1400; Döllinger, *Beiträge*, II, 368.

follower's house for the Chapter. Both texts describe three areas of activity in the General Chapter, taking the themes in the same order, though not using identical language.

De vita	*Practica*
(1) efficiuntur in eodem capitulo sandaliati, et ex tunc cum aliis sandaliatis 'magistri' et 'rectores' et 'sacerdotes' dicuntur. Item, in dicto capitulo ordinatur de hiis qui in dicta secta cupiunt profiteri et consolari . . .	(1) et in illis capitulis major omnium ordinat et disponit de presbiteris et dyachonibus,
(⟨some⟩ are made into the 'sandalled' at this Chapter, and from then on are said to be Masters and Rectors and Priests. Item, in the same chapter it is ordained about those in the said sect who want to profess and be consoled . . .)	(and in these Chapters the leader of all of them ordains about priests and deacons . . .)

While there is some ambiguity here – it is not clear that ordination and profession are envisaged in the *Practica* – there is none in the second and third categories. The second category is about choosing Waldensians to visit believers in various regions.

(2) in dicto capitulo deputantur et constituuntur visitatores amicorum suorum et credentium qui visitare debeant illo anno, et mittuntur duo in qualibet regione seu provincia in qua aliqui de eorum credentibus conversantur	(2) et ⟨ordinat et disponit⟩ de mittendis ad diversas partes et regiones ad credentes suos pro confessionibus audiendis
(And in the said Chapter the visitors of friends and believers who are to visit that year are appointed and constituted, and two are sent into each region or province in which some of their believers live)	(and ⟨he ordains and disposes⟩ about those to be sent to various parts and regions to their believers for the hearing of their confessions)

Though the *De vita* does not mention confessions at this point, its formal description of visits to believers, which is the subject of its sixth part, details these confessions. The third activity at the Chapter is the treatment of money.

(3) in dicto capitulo presentantur pecunia et helemosine per amicos et credentes eorundem sibi data et transmissa. Que quidem pecunia iuxta ordinacionem dictorum sandaliatorum distribuitur, et datur cuilibet certa porcio pro se et sua familia in victu et vestitu anno venturo sustinendo. Et si aliqui qui regunt hospicia presentes non fuerunt, mittitur pecunia per aliquos qui in illis partibus morantur, et de Alemania maior pars pecunie de qua vivunt ⟨et⟩ sustinentur apportatur.	(3) et ⟨ordinat et disponit de⟩ elemosinis colligendis, et audit et recipit rationem de collectis et de expensis factis.

(money and alms which their friends and believers have given and transmitted to them are presented at this chapter. The money is distributed according to the decision of the said 'sandalled', and a certain portion is given to each for himself and his household for maintenance in food and clothing for the coming year. And if some who rule *hospicia* were not present, money is sent to them by some who live in those parts. And the greater part of the money upon which they live ⟨and⟩ are maintained is brought from Germany.)

(and ⟨he ordains and disposes⟩ about the alms to be collected, and he hears and gives an account of ⟨the money⟩ that has been collected and the expenses that have been incurred.)

The point about Germany, which is made in the *De vita*, would have been manifest in a financial account of the sort which is described in the *Practica*.

These parallels are pretty strong, stronger than the parallels which can be found with the references to money and travel, quoted above, in the Anonymous of Passau. Much stronger, however, are parallels on two other points. One of these is prayer. In chapter 7 above I discuss the question Bernard Gui put to Waldensians about praying in the Waldensian mode, as specified in the *Practica*, variations in this question, and the various answers which can be deduced from the *culpe* and sentences of the *Liber sententiarum*. There is overwhelming emphasis in both of Gui's texts and in the *De vita* on the Waldensian mode of praying, and this emphasis finds no parallel in any other inquisition texts on the Waldensians. Details overlap, first of all praying by a bed or beds:[54]

De vita	*Liber sententiarum*
flexis genibus multociens ante lectus suos ponunt se ad oracionem	oravit flexis genibus inclinatus super quandam cayssiam juxta lectum
(they often put themselves to prayer on bended knees in front of their beds)	(he prayed on bended knees, bent over a bench beside the bed)

The senior Waldensian is noted as using the vernacular at the same two specified points, and most striking is the repetition of the same prayer formulae, one of which is a reference to Matthew 14. 17–21, while the other is from Apocalypse 7. 12:[55]

---

[54] *De vita* iii; *Ls*, p. 354.
[55] See also the description of blessing of the table before eating given by Raimon de la Côte, Fournier, I, 105.

De vita	*Practica*
Ante prandium ponunt se ad oracionem . . . In prandio ille qui regit hospicium benedictionem prandii facit in hunc modum, dicendo 'Benedicite'. Et alii respondent, 'Dominus'. Et postea dicitur oracio Pater Noster. Qua completa, dicit rector materna lingua, 'Deus, qui benedixit quinque panes ordaceos et duos pisces in deserto, benedicat cibum et potum et personas que recipient [See Mathew 14. 17–21]. In nomine Patris et Filii et Spiritus Sancti, Amen'.	antequam ponant se ad mensam benedicunt eam dicendo, 'Benedicite' 'Kyrie eleison, Christe eleison, Kyrie eleison', 'Pater Noster'; quo dicto, antiquior inter eos dicit in vulgari, 'Deus, qui benedixit quinque panes ordaceos et duos pisces in deserto discipulis suis benedicat hanc mensam et ea que sunt super eam et ea que apponuntur in ea'. Et facit signum crucis, dicendo, 'In nomine Patris et Filii et Spiritus Sancti, Amen'.
(Before dinner they set themselves to prayer . . . At dinner, the one who rules the *hospicium* does the blessing of the supper in this way, saying 'Bless'. And the others reply, 'Lord'. And afterwards the prayer 'Our Father' is said. When this is finished, the rector says in the mother tongue, 'May God, who blessed five loaves of barley and two fish in the desert, bless this food and this drink and those who are about to receive. In the name of the Father and the Son and the Holy Spirit, Amen.')	(Before they set themselves to the table, they bless it, saying 'Bless', 'Kyrie eleison, Christe eleison, Kyrie eleison', 'Our Father'. When this has been said, the oldest among them says in the vernacular, ''May God, who blessed five loaves of barley and two fish in the desert for his disciples, bless this table and those things on it, and those things which are placed on it'. And he makes the sign of the cross, saying, 'In the name of the Father and the Son and the Holy Spirit, Amen.')
Post prandium agunt gracias, et rector hospicii dicit materna lingua, 'Benedictio, et claritas, et retribue, etc'.	Item, quando surgunt de mensa in prandio vel in cena, reddunt gratias hoc modo, videlicet quod antiquior dicit in vulgari illud quod habetur in Apocalipsi: 'Benedictio et claritas . . .'
(After dinner they say grace, and the *rector* of the *hospicium* says in the mother tongue, 'Blessing, and glory, and repay, etc.')	(Item, when they rise from the table at after dinner or supper, they give thanks in this way, viz the elder says in the vernacular what is contained in the Apocalypse: 'Blessing, and glory . . .')

Finally, there is the question of the Waldensian Brothers' gifts to their followers of little objects. There are some traces of this elsewhere, among geographically far-flung communities. From the Bohemian inquisition of German-speaking Waldensians in the late 1330s there survives a curious story about a time when there was an inquisition in Steyr. Followers asked a Waldensian advice about responding to questions put by the inquisitor. 'When the question is put to you', he said, 'if men come to you, who hear confessions and do sermons, you should reply: "Men come to us, who ⟨sell things⟩ to us, and they bring other domestic things necessary for women."' [56] It is very possible that the cover-story was useful precisely because of its truthful element, that is, because the Waldensians were bringing such objects

---

[56] Patschovsky, *Quellen zur Böhmischen Inquisition*, p. 199 lines 16–20: 'Quando queretur a vobis, si veniunt ⟨homines ad vos q⟩ui audiunt confessiones et faciunt predicaciones, respondeatis: "Veniunt homines ad nos, qui nobis ⟨. . . . .⟩ et portant alias res domesticas necessarias mulieribus"'. Patschovsky reasonably suggests *vendunt* and some sellable object or objects for the missing word or words. Cf. general plotting of secrecy in ch. 5 above, p. 85 and n. 16.

as well as carrying out their secret pastoral activities. There is no other trace among the fragments which survive from this inquisition, but among the followers questioned in Stettin in 1392–4 there was one widow to whom the Waldensians had given a little knife.[57] While these traces are rare, there are more among the Waldensians tried in Piedmont from the 1480s onwards, and references to the gifts of pins (or needles) have been collected by Gabriel Audisio and Euan Cameron.[58]

I am side-stepping their interesting discussions of the possible meanings of these pins, and Cathar and monastic parallels, confining myself to the question, where among early texts can this material be found?[59] In Gui's *Liber sententiarum* we see Stephen Garini confessing in 1320 that between 1290 and 1295 he 'gave five Cahors shilling to John of Cernon, and received pins from the same man'.[60] John of Cernon was a Waldensian Brother attested in many of the other confessions, and there is monotonous repetition. Paulin (confessing in 1311 about contact around 1301), 'sometimes received from them the gift of a pin [*or* a gift, pins].[61] Uwnard (1311, 1293) 'gave from his money to some Waldensians, and received as a gift *gavinetos* and pins from some of the same men'.[62] Stephen of Cernon (1311, 1297)'often gave from his money to various Waldensians, and sometimes received little knives from them as a gift'.[63] Juliana (1303, 1312) 'received pins from them as a gift', while Hugonin (1309, 1312) 'received pins from the same ⟨men⟩ as a gift'.[64] Guilielma (1305, 1311) 'gave something to the Waldensians, and received pins from one of them'.[65] In addition to these, there are two confessions where an identical formula is used, 'he gave some things to the Waldensians and received from them', and these may both be summary versions of the more detailed confessions I have just listed.[66]

This is the only cache of early inquisition texts to carry this material: and

---

[57] Kurze, *Quellen*, p. 126, no. 15.

[58] G. Audisio, *Les vaudois du Luberon: Une minorité en Provence*, Association d'Études Vaudoises et Historiques du Luberon (Gap, 1984), pp. 244–5; E. Cameron, *The Reformation of the Heretics: The Waldenses of the Alps 1480–1580* (Oxford, 1984), pp. 118–19.

[59] See for example the reference to Good Men giving *pulcra jocalia* ('fine trinkets') to a follower (*Ls*, p. 11), and reference to Cathar followers and trading in pins in D25, fol. 45r; on monks' custom of carrying a pin (or needle) as a symbol of virtue, see Caesar, *Dialogus* vi.15–17 (I, 368–70).

[60] Gui, *Ls*, p. 242: 'dedit quinque solidos caturcenses Johanni de Cernone, et recepit acus ab eodem'.

[61] Gui, *Ls*, p. 222: 'aliquando recepit ab eis donum acus'.

[62] Gui, *Ls*, p. 233: 'dedit aliquibus Valdensibus de pecunia sua, et recepit dono ab aliquibus ex eisdem gavinetos et acus'.

[63] Gui, *Ls*, p. 240: 'pluries dedit de pecunia sua diversis Valdensibus, et recepit aliquando ab eis cultellos dono'.

[64] Gui, *Ls*, pp. 240, 241: 'recepit dono ab eis acus';'recepit acus ab eisdem dono'.

[65] Gui, *Ls*, p. 242: 'dedit Valdensibus aliquid, et recepit ab uno eorum'.

[66] Gui, *Ls*, pp. 216, 225: 'dedit aliqua Valdensibus, et recepit ab eisdem'.

it carries it in some abundance. And the *De vita* is the only generalizing text from anywhere in the Middle Ages to describe this feature of the Waldensians: 'in many places the said perfect heretics carry to their believers and their children and households some trinkets, that is to say, belts, knives, pincases and pins, in order to get more willing and favourable reception'.[67]

Fingerprinting, therefore, brings the *De vita* close to the Burgundian Waldensians tried by Bernard Gui.

The Form of the Text

The *De vita* refers at three points to the unnamed person 'who is attesting this', a man as is indicated by the gender of 'iste qui', 'he who'. The rubrics of the *De vita*'s sections, given at its beginning, conclude with the seventh: 'on the offence and guilt of the man who is attesting or confessing"de reatu et culpa deponentis seu confitentis'. This last section does not survive.

These few words point to two stages and their correlative texts.

First of all, inquisition. One man was questioned by an inquisitor. Much of what was said by the man who was attesting and confessing, the *deponens* or *confitens*, was translated into Latin and taken down by a scribe or notary in the written record, the *depositio*. One of the words in the *De vita* may be a clue to the original inquisitor or scribe. The word which the Dôle manuscript uses in Latin form, *agulherius*, 'is almost certainly an Occitan form'.[68] If the Dôle manuscript preserves the tradition of the original text, this would point to the Latin of Languedocian inquisitors, notaries and scribes; one such scribe used the very similar form *agulberius* when taking down the deposition of a Cathar follower in Toulouse in 1274.[69] There then followed, as in the procedure described by Gui in his *Practica*, the making of an extract from this deposition, summarizing those guilty acts (*culpe*) which related to the deponent's guilt (*culpa*), in a very short text which itself was also known as the *culpa*.[70]

Such depositions were at hand for inquisitors. After detailing some of the

---

[67] *De vita* vi.

[68] The opinion of the romance philologist Professor John N. Green, expressed in his linguistic commentary which is included in Biller, *Waldenses*, pp. 230–1.

[69] D25, fol. 45r, where *agulberius* denotes a man's trade, probably 'pinner' or 'pin-trader'. In the Latin record of the deposition of a woman (a Waldensian follower) interrogated in Valence in 1494, her vernacular is allowed to enter the Latin record when she says that 'when they were leaving her house they [the Waldensians] used sometimes to give her a certain quantity of pins' ('dum recedebant a domo aliquoties dabant sibi certam quantitatem acuum sive *d'aiguilles*'); P. Allix, *Some Remarks upon the Ecclesiastical History of the Ancient Churches of Piedmont* (London, 1690), p. 329.

[70] See ch. 7 above, p. 132 and nn. 17–18.

heresies of the Waldensian sect, Gui uses their existence as an excuse for stopping:[71]

> Item, in quite a few other things the said sect of the Waldensians is dissident and discrepant from the common way of life of the faithful, *in way of life and in customs*, as has been found and is apparent to inquisitors through the inquisition and questioning both of these Waldensians and their believers, and *especially through the confessions* of those who are converted away from this sect and heresy [my italics].

In a simultaneously formulaic and real fashion, Gui is saying that you can refer these specially informative 'confessions' for the details.

The second stage followed. The details of this remarkably informative deposition so impressed an inquisitor – or inquisitor's assistant – that he decided to edit it in order to produce a new text, a description of the way of life of the Waldensians: to convert a documentary record into a piece of literature. The original inquisitor's arrangement of questions to be put to and pursued with his extraordinarily knowledgeable witness will have led to a deposition which already to some degree grouped statements under general themes, as we see in the record of Jacques Fournier's interrogation of Raimon de la Côte, and if the deponent had some theological and Latin culture the deposition will have had more limpid Latin than is usual. Either or both will have lightened the editing needed.

Editing *could* have been lightened even further. Caterina Bruschi has suggested to me that the definitions and formal statements of organisation, belief and form of life could have been shaped in part by normative statements made by Brothers to the deponent, themselves in turn rooted in some oral or textual programmatic description of the Order. Such things as religious habit – sandals – are emphasized in order to underline the fact that the Waldensians constitute an Order and thus to make them appear more orthodox, and in this there is a parallel in the efforts made in texts produced by the Humiliati to give themselves an identity and the appearance of orthodoxy.[72] An attraction of this suggestion is that it would allow for the persistence within the description of archaic, even deliberately archaizing, elements in the description.

The extant work lacks its last section. The scribes of two of the extant manuscripts left a substantial blank space at the end of the sixth chapter. Perhaps they recognized that the last chapter had been shorn in one line of transmission of the text, and were leaving space for it to be copied in from

---

[71] Gui, *Ls*, p. 264: 'Item, dicta secta Valdensium in nonnullis aliis a conmuni conversacione fidelium vita et moribus dissidet et discordat, sicut per inquisicionem et examinacionem tam ipsorum Valdensium quam credencium eorundem, et precipue per confessiones illorum qui ab illa secta et heresi convertuntur inquisitoribus conpertum est et apertum.'

[72] See Caterina Bruschi's forthcoming 'Dall'eresia alla riammissione. Le cronache quattrocentesche degli Umiliati'.

another line in which it was intact – when Dondaine expressed the hope that the missing chapter would be found one day and published in a critical edition, he implied this view.[73] But there is another explanation, that the scribes were copying the text in a tradition which faithfully preserved the fact that it had been left unfinished by the original editor/author. The fact that he weeded most but not all traces of inquisition document, leaving in a few references to the deponent, indicates hesitation, a change of mind. We know that he originally intended to conclude with the deponent's *culpa*. Since a *culpa* abridged a confession, and the *De vita* is in any case a short adaptation of a confession, he may have come to see the appending of the *culpa* as pointless duplication.

Closer Fingerprinting: Sentences and *culpe* in the *Liber sententiarum*

Even after editing, the profile of the *De vita* must be close to the profile of the anonymous man upon whose confession it is based. There is first the range of knowledge. The anonymous knows a lot about such things as life in the 'hospices' of Waldensian Brothers, the Brothers' geographical spread and journeying, and the rite by which someone became a Brother or Sister. But he does not know two things, as the *De vita* specifically tells us:[74] 'Qualiter autem celebrent ignorat iste qui hoc deponit. Qualiter autem in sandaliatos ordinent ignorat similiter, sed audivit quod . . .' ('This particular man who is attesting this does not know how they celebrate [the eucharist]. Similarly, moreover, he does not know how they ordain ⟨some of them⟩ as the 'sandalled', but he has heard that . . .')

There is also a semantic profile: preferences for particular words. The *De vita* makes the unusual choice of *hospitium*, hospice, for the house in which Waldensians lived a formal religious life. It prefers to add *perfectus* or *perfecti* to *Valdensis* or *Valdensis hereticus*, or their plural forms, doing this no less than twelve times.

The next step, then, is to look at the sentences and *culpe* in the *Liber sententiarum*, in order to see what sort of confession would have had this profile. The Waldensians who appear in these texts can be put into simple categories: the Brothers who were obdurate, a Brother who converted, believers who were obdurate, and believers who converted. Let us first look quickly at examples of the two simple categories, the Brothers and believers who were obdurate. Gui passed a sentence of relaxation to the secular arm on John Brayssan, a full Waldensian Brother.[75] Part of the sentence referred to John's interrogation. He had refused to take an oath,

---

[73] 'Manuel', p. 184.
[74] *De vita* iv.
[75] Gui, *Ls*, pp. 207–8; see pp. 225, 240, 241 and 264 for followers' references to Brayssan.

quoting from a Gospel and St James's Epistle, and he had also indicated his full support of the Waldensian sect. Then the sentence goes on to list Waldensian beliefs in very formulaic fashion – 'Item, the aforesaid sect of the Waldensians asserts that . . .' – clearly now spelling out what it meant to support the Waldensian sect, not repeating what John had said when questioned.[76] His refusal to take the oath, his arguing about this, and declaring support for the Waldensian sect will have been enough for his condemnation, while his obduracy almost certainly meant that he refused to give names or answer further questions.[77]

Another sentence relaxed to the secular arm a follower, Ermenio, a widow from Alzonne. Produced from prison she refused to take an oath. Re-appearing the following day she did swear, and admitted that she had once appeared before an inquisitor at Najac, together with her father and husband and some others whom she named, probably all dead by now. She could not remember when, for this was all a very long time ago and she was now an old woman. Then she clammed up. 'Asked moreover and required to speak about herself and others on the matter and crime of heresy of the Waldensians, where she had seen and participated with Waldensians, which ones, and with what ⟨other⟩ persons ⟨she had seen them and participated⟩ with them, she replied that she knew nothing, nor did she want to confess anything.'[78] She appeared again four days later, because 'she did not want to confess anything about the matter of the heresy of the Waldensians',[79] and from then on she stuck to her guns, refusing to take an oath or say anything. So far I am just filling out one self-evident corollary of Bernard Gui's point. Most of the confessions from Waldensian Brothers or their followers who would *not* convert were unlikely to contain much of the sort of material that underlay the *De vita*, except on Waldensian rejection of oaths.[80]

Turning to those who converted, we begin with a Waldensian Brother, Stephen Porcherii, who was taken prisoner and led to Toulouse, where he eventually confessed and was converted in 1314.[81] Stephen 'had been

---

[76] Gui, *Ls*, p. 208, 'Item, secta predicta Valdensium . . .asserit'.
[77] While Jacques Fournier's interrogation of another obdurate Brother, Raimon de la Côte (Fournier, I, 40–122), found him very forthcoming on theology, it found him obstinately secretive about details of organization and names. See, for example, Fournier I, 55 and 74.
[78] Gui, *Ls*, p. 380: 'Interrogata autem et requisita quod diceret de se et de aliis super facto seu crimine heresis Valdensium, ubi et quos Valdenses et cum quibus personis vidisset et participasset cum eisdem, respondit se nihil scire, nec aliquid voluit confiteri.'
[79] Gui, *Ls*, p. 380: 'nollet de facto heresis Valdensium aliquid confiteri'.
[80] My four categories are, of course, too simple – those who converted might well also conceal, or have concealed; see Gui, *Ls*, pp. 235–6, for examples of women plotting to conceal information about Waldensians from the inquisitor.
[81] Gui, *Ls*, pp. 200–1; see pp. 221, 222 [bis], 223, 227 things being taken to him, 232, 233[ter], 235, 236, 237, 239, 240, 241, 242, 264 and 375 for other references to this well-known Brother.

received into the sect and rite of the Waldensians . . . by a certain Waldensian called Christian, in the presence of other Waldensians, whom he names in his confession'.[82] Though this *culpa* explicitly omits material contained in the confession and is short, it is still worth itemizing points of comparison with the *De vita*. First is the description of the rite of profession in the fifth part of the *De vita*, where a senior or wiser Brother in a hospice begins the ceremony, starting with a sermon preached to a gathering of all those, both men and women, who live in the hospice. In the passage just cited the two key elements are also the principal role played by a senior Brother, and the presence of others. Secondly, there is a miscellany of points where Stephen's activities or statements correlate with items covered in the *De vita*. He had once heard someone's confession, and imposed penance. Four of the articles of belief are similar to or overlap with the list of six articles in the *De vita* - on confession, purgatory, offerings for the dead, and oaths – though there is no marked similarity in wording.[83] But Stephen's participation with Waldensians 'in various places and towns and lands' ('in diversis locis et villis et terris') is fleetingly reminiscent of the *De vita*'s Waldensians living 'in various places, provinces and regimes' ('in diversis locis, prouinciis et regiminibus').[84]

More significant are the references to women. Stephen's *culpa* lists the names of the Waldensians he had known, beginning with two seniors ('majores'), including Christian, and listing sixteen Brothers, the last of whom is John Breyssan.[85] The text ends thus: '. . . and John Brayssan, and some woman who was called Raimonde of Castres, *who was of the same sect*, and he knew that *all* the aforesaid were Waldensians and held the life and sect of the Waldensians' ('. . . et Johannes Breyssan, et quedam mulier que vocabatur Raymunda de Castris, que erat ejusdem secte, et omnes predictos scivit esse Valdenses et tenere vitam et sectam Valdensium'). When we turn to the *De vita*, we find it generalizing about the reception of men and women: 'In this sect *both* men and women are received, and they are called "Brothers" and "Sisters".'[86]

Stephen's is the only evidence bearing positively upon the Sisters anywhere in the extant inquisition material from this period, and its individual emphasis parallels the emphasis of the generalizing statement in the *De vita*. Despite this, I must concede that not all of Stephen's confession brings it close to the sort of confession upon which the *De vita* was based. Nothing in Stephen's *culpa* helps with the areas of ignorance of the anonymous man who

---

[82] Gui, *Ls*, pp. 200–1: 'receptus ad sectam et ritum Valdensium . . . per quendam Valdensem qui vocabatur Cristinus, presentibus aliis Valdensibus quos in confessione sua nominat'. The list of Waldensians given later in the *culpa* is of *all* the Waldensians he admitted knowing, not those present at his profession.

[83] *De vita* ii.

[84] *De vita* iii.

[85] Gui, *Ls*, p. 201.

[86] *De vita* i.

confessed, nor is there any trace of the anonymous's penchant for the words *perfectus* and *hospitium*.

The fourth simple category is the *culpe* of the many Burgundian believers who confessed and were converted, but I shall pass these over, because even after forty-five years' involvement a believer's knowledge is unlikely to have had the range and *near* comprehensiveness of the confession upon which the *De vita* was based.

John Philiberti

I now turn to one strange half-way house person, a priest called John Philiberti.[87] His story needs retelling in some detail.[88] He was from La Chapelle-Saint-Sauveur (Saône-et-Loire), the son of the late Pons *de Boyba*, and he had once lived at Saint Laurent-la-Roche in the diocese of Besançon. At the time of his confession in 1319 he was living at Castelnau-Barbarens, in a diocese of Auch, and he was a priest of this diocese.

The earliest point in the story condensed in his *culpa* is around twenty-eight years before an earlier confession of 1311, in other words about 1283.[89] John was sent from Burgundy to parts of Gascony, together with someone else and equipped 'with the letter of an inquisitor' ('cum literis inquisitoris'). He was supposed to search for a fugitive Waldensian Brother called Rustus Jauberti. John arrived with his companion in the diocese of Auch. Later he

[87] A brief outline of Philibert's story appears in J.-M. Vidal, *Bullaire de l'inquisition française au XIe siècle jusqu'à la fin du grande schisme* (Paris, 1913), pp. 56–7 n. 2. The following have used or alluded to John: H. C. Lea, *A History of the Inquisition of the Middle Ages*, 3 vols. (New York, 1887), II, 148; G. Gonnet and A. Molnár, *Les Vaudois au moyen âge* (Turin, 1974), pp. 159–60; Jean Duvernoy, in Fournier, I, p. 100 n. 36, and in his 'Unité du valdéisme', 76; Schneider, *Waldenserthum*, p. 33; Cameron, *Waldenses: Rejections of Holy Church*, pp. 82–3; Given, *Inquisition*, p. 197. See also the next note.

[88] The texts which survive on John Philiberti are these: a *culpa*, drawn up by inquisitors, whose most recent reference is to a confession made in front of them in August 1319 (Gui, *Ls*, pp. 252–4; BL MS Add. 4697, fols. 139v–140v); a sentence by the inquisitors defining John as a relapsed heretic and sentencing him to be degraded from Holy Orders and relaxed to the secular arm (Gui, *Ls*, pp. 254–5; BL MS Add. 4697, fol. 141r); a sentence delivered by the archbishop of Toulouse degrading John from Holy Orders (Gui, *Ls*, pp. 274–7; BL MS Add. 4697, fols. 153v–155r). This last contains a papal bull relating to the case (Gui, *Ls*, p. 274), which was copied into Bernard Gui's *Practica* iii.23 (p. 120); it is calendared in Vidal, *Bullaire*, no. 26, pp. 56–7 (with reference to the original Vatican register). I have checked Limborch's edition of the *culpa* against the manuscript, finding no errors. On the two contemporary or near-contemporary marginalia, see n. 87 below. John also appears in the index of persons, under the place-name Castelnau-Barbarens, in the diocese of Auch, with two references to the folio numbers 123 (*culpa* and sentence) and 137 (degradation); see frontispiece.

[89] Given mistakenly as 1293 in Vidal, *Bullaire*, p. 56 n. 2.

returned from Gascon parts to Burgundy, back to those who had sent him. Then, after a certain amount of time, he came back to Gascon parts, this time doing it of his own free will.

Following this were two things, the passing of time and an event.[90] John 'lived for many years in the diocese of Auch. While he was living there he was led by some Burgundians – whom he names – into the love of and familiarity and participation with the Waldensians'.[91] The *culpa* goes on to say that John saw a great deal of them and got to know them very well – I shall return to the details. Then, after some time, Waldensian Brothers tried to recruit him. 'Item, at one time he was required and asked by the aforesaid Waldensians Christian and Humbert, and by some others whom he names, to want to become just like one of these Waldensians'. In the conversation John 'conceded to them that he did want to follow them and be of their sect and company'.[92] What happened then? Nothing.[93] John was a slippery character – as we shall see, in the eyes of one Waldensian Brother he was a great sinner. All that happened was the approach by Christian and others, and Philibert's expression of assent. There was no follow-up. John did not profess as a Brother.

One or two years before Pope Boniface VIII's indulgence, and therefore in 1298 or 1299, John appeared before brother Gui of Rheims, the inquisitor of Burgundy, and refused to take the oath because of what he had heard

---

[90] These two stages have been conflated by some historians, and the outcome of the second misinterpreted. H. C. Lea (1887) simply wrote that John 'formally joined' the Waldensians, while Jean Duvernoy wrote in 1974 that 'he converted to the heresy'. Writing earlier, in 1965, Duvernoy made the larger claim that, persuaded by the Waldensian Brother Christian, 'he made profession in the sect', and recently Euan Cameron has written that 'Cristinus persuaded him to become a Waldensian preacher'.

[91] '. . . moratus est multis annis in dyocesi auxitana, ubi morando fuit inductus per aliquos burgundos – quos nominat – ad amorem et familaritatem et participationem Valdensium'.

[92] 'Item, fuit requisitus et rogatus una vice per Cristinum et Hymbertum Valdenses predictos et per quosdam alios – quos nominat – quod vellet esse sicut unus ex ipsis Valdensibus et esse perfectus Valdensis sicut ipsi, et ipse concessit eis quod volebat eos sequi et esse de secta et societate ipsorum . . . Item, tunc dixit sibi dictus Cristinus, "Melius esset vobis quod essetis custos porcorum quam quod celebratis missam, quia estis in peccato mortali."'

[93] A comparison with Stephen Porcherii's *culpa* is instructive here. Stephen was formally received as a Waldensian Brother by the same Christian, and this fact, the most important charge of any, is naturally the very first item in Stephen's *culpa*. By contrast, nowhere in John's *culpa* is it said that he was received. Nowhere in the extant material is John himself referred to as a full Waldensian Brother. Nowhere is he described as carrying out a Brother's pastoral work. The *Liber sententiarum*'s index of persons lists four Waldensian Brothers, in each case spelling out 'perfect Waldensian', for example, 'Johannes Brayssan hereticus perfectus Valdensis relictus curie seculari xcvi⁰' ('John Brayssan, perfect Waldensian heretic, relaxed to the secular arm, 116th ⟨folio⟩'); Gui, *Ls*, p. 402; BL MS Add. 4697, fol. 11r. There is no trace of this in any of the texts relating to John Philiberti.

from the Waldensians.[94] He was then arrested and imprisoned at Saint
Laurent-la-Roche, appearing in a court in the formal setting of the
archbishop's palace at Besançon, in front of the inquisitor, ten or twelve
witnesses, and the inquisitor's notary. He confessed some things about the
Waldensians while hiding others, and after this, and when required by the
inquisitor Gui of Rheims, he swore and promised to bring about the
capture of Waldensians, whenever and wherever he knew they were, and
he abjured.

After this, John went away from Burgundian parts and went back to
Gascony, where once again he saw a great deal of the Waldensians – again,
I shall return to the details. John's independent activities as a Catholic
priest are laconically summarized: while believing the Waldensian sect to
be good, he 'nevertheless celebrated masses and administered the ecclesiastical sacraments'.[95] John persevered in his participation with Waldensians and adherence to their beliefs until he was once again taken prisoner,
and this time led to Toulouse in October 1311. He appeared before Bernard
Gui in Toulouse in November. At the beginning he did not want to confess.
Against his oath – clearly this time he had taken it without any fuss – he
denied the truth, but eventually he confessed and abjured. John's contacts
continued. At the prison gate in Toulouse John had a conversation with a
Waldensian believer, who told John that a Waldensian Brother, Hugonin
Pisaudi, was sending clothing to the former Brother Stephen Porcherii, who
was in the prison. John twice received clothing sent in this fashion by the
Waldensian believer, and he confessed these things in April 1318. His last
confession to an inquisitor is dated August 1319, but his case dragged on. It
was necessary for John to be degraded from the priesthood. Since this
needed the bishop of Auch but the bishopric was vacant, the matter went
to the Pope, from whom there came a bull (6 February 1320) empowering
the archbishop of Toulouse to degrade John. The bull was presented to the
archbishop on 5 March 1320 at Miélan (Gers). The archbishop had John
appear, together with two Dominicans acting as inquisitors in place of
Bernard Gui and delegates from the chapter and church of Auch, to
examine the bull, the truth of the inquisition, and the mode of proceeding.
John then appeared in the cathedral of St Stephen, in Toulouse, on 15 June,
for the solemnities of degradation. He was presumably executed shortly
after this.

Outstanding to begin with, as we look at John's case, is the amount of
documentation which it once generated, spanning at least thirty-six years.

---

[94] In fact, the dates of 1298 or 1297 would fit in better with the assessment at the time of
his later confession, made after his arrest in October 1311, that he had been in the
belief for fourteen years or thereabouts. There are references to the appearance of
others in front of Gui of Rheims: Gui, *Ls*, pp. 230–1, 264. One of them, Perrin Fabri,
like John confessed later that his confession to Gui of Rheims had been incomplete:
Gui, *Ls*, p. 230. On Gui see Vidal, *Bullaire*, pp. xiv–xv, xxx.

[95] '. . . nichilominus celebrabat missas et ministrabat ecclesiastica sacramenta'.

The precise nature of his first contact with a Burgundian inquisitor around 1283 is mysterious. If it included questioning there will have been written record, but all that we know surely is that it produced an inquisitor's letter. On the second major occasion of contact with inquisitors, in Besançon around 1298, there were at least two interrogations, and written record is implied by the spelling out of the presence of the inquisitor's notary at the second of these. The sentence could have been recorded. John's appearance in front of Bernard Gui and his confession to him in November 1311 will have been recorded, as also his later confessions to inquisitors in April 1318 and August 1319, and there should also have been a sentence following at least the 1311 confession. Meanwhile, Pope John XXII's bull refers to the *relatio*, the 'account' of the affair, which had been sent to him. Only a little can be said about what texts were available at what time. John Philiberti was telling Bernard Gui in 1319 about his *c.* 1298 appearances in front of Gui of Rheims. One approximation – that there were 'ten or twelve witnesses'('presentibus testibus x. vel xii') – suggests that the written record of Gui of Rheims's interrogation(s) may not have been available to Bernard Gui. The records of interrogations carried out in Toulouse, however, could be brought together, for the single extant *culpa* is explicitly based on the records of the three confessions of November 1311, April 1318 and August 1319. Finally, when the archbishop of Toulouse gathered with two deputy inquisitors and representatives of Auch, there was an examination of documentation, John XXII's bull and the *acta prioris iudicii*, the 'acts of the earlier court *or* judgement'.

Not only were there more documents, there was also more in them. If we can believe the 1319 confession, the record of the 1298 interrogations will have been lop-sided, containing material about the Waldensian sect in itself, but not names of individuals. John 'confessed some things about the matter of the Waldensians, and he knowingly hid ⟨what he knew⟩ about the Waldensians whom he had earlier seen in Gascony and with whom he had participated'.[96] In his 1311 confession to Gui he named the Burgundians who first led him into the love and familiarity of the Waldensian sect, as the *culpa* states, without repeating the names. He also named some Brothers who urged him to become a Brother, in addition to Christian and Humbert, but again the *culpa* does not include their names. The *culpa* also states that material about the Waldensians John had seen in Gascony, before his appearance in front of Gui of Rheims, 'is contained more fully in his confession' of 1319 ('in confessione sua plenius continetur'), as also the names of many believers of both sexes whose connections with the Waldensians he got to know in the period after the 1298 interrogations.

While John was not a Brother, his participation with the Waldensian Brothers far exceeded that of the usual Waldensian believer. During his

---

[96] '. . . confessus fuit aliqua de secta Valdensium, et celavit scienter de Valdensibus quos antea in Vasconia viderat et cum quibus participaverat'.

pre-*c.*1298 contact he visited them in their own 'hospices'. He often ate and drank and prayed with them, as an ordinary Waldensian believer might do, but he also 'sometimes kept the Waldensians company going from place to place' ('aliquando associavit Valdenses de loco ad locum'). This is followed by the statement that he heard their admonitions, sermons and instructions of the believers. In other words, he accompanied Brothers on their pastoral visits to their believers.[97] As we have seen, such was his involvement that several Brothers, led by Christian and Humbert, attempted unsuccessfully to persuade John himself to become a Brother.

From the statement in the *De vita* that only senior Waldensians were admitted to the General Chapter, it is clear that the ignorance of the anonymous confessor about ordination – which took place at the General Chapter – excludes such Waldensian Brothers from those who could have been this anonymous confessor. The anonymous had only 'heard' ('audivit') how ordination took place, presumably from one or several senior Waldensians, such as Christian. The anonymous, however, knew a great deal about virtually every other aspect of Waldensian life. This pattern fits John exactly. He was not a Waldensian Brother nor even a senior Waldensian, and therefore would never have been allowed to attend a General Chapter. But he talked to Waldensians, and his is the only *culpa* which preserves the fragment of a two-way conversation with a senior Waldensian, Christian. Afer the exchange about becoming a Brother Christian had said to him, 'It would be better for you to be a swineherd than to celebrate mass, for you are in mortal sin.'[98] What survives in the *culpa* of John's account of Waldensian beliefs is full and precise, as is also his description of the Brothers' pastorate among their believers, preaching, admonishing, hearing confessions and imposing penances. Comparison with the *culpe* of believers shows some slight nuances of wording. For example, where others heard things 'preached' ('predicari') by the Waldensians, John heard them 'taught' or dogmatized' ('doceri seu dogmatizari'), phrasing which suggests – possibly – a higher awareness rooted both in the theological culture of a trained priest and depth of knowledge of the Waldensians.

The anonymous knew much about life in Waldensian 'hospices', and so did John. 'On many occasions he saw and visited many perfect Waldensians in various places in ⟨their⟩ houses or hospices and in various towns' ('vidit et visitavit pluries multos Valdenses perfectos in diversis locis domibus seu hospiciis et in diversis villis'). John's *culpa* uses an unusual word, *prostratus*, when describing praying with the Waldensians, that the Waldensian was 'on bended knees, prostrate and bent over' ('flexis genibus, prostratus, et inclinatus'). Perhaps conflated here with posture while praying – genuflect-

---

[97] Most followers did not 'keep (the Waldesians) company' (*associare, sociare*) in this fashion; note three exceptions in Gui, *Ls*, pp. 222, 237, 239, and on p. 373 the milder case of a follower who 'led' (*duxit*) a Waldensian to someone's house.

[98] See n. 80 above.

ing and bent over – is the posture described in the *De vita* when begging forgiveness in a Waldensian 'hospice', lying on the ground.[99] The *De vita*'s word for Waldensian houses is *hospicia*, a word not found elsewhere in the *culpe* or sentences on Waldensians: apart from John's. A trained priest could have shared with an inquisitor a preference, occasionally manifested in inquisition texts, for schematizing people into two groups made precisely defined and distinct by a word, 'perfect' (complete or full) and others. John 'often visited many perfect Waldensians' (visitavit pluries multos Valdenses perfectos'), was asked by Waldensian Brothers to become 'a perfect Walden-sian like them' ('perfectus Valdensis sicut ipsi'), and refers twice to a 'certain perfect Waldensian, whom he names, Hugonin Pisaudi'. Among the other *culpe* and sentences there are only a few instances of this usage.[100] But John's penchant is shared by the *De vita*, which uses the word 'perfect' twelve times.

'The conversion, moreover, of heretics of the sect of the Waldensians or Poor of Lyons is very doubtful and suspect, and frequently they falsely return ⟨to the faith of the Church⟩ in order to evade the hands of inquisitors and ⟨afterwards⟩ revert to the vomit ⟨of heresy⟩.'[101] These words appear in Gui's inquisitors' manual, in a general contrast he makes between the firmness of conversions from Catharism, and the unreliability of those from Waldensian-ism. Stripped of theological odium, the words could well apply to John Philiberti. We already know some of his evasiveness with regard to inquisitors, namely his abjuration around 1298 and his promise to bring about the capture of Waldensians, followed by his reversion to Waldensian-ism. And it is possible that this was a repetition of an earlier pattern which he managed half to conceal from later inquisitors: that is, that his despatch to hunt a Waldensian fifteen years earlier, around 1283, was rooted in even earlier contact with the Waldensians, confession to an inquisitor, abjuration, and then a promise to go off and hunt down Rustus Jauberti. The Waldensian Brothers also found him a slippery customer. He kept them company, visited

---

[99] *De vita* iii.

[100] In the *Liber sententiarum*, as we have noted, *perfectus* is used in the index-entries of four Brothers. There is one occurrence in the *culpa* of a follower, Gerard *de Vincendat*, and another in the sentence on his brother Perrin, who was himself a 'full' Waldensian (Gui, *Ls*, pp. 232, 264), in references to Hugonin Pisaudi, who is elsewhere referred to without the term *perfectus* (Gui, *Ls*, pp. 223, 225[bis], 230). See one other instance, Gui, *Ls*, p. 375. There is also one instance where a careless mistake may be being made, where *perfectus* is applied to a married man who seems to have been a follower, not a Brother – the case is murky; Gui, *Ls*, pp. 241 and 262, and see also on this point Cameron, *Waldenses: Rejections of Holy Church*, p. 82. In the vast majority of material about Waldensian Brothers in the *Liber sententiarum*, *perfectus* is not used. *Perfectus* is used in Gui's *Practica*, to denote a 'full' Cathar or 'full' Waldensian heretic (see ch. 7 above, n. 10), and Gui will have found it in several of his literary sources, including the *De inquisitione hereticorum* attributed to David of Augsburg.

[101] Gui, *P* iv.3 (p. 220): 'Hereticorum autem de secta Valdensium seu Pauperum de Lugduno conversio multum dubia est et suspecta, et frequenter ficte redeunt, ut evadant manus inquisitorum, et ad vomitum revertantur.'

their 'hospices', and talked to them. At the same time he was himself a
Catholic priest, celebrating masses and administering the sacraments. The
very moral and moralizing men who were the Brothers saw him as being in
deep sin. Why did they attempt to recruit him? Because of the usefulness of a
man of experience and theological training? At any rate, he seems to have
been slippery here, allowing himself to say 'Yes' but not actually doing it.
Peering through the surviving data we glimpse the timeless moral and
psychological profile of the undercover man, the mole.

Clearly John fits very well the anonymous man upon whose confession the
De vita was based. This could well be John's confession of *aliqua de facto
Valdensium* to Gui of Rheims, or his 'fuller' confessions to inquisitors in
Toulouse. It could even be a confession, if he made one then, to an inquisitor
around 1283. This would correlate with the suggestion of some archaism in
the *De vita*, and the fact that Gui altered details when using it – omitting the
Sisters and the internationalism of general chapters – would make sense if he
was using a document produced about forty years or so earlier and therefore
in some ways outdated. I have not yet mentioned one tiny odd piece of
wording in John's *culpa*. 'Item, he *knew* and saw and heard that the
Waldensians' sometimes preached to their followers at night-time after
supper from the gospels and the epistles in the vernacular ('Item, scivit et
vidit et audivit quod Valdenses . . .'). The content of this is well-informed, but
not remarkable, but its qualification as a piece of knowledge is: 'scivit', 'he
knew' that. There could be a reminiscence here of the organisation and
presentation of material in a confession whose primary significance was not
implied guilt but *knowledge* and information. One of the two contemporary or
near-contemporary marginalia in Philbert's *culpa* is a cross in the margin by
the line containing the second part of this sentence.[102]

Some caveats should be noted. First, John's *culpa* contains material that was
not used in the *De vita*, most notably a sharp point about Waldensians and
life in a parish. They only go to church out of pretence, fearing otherwise to
be noticed. Secondly, I have been envisaging the editing of one confession,
the most economical explanation, and the most likely, but not the only one
that is possible. The references to 'the man who is confessing' could be
misleading: material from the confessions of another or others *could* have
been added. Thirdly, let us remember other Burgundians in the *Liber
sententiarum*. Earlier we looked at Peter Aymoni, one of various members
of this family from Alzonne, whose 1320 confession sketched contact going

---

[102] BL MS Add. 4697, fol. 140v: in the left-hand margin there are (1) a cross drawing
attention to a line containing the words that the Waldensians teach that one should
not swear on a book, but rather allow themselves to be killed before doing this (Gui,
Ls, p. 253, penultimate line, preceded by last word of previous line), and (2) a cross
drawing attention to a line containing the second part of the proposition that [the
Waldensians sometimes preach to their believers] 'after supper at night-time from
the gospels and the epistles in the vernacular' ('post cenam de nocte de evangeliis
et de epistolis in vulgari', Gui, *Ls*, p. 254).

back to about 1275.[103] Two years before this, in 1273, a man called 'Aymes', also of Alzonne and plausibly a relative, was one of a series of Burgundians questioned by inquisitors in Toulouse.[104] One of them had seen two Waldensians being burnt in Burgundy. Martin Schneider has gathered together references to the history of these Burgundian Waldensians, showing their earlier persecution and an existence in Burgundy which seems to go back to the first half of the thirteenth century.[105] We only have allusions to these earlier trials, no extant depositions, *culpe* or sentences, and consequently we have no way of investigating parallels between them and the *De vita*.

The broad fingerprinting leads us to the *Liber sententiarum*. The closer fingerprinting to John Philiberti. But the surviving fingerprints are part smudged. Too little survives for an exact match. The most that we can say is that John is the *most likely* candidate among the few whom we know and among the sources that are extant.

General Remarks

The *De vita*'s first significance is the role it played within a literary genre, and to get this into perspective we need to start with Gui's *Practica* and the tradition which lay behind it.

It is a commonplace that the fifth part of Bernard Gui's *Practica* is remarkable first for being directed at a *plurality* of sects and secondly for providing the combination, for each of them, of a special interrogatory and a description of the *ensemble* of the movement in question: history, way of life, and belief. A long development lay behind these two features.[106] At the broadest level, a sense of plurality in 'faiths' or 'laws' in the world – meaning in the modern term 'religions' – had been growing strongly since the earliest serious attempts to grapple with the law of Mahomet, by Peter the Venerable in the early to mid-twelfth century. This had its literary counterpart in the development both of works which looked at a plurality of sects and faiths or laws – of which the most notable early example was the direction of Alain de Lille's *Contra hereticos* against four of them (Jews, Muslims, Cathars and Waldensians) – and also of the literary genre of describing a 'law' or 'sect' as an ensemble of belief, organisation, and so on. Within this genre there are notable descriptions of the 'laws' (religions) of Mahomet (by Jacques de Vitry around 1220) and of the Mongols (by John of Pian del Carpine in 1247). And within the literature that more narrowly described sects there was foreshadowing. One early example was the combination to some degree of both

---

[103] See above and n. 23.
[104] D25, fols. 9v–10r.
[105] Schneider, *Waldenserthum*, pp. 31–3.
[106] For the following, see Patschovsky, *Passauer Anonymus*, ch. 5, and P. Biller, 'Words and the Medieval Notion of "Religion"', *JEH* 36 (1985), 351–69 (pp. 363–5).

belief and some description in the account of the Cathars and Waldensians, which Peter of Vaux-de-Cernai inserted into his history of the Albigensian crusade, between 1212 and 1218. In 1250 Raniero Sacconi's brilliant short account of heresy was in part rooted in an older tradition, in its concentration on doctrine. But interspersed in the theology was much descriptive material, such as divisions among the Cathars, rites, functions of particular ranks, numbers, divisions among groups, and the Waldensians were also included. The 1260s were decisive. Around 1266 an Austrian Dominican, the Passau Anonymous, compiled an anthology of texts, which was plural in subject-matter (Jews, Muslims and various heresies) and miscellaneously comprehensive, containing lists of doctrine, material describing heresy – for example, its cases, historical origin, and method of converting – and questions to be put to heretics. Whereas the diffusion of this work and perhaps its influence were largely a matter of German-speaking areas north of the Alps, another work of this decade, the mysterious *De inquisitione hereticorum* (once ascribed to David of Augsburg), was not so confined, spreading not only in these areas but also in France and Italy. Concentrating on the Waldensians, this treatise combined description *and* material for inquisitors, including advice about interrogation. The descriptive part is broken up into chapters, some extremely brief, on such themes as origin (here paralleling the Anonymous of Passau), belief, the two levels in the sect, clothing, houses, mode of teaching, and suchlike.

The *De vita* played a part in the development of only one of the elements in this tradition, the description. In sobriety of tone, in the solidity of its information and in its formal rationalisation of material into separate and numbered paragraphs or brief chapters, each dealing with one theme, the *De vita* marks a considerable advance from the *De inquisitione hereticorum*. Copied into a few manuscripts containing anthologies for inquisitors, it was clearly regarded as having some usefulness. Its high quality and many similarities to the account of Waldensian way of life in part five of Gui's *Practica* point to its role as a model. Not only will Gui have known and used it, when writing his own account he will have tried to improve upon it, just as he knew, used and improved upon the *De inquisitione hereticorum*. Gui's description marks an advance on the *De vita*. In a scholarly sense, in that it is based on the skilful use of many sources; in sheer coverage, in that it included history and also part of what the deponent behind the *De vita* said he did not know; and in literary polish, in that Gui left no explicit trace of his sources. For in being based on the confession of one man and in retaining references to this deponent, the *De vita* must have looked to Bernard Gui like a rough draft: not something in the imperiously objective and impersonal style at which he himself was aiming.

The *De vita*'s second significance is that it is a source of outstanding importance on the Waldensians. Here there is only room to insist upon three general points. When a group regarded as heretical by the Catholic Church – a religious order (such as that of the Poor of Lyons) or a Church (that of the

Cathar Good Men and Women) – is seen only through the Church's sources, it is often difficult to envisage an entity. Opposed in a polemical treatise, the group has a textual existence as a set of disembodied articles of belief. Glimpsed only through responses of followers to questions in trials, mentioning a few preachers and their sermons, the group may seem fragmented, without organisation: an anarchic group of local dissidents expressing religious particularism and dissent, only given firm definition by those inquiring into it, only body and structure in the fantasizing minds of the Church authorities persecuting it. All this is blown apart by the *De vita*. Here is something solid, a religious order, with rite of profession, and organized religious life in religious houses, organized pastorate, and international General Chapters, what is most important for administrators, money, and quite a lot of it. Like America in modern Catholicism, Germany in medieval Waldensianism supplied the gold. Then there is the language: a 'rector' 'rules' a house, it is 'governed', things are 'ordained', 'constituted' or 'commanded', people are 'appointed', and a 'determined' amount of money is 'assigned'. The very words breathe rule, order and organisation.

Secondly, the *De vita* portrays a group which presented itself as an Order, and which in fact continued to resemble the mendicant religious orders inside the Church, the Order of the Poor of Lyons.[107] Again, the language breathes this. The Order's members 'professed' the monastic vows of poverty chastity and obedience, and from then on they were called 'Brothers' and 'Sisters'. If only we translated *fratres* as 'friars' the semantic point would be clearer. They 'celebrated' regular meetings to deal with their affairs, just the Franciscans and Dominicans did and with the same name: 'General Chapters'. It is so long ago, 1935, that Herbert Grundmann insisted that hostility in the sources and confessional historiography obscures the generic similarity of religious phenomena, some of which became religious orders in the Church, others 'heretical sects'. The *De vita* reminds us how fundamental that point remains.

Finally, the *De vita* can contribute much to the question of continuity and change in this 'Order'. I take as an example here the Waldensian Sisters. Our view of the Waldensian Sisters is bedevilled not just by the paucity of the sorts, but also their variety of form. There *seem* to be differences: indicating change . . . or just the fact that the sources are so different and look from different angles at essentially the same phenomenon? Let us consider what the *De vita* says late in the thirteenth century, and then compare this with the beginning of the century.

The *De vita* insists that the Order of the Poor receives women as well, and that they are called 'Sisters'. Despite the grammatical predominance of the

---

[107] See Gui, *Ls*, p. 345, for the report of a conversation between a follower and a Brother, where the latter is asked whether the Waldensian *Ordo* had been approved by the Pope. See also Patschovsky, *Passauer Anonymus*, p. 67, for the term 'Ordo Pauperum de Lugduno' in the Anonymus.

male gender, much of the text applies to the Sisters as well as the Brothers. They 'profess' the three monastic vows, for at the end of this rite if the professing person is a woman the kiss of peace is given her by women. Silence in the *De vita* indicates that they are not allowed into higher ranks or the Waldensian priesthood, while it is made explicit that the Sisters are denied entry to the General Chapter, and this in itself implies exclusion from rule and matters of formal organisation. They are not mentioned in the description of the active pastorate among 'believers' and 'friends', but clearly there is some travel, for the *De vita* describes again how women give them the kiss of peace on their arrival if the Sisters journey from a hospice in one town to a hospice in another. They live in these hospices with Brothers, for the sake partly of pretense[108] – to the outside world they are wives or sisters of these men – and they take part in the religious life of these hospices, their intense and formal daily round of prayer, and the reception of reading or instruction in scripture. In addition, there is division of labour: they prepare the food. Sometimes the old Sisters live in hospices on their own, without Brothers, but they are frequently visited by the Brothers and food is prepared for them. Within the hospice there is prayer 'for Brothers and Sisters', while a Brother visiting 'believers' and 'friends' greets them 'on behalf of the Brothers', without, it seems, mentioning the Sisters. A clear contrast between the active and travelling pastoral life of the Brothers and that of the Sisters, much more confined within the walls of a hospice, is rubbed in by this contrast in naming.

The Waldensian letter of 1218, addressed to both Brothers and Sisters and reporting a council at which only Brothers took part, implies some such distinction already at this date. We can go back a little earlier, to glimpse Sisters living at the very beginning of the thirteenth century in Castelnaud-ary.[109] A clutch of depositions in 1245–6, bearing on a period forty years earlier, hence around 1205–6, when Waldensians lived 'openly' ('publice') in this place.[110] Deposing in 1246 one man from Castelnaudary, Peter Simon, stated that his mother, Aimengarde, and a certain unnamed sister were Waldensians. He had tried to persuade his sister back to the Catholic faith, on one occasion when he met her passing through Castelnaudary.[111] More illumination comes from Guillelme Michela, a woman of at least middle age when deposing twice in 1245. At her first appearance (7 July 1245) she said she had 'lived with the Waldensians at Castelnaudary for three years, and then the Waldensians were living openly in the country, and she used to be clothed, to eat, drink, pray and do other things as they did'. Re-appearing

[108] A question put to Raimon de la Côte about whether Waldensians cohabited with women (viz. lived in the same houses) could have been based on the inquisitor's knowledge of the *De vita*; Fournier, I, 74.
[109] See my earlier discussion, *Waldenses*, pp. 135–6.
[110] Toulouse MS 609, fols. 250v and 252v.
[111] Toulouse MS 609, fol. 252v.

on 12 July she opened up further, making it clear that these were Waldensian women, and that she might have been with them longer. She had 'seen Waldensians, and dwelt with the Waldensians Bernarde of Pomas, Rixende of Limoux and Christiane, for four years or thereabouts; item, she heard them saying that no-one ought to take an oath, for the sake of the truth or a lie, nor to bind themselves, justly or unjustly ⟨to do something⟩'.[112] We have to break through the formal dissimilarities between different sources when setting this beside the *De vita*. What is implied in Guillelme's first brief words is that she led a formal religious life with the three Waldensian women, wearing as they did a distinctive habit, and following their distinct observances in eating, prayer and a variety of other things which, though unspecified, clearly were done in a specific way. Manifest in these few words is the outline of a form of religious life for Waldensian women, which on the one hand is in place only thirty years after Valdes's foundation of the Poor of Lyons, and on the other hand is clearly in a line which leads to the form of religious life described for Sisters as well as Brothers in the *De vita*. There is fundamental coninuity.

This is not to deny any change. One Waldensian woman, Peter Simon's sister, is remembered while journeying, and half of what Guillelme tells us is of the Waldensian women – probably – instructing in doctrine. The fragments suggest a more open and active life than that which is glimpsed in the *De vita*, by which time the Sisters had come to be as 'cabined, cribbed and confined' as the Poor Clares. Then there was no secrecy: the Waldensians lived 'publicly' in Castelnaudary. By contrast, the *De vita* describes a later time which is full of secrecy, secrecy in holding General Chapters and secrecy in maintaining small mixed hospices of religious celibates. Above all, the Sisters were also concealed. Success at the time has in turn led to the Sisters' successful concealment from most modern historians.

---

[112] Toulouse MS 609, fol. 96r and v: 'dixit quod stetit cum Valdensibus apud Castrum Novum per tres annos, et tunc Valdenses stabant publice in terra, et induebat et comedebat et bibebat et orabat et cetera faciebat sicuti ipsi'; 'dixit quod vidit Valdenses, et mansit cum Bernarda de Pomars et Rixen de Limos et Xristiana, Valdensibus, per iiiior annos vel circa; item, audivit eos dicentes quod nemo debet jurare pro veritate vel mendacio nec condicere juste vel injuste'. On the first occasion the notary's use of male 'they', 'ipsi', may reflect his tendency to revert to male gender or Guillelme pretending at this stage; tendency to revert is the most likely explanation of the use of male 'they' ('eos') in the second case.

APPENDIX

Edition and Translation of the *De vita et actibus*

The following text is a transcription of Dôle, Bibliothèque Municipale, MS 109, fols. 32r–34r [= D], with variant readings from Vatican, Biblioteca Apostolica, MS Vat. Lat. 2648, fols. 71va–72vb [= V], and Milan, Biblioteca Ambrosiana, MS A. 129. Inf., fols. 182r–187r [= M]. For the eighty-one words of the beginning which survive in Rome, Arch. Generalices O.P., MS II 63, I rely on Opitz's edition [= O].[1] I do not note variant spelling in the high Renaissance Latin of the Ambrosian manuscript, in which, to take the most obvious example, 'e' becomes 'ae'. I do not note the Vatican and Ambrosian manuscripts' variant spelling 't' where Dôle has 'c', for example, 'hospitium' (Ambrosian, Vatican), 'hospicium' (Dôle). I distinguish 'u' and 'v', transcribing, for example, vel' rather than 'uel'. For the contraction which can be expanded to con- or com-, I have chosen con-. Variant readings are given against the main body of the Dôle text, *not* against its deleted errors. In other words, unless otherwise indicated, the assumption is that an error, which the Dôle scribe subsequently deleted, does *not* occur in other manuscripts.

My notes (from 1984) on variant readings in the Ambrosian manuscript contained errors, and I am greatly indebted to Caterina Bruschi for completely overhauling them.

[1] See n. 7 above.

fol. 32r / Sequitur de vita et actibus, de fide et erroribus hereticorum qui se dicunt 'Pauperes Christi' seu 'Pauperes de Lugduno'.

credentibus et *MV*

Primo, de ipsis hereticis et eorum amicis et de credentibus erroribus eorundem, et que sit differencia inter eos.

§ Secundo, de credencia et erroribus ipsorum.

3°] Tertio *MO* ertio *V*

§ 3°, qualiter in hospiciis conversantur.

consilia] concilia *OV* se] seu *MOV*

§ Quarto, qualiter sua consilia [*r*: concilia] se⟨u⟩ capitula celebrantur.

Quinto] uinto *V* qualiter] quando *M* aliqui *MOV omit*

§ Quinto, quando et qualiter ⟨ali⟩qui profitentur seu consolentur.

Sexto] exto *V*

§ Sexto, de visitacione credencium et amicorum eorundem.

§ Septimo et ultimo, de reatu et culpa deponentis seu confitentis.

sciendum *O breaks off* solidati] consolati *MV* et credentes *V omits*

Primo itaque est sciendum, quod de secta hereticorum predictorum alii dicuntur 'heretici perfecti' et 'solidati', alii 'amici' eorundem et 'credentes'.

doctores] rectores *MV*

Item, hereticorum perfectorum, alii dicuntur 'sandaliati', alii 'novellani'.[1] Sandaliati sunt illi qui 'sacerdotes', 'magistri' et 'doctores' dicuntur tocius heretice pravitatis, et possunt, ut asserunt, conficere corpus Christi sicut catholici sacerdotes.

supra] super *V* et caligas – calceate pedes *V omits* deferunt modo simili] modo simili deferunt *M* calceate] calciati *M* sandaliatos] sandalatos *M* tamen *MV omit* quam *MV* omits recipiantur] recipiuntur *MV* bona *MV omit* nil] nichil *V* sustinentur] sustintentur *M*

§ Item, sandaliati non tenent pecuniam, et sotulares decollatos seu perforatos supra pedes et caligas deferunt modo simili perforatas, iuxta auctoritatem 'Et calceate pedes vestros sandaliis'.[2] Et quicquid per ipsos sandaliatos ordinatur, constituitur vel eciam precipitur, ab omnibus inferioribus irrefragibiliter observatur, et eisdem tamquam capitibus obeditur. In ipsa secta tamen [*r*: tam] homines quam et mulieres recipiantur ~~non possident aliqua bona~~ et 'fratres' et 'sorores' nuncupantur. Non possident aliqua bona immobilia, sed propriis renunciant et sequuntur paupertatatem. Non laborant, nil acquirunt vel lucrantur, unde valeant sustentari, sed de bonis et elemosinis suorum amicorum et credencium sustinentur et vivunt studiis cum magna sollicitudine inherentes.

§ Item, amici eorundem et credentes possident inmobilia et utuntur coniugio, mercantur, negociantur, acquirunt eciam et lucrantur, et per ipsos hereticos perfectos visitantur, predicantur et inducuntur ad credulitatem eorundem, prout inferius apparebit.

[1] This perhaps rests on the sequence, novus > novellus > novellanus. I have been unable to find another example.

[2] Mark 6. 9: 'sed calceatos sandaliis'.

The following is about the way of life, doings, faith and errors of the heretics who are called the 'Poor of Christ' or the 'Poor of Lyons'.

First, about these heretics and their friends and the believers in their errors, and what the difference is between them.
§ Secondly, about their creed and errors.
§ 3rdly, in what way they live in the hospices.
§ Fourthly, how they celebrate their 〈Councils〉 [*D*: Counsels] or Chapters.

§ Fifthly, when and how 〈some〉 may profess or be consoled.

§ Sixthly, about the visiting of their friends and believers.
§ Seventhly and lastly, about the crime and guilt of the 〈person〉 who is attesting or confessing.
First, therefore, one should know that in the sect of the aforesaid heretics some are called 'full' and 'established' [*other manuscripts*: 'consoled'] heretics, others their 'friends' and 'believers'.
Item, of the full heretics, some are called the 'sandalled', others the 'novices'. The 'sandalled' are those who are called 'priests', 'masters' and 'teachers' [*other manuscripts*: 'rectors'] of the whole heretical wickedness, and they can, so they assert, consecrate the body of Christ like Catholic priests.

§ Item, the 'sandalled' do not keep money, and they wear shoes with the head cut off or pierced above the feet and boots pierced in a similar way, in accord with the authority, 'Have your feet shod with sandals' [*adapting Mark 6. 8-9*: 'He commanded them . . . to be shod with sandals']. And whatever is decided, constituted or even commanded by these 'sandalled' is inviolably observed by all those under them, and they are obeyed as heads. In this sect 〈both〉 [*D*: however] men and women may be received [*other manuscripts*: are received], and they are called 'Brothers' and 'Sisters'. They do not possess any immovable goods, but renounce their own things and follow poverty. They do not work, they do not acquire or earn anything by which they could be supported, but they are supported by the goods and alms of their friends and believers; and they live applying themselves with great zeal to their concerns.[1]

§ Item, their friends and believers possess immovable goods and engage in marriage, trade, act in business, also acquire and earn, and they are visited, preached to and led by these full heretics into their credulity, as will appear below.

---

[1] 'Studiis' could be 'devotions', 'studies', or 'areas of zeal' as well as 'concerns'.

Peter Biller

Secundo, sciendum est quod predicti heretici tenent, ~~credent~~ credunt et docent suis creditoribus et amicis septem articulos fidei et septem eciam sacramenta et alia pro maiori parte, que / fol. 32v / catholici credunt, exceptis erroribus qui sequuntur.

§ Non credunt quod dominus papa tantam potestatem habeat in terris quantam habuit beatus Petrus, nisi ita bonus esset et sanctus ut beatus Petrus erat.

§ Item, non credunt esse purgatorium nisi dumtaxat in hoc mundo.

§ Item, non credunt quod helemosine vel orationes animabus proficiant defunctorum.

§ Item, non credunt quod alicui liceat sine mortali peccato in aliquo casu de mundo hominem occidere vel iurare.

§ Item, credunt quod alter alteri sua peccata valeat confiteri, iuxta auctoritatem beati Iacobi: 'Confitemini alterutrum peccata vestra etc'.[3]

§ Item, credunt quod illi, qui inter eos in sandaliatos ordinantur, possunt ita bene corpus Christi conficere sicut catholici sacerdotes.

Tercio, sciendum est quod predicti heretici in diversis locis, prouinciis et regiminibus huiusmodi, tam in Alamania quam in aliis partibus, commorantibus per domos et familias, ~~per~~ duos uel tres in uno hospicio cum duabus vel tribus mulieribus, quas suas uxores esse fingunt vel sorores. Aliquociens antique mulieres sine hominibus in hospiciis commorantur, sed per alios hereticos sepe et sepius visitantur et eis alimenta prestantur. Talem in hospiciis vitam ducunt. Surgunt autem multociens et flexis genibus multociens ante lectos suos ponunt se ad oracionem. Et ille qui regit hospicium dicit quod orent pro regibus et ducibus et gubernatoribus seculi, ut Deus concedat eis ita mundum gubernare ut sit ad suam gloriam et ad eorum salutem, uel verba consimilia.

§ Item, orant pro fratribus et sororibus suis et eorum credentibus et amicis, quod in hoc mundo tanta bona et tantam penitenciam facere possint quod ad gaudia valeant paradisi pervenire, vel verba similia.

§ Item, orant pro inimicis et persecutoribus eorundem, ut ad penitenciam per Dei adiutorium convertantur, vel verba similia. Et pro omnibus dicatur sexies *Pater Noster*.

Apparatus:

sciendum] dicendum V

creditoribus] credentibus MV et amicis] amicis V

qui sequuntur] persequuntur V

helemosine] elemosine MV

mortali peccato] peccato mortali MV

sandaliatos] sandalatos M   possunt] possint V

regiminibus] regionibus M   commorantibus] commorantur MV

Aliquociens] Aliquot M

prestantur] parantur V

multociens] multoties MV   et flexis – qui regit hospicium V omits

gub-] gov- M   ut sit] quod sit MV

Item, orant – vel verba similia V omits

possint] possit M

sexies] septies vel decies MV

---

3 James 5. 16.

Secondly, one should know that the aforesaid heretics hold and believe and teach their believers and friends the seven articles of faith and also the seven sacraments and other things for the most part that Catholics believe, apart from the errors which follow.

§ They do not believe that the Lord Pope has as much power on earth as the Blessed Peter had, unless he is as good and holy as the Blessed Peter was.

§ Item, they do not believe that there is purgatory, except only in this world.

§ Item, they do not believe that alms or prayers benefit the souls of the dead.

§ Item, they do not believe that it is permissible for any reason in the world for anyone to kill a man, or to swear, without mortal sin,.

§ Item, they believe that one can confess one's sins to another, according to this authority of Blessed James: 'Confess your sins one to another', etc.

§ Item, they believe that those among them who are ordained as the 'sandalled' can consecrate the Body of Christ just as well as Catholic priests.

Thirdly, one should know that – in various places, provinces and regimes, both in Germany and in other parts – the aforesaid heretics ⟨dwell⟩ in houses and households, two or three in a hospice with two or three women, who pretend to be their wives or sisters. Sometimes old women live in hospices without men, but they are visited by other heretics frequently – and more frequently – and food is made available for them. They lead this form of life in their hospices. They often rise up and genuflecting often in front of their beds apply themselves to prayer. And the one who rules the hospice says that they should pray for the Kings and Dukes and governors of the world, that God should grant them to govern the world in a way that is to his glory and their salvation – or similar words.

§ Item, they pray for their Brothers and Sisters and their believers and friends, that they can do so much good and so much penance in this world, that they can win through to the joys of paradise – or similar words.

§ Item, they pray for their enemies and persecutors, that through God's help they may be converted to penance – or similar words. And for all of these they say the 'Our Father' six times.

§ Facta oracione, ille qui regit hospicium primo surgit et dicit, 'Deus sit nobiscum, si sibi placet'.

§ Post hoc illi tam homines quam mulieres, qui scripturas volunt addiscere, ⟨recipiunt⟩ a suis doctoribus lectionem, et lectionibus receptis et pluries repetitis faciunt postea id quod volunt, et mulieres cibaria preparant. Si aliqui offendant publice in aliquo, coram omnibus hospicii proicient se in terram postulantes veniam et penitenciam, et tunc eriguntur a circumstantibus et penitencia eis datur. Ante prandium ponunt se ad oracionem, ut superius continetur, et pluries in die. In prandio, ille qui regit hospicium benedictionem prandii facit in hunc modum, dicendo 'Benedicite', et alii respondent, 'Dominus', et postea dicitur oracio *Pater Noster*. Qua completa, dicit rector materna lingua, 'Deus, qui benedixit quinque panes ordaceos et duos pisces in deserto,[4] benedicat cibum et potum et personas que recipient. In nomine Patris, et Filii, et Spiritus Sancti. Amen'. Quandoque per illum qui / f. 33r / regit hospicium predicatur in prandio vel in cena, et facta cena et facta predicacione regraciantur [*r*. regraciatur] eidem per aliquem circumstantem et sua predicacio confirmatur. Post prandium agunt gracias, et rector hospicii dicit materna lingua, 'Benedictio, et claritas, et retribuere, etc'. ~~Et~~ Iterum ponunt se ad oracionem, ut supra.

Et familiares hospicii peccata sua rectori suo confitentur quando volunt, non tamen ad hoc conpelluntur nisi velint. Si aliqui credentes vel amici eorum ad eorum hospicium veniunt fit eisdem magnum festum et cum gaudio recipiuntur, et predicantur et exortantur in fide superius memorata, et quando confiteri ⟨volunt⟩ eis iniungitur penitencia per eundem ⟨vel⟩ ab alio de hospicio si rector non sit presens.

Item, cum aliqui heretici perfecti in una villa habitantes veniunt ad hospicium aliquorum perfectorum in alia villa commorancium, in adventu ipsorum dant sibi ad invicem osculum pacis, homines hominibus, mulieres mulieribus, et sic faciunt in recessu.

Quarto, sciendum est quod predicti heretici perfecti semel in anno in quadragesima celebrant concilium vel capitulum generale in aliquo loco Lombardie vel Provincie vel in aliis regionibus in quibus sandaliati vel eorum aliqui commorantur, et hoc fieri consuevit pocius in

[4] See Matthew 14. 17-19.

---

hoc] haec *M*   recipiunt *M V add*

id] illud *M*

et penitenciam] *MV omit*

respondent] respondunt *M*

rector] rector hospitii *MV*

Amen *MV omit*

et facta cena *MV omit*
regraciantur] regraciatur *V*   rengratiatur *M*

Iterum] Et iterum *MV*

Et *MV omit*

con-] com- *M*   ad . . . veniunt] ad hospitium veniunt eorum *M*
exor-] exhor- *M*
⟨volunt⟩] volunt a rectore seu maiore [maiori *M*] hospitii confitentur et *MV*
⟨vel⟩] vel *MV*
aliquorum] aliquorum aliorum hereticorum *MV*

quadragesima] quadragesima vel circa *MV*   concilium] consilium *M*
consilium] concilium *V*

§ When the praying is over, the one who rules the hospice rises first and says, 'If it pleases him, may God be with us'.

§ After this those who wish to learn scripture, both men and women, ⟨receive⟩ a reading from their teachers, and, after the readings have been received and often repeated, they do afterwards what they want, and the women prepare food. If any of them openly offends in some matter, they throw themselves to the ground in the presence of everyone in the hospice, begging for forgiveness and penance, and then they are raised up by those who are standing around, and penance is given to them. Before a meal they apply themselves to prayer, as is stated above, and several times a day. At the meal, the one who rules the hospice does the blessing of the supper in this way, saying, 'Bless', and the others reply, 'Lord'. And afterwards the 'Our Father' prayer is said. When this is finished, the rector says in the mother tongue, 'May God, who blessed five loaves of barley and two fish in the desert, bless this food and this drink and those who are about to receive. In the name of the Father and the Son and the Holy Spirit, Amen.' Sometimes at a meal or at supper there is preaching by the one who rules the hospice, and when the supper and preaching are over he is thanked by a bystander, and his preaching is corroborated. After a meal they give thanks, and the rector of the hospice says in the mother tongue, 'Benediction, and glory, and thanksgiving', etc. Again they set themselves to prayer, as above.

And household members of the hospice confess their sins to the rector when they want – they are not, however, compelled to do this unless they want to. If any of their friends or believers come to their hospice, there is a great feast for them and they are received with joy, and they are preached to and exhorted in the faith that is recorded above, and when they ⟨want to⟩ confess ⟨the confession is heard by the senior or rector of the hospice and⟩ penance is imposed upon them by him ⟨or⟩ by someone else from the hospice if the rector is not present.

Item, when some full heretics living in one town come to the hospice of some full heretics living in another town, on their arrival they give each other the kiss of peace, the men to the men, the women to the women, and they do likewise on leaving.

Fourthly, one should know that once a year, during Lent, the aforesaid full heretics celebrate a general council or chapter-general in some place in Lombardy or Provence or in other regions in which the 'sandalled', or some of them, live, and this used to happen more in Lombardy than elsewhere. Three or four full heretics come to this ⟨council⟩ [*D*: counsel]

Peter Biller

4^{or}] quatuor *MV*
Almania] Alamania *V*

quidam] quidem *MV*
consilio] concilio *V*

congregantur]
congregant *M*

subiectus] suspectus *M*

seu] vel *MV*

tempora] laudabiliter
conversati *V*
laudabiliter conversati
fuerint *M*
cum] una cum *MV*

assignatur] assignantur
M per⟨ma⟩ere]
permanere *MV*

presentantur]
presentatur *M*
helemosine] elemosine
MV

sustinendo] sustinenda
MV mittitur] mittitur
eis *MV* Alemania]
Alamania *MV*

⟨et⟩] et *MV* appo-] apo-
MV

celebrent *MV omit* hoc
deponit] deponit hoc *M*
ordinent] ordinentur *M*
ignorant] ignorat *MV*

Lombardia quam alibi. Ad quod consilium veniunt tres vel 4^{or} heretici perfecti de Almania habentes secum aliquem clericum vel alium interpretatorem, et fingunt aliquo modo se velle apostolorum Petri et Pauli limina visitare. In quo quidam generali consilio seu capitulo quasi omnes heretici hospiciorum gubernatores congregantur. In quo eciam capitulo credentes non admittuntur, nec perfecti heretici iuvenes, nec mulieres quamvis sint perfecte et antique, nec aliquis hereticus perfectus quamvis antiquus nisi eorum voluntati et obediencie totaliter sit subiectus et servet immobiliter sectam illam.

§ In predicto siquidem capitulo tractatur de statu omni dicte secte, et queritur a quolibet ut audivit de statu familie sue, et qualiter se gubernet, et si fuerint aliqui inobedientes seu rebelles mittantur et cum aliis sociis adiungantur.

§ Item, si aliqui heretici perfecti fuerint inter eos per longa tempora iuxta formam secte sue et fuerint sapientes in scripturis, efficiuntur in eodem capitulo sandaliati, et ex tunc cum aliis sandaliatis 'magistri' et 'rectores' et 'sacerdotes' dicuntur.

§ Item, in dicto capitulo ordinatur de hiis que [*r.*: qui] in dicta secta cupiunt profiteri et consolari, et illi de quibus conceditur postea consolantur et mansio seu societas assignatur eisdem in qua per⟨ma⟩ere debeant illo anno.

§ Item, in dicto capitulo deputantur et constituuntur visitatores amicorum suorum et credencium qui visitare debeant illo anno, et mittuntur duo in qualibet regione seu provincia in qua aliqui de eorum credencia conversantur.

§ Item, in dicto capitulo presentantur pecunia et helemosine per amicos et credentes eorundem / fol. 33v / sibi data et transmissa, que quidem pecunia iuxta ordinacionem dictorum sandaliatorum distribuitur, et datur cuilibet certa porcio pro se et sua familia in victu et vestitu anno venturo sustinendo. Et si aliqui qui regant hospicia presentes non fuerint, mittitur pecunia per aliquos qui in illis partibus morantur, et de Alemania maior pars pecunie de qua vivunt ⟨et⟩ sustinentur apportatur.

Qualiter autem celebrent ignorat iste qui hoc deponit.

§ Qualiter autem in sandaliatos ordinent ignorant [*r*: ignorat] similiter, sed audivit quod discalciantur per alios sandaliatos et ei traduntur calige et sotulares supra pedes perforati, ut superius continetur.

from Germany, bringing together with them some cleric or other interpreter, and they pretend that in some way they want to visit the holy places of the Apostles Peter and Paul. In this general ⟨council⟩ [D: counsel] or chapter, ⟨in fact⟩ [D: some] there are gathered together virtually all the heretics who are governors of the hospices. Still, in this council believers are not admitted, nor young 'perfect' heretics, nor women, however full and old they may be, nor any full ⟨male⟩ heretic, however old, unless he is totally subordinate to their will and obedience and unswervingly observes that sect.

§ The aforesaid chapter, in addition, deals with the whole condition of the said sect, and the question is put to anyone – as to what he has heard about the condition of his household, how it runs itself. And if any have been disobedient or rebellious they are to be sent off and attached to other companions.

§ Item, if any full heretics have been among them for a long time, ⟨leading a praiseworthy life⟩ according to the rule of life of the sect and have been wise in scripture, they are made 'sandalled' at the same chapter, and from then on – together with the other 'sandalled' – they are called 'masters' and 'rectors' and 'priests'.

§ Item, the said chapter decides about those who wish to profess and to be consoled, and those to whom this is granted are afterwards consoled and a residence or society is assigned to them, where they are to re⟨main⟩ that year.

§ Item, the chapter appoints and deputes visitors of their friends and believers, who have to visit that year, and two are sent into each region or province in which some of their creed live.

§ Item, the money and alms that have been given and remitted to them by their friends and believers are presented at this chapter. The money, in fact, is distributed according to the ordinance of the said 'sandalled', and a fixed portion is given to each for himself and his household for maintenance in food and clothing for the coming year. And if some who are to run hospices are not present, money is sent ⟨to them⟩ via some who live in those parts. And the greater part of the money upon which they live ⟨and⟩ are maintained is brought from Germany.

The one who is attesting this does not know how they celebrate.

§ Similarly, ⟨he does⟩ [D: they do] not know how they ordain as 'sandalled', but he has heard that they are unshod by the other 'sandalled', and boots and shoes pierced above the feet are handed over to them – as is contained above.

Quinto, est sciendum quod professio eorum qui inter ipsos recipiuntur fit hoc modo. Maior seu sapiencior de societate seu hospicii, in quo consolandus moraturus est illo anno, seu alius hereticus extraneus, si ibi presens fuerit et sapiencior reputetur, congregatis omnibus tam hominibus quam mulieribus que in illo hospicio commorantur, predicat, et, facta inquisicione, exponunt illi qui recipiendus est omnia que observantur in dicta secta ⟨et⟩ quod oporteat illum qui recipiendus est credere illud quod superius continetur, et quod de cetero castitatem servet, proprium non habeat, humilitatem et obedienciam promittat, et consilio et voluntati ipsorum hereticorum in omnibus obediat et pareat. Non iuret, non occidat, nec aliquod peccatum faciat pro posse suo, ymmo antequam in aliquo de predictis offendat mortem paciatur. Qui si predicta adimplere ⟨non vellet⟩ non reciperetur inter eos. Qui consolandus respondet se paratum omnia et singula supradicta pro posse suo fideliter adimplere et eciam observare ~~et pro~~ et tunc proiciens se in terram a circumstantibus erigitur et sibi a quolibet datur osculum pacis, si homo fuerit ab hominibus, si mulier a mulieribus. Et tunc ille qui sic receptus est solvet expensas pransi si habeat unde solvat. **Sexto**, sciendum est quod illi qui deputati et ordinati sunt ad visitandum credentes sic procedunt. Petunt que visitare debent, et antequam ad dicta loca veniant mittunt aliquem credentem, qui cognoscit eos quos visitare debent, ad eosdem et notificat eis quod tales fratres veniunt, et mandatur eisdem per dictos credentes et assignatur certa dies et hora ad quam venire debeant, ad quam veniunt una cum dicto qui conducit eos, aliquociens de die, aliquociens de nocte.

§ Non faciunt quoad presens congregaciones magnas, sed dictos credentes visitant de hospicio in hospicium, videlicet quoslibet in hospiciis eorundem, et ibi in quolibet hospicio manent per duos vel tres vel 4^{or} dies, aliquociens plus, aliquociens / fol. 34r / minus. Et predicant et exhortantur et instruunt ipsos credentes in fide et erroribus supradictis, et quod a predictis abstineant – non occidant, non menciantur, non iurent, non faciant aliquod quod sibi nolunt.

ibi presens] sibi presenes *V*   reputetur] reputentur *M*

inquisicione] predicatione *MV*

⟨et⟩ quod oporteat] et quod oportet *MV*

in omnibus obediat] obediat in omnibus *MV* pareat. Non mentiatur *MV*   iuret] iureat *V*   aliquod] aliquod mortale *MV*   in aliquo] aliquo *V* predicta] predictum *V* ⟨non vellet⟩] non vellet *V*   nollet *M*

receptus] acceptus *M* pransi] prandii *MV* habeat] habet *M* est quod illi qui] quod illi *V*   Petunt] Petunt enim loca *MV*   et antequam – visitare debent ad eosdem *V omits* debent, ad eosdem] debet *M*   mandatur] tunc mandatur *MV* veniunt] horam veniunt *MV*   una *VM omit* dicto] dicto credente *MV*   aliquociens de die] aliquando de die *VM*   aliquociens de nocte] aliquoties de nocte *M*   inhospicium] ad hospicium *M* eorundem] eorum *MV* tres] per tres *V*   4^{or}] iiij^{or} *V* quatuor *M* aliquociens plus *MV omit*   aliquociens] aliquoties *MV* predicant et] predicant *MV*   a predictis] ab infrascriptis *MV* occidant] occidat *M* aliquod] aliquid *M* nolunt] nolunt fieri *MV*

Fifthly, one should know that the profession of those who are received among them happens this way. The senior or wiser man of the society or hospice, in which the one who is to be consoled is due to live that year, or some other heretic from elsewhere if he is present and reputed to be wiser, preaches to a gathering of all those, both men and women, who live in the hospice. After the ⟨sermon⟩ [D: questioning], they explain to the person who is to be received all the things which are observed in the said sect; ⟨and⟩ that he who is to be received must believe what is contained above; and that henceforth he must observe chastity, have nothing of his own, promise humility and obedience, and obey and comply with the counsel and will of these heretics in all things. He must do his utmost not ⟨to lie⟩, not swear, not kill, nor commit any sin, in fact he should suffer death rather than offend in any of the aforesaid. Should he be unwilling to observe the aforesaid things, he would not be received among them. The one to be consoled has to reply that he is prepared to do his utmost faithfully to carry out and observe each and every one of the aforesaid things, and then he casts himself to the ground and is raised up by the bystanders, and the kiss of peace is given to him by each, if he is a man by the men, if a woman by the women. And then the person who has been received in this way has to pay the expenses of the meal if he has the wherewithal to pay.

Sixthly, one should know that those who are deputed and appointed to visit believers proceed in this way. They seek out ⟨the places⟩ which they have to visit; and before they arrive at the said places they send some believer, who knows those whom they have to visit, to them, and he notifies them that such and such Brothers are coming. And then, through the aforesaid believers, a certain day and hour at which they should come there is mandated and assigned to them [= the Brothers]. They come at this time, together with the said ⟨believer⟩, who guides them, sometimes by day, sometimes at night.

§ Up to now they do not have great gatherings. But they visit the said believers from hospice to hospice, that is to say, whomsoever in their hospices, and there in each hospice they stay for two or three or four days, sometimes for more, sometimes for less. And they preach to and exhort and instruct these believers in the aforesaid faith and errors, and that they should abstain from the aforesaid things: they should not kill, not lie, not swear, not do anything they do not wish ⟨to be done⟩ to themselves.

confessionem]
confessiones *MV*
iniungant] iniungunt
MV   credentibus]
credentes *V* eos] eis *V*
eius *M*   et in]
Aliquotiens etiam *V*
Aliquoties etiam *M*
deferunt] perferunt *VM*
perfecti *M omits*
cultellos] cutillos *M*
agulherios] achalberios
V acalberios *M*
favorabilibus]
familiarius *V*
familiaribus *M* fit] sit *M*
hyeme] hieme *M*
quam in] quam *MV*
ideo *MV omit*   quod]
quia *MV*   orant] orent
MV sic] sic dicti *MV*
et credentes]
credencium *V; M omits*
helemosinis sibi ipsis
elemosinas] elemosine
sibi datis ipsa *V*
elemosinis sibi datis
ipsa *M*   suum *MV omit*
easdem] eadem *MV*
ibidem] ibi *MV*
Septimo – est *MV omit*

§ Item, audiunt confessionem ipsorum credencium, et eis penitencias iniungant [*r*: iniungunt], et elemosinas recipiunt ab eisdem credentibus, et scripturas eos [*r*: eis] docent, et in aliis hospiciis dictorum credencium visitant isto modo. Et in pluribus locis deferunt dicti perfecti heretici suis credentibus et eorum liberis et familiis aliqua jocalia, videlicet zonas, cultellos, agulherios et acus, ut libencius et favorabilibus [*r*: favorabilius] recipiantur. Et dicta visitacio fit pocius in hyeme quam in estate ideo quod credentes melius vacare possunt. Visitatis credentibus salutant eos ex parte fratrum suorum omnium, et dicti credentes rogant eos ut ex parte ipsorum salutent omnes fratres suos et orant ad Dominum pro eisdem. Et sic visitatores et credentes cum pecunia et helemosinis sibi ipsis [*r*: datis] elemosinas reportant ad suum venturum capitulum generale et easdem ~~ibi p~~ ibidem presentantes dividunt, prout superius continetur.

Septimo sciendum est [*the rest of the leaf, which could have contained twenty-two more lines, remains blank*].[5]

---

[5] Like D, V leaves a large space blank – the end of the column fol. 72vb and all of column fol. 73ra – before continuing. There then follows in DMV account of Waldensian celebration of the Eucharist, the second part or chapter of a three very short chapters which often occur as a unit, and which Bernard Gui inserted virtually unchanged into his *Practica* V.ii.4. On manuscripts and editions of this fragment on the Eucharist, see Dondaine, 'Manuel', pp. 133 and 150; Gui, *P*, p. 247.

§ Item, they hear the confessions of their believers, and impose penances on them, and receive alms from these same believers, and teach them scriptures, and they visit in this way other hospices of the said believers. And in many places the said full heretics carry to their believers and their children and households some trinkets, that is to say, belts, knives, pin-cases and pins, in order to get more willing and favorable reception. And the said visitation takes place more in winter than summer, so that believers are better able to have free time. When believers are visited they [= the Brothers] greeted them on behalf of all Brothers, and the said believers ask them to greet all their Brothers on their behalf, and to pray to the Lord for them. And thus the visitors and the believers, together with the money and alms ⟨given⟩ to them [*D*: themselves], take them [= the money and alms] to the coming general chapter, and presenting them there they divide them up, as is contained above.

Seventhly one should know that [*blank space follows, for what the contents-list at the beginning states was – or was to be –* 'Seventhly and lastly, about the crime and guilt of the ⟨person⟩ who is attesting or confessing'].

The 'Register in the Register': Reflections on the Doat 32 Dossier

Caterina Bruschi

History of the Enquiry. Still on Doat

I was tracing the list of 'filters' imposed on the text of inquisitorial trials when Peter Biller drew my attention to another volume of Doat: D32. The extraordinary connection linking it to D26 added pieces to my 'deconstruction puzzle', and raised further problems and new methodological questions regarding inquisitorial sources. This paper's sole purpose is to start the analysis of this case-study, sketching a preliminary structure, which I intend to expand in the future.[1]

D32 appears to be quite an uneven register, bringing together a series of episcopal letters and papal bulls, mainly dating back to the period 1272–97. Behind it there lies a clear interest in *consilia*, the official advice offered by religious authorities and lay jurists about procedural queries, uncertain behaviour, and complaints. By the late thirteenth century the use of *consilia* had become widespread both among inquisitors whose doubts about application of the papal decrees needed a strong theological and juridical basis for their interpretation, and also among those who had to assess the inquisitors' management of the enquiries when there were complaints. It is interesting to list a few examples of those contained in D32:

1. (XIV *Kalendis Iunii* 1273): letters from John, cardinal of St Nicholas *in carcere Tulliano*, to the Dominican and Franciscan inquisitors *in partibus citra montanis* (Italy). John is asking them to make copies of Italian trial records, and send them to their colleagues in France, in order to instruct them on the suitable method of interrogation to adopt in similar cases.

2. (XV *Kalendis Ianuarii* 1286): Honorius IV's bull addressed to those inquisitors who could hardly find enough skilled notaries for the procedural recording of enquiries. The pope authorizes the prior of Dominican Order to name two notaries, according to the rules of the Holy Roman Church.

3. (IV *Idus Februarii* 1288): Nicholas IV's bull to brother Philip, inquisitor in the area of Treviso (Italy), ordering him to send to France the heretics he

---

[1] This was noticed first in Douais, *Documents*, pp. ccvi–ccx. I shall provide a fuller account of it in the forthcoming *Festschrift* for Ovidio Capitani.

arrested around Verona. Some of them are in fact French, and among them is one who is called 'bishop' of the heretics.

4. (1297): various letters from Philip IV, king of France, referring to the unjust and violent behaviour of the inquisitors; following them, a letter from the Carcassonne seneschal, on the same topic.

The case I wish to focus on comprises a complex sequence of events, linked to each other like a 'Russian doll'. The writer was an anonymous canonist, who had been appointed by the pope to judge the reliability of a suspicious inquisitorial register and to provide *consilia*. The register had been assembled following uncertain criteria, and in fact it had been considered suspicious for a long time. The canonist had received it via the inquisitor of Carcassonne, and, after conducting a thorough analysis of its contents, he was reporting the results of his enquiry to the pontiff.

The register brings together depositions of witnesses dating back to the period 1284–90 and recorded during inquisitorial trials in the Carcassonne area.

There had been investigation into eighteen cases of people 'deceased in the state of heresy', who had never gone on to confess. There had been the supposition that fourteen of them had been guilty of being present at rituals of *hereticatio*,[2] and that, having adored heretics, three had received the *consolamentum* just before death, and that the last one had survived his *consolamentum*, and had persevered in professing Catharism. Some of the characters involved here, named one by one, are well-known to readers of the Doat Collection. The first fourteen are:

a. *Arnalotus olim serviens* (formerly servant of) *de Cabareto*
b. *Peronella, uxor* (wife of) *Philippi de Montavilla de Pisenchis*
c. *Bernardus de Lercio de Ripperia Cabareti*
d. *Petrus Raynaudi de Tribus Bonis*
e. *Raymundus Regalis, olim rector ecclesie de* (formerly rector of the church of) *Pradalis*
f. *Bernardus Regino de Furnis*
g. *Raymundus Richardi, olim rector ecclesie de* (formerly of the church of) *Guerioserverio de Carcassona*
h. *Stephanus Cultellerii de Cannis, quondam rector ecclesie de* (the late rector of the church of) *Villa Lambert*
i. *Guillerma, mater* (the mother of) *Ysarni de Cannis de Narbona*
j. *Bernardus Egidii de Furnis*
k. *Bernarda Savortesia de Bastida de Praverenche*

---

[2] I shall use here the words 'heretication', 'hereticated' as literal translations of the Latin equivalents *hereticatio, hereticatus*. I shall also use 'heretic' (instead of 'perfect', or 'Cathar') to reproduce the inquisitor's *hereticus*, in order not to alter his lexical choices, while my translation 'believer', in quotation marks, stands for the Latin *credens*.

l. *Arnaldus Savorcesii, filius* (the son of) *Bernarde Savortesie*
m. *Arnaldus Regina de Furnis de Carcassona*
n. *Petrus Bernardi de Laurano de Narbona.*

The next three are:

a. *Iacobus, quondam rector de* (the late rector of ⟨the church of⟩) *Insulis*
b. *Raymundus Gayrandi, quondam rector ecclesie de* (the late rector of the church of) *Rippafera in Cabardesio de Carcassona*
c. *Rogerius de Mansa de Cannis de Narbona.*

The last to be named is *Philippotus de Montavilla.*

The depositions had been obtained in the years 1284–90 by the inquisitors Jean Galand and Guillaume of Saint-Seine, but they referred back to events between 1222 and 1243. Moreover, in 1309 Geoffroi (presumably Geoffroi d'Ablis), then inquisitor in Carcassonne, had proceeded to a second hearing of the witnesses, and Jean de *Belna*[3] had done the same in 1320, and neither of these had recorded substantial retractations of or corrections to the witnesses' first statements. The *doctor*, therefore, highlighted first the fact that for forty years no-one had been able to find material in the depositions that actually incriminated the deceased 'heretics', and also that these depositions 'have been recorded without interlinear ⟨material⟩, erasures, marginal additions, and omissions'.[4] He went on, secondly, to the point that the register did not record any reason why the *expeditio negotiorum* (the despatching of the case) had been so delayed, apart from the possibility that uncertainties and doubts about procedural legitimacy had led its being held back. It was on these uncertainties and doubts that the canonist focused his attention and analysis.

In fact, a further complication had been added to the case. According to the person who sent the register to the *doctor*, the volume had been assembled after a selection of documents which was itself dubious: presumably it excluded some important ones. What it did include were the original volumes called *liber decimus et undecimus diocesis Carcassone* (the tenth and eleventh book of the diocese of Carcassonne), about which – as he himself confessed – 'there has been murmuring for a long time'.[5] It is not surprising, then, that the collection was introduced by a papal document, included by the anonymous copyist to testify that Pope Clement V had seen the volume and had put his signature on one of the pages.

As far as we know, both the enquiry and – later – the register appeared suspicious and raised doubts about the thoroughness of the whole proceedings. As regards the enquiry, in fact, the inquisitors themselves had twice felt it necessary to repeat their interrogations and search for confirmation of the depositions, first ten and then thirty years later. As regards the register, this

---

[3] *Belna* in the manuscript: presumably Jean de Beaune.
[4] D32, fol. 169r: 'scripte sunt sine interlinearibus, cancellaturis, additionibus in margine, et remissionibus'.
[5] D32, fol. 168v: 'a longo tempore est murmuratum'.

had been constructed in such a confused way that most of the original features appeared to be lost, adding – to apply the phraseology I use in 'Magna Diligentia', in chapter 5 above – filters to filters. In D32 the two volumes *liber decimus et undecimus*, in fact, are accompanied by abstracts of the two earlier inquiries of 1309 and 1320, and by the records of a series of other unknown investigations held by the inquisitor who structured the whole *dossier*.

To put all this simply, D32 is the enquiry conducted by a canonist into a miscellaneous volume (now lost) which had included (a) a selection of the *liber decimus et undecimus* of the Carcassonne inquisition (containing the original trial interrogations) (b) excerpts from the further interrogations of 1309 and 1320, and (c) the record of some 'investigations' held by the last inquisitor, before assembling the volume. No other manuscript including the material of D32 is left, and the whole original *dossier* is lost.

According to a simple chronological criterion and to the names of the deponents, the connection between the 'dossier D32' and D26 appears quite an immediate one. D26 records from folio 79r onwards a whole section named 'Interrogations and depositions of the Albigensians in front of the defenders of faith, from 1283 to 1289'. The inquisitors Jean Galand and Guillaume of Saint-Seine had led this enquiry together.

Does D26 reproduce the *liber decimus et undecimus* of the inquisition of Carcassonne? The first point is that only eight out of the twenty-six witnesses heard in D26 are present in D32 as well:

a. *Guillelmus Gomefenx de Tureta*
b. *Arnaldus Macellarii*
c. *Richa Topina de Ripparia de Cabaret, uxor* (wife of) *Pascale Recordi*
d. *Bernardus Agassa de Carcassona*
e. *Guillelmus Sicardi de Cussac*
f. *Guillelmus Serra de Carcassona*
g. *Robertus Anglicus, serviens de* (servant of) *Cabaret*
h. *Iohannes de Nusiacho, serviens castello de* (serving at the castle of) *Cabaret*.

Why this difference? Why does only a limited number of deponents appear in D32? Are they *really* the same depositions?

There are two possible explanations to consider. The first hypothesis would be that the lost 'dossier D32' simply included a selection of the also lost Carcassonne volumes X and XI. This selection corresponds to a part of the D26 interrogations, while another part is now recorded in other volumes of the Doat Collection. According to Molinier, in fact, volumes 27 and 28 contain interrogations about the area of Carcassonne, Limoux and Lodève from 1318 to 1329. This first hypothesis is not implausible. It would not be unique: the well-known case of Peter de *Beauville*, for example, was recorded partly in D25 and partly in D26. It is therefore possible that when the Doat team assembled the whole collection the copyists split the original dossier into two parts, one of which ended up in other Doat volumes. Moreover, as we saw in chapter 5, Jean de Doat himself had often complained about lack of resources, sudden interruptions of the financial support to his enterprise, all elements that could have badly affected the continuity of the work. The suggestion is that behind the scenes a whole team of copyists and researchers had to face limitations in the availability of documents, and was consequently forced to make an arbitrary and personal selection of them.

As a logical consequence of this first hypothesis, one should look in the volumes D27 and D28, where the remaining depositions of the original books X and XI of the inquisition of Carcassonne should be contained. If they were to be found, none of my speculations about filters would be disproved. The copyists employed by Jean de Doat 'compact' registers that they find by chance in one specific place or moment, marking their division only with brief and concise titles. Therefore, the 'dossier D32', sent by the inquisitor of Carcassonne to the canonist, would be not only the 'collection' of the original registers X and XI, but also a selection of their contents. It is crucial to remember that, whatever the case, we do not have the dossier, the original source of the enquiry.

The second hypothesis – and in my opinion the most likely – differs slightly from the first. The well-known mobility of the inquisitors, in fact their almost complete freedom to organize and manage the activity of the tribunal, allowed them to conduct more than one enquiry at the same time. It is therefore equally possible that those eight witnesses who gave depositions in both D26 and D32 actually did do so in the same years and months, and in front of the same two inquisitors, but that their depositions concerned different enquiries or suspects. What they said could have been fragmented and recorded as 'portions' in different registers, in relation to different enquiries. What we could call 'fragments of deposition', although collected on one occasion, ended up in different volumes, according to the case in question.

The case of Bernard Agasse can cast light on our hypothesis. In D26 his deposition is the crucial testimony in the case of the theft of books of the inquisitors in Carcassonne, while in D32 he is questioned about the involvement of some deceased people in heretical activities. This suggests that during the hearing of a witness implicated in more than one case, the notary had to split his interrogation into several parts, and to record each 'fragment' in the appropriate register. If this is correct, we are led to see our original registers as rather thematic. This adds further structural filters (that is, those depending on the internal criteria of the enquiry and its records) to our previous list.

One point needs to be kept in mind which does not materially affect either hypothesis: a witness could be summoned several times, depending on the number of cases s/he could contribute to with his/her deposition.

Content: Main Doubts

When conducting his enquiry the canonist applied himself to a series of clear issues: the elements of the dossier that raised doubts about its own legitimacy, the legitimacy of the condemnation, and the supposed fairness in conducting the interrogation. He listed them rather neatly and precisely, and on each point he supported his statements with examples taken from the text. A brief survey of the main ones illuminates the juridical review's most crucial worries.

The first three points focused on the constitution of our dossier. The canonist seemed puzzled by (a) the delay in resolution of the case (b) the necessity of a repeated summons of the witnesses to confirm their first declarations (c) some arbitrary omissions of witnesses' names by the last inquisitor (the one who assembled the dossier) and chronological data regarding the depositions, and the cancellation of the notaries', inquisitors' and judges' names.

Further points needing careful enquiry were often repeated by the canonist. Are a perjuror's depositions – other than those particular ones where perjury has been specifically demonstrated – trustworthy? And to what extent? What are the connections between deponents, and how can these links affect the reliability of their words? The *doctor* seemed particularly concerned to carry out an exhaustive survey, to remove every possibility of misunderstanding, or chance of mistake. A long series of cases was analyzed with extreme care and attention, and their details dissected and cross-referenced. Special care was applied when studying any case of one person informing on another. The canonist was interested in the reasons that might have led a Cathar to betray his companions. To distinguish those who – although *socii* of (affiliated to) the Cathar church – are telling the truth, from those who are not, he wrote that

> one needs to believe them, against others, if on the basis of probable conjectures and the number of them or the quality of the persons (both the ones attesting and those against whom they are attesting) and other circumstances – one thinks that they are not testifying falsely.[6]

> (tunc demum eis credi debeat contra alios si ex verisimilibus coniecturis, et ex numero ipsorum aut personarum – tam deponentium quam eorum contra quos deponitur – qualitate, et aliis circonstantiis sic testificantes non falsa dicere presumentur.)

Further, when confronting a dubious witness, the *doctor* checked if he/she had already attested in other cases, and had been reliable then, and if his/her attitude towards the inquisitor had been 'predominantly' honest or not.

---

[6] D32, fol. 170r.

He then examined the affective links between people, together with the relations that connected them with the group. Moving later to the reasons why these relations had begun to deteriorate and had led to the inculpating confession, he put together in a large category betrayals of companions and the cases of real plots directed against a scapegoat. He presented to the pope a series of elements to understand their dynamics, applying almost a mathematical logic to studying the contradictions of the deponents during the trial.

[The *credentes*] who had suffered an injury are very fond of each other and when one of them is harassed by some believer, they are ready to plot against him, and to impute to him the crime of heresy. And one of them denounces ⟨him⟩, evidence is given, he names others as witnesses – ⟨people⟩ with whom, as has frequently been found, he had conspired. For this reason the inquisitor has to be very meticulous when 'believers' of heretics, freed from prison, come and testify against others, especially against those earlier believed to have been faithful about those matters which took place before the imprisonment [of the just released 'believers']. Because their depositions, additions and corrections are very dangerous – since they know not only the heretics' way of living, moving around, and escaping, and their way of coming into the houses of those waiting for *heretication*, but also the heretics' mode of heretication, and adoration – they easily agree when bringing evidence against whatever faithful person they dislike. And, as has often been seen, ⟨they do this⟩ very plausibly, agreeing with each other.[7]

([The *credentes*] qui iniuriati fuerunt multum se mutuo diligent, et quando per aliquem fidelem molestiam aliquis eorum patitur, inter se sunt prompti ad conspirandum contra eum et imponendum crimen heresis, et unus eorum denuntiat, et testificatur, et nominat alios pro testibus, cum quibus conspiravit sicut frequenter inventum est, propter quod magna diligentia est habenda per / inquisitorem quando tales qui fuerunt hereticorum credentes liberati a muro veniunt ad deponendum contra alios, et maxime fideles reputatos ante de factis prius commissis, antequam ipsi inmurarentur. Tales cum eorum depositiones, additiones, et correctiones, multum solent esse periculo se, quia cum ipsi sciant modo vivendi, incedendi, et tacitandi [*probably a mistake for* latitandi] hereticorum, et veniendi ad domos hereticandorum, sciant etiam modum hereticandi, et adorandi hereticos, faciliter concordant ad ferendum testimonium contra quemcumque fidelem qui eis displicet verisimiliter, et concorditer, sicut frequenter visum est.)

The procedural criterion for summoning the accused was another interesting element in scrutinizing the case. Were the accused free to defend themselves in a convenient way, or rather did the delay in concluding the case prevent regular and fair process? And, consequently, did inefficiency in

---

[7] D32, fols. 171v–2r.

the judicial system have a bearing on their death without repentance? Did they die as convicted heretics because of the negligence of their persecutors? Here the canonist displayed considerable humanity, 'defending' the rights of the dead heretics:

> perhaps one could allege many things better against them [the witnesses] if they were ⟨still⟩ alive; and they could also themselves be re-questioned, and their faces could be seen, and their words could be understood better in their own voices than from a script. Maybe, in fact, the witnesses for the defense are already dead, witnesses who knew the state of their parents, their rivalries, and other relevant objections against the witnesses of our case.

> (contra quos melius forsan possent multa opponi si viverent, et ipsi etiam possent repeti, et facies eorum videri, et verba ipsorum melius ex ore eorum intelligi quam ex scripto. Sunt etiam forte mortui eisdem deffensoribus [*perhaps Doat copyist mistake for* deffensionibus] testes qui noverunt conditiones parentum defunctorum et inimicitias et exceptiones alias contra testes de quibus agitur competentes.)[8]

What is surprising here is the extraordinary care with which the canonist almost 'surgically' dissected the depositions: he established some recurring themes within them, and then verified their validity, through cross-referencing of the depositions. There is a good example of his way of proceeding in the case of *Arnalotus serviens defunctus de Cabareto*.[9] Fourteen witnesses had been asked to confirm his presence at a Cathar *consolomentum*, and his act of genuflection in front of the heretics. The canonist examined various elements: time of the fact, place of the fact, presence of a formal act of *reverentia* (reverence), names of the participants, and so on. He acted as though he was setting out a spreadsheet. For each of them he wrote own what the fourteen witnesses had said, and noted if there were any discrepancies. He assigned a number to each witness. Then he noted, for example, as regards the time, how five said that the facts had taken place during the day – numbers follow – but disagreed on the precise hour, while nine others claim that it had been at night – numbers follow. As regards the place, however, all agreed on the name of the place, witnesses one, five, and eleven even on the house, witnesses six, seven, eight and nine on the room in which the rite had been held. About the day, nobody could recall it precisely enough, but witnesses two and eight were not asked about it.

Modern historians assume a 'grille' of questions lying behind inquisitorial depositions. Here the results of the canonists's analysis are very interesting. He implicitly acknowledged that a rigorous application of such a grille cannot be taken for granted. Or, rather, while its lax application had probably already become usual in inquisitors' enquiries, this was not assumed to the

---

[8] D32, fol. 173r.
[9] D32, fols. 188r–196r.

same extent by the canonist – I shall return later to this point. The canonist appreciated how

> many of the said witnesses seem to have been imperfectly examined and interrogated, and not only about the above mentioned matters, but also about the mode of heretications, and adorations – not just imperfectly, but also with very different procedures. And [for this reason] sometimes the afore-mentioned witnesses appear to clash in their depositions.[10]

> (videntur multi de dictis testibus imperfecte examinati, et interrogati fuisse, et nedum circa premissa, seu etiam circa modum hereticationum et adorationum, non solum imperfecte, imo multum diversimode, et quandoque contrarie deponere videntur testes predicti.)

In his opinion, the inquisitors had been wanting in procedural rigour. Given the way in which our jurist was 'deconstructing' the text, we are not surprised to see him upholding a degree of rigour that seems far removed from inquisitors' practice. This is clearly shown when the *doctor* gives examples of the way in which some of the witnesses contradict themselves. During the ritual of Cathar *consolamentum*, the heretication – he said – it is usual for the two 'heretics' to have different roles. The first, and the eldest, actually 'consoles' the believer, while the second, the junior one, simply acts as an assistant. Despite this well-known practice, the D32 witnesses confessed to having seen both 'consoling', 'X and Y, 'consoling' the *credens*', and 'two unknown men', 'two heretics', 'X and his fellow', or 'X and his fellow, whose name I cannot recall'. With these differences in describing the same episode, could such testimonies still incriminate the suspect?

Such a little detail – which I initially interpreted merely as variation in writing down these long depositions – evidently had a different 'weight' in the canonist's reading of the record. Every tiny discrepancy was important to him and could determine the reliability of a particular record.

The practical management of the enquiry, its recording, the cross-referencing of all the registers behind the 'dossier D32' – all these were of vital concern to the canonist. Following his deconstruction, some further considerations immediately arise. To begin with they concern the latitude allowed to inquisitors in the interpretation of the canonist/papal rules in this area. Was it permissible to hide the names of the witnesses? Or to alter the order – and, consequently, the record – of depositions? The writer in fact underlined the fact that 'frequenter primo deposita inveniantur ultimo in libro scripta' (often those things attested at the beginning [of an enquiry] are the last to be written down in the book).[11] At the end of each section the

---

[10] D32, fol. 175v. If influenced by vernacular usage, *multi de dictis testibus* means 'many of the said witnesses', rather than 'many' of them were examined 'about the said witnesses'.

[11] D32, fol. 179v.

writer asked if depositions assembled in such a way were enough to establish the *post mortem* condemnation.

While continuing to apply his rather mechanical criteria of truthfulness, our jurist never looked directly at the truthfulness of the content of the depositions. For example, in a case where witnesses saw and adored heretics, their failure ever to mention heretical beliefs was a problem: was there enough to accuse them? Was the attestation of only *some* elements of heretication enough to prove that they had been hereticated? The writer seemed to support a 'no' in answer to this, when asking,

> If the simple fact that a heretic had taken the hands of the 'hereticated' person into his hands constitutes proof that this person was 'hereticated' – and the fact that he had put the book in which the gospel of the blessed John is written on the 'hereticated' ill person's head, while reading the blessed John's gospel? Or, assume that it is proved that someone had actually been at such a 'heretication' and had adored heretics there: nevertheless this may not prove that on that occasion the heretic had taught some doctrinal errors, or that he had dogmatized against the Catholic faith, nor may it show that the 'hereticated' person or he who is proved to have been present at the rite of 'heretication' had listened to the errors of the Manichaean or other heretics – should such people be held to be 'believers' of heretics' errors?[12]

> (Si probatur aliquem hereticatum fuisse ut quia hereticus posuit manus ipsius heretici inter manus suas, et librum in quo scriptum est evangelium beati Iohannis super caput ipsius infirmi heretici legendo evangelium beati Iohannis, vel probetur aliquem tali hereticationi interfuisse, et ibidem hereticos adorasse, non tamen probetur quod hereticus tunc aliquod errores docuerit, seu contra fidem catholicam aliquid dogmatisaverit, aut quod hereticatus, vel ille qui dicte hereticationi interfuisse probatur aliquos errores hereticorum manicheorum aut aliorum audiverint, utrum tales credentes hereticorum erroribus debeant reputari.)

As a general rule, it seems that either the jurist believed that what he read in the documents actually corresponded to the real dialogue that had occurred between the two parties, inquisitor and deponent, or, alternatively, that he did not consider that the filters superimposed by the grille of questions, or by the biases of both actors, deserved in any way to be taken into account in the evaluation of the enquiry.

So, he carried on with his analysis, moving on to another point, the lack of summons of lay and ecclesiastical witnesses to the interrogations. According to him this negligence suggested doubts about procedure. He suggested that the system of *deffensiones*, that is, the formal delivery of charges to the suspect or to his /her representative, to allow them to organize a line of defence, had been blatantly disregarded.

---

[12] D32, fol. 182r–v.

There is doubt whether the *deffensiones* (= the allegations) given to the heirs and relatives of the deceased ones were given to them properly, since the *deffensiones* given to them were like those contained in the book which has come to us, that is, without the names of the witnesses. If the names of the witnesses and the aforesaid notaries are also not contained in the original, there is doubt whether such proceedings against the dead can be valid.[13]

(Dubitatur an deffentiones date heredibus et propinquis dictorum defunctorum sint sufficienter eis date, cum tales eis date fuerint quales in dicto libro nobis tradito continentur, tacitis nominibus testium. Si vero nec in originali continentur nomina testium et notariorum predictorum, dubitatur an tales processus possint valere contra defunctos.)

A careful reading suggests that the canonist's main purpose was to 'strip' from the text all the elements that could invalidate the *post mortem* condemnation. If read in this light, his deconstruction provides for us a unique benchmark of what he considered to be an 'ideal enquiry'. Ideal, of course, from the point of view of a theoretician rather than a practitioner, a canon lawyer rather than an inquisitor. The view of a canonist is not to be underestimated or dismissed as irrelevant. Historians have failed to take sufficiently into account the gap between canonical decrees and official documents on the one hand and practice on the other. While the law and its application are evidently linked in this case, what happens in one does not necessarily happen in the other. One thing is the norm, another thing the actual *consuetudo* (practice) of everyday trials and auditions.

Problems for the Historian

To continue with a metaphor derived from this inquisition into inquisitions, I myself have been the inquisitor of Doat volumes, in chapter 5 above, *Magna diligentia*. I felt it rather odd to realize that the same worries about the records were stimulating the canonist's enquiry of D32, that the same doubts were leading to their deconstruction. It is time therefore to say a few things about the problems that such a textual process poses for the historian. For we have a rare opportunity to juxtapose two views of the enquiry, ours and that of the fourteenth-century canonist.

On what grounds was the D32 enquiry felt to be irregular from a procedural point of view? What was the *discrimen* applied, the 'limit' beyond which the supposed irregularity could even lead to invalidation of the condemnation?

Undoubtedly, the first question was the most important one: it was the very basis of the whole enquiry. The problem of procedural irregularity emerged from the substantial clash between the theory of canon law and trial

---

[13] D32, fol. 183r.

220

Caterina Bruschi

practice. How one was received and absorbed into the other must be our starting point: to what degree did the structural problems of our 'dossier D32' cause irregularity for the canonist? To what degree, then, was what what the canonist saw as irregular the direct consequence of a formal fault, common to most enquiries in the Doat Collection?

This inevitably leads to the further question, which points of the enquiry about the 'dossier D32' generated doubts among contemporaries? What elements of its procedure provoked complaints and caused the 'enquiry into the enquiry'? Since it was a *post mortem* case, it is most likely that it was the relatives of the deceased heretics who protested about it. Was it something to do with the confiscation of the heretics' property? Apparently even to the first observers – the relatives? – some elements in the conduct of the case did not match the rules for interrogation, and the consequent condemnation of the suspects: what are the characteristics of those elements?

Thirdly, establishing a definition of the conceptual criterion of 'irregularity' seems fundamental. This enquiry appeared suspect or irregular to contemporaries, who urgently requested its revision. At the same time its conduct and conclusion, the sentence, preoccupied the canonist. Were both contemporaries and canonist in agreement on one conceptual definition of 'irregular', or 'legitimate'? Did this concept vary, depending on their different purposes? To what extent could such preconceptions have invalidated the accusations and, consequently, the development of the case?

This last question brings historians onto the stage. It is our task, as it was the canonist's before us, to establish the validity of the case, in the absence of the first enquiry. In addition to this, historians have to evaluate and assess the canonist's work, and the effectiveness and fairness of his survey.

Without expressing judgements on legitimacy or illegitimacy, it is our task to de-construct the logical mechanism that gave life to: (1) the construction of the first enquiry; (2) the creation of the second 'dossier D32'; (3) the definition of an ideal sort of enquiry, the one that the canonist wanted to verify with his work.

As to the first point, it is probably sufficient refer back to chapter 5 above and to its list of 'filters', while the second, third and fourth points need to be developed in the future. This I shall do on the basis of the story of the *affaire* D32, the last and only witness of this extraordinary textual process.

Which Wyche? The Framing of the Lollard Heretic and/or Saint

Anne Hudson

I should like to start by recalling the story behind the Wife of Bath's familiar question 'Who peyntede the leon, tel me who?', for it is the text of the present sermon.[1] The question is the lion's when shown a picture by a peasant of the killing of a lion by a man with an axe; in Marie de France's recounting of the fable the lion follows up his question by describing to the peasant how *he* would have represented a man and a lion.[2] The story here concerns not a peasant and a lion, but a series of ecclesiastical figures and a man called Richard Wyche, or, to use the loaded terms of conventional history, investigating authorities and a heretic.[3] The story – the case, the legend – of Richard Wyche is one of the rare instances where we have two pictures, one painted by the man, the other by the lion. I propose to start by describing these two pictures, one by one, using the terminology that each uses about its own story. As will be seen, the identity of man and lion is not a fixed one.

The Official Story

It may be unfair to start this version from the end, but I will do the same with my second. The official picture of Wyche is crystallized and dominated by the account of his death: on 17 June 1440 Richard Wyche was burned as a relapsed heretic on Tower Hill in London. This fact is recorded

---

[1] *The Riverside Chaucer*, ed. L. D. Benson et al. (Oxford, 1987), 'Canterbury Tales', iii.692.

[2] See the edition and translation by H. Spiegel (Toronto, 1987), no. 37.

[3] An account of the case is to be found in J. A. F. Thomson, *The Later Lollards 1414–1520*, 2nd edn (Oxford, 1967), pp. 15–16 and 148–50 (to which, as will emerge below, some details can be added); see also C. von Nolcken, 'Richard Wyche, a Certain Knight, and the Beginning of the End', in *Lollardy and the Gentry in the Later Middle Ages*, ed. M. Aston and C. Richmond (Stroud, 1997), pp. 127–54. Much important detail of the background to Wyche's case is to be found in M. Jurkowski, 'Heresy and Factionalism at Merton College in the Early Fifteenth Century', *JEH* 48 (1997), 658–81. Since this paper was written Rita Copeland's study of Wyche has been published in her *Pedagogy, Intellectuals, and Dissent in the Later Middle Ages: Lollardy and Ideas of Learning* (Cambridge, 2001), pp. 151–90; I have added a few points of factual disagreement to the notes here, but have not otherwise modified the text.

in various London chronicles.[4] Two weeks later, on 2 July 1440, the patent
roll records the grant of Wyche's goods and chattels to the king's servant
John Somerseth, Wyche having been executed 'for certain articles and
untrue opinions held by him against the faith of Christ and of Holy
Church'.[5] At the time of his burning Wyche was vicar of Harmondsworth,
Middlesex, to which he had been presented in January 1437, the patrons
being Winchester College.[6] Episcopal registers allow his previous livings to
be traced: he went to Harmondsworth from Leaveland in Kent in 1434, a
living in the patronage of the king; he had been admitted as vicar of West
Greenwich, now known as Deptford, in 1423, and had probably held that
living until he moved to Leaveland.[7] That paper trail is entirely neutral: the
moves are part of the normal process of clerical appointment, and the
documentation does not differentiate Wyche from any other priest. Where
Wyche was before Deptford is not declared – nor need it be, there is
nothing incriminating about that. Thirty years earlier a Richard Wyche
appears to have resigned from the living of Hartley, also in the Rochester
diocese, in June 1394; whether he is the same man is typically unresolvable.[8]

Between 1394 and 1424 Wyche, if indeed the two are the same, had,
however, appeared in ecclesiastical records in a much less conventional
guise. The earliest surviving document is one found in a brief collection of
heresy material in BL Royal 8 F. xii, fols. 16–17.[9] There appears a formal
recantation before Bishop Walter of Durham by *Ricardus Wyche, presbyter
Herfordensis*, of fourteen heresies,[10] followed by a further six articles whose
veracity Wyche was apparently required to affirm; he was forced to read out

[4] See *Six Town Chronicles of England*, ed. R. Flenley (Oxford, 1911), pp. 101 and 114;
C. L. Kingsford, *Chronicles of London* (Oxford, 1905), pp. 147 and 153–4, and the
material added to the same author's *English Historical Literature in the Fifteenth
Century* (Oxford, 1913), p. 339. Also *CCR 1435–1441*, pp. 385–6.
[5] *CPR 1436–1441*, p. 426.
[6] See G. Hennessy, *Novum Repertorium Ecclesiasticum Parochiale Londinense* (London,
1898), p. 203, from London reg. Gilbert fols. 5r and 32v. Here, and in the following
notes, references to bishops' registers are given in the form diocese, bishop's name,
folio, page or opening; the registers are listed in D. M. Smith, *Guide to Bishops'
Registers of England and Wales* (London, 1981).
[7] For the institution to West Greenwich see C. H. Fielding, *The Records of Rochester
Diocese* (Dartford, 1910), p. 81, from Rochester reg. Langdon fol. 66r; for the move to
Leaveland, *The Register of Henry Chichele*, ed. E. F. Jacob and H. C. Johnson, 4 vols.,
Canterbury and York Society 42 and 45–7 (Oxford, 1937–47), I, 342. The exchange of
Leaveland for Harmondsworth is recorded in *CPR 1436–1441*, p. 32.
[8] Rochester reg. de Bottlesham, fol. 49v.
[9] The material directly relating to heresy cases begins with this, followed by the
recantation of Purvey in 1401, the parliamentary writ for the burning of Sawtry also
in 1401, and a copy of Courtenay's reissue on 13 December 1384 of the Blackfriars
Council condemnation of articles from Wyclif's works. The Wyche material is
reprinted in the appendix to *FZ*, pp. 501–5.
[10] The *FZ* text, p. 501, reads *Willelmus . . . Dinolmensis episcopus* but the personal name
in the manuscript is clearly *Walterus*.

all of this, to sign the document, and to promise that he would not in any way propagate the heresies in future but would abide by the teachings of Holy Church. The document is formally undated, but Bishop Walter of Durham is clearly Walter Skirlawe, bishop from September 1388 till his death in March 1406; equally the final affirmation that Wyche made speaks of 'dominus Innocentius . . . papa septimus', and hence cannot have been made until October 1404 when Innocent was elected.[11] In the opening section, couched in the first person but, from its vocabulary and demeanour, almost certainly in wording provided by Wyche's accusers, Wyche acknowledges that he had failed to respond to the bishop's summons and had consequently been twice excommunicated – this is, it is reasonable to conclude, a case that has been pursued by the authorities over some time. The fourteen errors are stated in bald terms: images are not to be worshipped, each lay person is bound to know the whole gospel and to preach it, no priest should beg anything, every place is as suitable for prayer as every other, and so on; ominously the last two are 'they act wrongfully who burn men', and 'foolish are those who say that Richard Wyche has erred in any point'.[12] The six statements that Wyche was required to affirm cover matters not directly addressed in the fourteen errors: the first two provide an orthodox formulation of eucharistic doctrine, the third affirms that obedience is due to all parts of canon law, the fourth that the four orders of friars are approved by the Church and should be received and helped in their work, the fifth that no priest should preach outside his own parish save by special licence from the relevant bishop, and the sixth that anyone entering an order of mendicants, even if he were able-bodied and capable of labour, is entitled to beg. No further comment is made. We may surmise that the bishop had doubts about Wyche's opinion on all six final matters, but that is our deduction: their presence in the picture is, in view of the general economy of its delineation, doubtless significant but it would strictly be going beyond the evidence to affirm that Wyche had taught their opposite.

That recantation stands, as I have said, on its own, followed by a comparable recantation by John Purvey dateable to 1401. No word is given of Wyche's sentence, if any, after he had recited it. From other sources we learn that Skirlawe had prosecuted a number of Durham parish priests over the winter of 1402/3; the case against Wyche probably, though not decla-redly, started at the same time.[13] In date the next official record derives from

---

[11] *FZ*, p. 505. Copeland (above n. 3), pp. 152–4, dates the enquiries of Bishop Skirlaw, and this document, more precisely than the evidence warrants; her statement there on the source for this document should be modified by the information given p. 184 n. 91 – only the undated reply of Wyche, discussed here pp. 228–9, appears in the manuscript of the *FZ*.

[12] *FZ*, pp. 501–3.

[13] See the material collected together by M. G. Snape, 'Some Evidence of Lollard Activity in the Diocese of Durham in the Early Fifteenth Century', *Archaeologia Aeliana* 4th s. 39 (1961), 355–61.

the instigation of Wyche himself: in the autumn of 1416 Wyche filed a suit of debt and detinue in Oxfordshire against William Warde, fellow of Merton, alleging that Warde detained from him 54s. 6d. and a book worth five marks. Four years later, 13 June 1420, Warde failed to appear and was outlawed, but in October 1421 appealed. The outcome of the case is unclear, but its process suggests Wyche was near Oxford around the time of proceedings against Oldcastle's followers.[14] From there he may have gone further south, since the next record concerning Wyche occurs in the Exchequer rolls, enigmatically granting payment to a sergeant of the sheriff of Southampton on 21 October 1417 for expenses incurred in arresting, following divers writs from the king, Wyche and another priest William Broune, and delivering them to the King's Council at Westminster 'to make disclosures to them concerning certain sums of money' that belonged to Sir John Oldecastell, knight, forfeited to the king'.[15] Again no record survives of the immediate process against either man, though the potential charge now presumably involved treason as well as, or even rather than, heresy.

Two years later, however, both men appeared before the Canterbury Convocation on 20 November 1419. In the fuller record of Chichele's register some part of Wyche's earlier history is rehearsed: Wyche had been investigated by Skirlawe, and also by Richard Holme, and had been imprisoned 'for a long time . . . in northern parts'.[16] If, as seems to be implied, Holme's investigation was separate from that by Skirlawe, its date and its locality seems to have been similar.[17] The precise dates for which Wyche had remained in prison is unclear, but, it is said, Wyche had been brought south by a royal summons called *corpus cum causa* to Westminster, where he had been freed. At what point, or why, this had happened is unclear. But what is stated is that the 1417 arrest had been followed by imprisonment in the Fleet prison, whence the two had come before Chichele and Convocation. But if Chichele's clerk recorded the antecedent history in some detail, albeit maddeningly undated, he did not continue to the archbishop's own questioning: Broune was allowed to recant, but of what

---

[14] For this case, and the documents (largely unprinted) on which it is based, see Jurkowski, 'Heresy and Factionalism', pp. 679–80.
[15] *Issues of the Exchequer . . . from King Henry III to King Henry VI inclusive*, ed. F. Devon (London, 1837), pp. 352–3.
[16] *Register of Henry Chichele*, III, 57.
[17] For Holme see A. B. Emden, *A Biographical Register of the University of Cambridge to 1500* (Cambridge, 1963), pp. 311–12. Holme was commissary to Bishop Thomas Langley whilst the latter was chancellor to the king, between March 1405 and January 1407, and later to Arundel in his resumed chancellorship, January 1407 to December 1409: see R. L. Storey, *Thomas Langley and the Bishopric of Durham 1406–1437* (London, 1961), pp. 15–17, 25 and 169, and CPR 1405–8, p. 313. The enquiry concerning Wyche was probably under the former of these two tenures. Copeland (above n. 3), p. 184, suggests that Holme was Skirlaw's chancellor, but there is no evidence for Holme's association with Durham until the episcopacy of Langley.

is unspecified, but Wyche was returned to the Fleet prison to await a decision on appropriate action.[18]

Chichele's register gives no more. Six months later, on 15 July 1420, Wyche was released from the Fleet prison on the security of £200 from five men, three from Herefordshire or Worcestershire, two from London, to appear again at Michaelmas before the King's Council 'to answer touching what shall be laid against him.'[19] End of story. The most that it seems legitimate to deduce from this is that Chichele had not been convinced of Wyche's unorthodoxy at this point, but that questions still remained about his involvement with Oldcastle and that the charges would come before a civil court. Since Wyche was appointed to Deptford in 1423, however, it would seem that he was not found to have been seriously implicated in Oldcastle's rising.

Here then is a coherent, if incomplete, picture: from the documentation by Church and state we are allowed to see a man recurrently under suspicion, required to recant at least once in the first decade of the fifteenth century, examined by Convocation and by Council or their agents between 1417 and 1423, holding a series of livings near London, and executed on Tower Hill in 1440 after being again found guilty of heresy. The paper trail is not complete, but sufficient remains to produce a background to that final stark image of the flames on Tower Hill. But it is a schematic picture in black and white, and neither Wyche nor his opponents emerge as more than flat figures. Even the names of those opponents are few: Skirlawe, Holme, Chichele; beyond that are a shadowy host of clerical officials and underlings, minor officers responsible for arresting, supervising, producing the offender; faceless notaries and scribes who recorded in formulaic terms crucial moments of recantation or trial, but who either had not the knowledge or did not care to record anything beyond a few crucial moments. As for the central figure, we learn his name and the fact that he derived from the Hereford diocese, that he was a priest, that he had travelled, probably lived, widely in the north as well as in the vicinity of London, that equally he had resided – or at least that he had not been charged as non-resident – in several livings around London for nearly twenty years. As far as his heresy is concerned, the crime for which he was finally burned, all we are firmly told are the fourteen errors he recanted thirty-five years before that burning. No further opinions, no explanation for the views allegedly held, no reasoning for, or linkage between, the opinions. Those opinions, furthermore, were found offensive by the authorities, but no definite label was attached to them or to Wyche. Wyche had been fitted in to the stereotype of the heretic, treated in the prescribed fashion, and recorded in the traditional formulae.

---

[18] *Register of Henry Chichele*, III, 57. Dr Maureen Jurkowski kindly tells me that her searches for this writ through Public Record Office files have not uncovered it, or related, documents.

[19] *CCR 1419–1422*, p. 82.

As a transition to the next section it is worth mentioning one vignette preserved in this hostile record of chronicle and official document. At the site where the ashes from Wyche's fire were buried a shrine was set up by his followers, where they made prayers as to a saint.[20] The irony of this escapes the contemporary notice: that, to judge by several items in the recantation at the end of Skirlawe's process against him, Wyche had taught against images, pilgrimages and prayers in special places. 'Orthodox' behaviour is here decried by 'orthodox' sources; the 'heretic' would have denounced that behaviour as strongly as the 'orthodox' authorities.

The Individual's Story

Like the ecclesiastical story, this picture is radically incomplete – just as the ecclesiastical picture is riddled with holes, so half of the picture drawn by the individual does not survive. We have nothing from the second half of Wyche's career, no record from him of events after his alleged involvement with Oldcastle. But for the first decade of the fifteenth century a surprising amount of his own record survives. The first, and fullest, item is a long letter from Wyche to his friends, written whilst he was imprisoned and under interrogation by Bishop Skirlawe; when he wrote he had been excommunicated and sent to wait in prison for his degradation from clerical office.[21] No year is specified within the text, though the sequence of events from Wyche's arrest in late November through to the excommunication in the middle of the ensuing Lent is carefully set out. The purpose of the letter was apparently twofold: its final section makes requests of his friends, for prayers, for various minor objects and books (pp. 541/28–544/9), but the main part details the immensely complicated processes of the investigation, recounting conversations, specifying the interrogators and intermediaries sometimes by their office, sometimes by their name.[22] Wyche clearly apprehended that Skirlawe wanted a recantation, not just a conviction for heresy; his officials, by Wyche's account, were prepared to resort to elaborate guile to achieve this. Wyche declares he was arrested in Chester le Street (p. 531/7), and first came before Skirlawe on 7 December, accused of preaching errors, and questioned on his views about the mendicancy of the friars (p. 531/13); the bishop's

---

[20] See Caroline Barron's review of Thomson (above n. 3), in *Journal of the Society of Archivists* 3 (1967), 257–9; the place of Wyche's burning is there said to be West Smithfield, but this is contradicted by all of the chronicles listed above, n. 4.

[21] The text was printed by F. D. Matthew, 'The Trial of Richard Wyche', *EHR* 5 (1890), 530–44; references here are by page and, following a slash, added line numbers. For the final situation, see pp. 540/49–541/3.

[22] Snape, 'Lollard Activity', may be over-confident in preferring the date of the winter of 1402/3 for the events recorded; he mentions, but as less probable (p. 358), 1403/4. But the recantation reference to Innocent VII (above, p. 223) requires the end of the case to be dated after October 1404.

officials required him to swear that all Christians were bound to accept and obey all parts of canon law (p. 531/19); Wyche asked for time and counsel, was given until after dinner but then repeatedly refused to swear; he was denounced as excommunicate and consigned to prison (p. 531/22–7). A few days later he was taken before the bishop, and asked who had licensed him to preach in the diocese (p. 531/31). By this time the bishop had learned that Wyche was 'one of the sect of Lollards who do not believe the truth about the eucharist' (p. 531/40).[23] Thereafter the eucharist formed the overt central issue of enquiry, though, as Wyche apprehended, the heart of the matter was the question of ecclesiastical authority: Skirlawe was demanding that Wyche should abandon individual judgement to blind obedience. Wyche was left in prison until after Christmas (p. 532/23), but then intermittently was questioned and persuaded for at least a further two months.

There is not time here to recount the circumstantial story that Wyche sets out, a story whose time scale is precisely timetabled,[24] and whose scene is often lit by vivid visual detail and nuanced phraseology. A few points must be highlighted from this fascinating document. The first is the awareness that Wyche shows of legal procedure and its rules. Twice he attempted to stop the enquiry by questioning its legality: in one instance he disputed the validity of the charge since it named him erroneously as from the Worcester diocese (p. 541/9), in the other more extensively he claimed that, since Skirlawe and his officials had not kept to their own schedule but had failed to summon him when they had stated they would, the charges against him must lapse – only a new charge, based on new evidence, could resume the investigation – and for this he cited precedent in the southern province.[25] The second point is that, whilst the enquiry was largely conducted, as would be expected, by the bishop and his clerical officials, an unnamed knight was used as an intermediary; the purpose of the knight was to persuade Wyche to agree to swear an oath to the bishop *in corde tuo limitatum*, 'with reservation in his heart' – such an oath would, the knight averred, satisfy Skirlawe at the same time as salving Wyche's own conscience.[26] The manoeuvres on both sides about this oath dominate much of the account in the letter: Wyche ruefully admits that it was inevitable that Skirlawe would manipulate the oath, and

[23] Von Nolcken, 'Wyche, a Certain Knight', pp. 133–5, summarizes Wyche's Lollard views as they emerge from this text.

[24] The intervals between interrogations are clearly signalled (see pp. 533/7 and 16, 534/2, 535/2–3, 536/22 and 24, 537/13, 18 and 47, 538/14 and 18, 539/16 and 540/16). The latest date is two weeks after Ash Wednesday. For the argumentation, see von Nolcken, 'Wyche, a Certain Knight', pp. 136–9, though inevitably interpretation colours the summary.

[25] See pp. 537/14 and 540/22. It is tempting to wonder whether the precedent he has in mind was that of William Thorpe, and whether this was how Thorpe had escaped from the clutches of Bishop Braybrooke of London in early 1397 (see *Two Wycliffite Texts*, ed. A. Hudson, Early English Text Society 301 (Oxford, 1993), pp. xlix–l); for the possible connections between Wyche and Thorpe, see there pp. lviii–lix.

[26] See p. 534/30, and then persistently to p. 540/6.

would not be satisfied, contrary to what the knight had assured Wyche, with the single noncommittal promise (p. 539/31ff). The third point that deserves highlighting in this picture is the constant psychological pressure on Wyche: at an early stage Skirlawe threatened him with burning (p. 533/13), later the revocation of Purvey (in 1401) was read to him (p. 537/19), and he was threatened with the amount of evidence the officials had against him (p. 539/ 11), and then (rather obscurely) threatened that he must be regarded as a relapse (p. 540/11) – a condition which by current legislation meant that, even if he recanted, he could be held indefinitely in prison, and if he did not he would instantly be resigned to the lay authorities for execution.[27] Finally, as befits a personal letter, friends are named, individual messages sent, the writer's variable states of mind indicated, and his requests set out.[28] Most strikingly we are given an impression of the demeanour of the officials to Wyche. As has been said earlier, some are identified by name, some by position only – 'the archdeacon', 'the chancellor' are the most prominent. Some in both categories cannot be identified now, others can.[29] Doubtless the recipients of Wyche's letter could have named most: 'the chancellor' we can be certain they knew – certain because Wyche, very unusually in Lollard texts at one point but unnecessarily mentions *bonus Wicleff* as his teacher; 'the chancellor' at this point in the Durham diocese was Robert Wyclif, probably his nephew, the unnameable but implied *pessimus Wicleff*.[30]

Before I comment further on the picture that emerges here, it is worth turning to two other texts from the individual's side of the story – albeit neither is so long or so directly informative. The first, like the transition vignette, derives from hostile recording. In the single manuscript of the *Fasciculi zizaniorum* appears an undated reply of Richard Wyche on articles of which he has been accused, the suspect 'protesting that whatever I shall write

---

[27] See *Chichele reg.* I, cxxix–cxxxvi for early fifteenth century refinement of the rules concerning what constituted relapse.

[28] See pp. 541/28ff. Snape, 'Lollard Activity', suggested identities for some of these friends amongst the excommunicated persons of the surviving documents. For 'James' (p. 535/48), see Jurkowski, 'Heresy and Factionalism', p. 618. C. Kightly, 'The Early Lollards: A Survey of Popular Lollard Activity in England, 1382–1428' (unpublished D.Phil. thesis, University of York, 1975), p. 17 n. 3, dismissed the likelihood that *Robert Herl* (p. 542/27) is to be identified with Robert Harley who was executed in 1414 for his part in the Oldcastle rising, but in view of the connections between Wyche and Oldcastle this should perhaps be reconsidered.

[29] The archdeacon of Durham (p. 532/13 and elsewhere) till 1408 was Thomas de Weston (*Fasti Ecclesiae Anglicanae 1300–1541* VI [London, 1963], 112); Paris, a Dominican (pp. 539/19, 540/17ff), was John Paris O.P. (see A. B. Emden, *A Biographical Register of the University of Oxford to 1500*, 3 vols. [Oxford, 1957–9], III, 347 and 357; Emden, *Cambridge*, pp. 441–2; FZ, pp. 286, 498 and 343); the monk called Rome is doubtless Thomas Rome O.S.B. from Durham Cathedral Priory (Emden, *Oxford*, III, 1587–8). One who should be identifiable is the Augustinian prior of Newcastle (p. 539/19).

[30] See p. 536/14; for Robert see *CPR 1401–1405*, p. 459, where in a document of 20 October 1404 Robert de Wyclif is named as Skirlawe's chancellor.

or say which cannot be grounded in scripture I will in repentance revoke and retract, and I ask that the Church should regard as error'.[31] There follow fourteen sections – despite the identity of numbers *not* in all instances identical with those in the recantation – listing views, and, in most but not all cases, the evidence Wyche would adduce for their legitimacy.[32] Part of the first is included by Thomas Netter in his later refutation of Lollard views as deriving from 'quidam dictur Richardus Wyth respondendo pro se in libello oblato judici ad defensionem huius'.[33] The evidence cited by Wyche is primarily biblical, but in addition patristic and canon law authorities are cited, sometimes at length and most with precise referencing, together with 'venerabilis doctor Lincolniensis', that is Grosseteste.[34] Wyche emerges from this as erudite: most striking is his knowledge of the gloss on a section of the *Decretum* by 'the archdeacon', that is Guy de Baysio.[35] But, although this may help to fill out the intellectual background, little of Wyche's own reasoning emerges – or perhaps, given the source, is allowed to emerge. The veracity of the record, even if it has been abbreviated, is supported by the existence of numerous other comparable lists produced between 1380 and 1450 to justify claims that the authorities regarded with suspicion, lists which are preserved not only, as this one, in sources deriving from the ecclesiastical establishment, but also from manuscripts more favourable to innovatory ideas.[36]

The second text is the more surprising and arguably the more informative. This is a letter written by Wyche to Jan Hus, dated from London on 8 September 1410; since all the surviving seven manuscripts derive from Bohemia, there is a Czech translation in a further copy, and two copies of a reply from Hus are likewise found in Bohemia, it seems reasonable to conclude that the letter was indeed sent and reached its destination.[37] In

---

[31] *FZ*, pp. 370–82, here p. 370/2.

[32] Articles 1 and 2 are parallel to the items listed in the recantation 1 and 9, but the remainder are not the same. The articles here, like those of the recantation, are an eclectic mixture of views commonly found in Wycliffite texts (e.g. here 1 on images, 2 on mendicancy, 3 on the equal power of all good priests, 4 on the invalidity of papal excommunication) and the idiosyncratic (e.g. 8 that bastards cannot be saved, 9 that the only lawful offerings are animals).

[33] *Doctrinale* vi. 161, ed. B. Blanciotti, 3 vols. (Venice, 1757–9), III, 967, quoting most of the authorities cited in *FZ*, pp. 370–1.

[34] For patristic references see, for example, *FZ*, p. 370, from Gregory's *Registrum* x. 30 (modern xi. 13, *PL* 77, 1129), and, for canon law, *FZ*, p. 373, referring to Jerome on the epistle to Titus (*PL* 26, 562–3) found 'in canone dist. 95' (D. 95 c. 5, Friedberg, I, 332–3) from which Wyche is evidently quoting; for Grosseteste see *FZ*, pp. 381–2.

[35] *FZ*, p. 380, referring to commentary on D. 32 c. 6, 1 (Friedberg I, 117–18).

[36] For lists in Wycliffite texts cf. *An Apology for Lollard Doctrines*, ed. J. H. Todd, Camden Society old s. 20 (London, 1842).

[37] The edition in V. Novotný, *M. Jana Husi Korespondence a dokumenty* (Prague, 1920), no. 22, lists, and gives variants from, the seven manuscripts, and as 22* prints the Czech translation from the single surviving manuscript. Hus's reply is in the same edition no. 24. The heading of one copy of Wyche's letter, in Stará Boleslav MS C. 132 (now Prague, University Library, MS Cim D 79), 'Magister Richardus *Oxoniensis* ad Magistrum Johannem Hus' (my italics) is interesting. There is a modern English

many respects the content of the letter is uninstructive: it is devoted to brotherly encouragement to persistence in evangelical living and is couched in language rich in biblical resonance with parallels drawn between present suffering and the experiences of Christ and the early Church. But some interesting points emerge: Wyche has evidently heard of Hus's constancy amidst the troubles afflicting him and his friends in Bohemia, though, whether from ignorance or tact, ascribes these to 'antichrist';[38] he mentions the situation in England where 'God has so greatly strengthened the hearts of some people, that they gladly endure imprisonment, exile, and even death for the Word of God';[39] more specifically, Wyche knows the name of *Jacobellum* as a 'co-worker in the gospel' with Hus – *Jacobellum* is Jakoubek of Štríbro, one of Hus's foremost assistants.[40] Less well attested than Wyche's letter is another, dated the same day, 8 September 1410, and addressed to Woksa of Waldstein, a noble who supported Hus, deriving from Sir John Oldcastle.[41] Again the content is entirely conventional, but the interest lies in the coincident dating: even though Oldcastle's letter is addressed from his manor of Cooling in northern Kent, it is surely stretching credulity too far to think that two Englishmen should independently write on the same date to two associated figures in Bohemia on comparable lines. Though from hostile sources the outcome of the charge against Wyche of association with Oldcastle does not emerge, these letters surely guarantee its veracity – even if they do not indicate whether that association was innocent or treasonous.

Here then the individual's story is unusually full: even if the latter half of the picture, after 1410, has been torn away, the earlier half is in full technicolour, 3-D if not wrap-around, with quadraphonic sound system. But, despite all its verisimilitude and circumstantial detail, can we believe it?

translation of the letters by M. Spinka, *The Letters of John Hus* (Manchester, 1972), pp. 213–15 (Wyche), 45–8 (Hus's reply).

[38] Novotný, p. 76: 'Audivi, fratres, quam acriter vos turbat Antichristus, tribulaciones varias et inauditas Christi fidelibus inferendo' ('I have heard, brethren, how bitterly the Antichrist troubles you, inflicting various and unheard of tribulations on Christ's faithful'; translation is that of Spinka, p. 213).

[39] Novotný, p. 78: 'in regno nostro et alibi deus corda quorumdam adeo animaverat, quod eciam usque ad carceres, exilium et mortem gaudenter sustinent propter verbum Christi'; translation Spinka, p. 215.

[40] Novotný, p. 78: he greets the lovers of God's law 'et specialiter vestrum in ewangelio coadiutorem Jacobellum' ('and especially your co-worker in the gospel, Jakoubek'; Spinka, p. 215); for Jakoubek see H. Kaminsky, *A History of the Hussite Revolution* (Berkeley and Los Angeles, 1967), pp. 75–80, and see further pp. 98–126 for his later radicalism.

[41] Again printed in Novotný no. 21; two copies, both Bohemian, survive. Woksa was amongst those excommunicated by the archbishop of Prague 2 May 1411 (*Documenta Mag. Ioannis Hus vitam*, ed. F. Palacky [Prague, 1869], p. 430), and he appears in later documents (pp. 581, 584 and 591) favourable to Hus. Failing Woksa, the letter is directed to Zdyslaus of Zvířetic who appears also in these documents, and in the defence of Wyclif's books (below p. 234).

There are, I would like to suggest, problems of various kinds. First of documentation. The absence of an English copy of Wyche's letter to Hus may not be surprising, but the similar absence of the longer document is odd.[42] Furthermore, why should a Bohemian audience be interested in such a detailed account of experiences in a north-country English prison, and in its requests for trivial items from unknown friends with rebarbative names, especially when that distant audience could not furnish the personal identities for the officials pictured?[43] Even if it may be granted that, along with the knight as *agent provocateur*, there was in the prison a sympathetic warder prepared to transmit the suspect's letter to his rural friends, how or why did that apparently personal document travel from northern county Durham to Bohemia?[44] To suggest that the whole document is a forgery would raise more difficulties than it solves; but simple preservation should suggest that the actual reception of the letter is revealing: that it is found so far from home must imply that its intended recipients saw it as more than locally significant, more than just a private record of a single experience. Turning attention to that wider significance, features that the historian tends to 'read over' emerge: far from being a spontaneous and artless account of personal experience, the whole is couched within a well-developed rhetorical frame. Echoes of the Pauline pastoral epistles abound, especially in the mingled exhortations and salutations to friends at the end;[45] the vocabulary of bible and hagiography combine to present the writer in the role of incipient

---

[42] John Bale's knowledge of the letter of Wyche (given by Bale as *Wichewith vel Wichewurth*) to Hus in his *Index Britanniae Scriptorum*, ed. R. L. Poole and M. Bateson, rev. C. Brett and J. P. Carley (Cambridge, 1990), p. 363, derives 'ex opusculis Ioannis Hussij' and is certainly the 1558 Nuremberg edition of texts by and documents concerning Hus (i. fol. 101r–v, with the surname *Vuychewitze*). Foxe's knowledge of the letter (see *The Acts and Monuments of John Foxe*, ed. S. R. Cattley and J. Pratt, 8 vols. [London, 1853–70], III, 506–7) almost certainly derives from the same source (surname *Wichewitze*) since it is not clear that Foxe identified its writer with the Wyche whose burning in 1440 he records elsewhere (III, 702–4).

[43] The manuscript, Prague, University Library, MS III.G.11 (Wyche fols. 89v–99v), is an interesting collection: in addition to that letter it also contains twelve sermons and twenty-three other short works by Wyclif, and the Latin version of William Taylor's 1406 sermon at St Paul's Cross London (see my paper 'William Taylor's 1406 Sermon: A Postscript', *Medium Aevum* 64 [1995], 100–6). The claim that the *Quaestio ad fratres de sacramento altaris*, usually thought to be by Wyclif, is in this manuscript ascribed to Wyche (see W. R. Thomson, *The Latin Writings of John Wyclyf* [Toronto, 1983], p. 74, recording an older view) derives from a dubious claim concerning an erasure in the medieval list of contents on fol. i (a claim repeated by von Nolcken [above, n. 3], p. 149 n. 60, and by Copeland [above, n. 3], p. 152 n. 5).

[44] A similar problem exists both with Thorpe's *Testimony*, declaredly written in prison, which survives in one medieval English copy and in two Bohemian Latin manuscripts, and with the longer *Opus Arduum* (for which see my paper in *Lollards and their Books* [London, 1985], pp. 43–65).

[45] See pp. 542/1ff, 542/27ff and 543/20ff.

saint[46] – Wyche may have preached against the worship of saints, but he had certainly absorbed the literary techniques of their biographies.[47] And his apparently private letter was carefully designed for a wider audience. That awareness of rhetoric is much more evident in the letter to Hus: this is an exercise in the consolatory epistolary style rather than a meaningful transmission of information, whether personal or sect – Hus's reply, interestingly, is the more 'informative', both in regard to the immediate situation in Bohemia and also in its use of established Wycliffite vocabulary.[48]

Reconstruction?

> Look then upon this picture, and on this:
> The *counterfeit presentment* of –

not two brothers, but the same person. Can one picture be made from the two? Or is the *presentment* so rhetorically coloured that the two *counterfeits* can never be combined? Of course it is possible to elicit the 'facts' from both pictures, and weld them together to provide an outline biography. In such an enterprise, however, hypotheses have to be accepted, incipient contradictions ironed out, and the danger is that the resulting picture may resemble a diagram. The interest of this case lies not just in the two, arguably unresolvable, pictures, but in the way it highlights the simplification of the cases where only *one* picture survives: usually, as with Swinderby, Robert Hook, William Drayton and probably John Purvey, it is the ecclesiastical authorities' picture which alone survives, rarely, as is almost the case with William Thorpe, the individual 'heretic's' picture.[49] But each is rhetorically framed: Thorpe's dramatic identification of antichrist with Thomas Arundel is no less contrived as propaganda than the episcopal register that brands the captive as 'hereticus, pessimus Lollardus'.[50] It is for

---

[46] See the sequence of biblical quotations and their surrounding appropriation on pp. 541/32ff and elsewhere in this concluding section, but also earlier on pp. 533/14, 536/24–537/12 and 541/20–7.

[47] In Wyche's recantation (above, pp. 222–3) hostility to saints, their images, pilgrimages to their shrines and prayers to them, is seen in errors 1–2, 7 and 11–12; in the undated *responsio* (above, pp. 228–9) in answers 1 and, implicitly, 14.

[48] See Novotný, no. 24 pp. 84–5; for the Wycliffite vocabulary, reflecting the concept of the Church as the *congregatio predestinatorum* ('the congregation of the predestined'), see the final salutation from 'Christi ecclesia de Boemia' ('The Church of Christ in Bohemia') to 'ecclesiam Christi in Anglia' ('The Church of Christ in England'); Spinka, p. 48.

[49] For some references to the documentary materials on the first two, see Hudson, *Premature Reformation*, pp. 74–7, 154 and 164; on the third, *Two Wycliffite Texts*, pp. xix–xxi, and for the fourth, *Lollards and their Books*, pp. 85–110.

[50] See Thorpe's *Testimony* in *Two Wycliffite Texts*; materials concerning the early stages of Thorpe's 'heresy' survive from hostile sources (see pp. xlvii–l). Maureen

a modern audience easier to exonerate the individual than the official, to portray sympathetically the captured and interrogated suspect than to persuade of the disinterest of a 'caesarian prelate', simpler to discern the official formulae of the episcopal or civil document than the rhetoric of hagiography. But we should be careful. Which *was* the lion, which the peasant?

The Researcher's Story

If there is an inherited rhetoric that seeks to convince in both the Official Story and the Individual's Story, there is also a conventional art of persuasion in the language of the present-day researcher. The material here must candidly be admitted as a series of hypotheses, clues that cannot in the final analysis construct a watertight case – for the present, at least. But, in the hope that more may subsequently emerge, or be seen by other investigators, it seems worth setting out the trail so far.

The final sentence of Hus's reply to Wyche's 1410 letter thanks him for the trouble he has taken over manuscripts on behalf of the Bohemians: 'quod tantis laboribus exemplaria nobis egentibus ministrastis'.[51] What were these manuscripts? It seems clear from the wording that they were more than just the letter from Wyche, or even the two from him and from Oldcastle: the reasonable implication of the words is that they were books which Hus and the Bohemians had requested, and which Wyche had supplied, or had been influential in supplying. The use of the term 'exemplaria' rather than 'manuscriptas' suggests that the books supplied were to furnish the masters from which further copies might be made. The texts which Hus and his followers are most likely to have wanted from England are those of Wyclif's writings.

Hus in this letter earlier refers, in infuriatingly allusive terms, to two of the intermediaries in the correspondence: 'Nicholas, to whom I am writing, will inform you of other things. The letter was first delivered to us on the second Sunday in Lent, because Simon was in Hungary with it.'[52] Presumably Hus could be sure that Wyche would be able to identify these two just from their Christian names. The identity of the Nicholas, who will be physically present

---

Jurkowski has also discovered important new information about Thorpe's arrest in 1407; for this see below, p. 236.

[51] Novotný, p. 85; Spinka, p. 48; one of the two copies reads *exempla* for *exemplaria*. Stephen Páleč also reports that Hus mentioned '*literas* de Anglia et presertim unam bonam epistolam quam . . . michi scripsit Richardus Witz presbiter magistri Johannis Wicleff' (Novotný, no. 29, quoting from the extracts from Páleč's unprinted *Tractatus de ecclesia* in J. Sedlák, *M. Jan Hus* [Prague, 1915], ii.248*). Hus's letter is not among those whose authenticity has been questioned by B. Kopičková and A. Vidmanová, *Listy na Husovu obranu z let 1410–1412* (Prague, 1999).

[52] Novotný, p. 85; Spinka, p. 48; the names are identical in both copies.

when Hus's letter arrives, can be suggested with fair certainty: Mikuláš Faulfiš, to give his name in Czech form, was one of two Bohemians who visited England in 1406–7, and who, by Hus's own testimony at Constance, died travelling between Spain and England some years later.[53] His death can be shown, from documentary evidence relating to a dispute over his inheritance, to have occurred by the end of November 1411.[54] The purpose of Faulfiš's earlier journey was the collection of materials concerning Wyclif: he, and his companion Jiri Knĕhnic, gathered a chip from Wyclif's tomb at Lutterworth, obtained through the assistance of Peter Payne (later to follow them back to Bohemia) a testimonial from the University of Oxford to Wyclif's repute and orthodoxy,[55] and copied at least three of Wyclif's longer theological writings. Their copy miraculously survives as Vienna, Österreichische Nationalbibliothek MS 1294: notes before and after the three texts and at the end of some chapters provide the testimony to its origins, and allow an itinerary for the two Bohemians to be constructed.[56] The 'Simon' of Hus's letter has been taken to be Simon of Tišnov, one of the masters, along with Hus himself and Jakoubek of Stříbro (the Jacobellus of Wyche's letter), who had spoken in defence of Wyclif's books in July and early August 1410 after the bonfire of the master's books ordered by the archbishop of Prague; Simon had defended *De probationibus propositionum*, better known to us as part 2 of *De logica*.[57] Suggestively, ÖNB 1294 has as a flyleaf a document naming Simon of Tišnov as the beneficiary of a newly founded chapel.[58] Equally, a connection between Simon and Faulfiš is assured by the fact that the former appears as a creditor of the latter in the legal negotiations which followed Faulfiš's death.[59]

Was Wyche then involved in some way in facilitating the production of ÖNB 1294? Directly, the answer must probably be negative: Wyche is likely to have been still in prison in the north in 1406–7. But the itinerary and

[53] Novotný suggests this identity with a question mark. For the 1406–7 journey see below; Hus's comment on his death is reported by Peter of Mladoňovice, printed F. Palacký, *Documenta Mag. Johannis Hus* (Prague, 1869), p. 313, trans. M. Spinka, *John Hus at the Council of Constance* (New York and London, 1965), p. 220.

[54] See *Archiv Český* 36 (1941), p. 440.

[55] The testimonial, obtained on the signature of Congregation, is printed in *Concilia Magnae Britanniae et Hiberniae A.D. 466–1717*, ed. D. Wilkins, 4 vols. (London, 1737), III, 302 from BL MS Cotton Faustina C.7, where it is dated 5 October 1406. Memory of the visit, and of the testimonial, was still vivid at Hus's trial in 1415, judging by the testimony of Peter of Mladoňovice (above n. 53) p. 313.

[56] See below for its details.

[57] For the events leading to the bonfire and the defences, see Kaminsky (above n. 40), pp. 70–4 and esp. p. 73; Simon's text is printed by J. Loserth, *Wiclif and Hus*, trans. M. J. Evans (London, 1884), pp. 309–16. Another spokesman was Zdyslaus of Zvířetic (above n. 41).

[58] See flyleaf I at the start, dated at the end 1401; mentioned in the most recent catalogue listing, *Katalog der kroatischen, polnischen und tschechischen Handschriften der Österreichischen Nationalbibliothek*, K. Schwarzenberg (Vienna, 1972), p. 12.

[59] See above, n. 54.

dates found in the manuscript warrant closer attention. Three texts appear in the manuscript, each originally in separable sets of quires;[60] their present ordering is *De veritate sacre scripture*, *De ecclesia* and *De dominio divino*. Copying of the first of these was, by the note added at the end of chapter 20, in train on the vigil of St James, 24 July; it was corrected, according to the note at the end, by Faulfiš and Kněhnic in Oxford on 1 February 1407.[61] The second text is said at the end of chapter 2 (fol. 134va) to have been copied at Kemerton, but its writing is only dated once, at the end of chapter 4 'in vigilia pentecostes' (fol. 141ra). The third text was copied at Braybrooke (end of book iii chapter 5), and is twice dated by liturgical occasion, Maundy Thursday and Good Friday (fols. 223va and 225va, at the end of i.10 and i.11). It seems not unreasonable to think that the shortest timetable compatible with these dates is the most likely: the Bohemians had a mission in England, but no reason to delay there. This suggests that they first copied *De veritate* in an uncertain location, possibly Oxford; they were certainly there to collect the Wyclif testimonial, and in February 1407 to correct the text. They then went to Braybrooke where they worked on *De dominio divino* in March 1407, the occasions mentioned being 24 and 25 March that year; then on to Kemerton, where they were at work on *De ecclesia* on 14 May (Whit Sunday that year fell on 15 May). Their hosts outside Oxford are not directly relevant to the present question, but can be identified as Robert Lychlade, rector at Kemerton after investigation for heresy in 1395 whilst at Oxford, and the Latimer household at Braybrooke.[62] A visit of eleven months, and a journey to three places at least, could certainly explain Hus's assumption that 'Nicholas' needed no further specification.

Indirectly, however, Wyche may be connected with the details that emerge from the notes in ÖNB 1294. In addition to the notes that date and localize the copying, a few other comments are to be found. Relevant here is a Czech couplet at the end of chapter 11 of the copy of Wyclif's *De ecclesia*:

> W Anglii wyerna dwa knyezy
> Pro slowo bozye w zalarzy wyezye   (fol. 163vb)

'In England they have imprisoned two true priests for preaching the gospel.' This note is likely to have been made at Kemerton in May or early June 1407.

[60] Their separation is now disguised by the indexes provided by a different hand at the end of the first two items: the second of these covers an added bifolium (now fols. 208–9) plus the first leaf of the ten-leaf quire on whose third the final text begins.
[61] Fols. 68va and 119vb; the notes relevant to the itinerary are all entered within the ruling of the columns, directly after the last word of the chapter; consequently, save at the end of the text, they cannot have been added later but must have been entered as the writing proceeded. The note concerning the correction of *De veritate* is at the foot of the column, whilst the text ends halfway down.
[62] See Hudson, *Lollards and their Books*, p. 78, and references there given.

A recent discovery by Maureeen Jurkowski suggests the news that could have provoked that couplet: on 17 April 1407 William Thorpe and his assistant John Pollyrbache were arrested in Shrewsbury, interrogated, and then in late June or early July taken under guard to imprisonment by Archbishop Arundel in Canterbury; the charges against the pair were indeed that they had preached errors.[63] Since chapter 2 had been completed by 14 May, news of the arrest could well have reached the Bohemians by the time they had copied as far as the end of chapter 11.

If this last identification is plausible, and if the earlier suggestions concerning the allusions in Hus's letter are credible, then Wyche can be linked much more closely to the group of Wycliffites influential in facilitating the transmission of books to Bohemia; indeed, if all these hypotheses are put together, a much clearer picture emerges of that transmission than has hitherto been discernible. Wyche can be seen to have been acquainted not only with two Bohemians, Nicholas and Simon, and to have known of Jakoubek of Stříbro, but also with other English Lollards. The misspelled 'Willelmi Corpp' of his prison letter can be more firmly identified with William Thorpe, long elusive not only to his contemporaries but also to modern researchers; the suggestion that Wyche's letter could have been the inspiration for Thorpe's *Testimony* gains in credibility.[64] If Faulfiš and Knĕhnic heard of Thorpe's arrest in Gloucestershire, and thought it worth recording, it reinforces the idea that the Bohemians' journeyings round England were the result of a concerted effort by a number of native Wycliffites to facilitate their endeavours. And there is no reason to suppose that ÖNB 1294 comprised the full extent of the Bohemians' new baggage on their return home: particularly in the first half of their visit there are gaps in time for more copying. One credible addition might be the exemplar for several of the texts now surviving in Prague University Library MS III.G.11: a Latin version of William Taylor's 1406 sermon at St Paul's Cross, some three dozen short works by Wyclif, and the sole copy of Wyche's prison letter.[65] William Thorpe's *Testimony* must have been a later migrant: again two Latin copies are found in Hussite territory, but the work cannot have been written at least until after 7 August 1407, or, if the colophon to the single medieval English manuscript is believed, until after the death of archbishop Arundel in February 1414.[66] Hus's thanks for the *exemplaria* become comprehensible. Dimly and tentatively, we may see two groups of associates: the Bohemians Hus, Jakoubek, Faulfiš, Tišnov, Waldstein, Zvířetic, and the English Wyche,

[63] M. Jurkowski, 'The Arrest of William Thorpe in Shrewsbury and the Anti-Lollard Statute of 1406', *Historical Research* 117 (2002), 273–95. I am very grateful to Dr Jurkowski for advance information on this discovery, and for her comments on an earlier draft of this paper.

[64] See my edition (above, n. 25) pp. lvii–lix.

[65] Above, n. 43 and references there.

[66] See edition pp. xxviii–xxx and lii.

Oldcastle, Thorpe, Payne, even Taylor, and the multifarious interchanges and connections between them.[67]

This story, as I warned, is full of hypotheses; the picture has been fragmented into tiny pieces, only a few of which survive – or, at least, have so far come to light. The outline that I have been suggesting would go some way to explaining Bohemian interest in Wyche. Insofar as any narrative emerges, it fills in the background to Wyche's career up to the writing of his letter to Hus in 1410. It does not help towards filling the hiatus between Wyche's release from the Fleet in 1420 and his burning for heresy in 1440: the sequence of benefice changes testifies to Wyche's presence in England during that time, but not much more. Whether he remained true to his Wycliffite beliefs throughout that time, how he propagated heresy or finally came into the authorities' power, these are only the most obvious questions that remain unanswered.

---

[67] Purvey because his 1401 recantation was mentioned to both Wyche (above, p. 228) and Thorpe (*Testimony* 499, 541–8), and both evidently knew something of his history; Taylor because Thorpe refers to the scandal of his November 1406 sermon (*Testimony* 1967–89 and notes) – a time when Faulfiš and Knĕhnic were in England. The Bohemian Jerome of Prague is another tempting addition: he had been in Hungary just before Simon of Tišnov in 1411 (see F. Šmahel, 'Leben und Werk des Magisters Hieronymus von Prag', *Historica* 13 [1966], 81–111 esp. pp. 86–9).

Index

Medieval people are listed by their first names. These names and the titles of works have not been standardized to one language.

256 *Index*

Walter Skirlaw (*cont.*):
  proceedings against Durham priests: 223
Wazo, bishop of Liège: 34
West Greenwich (Deptford)
  vicar: 222, 225
William VIII, count of Montpellier: 38
William, archdeacon of Paris: 46
William Arnaldi OP, inquisitor: 85, 100, 102–4
William Audebert, Cathar believer: 97
William Broune, Lollard (?): 224–5
William Courtenay, archbishop of Canterbury: 222 n. 9
William *de Plainha*, Avignonet conspirator: 103
William *de Turreta*, Cathar believer: 95
William Drayton, Lollard: 232
William Fabre, Good Man: 97
William Fabri, Avignonet conspirator: 100
William Feraut, Cathar believer: 97
William Garini, Waldensian believer: 145
William Garcia OFM: 96
William of Ockham OFM: 27, 41
  Dialogue: 26
  heretic: 25–6
William Sawtry, Lollard
  execution: 222 n. 9

William Swinderby, Lollard: 232
William Taylor, Lollard: 237
  sermon: 236, 237 n. 67
William Thorpe, Lollard: 227 n. 25, 236, 237
  Testimony (account of his trial): 231 n. 44, 232, 236, 237 n. 67
William Tron, notary, heretic: 92
William Warde, fellow of Merton: 224
Winchester College: 222
wine: 94, 127
Woksa of Waldstein, Hussite: 230, 236
Women
  heresy: see Cathars, Waldensians
  orthodoxy: 50–1
Worcester
  diocese: 227
Worcestershire: 225
Wyclif
  See John Wyclif

York: 3

Zerner, Monique
  Inventer l'hérésie?: 15
Zdyslaus of Zvířetic, promoter of Wyclif: 230 n. 41, 234 n. 57, 236

Latin and Vernacular: Studies in Late-Medieval Texts and Manuscripts, ed. A. J. Minnis (1989) [Proceedings of the 1987 York Manuscripts Conference]

Regionalism in Late-Medieval Manuscripts and Texts: Essays celebrating the publication of 'A Linguistic Atlas of Late Mediaeval English', ed. Felicity Riddy (1991) [Proceedings of the 1989 York Manuscripts Conference]

Late-Medieval Religious Texts and their Transmission: Essays in Honour of A. I. Doyle, ed. A. J. Minnis (1994) [Proceedings of the 1991 York Manuscripts Conference]

Prestige, Authority and Power in Late Medieval Manuscripts and Texts, ed. Felicity Riddy (2000) [Proceedings of the 1994 York Manuscripts Conference]

Middle English Poetry: Texts and Traditions. Essays in Honour of Derek Pearsall, ed. A. J. Minnis (2001) [Proceedings of the 1996 York Manuscripts Conference]